CRIMINAL
JUSTICE
HISTORY

CRIMINAL JUSTICE HISTORY is an international forum for the history and analysis of crime and criminal justice. It annually publishes research and historiographical articles, comparative and interpretive essays, conference assessments, research notes, book review essays, and reviews. The annual encourages submissions from authors in any part of the world in disciplines such as history, law, anthropology, sociology, political science, and the criminal justice sciences that relate specifically to the history of crime and criminal justice and to its broader social, historical, legal, and institutional contexts in any geographical area or period.

Board of Editors

CRIMINAL
JUSTICE
HISTORY

AN INTERNATIONAL ANNUAL

Volume 15
1994

Greenwood Press
Westport, Connecticut • London

British Library Cataloguing in Publication Data is available.

Copyright © 1996 by Greenwood Publishing Group, Inc.

ISBN: 0–313–28737–6
ISSN: 0194–0953

First published in 1996

Greenwood Press, 88 Post Road West, Westport, CT 06881
An imprint of Greenwood Publishing Group, Inc.

Printed in the United States of America

The paper used in this book complies with the
Permanent Paper Standard issued by the National
Information Standards Organization (Z39.48–1984).

10 9 8 7 6 5 4 3 2 1

Contents

Book Review Essay

Book Reviews

Preface

The secular rise in recorded crime that has come to dominate the media and the press in North and South America, as well in Eastern and Western Europe, has been accompanied with an equal attention to policing. The crime wave and policing have had their impact on the interests of the scholarly community as increasingly historians, lawyers, and criminologists have turned their research agendas to these fields. While last year's volume of *Criminal Justice History* (*CJH*) had a number of chapters on crime, this year's volume features an even larger number on police, and the policing of urban society, in Europe and North America.

The role of the police in the context of communities and the state figures prominently in the studies of Michael Broers, Roger Swift, and Ian Bridgeman. Broers, in an extensive examination of the development of a police state in Piedmont, Hesperia, which was annexed by France in the course of the French Revolution 1789–1821, describes the rise of organized banditry and the wave of petty crime in the late eighteenth century. The failure of lords and monarchs to enforce judicial duties contributed to collective forms of law-breaking, especially smuggling, where groups of bandits established commercial relations with city buyers for their goods. But Napoleon's introduction of the *gendarmerie*, together with the enforcement of conscription, enabled the Savoyard monarchy to instill law and order in the countryside. The enforcement of the policing function by the *carabinieri* was successful because of its support by noble families, the propertied class, and a Catholic theocracy based on the moral order of family life.

The policing of the Irish in nineteenth-century England bears some similarities to the Piedmontese. On the one hand, the intracommunal disorders of the Irish in cities such as Liverpool, Manchester, and London were of no concern to the English police. But the large migration of the Irish at mid-century due to the Great Famine brought public pressure to bear upon the police to exercise a social control function as they had practiced on the navvies who worked on the building of the railways in the 1830s and 1840s. This action in turn caused Irish assaults on the police, and a widening of violence, in mid–Victorian England. These "class B disturbances" are regarded by Swift as a subject worthy of further investigation. The policing of the Irish in England, however, is in sharp contrast to the operations of the police in Ireland itself. As Bridgeman demonstrates, the development of a secret police (G Division) within the Dublin Metropolitan Police to combat the rise of political crimes and subversion in the cities was unsuccessful. Effective policing in Ireland came eventually from the professionalization of the police forces and the links they established with local prosecutors, court clerks, justices of the peace, and stipendiary magistrates.

Policing in North America is the focus of two studies by David Barlow and Greg Marquis. Barlow provides a history of the tribal police in the United States from the Indian Interstate Act of 1790 to the 1970s. Several important observations emerge from this study. In the early national period, Indians were victimized as much by their own people as they were by outlaws. When Indian Affairs was transferred from the War Department to the Department of the Interior in 1849, the military remained the primary law enforcement agency until the tribal police were established in 1869. But once the federal policy of assimilation took root in the late nineteenth and early twentieth centuries, the breakup of tribal cohesion was accompanied by the dismantling of the tribal police. Only with the reconstitution of tribal government in the Reorganization Act of 1834 did a tribal justice system return, although restricted to the enforcement of misdemeanors. Barlow draws some interesting parallels between tribal minorities policing minorities and black minorities doing the same, and in the development of self-government on Indian reservations and the empowerment of African-American communities. Social control has remained the predominant concern of policing, and Native and African-Americans who have been brought into the structure of policing have not yet been able to change it.

The police have been central to the development of the modern state, and the professionalization of the police has been an integral component. Anthropometric identification, fingerprinting, and photography were key elements in crime detection from the 1890s to the 1930s. The linking of physical characteristics to behavior was pioneered by Europeans in the nineteenth century, and at first the idea that a small, identifiable criminous class was responsible for a large amount of criminal behavior was attractive to police authorities in North America. Greg Marquis, in examining the background and history of the Canadian Identification of Criminals Act of 1898, notes how some of the police forces in the country used the act to arrest "suspicious" persons, and apply Bertillon measurements to construct an information pool with which to discipline and control these "marginal" elements of society. Curiously, however, it was the more hierarchical and less democratic Canadian society that opposed the extension of "criminal identification" to nonfelonious crimes, and Canada failed to develop the universal system of identification that was instituted in the United States.

A second major subject found in this volume concerns the administration of justice in the courts. The records of medieval local, criminal courts seldom survive in long runs. There are some extent criminal registers, however, for the Dalmatian town of Dubrovnik from the early fourteenth century, and Nella Lonza has brought them alive. Under the jurisdiction of the Venetian Great Council and the governorship of the count of Dubrovnik, the court of the commune operated under Roman law both by statute and local custom. Although the court used both accusatorial and inquisitorial procedures, Lonza has found that in practice both procedures were similar, and that custom was the primary authority for judgments. The court of this commune, moreover, looked to witnesses as the major source of evidence. The registers reveal that personal assaults comprised the great majority of criminal cases, while property offenses were the least in number. Most sentences were of fines, and curiously only the wealthy were committed to detention when they refused to pay. In the end, the judges used considerable discretion in their handling of court procedures, and their admonitions were an effective tool for keeping the peace.

Judicial discretion and independence are also at the heart of McElligott's examination of the background of the rise of the police state in the Third Reich, 1930–1934, where he assesses the rise and fall of the *Sondergerichte*—the summary courts of 1932, in the northern German industrial town of Altona. These courts, which denied pretrial investigations, defendants' rights, and trial by jury, were marked by vigorous prosecutions and strong judges. The courts tried over 16,000 people in Prussia alone before they were rescinded in December of that year. But McElligott's examination of the cases in Altona, and of the famous case of the "Altona Fifteen," explains how the rationale of the courts to thwart the violence of Communists—was fallacious. The violence was actually perpetrated by Nazis, and the injustices catalogued by the courts led to their abolition. The study also shows how the judges—who were on the whole not politically appointed—remained independent minded and only acquiesced to this draconian criminal justice system because of their fear of the rise of a criminous proletariat.

The impact of war on the civil courts is the subject of Philippe Chassaigne's study of Bordeaux, 1914–1918. The mobilization of Frenchmen in 1914 brought a drop in recorded crime of more than half, and the end of offenses such as vagrancy. Assaults, however, rose above the prewar level, and economic delinquency increased as merchants and shopkeepers tried to profit from wartime conditions. But Bordeaux, unlike other French cities, witnessed only a slight increase in recorded crime with the end of the war. One significant result of the war, however, was an increase in prostitution, which led to laws against soliciting. As Augustine Brannigan suggests in his review of the literature on prostitution, the problem of the victimization of women that arose in the late nineteenth century is still with us today. While the jury is out as to whether prostitution should be viewed as a crime or a nuisance, the soliciting laws of the "modern" era still predominate in our postmodern times.

The twin-edged sword of law reform is the third major subject that can be found in the chapters of this volume. James Donovan explores with considerable dexterity the great movement of French law, police, and the courts to combat pedophilia in the nineteenth century. The view of childhood as a distinct phase of life separate from adulthood that began in the eighteenth century lay behind a transition from the tolerance of the sexual abuse of minors to a large increase in prosecutions for sex crimes against children in France. This transition did not reach Britain until the late nineteenth century, and Austria and the United States until the twentieth. In spite of the fact that most cases were never reported, Donovan's research has revealed a sixfold rise in prosecutions from 1825–1830 to 1876–1880, and a rise in the prosecution of rape and indecent assault of minors from 1.9 to 18.5 percent of all felonies 1825–1880. The reasons for this change are explored in considerable depth. They include simple majority jury verdicts, reduced sentences for "extenuating circumstances," the new literature of forensic medicine, child welfare reform, and the rise of a conservative political culture.

The study of children and youth in the criminal justice system has been led by social historians examining family and gender issues. Malcolm Feeley, in an extensive survey of the evidence for the history of female criminality—the long durée of the seventeenth to the late twentieth centuries—has surveyed much of the evidence presented to date and offers some interesting and controversial suggestions. He concludes that women comprised 30–50 percent of all culprits in Europe and North America in the seventeenth and eighteenth centuries, and only 5–15 percent from the late nineteenth to the late twentieth century. After dismantling many of the current theories for this change, Feeley argues that potential explanations lie in the historical developments of capitalism and patriarchy. A shift of industry from the family household to the factory took women away from their diverse economic roles and relegated them to the family, feminized domestic service, eulogized women as subservient, virtuous, and pious, and only allowed them into the new workforce for "slopwork." Feeley's paradigm will be a subject of considerable research and discussion in the coming years.

Research and writing in the criminal justice history area has become increasingly revisionist, and several of the reviews in this volume bear testimony to that phenomenon. Rousseaux's review of Brackett's study of crime and criminal justice in Renaissance Florence notes how the dukes failed to gain control of the criminal courts. Lacking effective police, courts, and prisons, they even lost money in dispensing justice. As Lonza has shown in her study, state control was not profitable in preindustrial times. In a similar vein, Garton's review of Byrne's study of the criminal law in early nineteenth-century New South Wales shows how the criminal law was used both for and against authority, challenging once again state formation theories. Convicts forged freedoms within their system, working-class women used courts for redress more than men did, and workers used the law to modernize labor relations.

Revisionism in an Anglo-American context is evident in two reviews. According to Bailey, a keen scholar of British policing and punishment, Hirsch's *The Rise of the Penitentiary* demonstrates how early nineteenth-century U.S. carceral ideology was derived from the English workhouse of the sixteenth and seventeenth centuries, and was not a uniquely American solution to a uniquely American problem. The rehabituative ideology that emerged was a practical blending of hard labor by day and confinement by night. This forming of some common Anglo-American legal traditions is also at the heart of the collected essays on the North American West— *Law for the Elephant, Law for the Beaver.* As Marquis notes, the settlers of the Canadian and U.S. West may have had more in common than they had differences. The development of both of their criminal justice systems had elements of race and class, and the Canadian West is coming to be viewed in much less idyllic terms than it has been. In the end, the sources on which the history of crime and justice has been written must be expanded to yield the answers to some of these new questions. Mark Finnane counsels us to take heed of the influence of the new cultural history on the social history of crime, as evidenced in the collection of essays on crimes and trials in Australia.

The social and cultural history of crime has also led in new directions. Doggett's study of wife-beating and the law in Victorian England goes back to Anglo-Saxon times to explain the assimilation of wives into husbands. Her analysis of the history of coverture (the legal disabilities of wifehood) tries to answer the question of why it took so long in England (1891) to make it unlawful for a husband to beat and imprison his wife. The Victorian era was, as well, a time of profound change. As Cowman notes in her review of Walkowitz's *City of Dreadful Delight,* English women were becoming marching lawbreakers. Active in their use of the law, they were suing doctors, escaping asylums, stealing and burning pornographic literature, vandalizing sex shops and cinemas showing erotica, and forcing their husbands by judicial writ to return to the conjugal bed.

In spite of searching for new horizons, the process of synthesis continues. Emsley's political and social history of the English police is seen by Philips as offering a corrective to the Whig interpretation of the past, as well as to the view of the police as an instrument of class power to discipline and control the industrial proletariat and subversive groups. Marquis's history of the Canadian chiefs of police is seen by Edgerton and Swainger in different lights—from a rigid law and order mentality to a professional liberalization. Harriger's history of the U.S. federal special prosecutor shows the interaction of politics and the criminal law from the bottom up. Perhaps the last word on synthesis, however, should belong to Moczydlowski's *Hidden Life of Polish Prisons*. With double the prisoners per capita of any Western country, the former Director General's landscape resembles that of an exotic tribal culture at work.

Louis A. Knafla

"Coram Domino Comite et suis Iudicibus": Penal Procedure in Early Fourteenth-Century Dubrovnik

Nella Lonza
University of Zagreb

SOURCES: COURT REPORTS AND LEGAL FOUNDATIONS

The register "*Liber de maleficiis et dampnis datis tempore nobilis viri domini Bartholomei Gradonici honorabilis comitis Ragusii in suo secundo regimine*," from 1312–1313,[1] provides an insight into the life of the central court of the Dubrovnik commune.[2] It is obviously a part of a broader volume because the last report is not complete; it covers a nine-month term (from 22 July 1312 to 18 April 1313), while other office registers, kept under the administration of the same count Gradonicus, lasted for another year.[3] The *Liber* contains eighty-seven *casus;* reports are always short, and give only summaries of procedural actions and results of evidence. Although we know that such criminal court records had been kept in Dubrovnik since at least as early as 1279,[4] only a few fragments from the thirteenth century are extant today.[5] The materials of penal proceedings from the fourteenth century are scarcely extant, and survive more consistently only since the following century.

The substratum of legal reality in Dubrovnik at the beginning of the fourteenth century was based on the Statute of 1272.[6] Analysis of its content shows, however, that the core of penal norms was actually taken over from an older statute of 1238 that has not been preserved.[7] The regulations brought later on by the Dubrovnik councils were added at the end of the statute or interpolated—where they logically fitted in, or were put into new legal collections. The first one, *Liber omnium reformationum,* was initiated in 1335 and covered the norms from the beginning of the century, including some from the penal law.[8] The statute placed customary law (*consuetudo*) in a secondary position, leaving it to the area that the written law did not cover.[9] However, in times of social polarization, the norms of customary law (and of morale) will clash with regulations to such an extent as cor-

Historical Archives of Dubrovnik, Dubrovnik Republic, Lamenti Politici, 1, Fol. 7.

Liber de Maleficiis, 1312–1313

responds to the force of the social group standing behind the customary law.[10] Finally, although it appears that in the legal system of Dubrovnik, as with all others of the "Venetian circle," legal holes were filled in not with the help of *ius commune,* but with the creative activity of the court,[11] the Dubrovnik legal system undoubtedly was inspired by the substantive solutions and forms of the common European legal tradition.[12]

JURISDICTION AND COMPOSITION OF THE COURT

During the Venetian dominion over Dubrovnik (1205–1358), the central constitutional position was held by the count of Dubrovnik, appointed by the Venetian authorities. According to the statutory provisions of 1272, he appointed judges and members of the Minor Council, and every year together with them chose the members of the Great Council.[13] Such a structure and composition of the most important bodies suggests enormous power on the part of the count, who could function with absolute power. In spite of the incomplete data that have been preserved, the extant materials outline the real system as a sensitive organism based on not only his power, but also on opportunism and a balance of interests and compromises.

In spite of the statutory grants, the count did not carry out an aggressive and arbitrary personal policy that would exclude the influence of individuals, families, and groups within the city. The circle of persons acting as the governing group in both the court and in the Minor Council was more constant[14] than the person of the count, who changed every two years. The new count "inherited" those with whom he ought to have shared power. During the first decades of the fourteenth century the Great Council was gradually transformed from an electoral organ into a body with a constant structure, composed of all male patricians of legal age.[15]

The count of Dubrovnik, as well as of other subordinate towns, was appointed by the Venetian Great Council for a two-year term.[16] He received instructions (*comissio*), containing the basic guidelines as to his rule,[17] including some instructions about punishment. As his income was more than 1,000 *perperi* per year[18] and his position on the scale of honor was significant, it is therefore not surprising that this duty was entrusted to members of the most distinguished Venetian families, often even to the sons of the doge.[19] This office was a good opportunity for the Venetian authorities to test the capabilities of an individual so as to plan his future political career.

Bartholomeus Gradonicus (Gradenigo) was, during this period, the count of Dubrovnik for the second time.[20] Not elected at the usual term, he started his duty in July 1312[21] due to the vacancy caused by the death of the count Peter Michael. He was re-elected the count of Dubrovnik for the third time from 1320 to 1322.[22] Later on, he held high honorary positions in Venetian political life, being referred to as "*capitaneus generalis*" in the documents of 1335–1337, and as doge from 1339 until his death in 1342.[23]

The Grand Tribunal (*Curia Maior*) tried, under the guidance of the count, both civil disputes of the value above five *perperi*[24] and criminal cases.[25] Based on some extant civil and other legal registers from the same years,[26] we know that the same judges also participated in civil litigation.

Two groups of judges are found in this court register. Five of them held office until 1312: Marinus de Petregna, Johannes de Çelipa, Luce de Bona, Martulus de Tedusio, and Tefla de Tefla. Since the judges' term of office lasted for a year and could not be prolonged,[27] they were then replaced by other patricians who were chosen on St. Michael's day (29 September) in 1312: Petrus de Prodanello, Petrus de Pabora (on 3 June 1313 he was replaced by Pancratius de Saraca), Nicola de Sorgo, Ursacius de Bodaça, and Nicola de Gundula (on 26 April 1313 he was replaced by Matheus de Petregna, because just one day before that Gundula had been designated commander of a galley that had to sail to Venice).[28] Matheus Petregna and Pancratius de Saraca are mentioned as judges from 23 October 1312, which was prior to their formal appointment, and they always appeared together with the count's assistant in less important procedural stages.[29] This suggests that they were asked to function from time to time as judges' deputies in less serious procedural stages, and were promoted to be judges of the Grand Tribunal when there was a need for a permanent substitute.

These five judges did not act as a *collegium*. Only those who were asked by the count to participate in the disposition of procedures would take part.[30] Therefore, neither the number nor the composition of the tribunal was constant.[31] Most of the time there were two members, sometimes more.[32] It was not prescribed what the structure of the court should be in the case of different offenses. However, there was a tendency with more complicated and delicate cases to have a larger tribunal[33] (e.g. at inquisitional trials,[34] or when the accused were members of the count's escort).[35] It is not possible to determine from these sources whether the count manipulated the summoning of judges for a proceeding. For example, when a member of the count's escort was involved in some injury, the count engaged three judges, although we would expect that sympathy for the accused may have led the count to reduce the number of tribunal members.[36] In order to avoid permanently held judiciary positions (of particular sensitivity), renewed appointments of judges was forbidden.[37] Also, in spite of the fact that a corresponding statutory ban was not yet formulated,[38] members of the same noble family would not be judges at the same time,[39] thereby preventing the abuse of justice.

The Petregna family, which was considered among the most eminent of Dubrovnik, provided two judges: Marinus was one of the most politically engaged patricians, and his brother Matheus was more concerned with commerce.[40] Johannes Çelipa, who was not from a particularly rich family, was actually one of the most respectable Ragusean patricians of his time, and was regularly a member of the *Consilium Rogatorum,* and often a member of the Minor Council. Like Marinus Petregna, he was sent on delicate missions.[41] Just at the time when his family influence began to rise, Luca Bona also presented himself as a judge of *Curia Maior.*[42] From the family Tudisio, particularly outstanding was Martolus Stançii de Tudisio, known for his lively commercial activity and political engagement in legations and different offices. He was always a member of the *Consilium Rogatorum* and a frequently appointed judge.[43] Tefla de Tefla is a lesser-known patrician, mentioned only in a few contemporary documents.[44] Petrus de Prodanello cannot be identified quite accurately because there were two nobles in that family with the same name. He was most probably Petrus Ursacii, who was a permanent member of the *Consilium Rogatorum* and often a judge.[45] In the large family of Bodaça there were at that time two by the name Ursacius,[46] but in regard to public life it was most probably the more prominent and distinguished Ursacius Nichifori de Bodaça.[47] The judicial role was also performed by Nicolaus Sorgo, a representative of the family whose members just managed to get a position in the Minor Council and in some other important bodies.[48] Nicolaus de Gundula was engaged in commerce, particularly with Apulia and Venice, where he often went for legations.[49] Pancracius de Saraca also belonged to the circle of distinguished patricians.[50]

Therefore, most of the judges were representatives of the eminent patrician families. It is interesting to note some very clear exceptions when the members of not particularly powerful families were repeatedly appointed as judges,[51] sometimes as soon as the ban period for re-election elapsed. In such cases it was persons whose reputation and personal talent placed them among the political elite.

As opposed to other members of the judiciary (count, assistant, chancellor) who were, each in a different way, paid for their work, there is no evidence that judges received any kind of compensation.[52] Neither, however, were their economic activities disadvantaged. An analysis of their work shows that they usually participated in less than one criminal procedure a week,[53] while they were probably more engaged with civil proceedings. Their economic activity was mainly based on business associations, commonly involving an economic community of brethren.[54] Taking into consideration the principle of the representation of families at important offices, it is obvious that commercial operations and public service duties—which caused loss of time but did contribute to the family reputation—were distributed and shared among relatives.

A count's personal policy was defined mainly by the existing social structure and distribution of political power. He would not find it reasonable and opportune to be obstinate by engaging only "his men," as evidenced by the fact that during the time of several counts the same persons appeared as judges.[55] In addition, after the cessation of the Venetian domination in 1358, when members of the Minor Council as well as judges were appointed by the Great Council (patricians' assembly), no significant change could be noticed.[56]

However, the count's position at the trial should not be underestimated. In addition to selecting and summoning judges, he presided over the tribunal and had the most active role during the judicial process. Judges were present at hearings of witnesses and participated in pronouncing the sentences. During the trial the composition of the *collegium* usually did not change, due to the concentrated nature of the procedure. There was one case where the *collegium* members did change during a trial, but this had no effect on the course of the procedure,[57] suggesting the judges had a secondary role. Nevertheless, if they had been mere observers, neither the provisions on the banning of re-election nor the necessity to have patrician families represented in order to avoid the concentration of power would have been needed. The extant court materials unfortunately do not permit an examination of the relations within the tribunal, particularly not in respect of possible dissensions between the count and the judges.

Although the judiciary in any system may be a very efficient lever of the government, the judicial power of the Venetian count should not be overestimated. There were situations of negative reaction of the "diffuse social community" toward the count's criminal policy, either because of opposition to his jurisdiction,[58] or because a different value system built into local morals and customs would lead to a solution of a case different from what the public authority had planned.[59] It is important to note that in the cases mentioned, the Venetian response was either to give in or make a slight reproach, and not to use sheer force. Conflicts were resolved through negotiation and compromise. The relation between the Venetian superior and the Dubrovnik commune was complex, and the extent of the power of the Venetian Republic is questionable.

This balance of power can be seen in the example of one procedural norm that occurred in 1305. Venetian authorities reacted to the regulation of Dubrovnik that testimony given by a foreigner against a citizen of Dubrovnik would not be accepted in criminal or civil cases. The Venetian Great Council wrote to the count of Dubrovnik and to the commune, stating that the provision had to be repealed with regard to relations with Venetians; otherwise the Venetian authorities would enforce the regulation reciprocally.[60] Therefore, we can assume that the Venetian authorities had no power to intervene in the Dubrovnik legal system and to change unfavorable and humiliating provisions, but could only apply the same regulations against the citizens of Dubrovnik. As the commune persisted in maintaining its regulation, the dispute was solved only three years later, again on the ground of reciprocity.[61]

Ordinarily the count would bring along his assistant (*"socius"* or *"miles"*)[62] to take his place when needed, especially for less delicate duties.[63] With members of the Minor Court (*Curia Minor*), the assistant adjudicated in less serious civil disputes and helped the count in criminal cases as well.[64] He mostly heard the testimony,[65] in one case he received the claim instead of the count,[66] and once he pronounced the admonition.[67] Sometimes the count gave him particular procedural tasks, but he always substituted for him in the case of absence.[68]

The count's assistant in this period was Marcus Gradonicus, for whom it was obviously one of the first steps in his *cursus honorum*. One can conclude from various sources that he was the count's son.[69] The Venetian authorities had a positive attitude toward such personal solutions.[70] It was in their interest for the count to have a reliable and devoted assistant, and for the young patrician to acquire some governing experience by working with his father.

The mechanism of central criminal jurisdiction was spreading over both land and insular territorial units in the fourteenth century. Local counts and judges were authorized to resolve only smaller civil disputes.[71] In criminal prosecutions their task was to undertake the necessary investigative operations urgently and to arrest the culprit. They had to inform the count of Dubrovnik immediately, and to present the case to him.[72] Their statements were used in the proceedings that followed before the count and the Major Court.

The criminal justice records were made by the chancellor.[73] Due to the lack of Ragusans with adequate knowledge and skills, and to the delicacy of the task itself, educated chancellors from Italian towns were engaged.[74] Although they were under annual contracts, there was no obstacle to renewing these and letting them stay on as long as they worked professionally and efficiently.[75] Thus, in March 1312, the Minor Council prolonged the engagement of *magister* Albertinus from Cremona,[76] who acted as chancellor in Dubrovnik until 1315—when he was chosen for the notary of the Venetian *Curia Maior*.[77] Although his name had not been written down, he was probably the scribe of this register.

It is difficult to evaluate the chancellor's contribution in framing criminal procedures. When a reader is faced with a court register, there is always a dilemma. Were all the described formalities really carried out, or was it actually the scribe who gave them a perfect form? There are also some very general questions about the role of the chancellor in the development of criminal law. Traces of medieval legal doctrine can be positively recognized here and there in the court registers.[78] Since chancellors were the only "professionals" at the court, we can assume that they were to be thanked for the reception of the *ius commune*.

PARALLEL DISPUTE-SOLVING MECHANISMS

Although the register of 1312–1313 is a product of the state court, it contains elements that allow insight into other ways in which social conflicts and disputes were resolved. A large number of tense situations were solved within the same social group in which they had taken place. Either the group members agreed, not wanting the conflict to become known outside their circle, or the public authority wanted to leave "disciplinary" adjudication to narrower social communities. For example, family offenses met with sanctions within the family—the *pater familias* punished his family members.[79] Similarly, the master punished his servant, and so forth.[80] The adjudication for some crimes was kept within the village community.[81] In some cases the central authority would even encourage this by the introduction of collective liability for obligations resulting from an offense, and by leaving the community to find the offender and place the burden of judgment on him.[82]

From the total number of eighty-seven reports in our register, only about half (forty-five) end with the pronouncement of a sentence.[83] It is sometimes clear that the normal flow of the procedure was interrupted for a non-legal reason, probably an out-of-court agreement and settlement.[84] Sometimes the parties had agreed in advance not to turn to the court at all,[85] as if it were a civil dispute that depended on their disposition. But the Dubrovnik authorities would only leave the adjudication to other subjects in the question of a particular type of crime. It would have been too risky to allow generally the aggrieved party or his locale to avoid regular judicial channels in order "to take justice in its own hands." Public authorities did not like such behavior because it jeopardized their power and threatened an escalation of violence.[86] In Dubrovnik, the court often pronounced an admonition by which it tried to prevent revenge, especially within the urban community.[87] This proves indirectly how seriously the court considered that particular danger.

CRIMINAL PROCEDURE

Criminal procedures were generally initiated with a claim to the count by the aggrieved party or any other person in his or her name.[88] The statutory provisions determined a preclusive and subjective term of three days, and in the case of crimes in out-of-town areas within eight days.[89] If the offender was not known, fell under, or was not available for Dubrovnik jurisdiction, there was a special procedure directed mainly to the collection of evidence that might be of help in the future.[90]

The initial action was really undertaken before the count himself, which corresponds to the formality of an act meant for the engagement of the state authority. The claim could, in very exceptional circumstances, be submitted to the count's assistant, but it was clear that he was just an inter-mediary. The procedures were always initiated by the aggrieved party or a proxy, usually a relative. A husband could initiate an action on behalf of his wife,[91] but aggrieved women had the procedural capacity to appear as accusers. There was a case in which a father sued a person who had beaten his son,[92] and in two other cases a brother sued on behalf of his brother.[93] In one *casus* the procurator was in no obvious or close family relationship with the accuser but acted as a proxy.[94]

For these eighty-seven cases, in only a few did the count start the pro-cedure *ex officio,* usually when there was a special interest on the part of the authorities due to the sensitivity of the issue or seriousness of the deed. For example, the count initiated a procedure when there was a serious fight between citizens of Dubrovnik and some Vlachs (citizens of the hinterland) who complained to the count,[95] when there was an illegal armament of a ship,[96] and in the case of death caused by a wound or some injury.[97] Also, the count once started a procedure of an inquisitorial type on the basis of a denouncement by the aggrieved person who did not know or suspect who the offender was.[98] Sometimes he was motivated by an official claim submitted by *justiciarii* who were performing market control,[99] and once it was upon a notice by a third person who was an eyewitness.[100] In very serious cases the authorities promised high rewards for those who reported crimes.[101]

Defense of the accused was rarely recorded, thirteen times (15 percent). The accused was only obliged to respond to the summons and did not have to say anything.[102] His statement did not have a fixed procedural position, and was significantly different from testimony by witnesses.[103] There was no indication of the accused receiving legal assistance. If he was innocent, he could only have hoped that the court would carefully establish the truth. The protection from false accusation was guaranteed by punishing the ac-cuser through the retaliation principle.[104]

When reading the reports, we can see that it was not unusual for the aggrieved party to bring along witnesses at the submission of a claim so that they could give their statements right away.[105] Alternatively, they would simply give their names to be summoned by the court. It was also possible for the accused to bring along a person who would confirm his or her innocence.[106] When hearing from the witnesses, the chancellor would note what was spontaneously said, as well as the questions asked and the answers received. If a witness was giving the already known facts, only very brief notes were recorded.[107] From the end of the thirteenth century, we can find that it was possible to require the questioning of absent wit-nesses.[108]

The questions asked by the court are of particular interest because they tell us what circumstances were considered relevant. Some of them sort out statutory norms as circumstances that have to be examined because they connected some substantial consequence; for example, the question of whether blood had accompanied a corporal injury would have been important in evaluating the deed and choosing the penalty.[109] The fact of who started a fight could have been decisive in determining the guilt and punishment of the accused.[110] Sometimes it was necessary to determine some particular fact in order to better understand the case, even if, according to legal rules, the circumstance had no qualifying role.[111] Other questions were asked to make progress in the case. For example, asking about the presence of other persons gave the court some information about potential witnesses.[112]

The note on the pronounced sentence was usually very short, and was either at the bottom of the page or in the margin. The chancellor would cross out the finished or suspended procedures in order to make the records as orderly as possible. Since acquittals were not recorded, it is not possible to distinguish them with certainty from decisions that suspended the procedure for some other reason.[113] In some cases, it is clear from the very beginning that the procedure could not continue because the accuser did not have witnesses who would support his or her assertions,[114] or had some who were not trustworthy. Sometimes we come to the conclusion that the procedure was stopped by the will of the accuser. It is important to mention that quite a number of case reports (as many as fourteen)[115] contain only the claim, sometimes with the names of proposed witnesses, with some empty space left for the recording of procedural matters. We can suppose that in these cases either the parties came to an agreement, or the accuser realized there was insufficient evidence or lost interest in finding court satisfaction for some other reason.

There are two types of procedure recorded in the register, accusatorial and inquisitorial.[116] A content analysis that excludes terminological pretense shows that the division is not very strict, and if the activities of the court and of other procedural participants are analyzed, no significant differences between accusatorial and inquisitorial procedures can be found. Indeed, they are actually one and the same procedural type.

An examination of the reports on "accusatorial" procedures leads to the following conclusions. The court, during the presentation of evidence, carried out the questioning of witnesses, of the accused, and of the defendant, freely formulating questions and asking also those questions relating to the facts beyond the accusatory act.[117] In addition, the court questioned witnesses not proposed by the accuser,[118] and pronounced penalties for the accuser even when there was no counterclaim.[119]

However, official practise was obviously no precondition for calling a procedure "inquisitorial." The count could have initiated such actions on the ground of rumors, or on his own suspicions that some criminal offense had been committed.[120] But an inquisitorial procedure could be carried out even when the aggrieved party submitted the claim.[121] The only obvious difference from "accusatorial" proceedings was that the court used the inquisitorial form when the question was more serious and the crime more complicated,[122] saving only exceptions.[123]

Some older court records from Dubrovnik show that the procedure was of a mixed type,[124] while in the materials from the Dalmatian commune of Trogir, for example, the accusatorial principle was more obvious.[125] However, only a complex comparative study of criminal sources of other Dalmatian communes could lead us to a justified conclusion about the diffusion and development of different procedural models in that area.

EVIDENCE

The most common type of evidence found are testimonies by witnesses, aggrieved parties, and the defendant, as well as confessions extracted by torture or medical expertise. All these methods are within the framework of rational means of evidence,[126] which was to be expected in regions like Dubrovnik, open to influences of the Roman-canon legal tradition.

Provisions of the Dubrovnik statute that relate to types of evidence in criminal procedure are not particularly elaborate. They do not even mention, for example, some of the known judicial practices at the beginning of the fourteenth century. It is typical that these topics are not treated as a whole, nor even at one place; rather, they are mingled with provisions on witnesses in civil disputes,[127] or mentioned with the description of specific crimes.[128] Particularly interesting is statutory chapter III,33, which introduced novelties[129] in the system of statutory evidence rules.[130] It set up the principle that death or mutilation sentences had to be based on the testimony of at least two witnesses; in other cases, they could, as had been the case until then, be based on only one.[131]

The statutory evidence rules were a prescribed minimum for a convicting judgment, and not a rigid system that negated judicial evaluation of the given facts. The court established whether there were weaknesses in the personality of the witness that made him or her inappropriate to testify.[132] Attitudes of judicial practice as to the capacity of a person to be a witness seem to have followed statutory rules. Negative personal characteristics,[133] as well as a relationship of dependence,[134] resulted in an *a priori* elimination of a person being considered as a witness. Previous conflicts with the accused could be a reason for rejecting someone's testimony.[135] In each concrete case, the court determined freely to what extent it would trust a person's testimony.[136] As to their capacity to testify in criminal cases, the statute discriminated against women, having determined that in the case of offenses committed at night their testimony could be accepted only if there were no male witnesses; then it was possible to pronounce a mitigated penalty.[137] The judicial practice was more flexible on that point,[138] but it is a fact that women rarely appeared as witnesses.[139] These solutions corresponded to the developed medieval procedural doctrine that was, with more or less intensity, accepted in all regions where the *ius commune* was resident.

When we examine the medieval court materials of other Dalmatian towns, we come to the conclusion not only that testimony from witnesses was the most important and the most common form of evidence, but that the essence of the evaluation of evidence was often hidden in preliminary decision making on the permissibility and acceptability of testimony. The court at that point actually switched to some content problems, evaluating every given testimony.[140] We can say, therefore, that boundaries of procedural and substantive decisions were more flexible than in more modern times.

The Dubrovnik statute of 1272 does not mention torture, but this does not mean that it was not known in judicial practice.[141] Torture appears only once in our register, in the case of stealing wax of higher value.[142] The court resorted to it because, without any eyewitnesses, it did not have any other way of checking the existing suspicions. It is clear that a confession under compulsion is of a dubious verity. Therefore, the legal doctrine tried to consolidate its rational foundations by considering a confession valid only after the accused had repeated it without being tortured.[143] The confession on torture written in our register was given before the count, but in order to make it valid, the accused had to confirm it afterwards in the presence of the whole court.[144] He would then give numerous particularities about how he committed the crime so that it would confirm the allegations he had been charged with.

In establishing relevant facts for a murder or serious wounding, the court relied on the expert opinion of a physician. In some cases, he only had to determine that the life of a wounded person was no longer in danger.[145] When the case involved a knife stab that caused someone's death, the physician's statement was very precise and thorough—it had to involve the position and the shape of the wound, the cause of death, and the weapons that were used.[146] It was during this period that physicians from Dubrovnik had to report any wound that was alleged to be the consequence of violence.[147] A few decades earlier, such a regulation had been introduced in Venice to enable the state authorities to intervene successfully, not only with prosecution, but also with some actions that would prevent the escalation of violence.[148]

With regard to the evidential foundation of sentences, we have to bear in mind that the statute did not require the same information for all offenses. For those involving the most severe sentences, the degree of cognitive certainty had to be higher. Pursuant to the rules of Roman-canon law procedural doctrine, serious crimes were proved by corresponding testimonies of two eyewitnesses, confession of the accused, or on the grounds of a document.[149] This principle, general to medieval Europe during the period, was reflected in Dubrovnik. More serious offenses were those for which the death penalty or mutilation may have been pronounced.[150] If we compare these with the crimes from our register, only one case of murder may be separated as to its seriousness.[151] This involved an inquisitorial procedure where seven witnesses were examined, among whom were two women. All the witnesses elaborated on *indicia* very thoroughly, but they all stated that they did not see who had stabbed the victim. The accused was sentenced to banishment as the murderer on the basis of a statutory contumacy provision, not based on the evidence presented. We cannot, therefore, be sure if the above-mentioned two-witness rule would be strictly applied here or not. All other cases, being less serious, did not undergo such an abstract demand for an evidence minimum. The court could have decided alone whether the elaborated evidence represented sufficient grounds for its conclusion. In most of the cases there was enough room for a free evaluation of evidence. The condemnatory sentence may also rest on a weaker evidence base, even on some *indicia*. By acting conscientiously in determining the facts, the court came to its conclusion according to the rules of logic and experience.

An analysis from the reports in the register in which the results of the procedure were known has shown that the evidence substratum in accusatorial sentences varied. Some sentences were based on the confession of the accused,[152] or on the statements of several eye-witnesses.[153] Quite a number of them were based on the testimony of only one witness about directly relevant facts,[154] as well as on some *indicia*.[155] In some cases of petty offenses (punished by very low penalties), however, there was obviously no need to insist on a complete web of evidence.[156]

By looking at all the recorded cases, it is clear that often more witnesses were examined than would have been necessary if the legal evidence rules had been strictly followed.[157] That is, the principle of looking for material truth surpassed procedural economy. In the case of more serious offenses the court paid more attention to the presentation of evidence, and applied a great deal of pedantry at thoroughly establishing the relevant facts.[158] Least certain are the cases in which no convicting sentence has been recorded, although there seems to be a fairly firm evidential basis to expect it according both to rules of evidence and free evaluation.[159] Since the argument *a tacito* seems too risky, we can only speculate that these cases were brought to an end by out-of-court compensation, and that the public authority did not have a motive to insist on further prosecution.

COURT ADMONITION

The court records reveal a very special and effective legal tool, in the form of an admonition (*"preceptum"*), by which a person or persons were prohibited from behaving in a certain way, accompanied by a sanction. Juridically speaking, the court acted as the creator of individual norms that had a full structure (hypothesis-disposition-sanction). The creation of the admonition was motivated by the understanding that unhealthy relations, having caused one delict, could continue causing a whole series of crimes. These norms were within the competence of the same court authorities, and it was quite logical for the court to see its task as including the prevention of continuing conflict. After all, the constitutional system of the time was not based on the separation of powers.

Out of forty-three records ending with a sentence, court admonitions were pronounced in ten cases.[160] With only one exception, they occurred in procedures in response to physical attacks—fights and injuries—and were used in one-third of twenty-seven completed trials for such charges. Because the court admonition was meant to control revenge, it was pronounced on the defendant, but in half of the cases, the accuser, that is, the aggrieved party, was not spared, either. Even if the accuser did address the state authorities by initiating the court action, that did not guarantee that he or she would not react later by revenge. It is interesting that the count pronounced admonitions that applied not only to persons subject to the trial, but also to a broader circle of relatives (sometimes up to five additional people were included).[161] The admonition could apply to persons outside the family structure, or to all those who were rationally suspected of being capable of joining the revenge chain. Also, the banned behavior was not always to the accuser's disadvantage only, but could be directed to another person involved in the initial conflict.[162] It was also foreseen that one of the parties in conflict could engage a third person to perform the revengeful act, and this, too, would be addressed in the admonition, so that all the possibilities were covered.[163] The court admonitions in *Diversa cancellariae* registers are even more detailed, and they demand a removal or report of the assault by the third person, thus increasing the feeling of joint responsibility.[164]

The admonition was pronounced during the trial and was written down above the sentence, often before the witnesses' testimonies.[165] It is not clear how long the admonition would be in effect, it appears that it was not limited to the procedural time limits but was of a longer duration. It was left to the court to appraise the situation, and to foresee what kind of secondary conflict could arise as well as to provide an efficient prevention. The forbidden behavior ranged from acts to words and from fights to insults. Due to its purpose and aim, no penalty was considered exaggerated. The sanctions provided were very high and, as a rule, they far exceeded the penalty pronounced in the same case. For example, in one case the fine was six *perperi,* and the sanction from the court admonition twenty-five *perperi;* in another the penalty was ten *perperi* and the court admonition sanction was one hundred *perperi.*[166] The admonition sanctions rose to fifty, or even one hundred *perperi,*[167] sums that very rarely occurred with primary penalties. In order to make the court admonition efficient, the amount had to be such so as to deter or discourage one from entering into the conflict. There were *casus* when, in the same procedure, the same sanctions were not prescribed for all persons.[168] They were in proportion with the danger that was threatened (as in the case of a fight with knives), and perhaps with the income of the person in question.

Court admonitions were not typical for Dubrovnik only; they appear with some minor differences in sources from Šibenik in the fifteenth century.[169] We can assume that it was among the practices known to the courts of other Dalmatian towns,[170] and it would be interesting to find out whether admonitions resulted from Venetian law directly or whether they derived from a common European legal heritage.

MEASURES TO SECURE THE PROGRESS OF THE TRIAL: DETENTION, WARRANTY, AND CONTUMACY

Judicial practice of Dubrovnik at the turn of the thirteenth century did not include prison sentences, but it did recognize detention as a measure for dealing with suspected persons to secure court appearances and to prevent further disturbances.[171] In addition, it had to apply pressure on the accused to look for the warrantor,[172] or to contribute to the execution of the punishment.[173] Detention was particularly appropriate in the case of more serious crimes, or when there was a possible danger of escaping. Detention was applied only once in this register in a more complicated case of stealing. Because of the count's warrant, the suspect had been arrested within the region and was imprisoned. Detention did not achieve the expected results, however, as the culprit ran away after the sentence had been pronounced.[174] Due to concentrated and short-lasting procedures, detention was not at that time accompanied by problems that occurred later on. In fifteenth-century Dubrovnik, long-lasting detentions were not rare and lasted up to one year.[175]

Another institute by which the court tried to ensure the appearance of the accused was the demand to have a warrantor (*"pleç de presentando ad racionem"*).[176] Finally, the contumacy procedure allowed bringing a condemnatory sentence if the accused person failed to appear in court.[177] The presumption prescribed that by failing to face the justice the accused actually demonstrated his or her guilt and the inability to defend himself or herself by legal arguments. However, the court was thus not deprived of the duty to bring about evidence and to enter *in meritum*.[178] In the contrary case, it would have been very difficult or even impossible to establish the facts if, later on, the regular procedure was reactivated.[179] In practice it usually happened that the court had already gathered considerable evidence when the contumacy occurred.[180]

The contumacious penalty was in the form of an additional sum of money or banishment from the city and its surroundings.[181] In some very serious cases, a banished person appearing in the forbidden territory could have been killed with impunity.[182] In the case we have analyzed, the contumacious sentence would appear in the form of an additional sum of money half as large as the prescribed fine.[183] Only a murderer would have been given a banishment, which corresponded to the seriousness of the crime and to the death penalty.

PENALTIES

The penal system of Dubrovnik at the end of the thirteenth and beginning of the fourteenth centuries was based on fines, as in other similar environments at that time.[184] This did not always contribute to public morale, and was proved with a case from 1284. Relatives of a nun whose nose had been cut, as well as other people, reacted bitterly when the accused was subjected only to a fine of seventy-five *perperi*. To them, he deserved corporal punishment (amputation of the nose, hand, or leg), or even death.[185] The statement of the participants that *ratio* (judicial justice) and *iusticia* (equity) were confronted was a typical example of the heteronomy of different parts of the legal system.[186] The intention of the rebellious group to take justice in its own hands and get revenge was brought to an end by an intervention of the state authority and the judicial prosecution of the initiators of disobedience.[187]

The Dubrovnik statute, apart from fines, also provided for some corporal punishments (mutilation, whipping, and branding) as a deterrent for not having paid a fine.[188] These sanctions were probably not often carried out, but we have some indirect confirmation that such punishments did exist.[189] The death penalty was provided for the case of murder.[190] The most frequent remedies, listed in the register, however, were monetary ones.

An analysis of fines pronounced by the court reveals considerable correspondence to the fines provided by statute.[191] It would be anachronistic to explain this fact by a strict obedience to the legal rule, and there are a few cases that refute it. Naturally, statutory norms were models and examples to be followed, but not so rigidly as to preclude the court from acting with flexibility. Because of the relatively short period of time from the passing of the statute, such conformity is not unexpected, because the court evaluation of the punishment was based on the value system of the society that could not yet be changed. However, in some cases, the pronounced fine did not fit into the statutory framework, which suggests that the circumstances of a concrete act had some influence on the judgment. Quite differently, the extent of the fine for an insult was left by the statute to court discretion, allowing the evaluation of each particular case;[192] the pronounced sentences were low, mostly only one *perper*.[193]

The severity of the punishment reveals the social value scale. High penalties and strict trials for thefts, in both the statute and judicial practice, showed what was considered to be extremely dangerous for public order. The authorities reacted with the most serious punishment to the actions that jeopardized the constitutional foundation; thus, the patrician who refused to go to legation was fined five hundred *perperi*.[194]

We do not have at our disposal a sufficient number of *casus* for a reliable examination of the hypothesis of whether belonging to a certain social stratum had an influence on the punishment. In the examples we have compared, no such difference can be seen,[195] and the judiciary in that respect had been more neutral than one would usually tend to expect.[196] However, we do not want to suggest that social status did not have any influence on punishment policy. It is also obvious that the same fine did not affect the poor and the rich in the same way.

To what extent the usual fines affected the common people can well be shown by the comparison with essential prices and values in Dubrovnik during the period.[197] For one *perper*, which was the usual fine for an insult, it was possible to buy almost twenty-four gallons of wine. A one-year rent for a small house was five to eight *perperi*, and that corresponded to the fine for a physical attack with no blood. In order to pay that fine, a day-laborer had to work for over two months, and the punishment for an insult corresponded to ten days' wages. A mason's income was such that a fine for an insult would have taken almost five days' wages, and a corporal injury with blood would have been equated with two average months' pay. Thus, the amounts were not low, and could not be paid without serious consequences. Therefore, it seems that the penal policy was severe enough with these pecuniary fines.

Since the system based on fines obviously bears many defects—due to the inability to collect the money—that can generally jeopardize the efficacy of punishing, the statutory regulations foresaw some supplementary penalties as well. The Dubrovnik statute, like many others, brings the system of accompanying corporal punishment of different kinds. We have not found them in our register, but it was not actually obligatory to mention them in the court sentence since their application followed *ex lege*, when the primary sanction had not been carried out within the given period of time.

The accused tried to avoid the danger of supplementary corporal punishment by finding warrantors for the pecuniary fine. The state authority also encouraged it, preferring the collection of an amount of money that would enlarge its revenues. In this register, warrantors appeared in thirteen procedures,[198] and represented the usual way by which the defendant tried to convince the authorities that the fine could be collected with no difficulty.[199] The circle of people who appeared in the role of warrantors was very wide. Sometimes they were members of the defendant's family who were helping him or her out of solidarity; often it was a contractual relationship with third persons, probably some sort of a loan that enabled the accused to gain some time and secure the necessary amount of money.

When authorities were unable to collect a fine and no supplementary corporal punishment was provided for, they probably began introducing detention. However, that could have been an efficient measure of pressure only on a wealthy person. In fifteenth-century Dubrovnik, there was also a possibility to commute the pecuniary penalty into an imprisonment, which gave the poor a possibility to avoid the pecuniary burden that threatened to have long-lasting effects on his living standards.[200] The public authorities did not need to be disappointed: They did lose the income (that was not very certain anyway), but they also demonstrated their coercive power. It has to be mentioned, finally, that in the middle of the fifteenth century this possibility of substitution of imprisonment for a fine was possible only for the offenses that had a relatively low public significance.

The commutation of the pecuniary penalty into a prison sentence signalled the beginning of a gradual transition to the new sanction system, having given a more distinguished role to imprisonment. The results of this process in Dubrovnik—as well as in other Dalmatian communes—have still not been systematically examined. But it seems that they follow basically the process of transformation of the penal system that had taken place in thirteenth-century Venice.[201]

CRIME IMAGES[202]

Among the pronounced sentences, the most numerous crimes are batteries (fights, strokes, injuries), comprising 63 percent, that is, twenty-seven out of forty-three trials of all offenses. The same can be said for the claims of unfinished procedures: 66 percent (fifty-seven of eighty-seven cases) were submitted because of a physical attack, and in two of them there was a question of threat.[203] Punishment for an insult was pronounced in four cases (in another case together with the punishment for striking).[204] It is surprising that pure property offenses were rarely (twice) tried.[205] This does not mean that property disputes did not exist in everyday life, but indicates that they were either solved by self-help or were hidden motives for violent assaults. Some were solved by a civil claim for restitution or for compensation. A group of seven sentences relates to the violation of the city order: Violations of commercial norms (by refusing to sell[206], by having false weights[207]), by equipping a galley with inadequate arms,[208] by refusing the entrusted legation,[209] or by not caring for the office of taxation.[210]

The evidence suggests that crime reflected the escalation of violence, ranging from insults to batteries.[211] By sometimes beginning with harmless teasing or insulting words or curses,[212] emotions led to vehement reactions often ending with serious consequences.[213] The fact is that almost two-thirds of the cases reaching the court of Dubrovnik at that time concerned physical attacks. Bearing in mind the expected "black number," violence has proved to have been part of Dubrovnik everyday life—on the square, in the street, and in the shop.[214]

The public authority, by trying to reduce conflicts to a minimum in order to enhance its stability, tried to make a prognosis about which situations were dangerous and could provoke the spiral of violence. Apart from strict admonitions by which the authorities tried to prevent new crimes from happening out of already disturbed relations, there was a preventive prohibition of behavior that could have caused riots.[215] Just like any other medieval commune, Dubrovnik also had a curfew after the third ringing of the bell, when inns had to be closed.[216] It was forbidden to walk around at night (particularly with no light),[217] to carry weapons,[218] or to wear disguises[219]—all these things were considered risky for the peace of the urban community.[220]

We have to ask ourselves, to what extent do the crimes described in the register actually reflect the whole picture of "criminality"? Research in historical criminology is naturally far from reliable, because court register analysis of this era can rarely be supplemented by other sources. We can hardly object to the reasonable warning by Mario Sbriccoli who says that court archives are very useful for examining the functioning of the judiciary, but not for making more complete conclusions on criminality.[221] Therefore, all we have tried to say above ought to be taken only conditionally.

FINAL OBSERVATIONS

The Dubrovnik register, from the beginning of the fourteenth century, represents a rare source of information about criminal behavior and the penal system in communal societies of the Dalmatian coast. An insight into the functioning of the judiciary, however, would not be complete without an analysis of the court system, its composition, and changes in personnel. The leading appointive and procedural roles provided by the count sent from Venice would suggest that the judicial power was concentrated in his hands. However, a prosopographic analysis shows that a stable social structure and the distribution of political power among patrician families had some influence on his appointments. The statutory rules on the representation of noble families and the rotation of judges show the importance of judicial duty.

Criminal procedures were mostly initiated by the claim of the aggrieved party or his proxy, and were started *ex officio* only in very serious and complex cases. If the committer was not known or could not be reached by the Dubrovnik judiciary, there were some procedural actions to secure and collect evidence. Accusatorial and inquisitorial procedures differed only in some unimportant formal elements. There was already in place a unique procedure with the more expressed inquisitorial principle. Almost half of all procedures initiated were not finished. The reason was usually hidden, but we could assume that there was an out-of-court settlement or that a crisis in the presentation of evidence occurred.

The system in the court practice for gathering evidence was far more complicated than that according to the statute (the application of torture and of medical expertise, for example), as well as according to the way the court reached its decisions. It proves an ahistorical overrating of the place that statutory norms have among other components of the legal order. The system of evidence rules established a minimum proof only for the most serious crimes, so that the court was not usually bound by them. One can see that the principle of seeking material truth was more prevalently expressed than one would expect. The decision whether to accept a witness's testimony included the judgment as to his or her general veracity and an evaluation of the statement itself, so that a seemingly procedural decision often hid the crucial outcome. Questions asked by the court during the presentation of evidence widened the circle of relevant facts more than the statutory provisions considering elements of guilt.

At this point, our attention is drawn to the court admonition, which was introduced through judicature. The court evaluated the entire conflict situation. It could pronounce admonition not only for those involved in the crime but also for their families and third persons. The sanction was established according to the danger of revenge. As we can see, the elements of the admonition were flexible and were adapted to each case. It was clear from the judiciary records that in everyday life violence tended to escalate, and the admonition was an attempt to break the chain of vengeance.

The penal system was founded on fines that were still efficient and useful for the authorities as a form of cryptotaxation.[222] Pecuniary penalties were also preferred in other similar surroundings, representing a transition from corporal punishment to imprisonment. Threatening by supplementary corporal (mutilation) penalties expressed in the statutory norms was avoided in practice by the introduction of warrants. The pronounced penalties correspond to the ones foreseen by the statute. However, that is not considered to be a proof of the application of the principle of legality. It only shows that the value system did not change in the last thirty years. Absolute amounts are quite high in comparison with wages and living costs. The amount of the fine indicated the evaluation of the crime from the point of view of a social mischief, and also took into consideration subjective elements. There was no significant difference in the fines imposed on patricians and plebeians, which may be significant in examining the stratification of Dubrovnik society in the early fourteenth century.

The examination of criminality is limited by the nature of the sources and by the unknown "dark figure," and the tendencies noticed may only be sketched. Two-thirds of all the procedures from the register were held because of corporal attacks, and purely property offenses were rare. They were probably covered by the civil judiciary or out-of-court actions. Not all physical violence came before the court, either because the punishment was partly left with the narrower social groups (e.g., families), or because of concrete relations that initiated informal agreement mechanisms and not the aegis of state repression. The public authority fought criminal behavior by punishment and admonition in an already-existing conflict situation. It sometimes acted preventively by prohibiting the kinds of behavior it considered risky for the preservation of social peace.

There is a question whether it would be possible to generalize the conclusions derived from the Dubrovnik register analysis to the other Dalmatian communes. The court materials of other towns have not been studied yet, so a definite answer is not possible. The elements of statutory regulations suggest that there are no important differences. At the beginning of the fourteenth century other Dalmatian communes also had the same type of the criminal procedure with more expressed inquisitorial elements. The law of proof was basically the same (types of evidence, evidence rules) and the penal system was in the same stage of development (fines were prevalent). The criminal law of Dubrovnik and other Dalmatian towns was closely related to the legal system of Italian communes. There was a slight delay in the formation of public institutions and legal order, but the receptivity to new penal institutes (e.g., inquisitorial elements, torture) was becoming higher. It is not always possible to establish where some particular influence came from. The mark of the Venetian domination on the Dubrovnik legal system is indisputable. Still, the rise of the Dubrovnik patriciate and economic growth resulted in a fairly obvious level of autonomy at the turn of the fourteenth century. The receptivity of such a developed environment was significant, and it would be difficult to say with certainty whether some criminal law novelty had come directly from Venice or had been accepted from the legal heritage of the *ius commune*. Dubrovnik had to face similar problems in the functioning of government and in keeping social stability as did other developed Mediterranean communes. It is therefore natural for Dubrovnik to have to reached for the same procedural solutions and to formulate or similar penal policy.

NOTES

An earlier version of this article was published in the Croatian language in *Anali Zavoda za povijesne znanosti Hrvatske akademije znanosti i umjetnosti u Dubrovniku* 30 (1992): 25–54. Acknowledgment is due to Louis Knafla for his suggestions and encouragement.

1. Historical Archives of Dubrovnik, the Dubrovnik Republic Fund (cited hereafter as: HAD, DR), series Lamenti politici, I. At the beginning of this century the court materials of the Dubrovnik archives were inconsistently classified, and the

series were made without a valid criterion: "*Lamenti politici*" is neither an original, nor by content a linked whole. The register has recently been published by Nella Lonza and Zdenka Janeković-Römer, "Dubrovački 'Liber de maleficiis' iz 1312– 1313. godine," *Radovi Zavoda za hrvatsku povijest Filozofskog fakulteta Zagreb* 25 (1992): 173–228. A few records from this register were mentioned by Bariša Krekić, "Crime and Violence in the Venetian Levant: A Few XIVth Century Cases," *Zbornik radova Vizantološkog instituta* 16 (1975): 128.

2. At the beginning of the fourteenth century, Dubrovnik (Lat. *Ragusa*, Croatia) had already been included in the Venetian dominion on the Adriatic for about 100 years. The content of dependent relations was changing according to the balance of power, but within the trend of the ever-increasing emancipation of Dubrovnik until finally Venice, weakened by wars, had to withdraw in 1358. Since then, and until 1808, Dubrovnik was developing as a free republic under the supreme protection of one of the great powers (the Croatian and Hungarian kingdoms, the Ottoman Empire). Successful economic development of the community was based on maritime trade and commerce. Some tensions among the social classes (especially the patricians and the wealthy merchants who did not have any ruling power) did not develop into durable confrontations. The structure of the governmental bodies was being built from the thirteenth century, (*Consilium Maius, Consilium Minus, Consilium Rogatorum, Magna Curia,* etc.), reaching its final form in the middle of the fourteenth century. At the end of the thirteenth century, the city without the district had about 3,500 inhabitants. The territory included the coast in the length of thirteen miles, and a quite wide archipelago.

For a review of Dubrovnik history, see Vinko Foretić, *Povijest Dubrovnika do 1808. godine* (Zagreb, 1980), 2 vols. (emphasis on political history); and a short but well-balanced book of Bernard Stulli, *Povijest Dubrovačke Republike* (Dubrovnik-Zagreb, 1989). For volumes published in English: Bariša Krekić, *Dubrovnik in the 14th and 15th Centuries: A City Between East and West* (Norman, 1972); Francis W. Carter, *Dubrovnik (Ragusa): A Classic City-State* (London and New York, 1972)—emphasis on economic history, a very extensive bibliography, and a review of archive series; and Josip Lučić, *Dubrovnik, City of Croatian Freedom: A Chronology* (Zagreb, 1991).

3. "Liber de consiliis et reformationibus" (HAD, DR, Reformationes, V, fols 1–36), "Capitulum de litteris citatoriis et preconiçationibus" (ibid, fols 47–62), "Capitulum de procuratoribus" (HAD, DR, Diversa cancellariae, V, fols 112– 149v), "Capitulum de venditionibus possessionum" (ibid., fols 171–214).

4. "*Scriptum in libro maleficiorum*" (*Istorijski spomenici Dubrovačkog arhiva: Kancelariski i notarski spisi g. 1278–1301,* ed. G. Čremošnik, (Beograd, 1932): 21).

5. Fragments of the "Liber de maleficiis" from 1284 to 1285 are bound into the volume of HAD, DR, *Diversa cancellariae,* II, and published in *Spisi dubrovačke kancelarije* III, ed. J. Lučić, *Monumenta historica Ragusina III* (Zagreb, 1988), cited hereafter as DC II. There is another register from the fourteenth century still kept in Dubrovnik: "Capitulum maleficiorum et maledictorum" (1348–1350), included in the series *Lamenta criminalia,* X.

The situation is similar with other archives on the Dalmatian coast. The only larger pile of materials until the middle of the fourteenth century are the court records of Trogir, among which there are also some criminal documents: *Zapisci sudbenog dvora općine trogirske* I, ed. M. Barada, *Trogirski spomenici II* (Zagreb, 1951), cited hereafter as TS I.

6. A critical edition is *Liber statutorum civitatis Ragusii,* eds. V. Bogišić and C. Jireček, *Monumenta historico-iuridica Slavorum Meridionalium IX,* (Zagreb 1904). The statutory provisions are cited hereafter as Statute.

7. It is mentioned in 1254 in the text of the count's oath (Bogišić-Jireček, *Liber,* LXIX), and in the fourteenth-century dispute about the application of relevant law (Statute VIII, 58). These data are supported by a comparison of the contents of sequence and style of criminal norms of the Dubrovnik Statute, the Korčula Statute of 1265, and the Venetian *Promissio de maleficiis* (1232). It shows that the Dubrovnik norms must be older than the ones of Korčula, and closer in time to the Venetian ones. See *Statuta et leges civitatis et insulae Curzulae 1214–1558,* ed. J. Hanel, *Monumenta historico-iuridica Slavorum Meridionalium 1* (Zagreb, 1877), cited hereafter as Statute Korčula; and *Volumen statutorum, legum ac iurium D. Venetorum, Promissio de maleficiis* (Venetiis, 1632).

8. "Liber omnium Reformationum Civitatis Ragusii," ed. A. Solovjev, in *Istorisko-pravni spomenici I, Dubrovački zakoni i uredbe. Zbornik Srpske kraljevske akademije za istoriju, jezik i književnost srpskog naroda,* III, 6 (Beograd, 1936), 1–348.

9. Statute II, 4.

10. See the examples in the text below.

11. Statute, Proemium and II, 4. See Lamberto Pansolli, *La gerarchia delle fonti di diritto nella legislazione medievale veneziana* (Milano, 1970); and Ugo Nicolini, "Diritto romano e diritti particolari in Italia nell'eta comunale," *Rivista di Storia del Diritto Italiano* 59 (1986): 13–172.

12. On the *ius commune* see Manlio Bellomo, *L'Europa del diritto comune* (Roma, 4th ed. 1989).

13. Statute I, 3.

14. The data about the composition of the Great Council from the beginning of the fourteenth century are incomplete because the materials have not been preserved as a whole. We have those from 1301, 1302, 1303, 1312, 1319, 1322, etc.: *Libri reformationum I, Monumenta Ragusina, Monumenta spectantia historiam Slavorum Meridionalium* X (Zagreb, 1879), cited hereafter as MR I.

15. In 1322 the count formally lost the possibility of electing the council members, and the Great Council was "closed" (*Libri Reformationum V, Monumenta Ragusina, Monumenta spectantia historiam Slavorum Meridionalium XXIX* (Zagreb, 1897), 349; cited hereafter as MR V. It is necessary to accept the observation by Milan Rešetar ("Dubrovačko veliko vijeće," Dubrovnik 1 (1929): 60), stating that the number of members suddenly increased from 1303 to 1312 (from 66 members to 190). If we keep in mind the estimation that in 1312 there were about 300 adult male patricians (Irmgard Mahnken, Dubrovački patricijat u XIV veku, I, Posebna izdanja SANU CCCXL, Odelenje društvenih nauka 36 (Beograd, 1960), 9), we could come to the conclusion that the selection principle on the part of the count was still not dominant.

16. Šime Ljubić, "Ob odnošajih dubrovačke sa mletačkom republikom tja do g. 1358.," *Rad Jugoslavenske akademije znanosti i umjetnosti* 5 (1868): 98.

17. The nucleus of the *commissio* was transferred and supplemented with new regulations if necessary. Just at his second appointment for the count of Dubrovnik,

Bartholomeus Gradonicus received supplemented instructions (Šime Ljubić, *Listine o odnošajih između južnog Slavenstva i mletačke republike I, Monumenta spectantia historiam Slavorum Meridionalium I.* (Zagreb, 1868), 262; cited hereafter as *Listine I.*

18. *Listine I*, 208. For the value of the *perper* see below.

19. Foretić, *Povijest I*, 65. Johannes and Petrus Teupolo, Marcus and Andreas Dandulo were, for example, the doge's sons (Statute VIII, 22 and 52; Bogišić-Jireček, *Liber*, LXVII-LXVIII; MR V, 48).

20. He became the count for the first time in 1309–1311 (Bogišić-Jireček, *Liber*, 461; *Listine I*, 246, 254).

21. For the dates of the beginning and ending of the office see MR I, 9 and 42; HAD, DR, Diversa cancellariae, Va; *Listine I*, 273.

22. Bogišić-Jireček, *Liber*, 461.

23. See *Listine II* (Zagreb, 1870), 15, 63 *et passim*; *Listine III* (Zagreb, 1872), 445; Adriano Cappelli, *Cronologia, Cronografia e Calendario perpetuo* (Milano, 6th ed. 1988), 347.

24. It was approximately a one-month salary of a stonemason. See Vuk Vinaver, "Prilozi istoriji plemenitih metala, cena i nadnica (srednjevekovni Dubrovnik)," *Istorijski glasnik* 1–2 (1960): 70. Later in the text we shall give some other examples of the values and prices.

25. Separate judicial bodies for civil and criminal procedures exist only from the middle of the fifteenth century. See Kosto Vojnović, "Sudbeno ustrojstvo republike Dubrovačke," *Pad Jugoslavenske akademije znanosti i umjetnosti* 105 (1891): 1.

26. DC V; HAD, DR, Reformationes V, fols 47–62, published in MR I, 42, etc. (especially 44–50).

27. Statute I, 3.

28. MR I, 11 and 26. The case of the replacement of the judge was regulated by Statute VIII, 14, 2 from 1305.

29. Fols 15, 18v, 19, 43, 45v, 46.

30. Statute II, 4, 3.

31. It is interesting to note that on 24 Feb. 1313 Petrus de Prodanello and Ursacius de Bodaça appear, and also Nicola de Sorgo and Ursacius de Bodaça, because it shows that judges could also have been replaced on the same day (fols 34v, 36). Since it was a matter of routine, there is no particular legal reason that would speak in favor of a deliberate change in the court composition. It probably happened out of some practical reason, or perhaps one of the judges had some other obligations.

32. See Statute II, 4, 8.

33. In six procedures three judges take part (fols 17, 20, 27v, 31, 37, 39); in four procedures, four (fols 20, 25, 27, 29v); in one procedure there are five judges (fol 21). In documents from the end of the thirteenth century there are cases in which, besides the count and elected judges, members of Minor Council also take part at the trial (DC II, 158–59).

34. Fols 20, 21–23, 37.

35. Fol 39.

36. Ibid. The Korčula Statute (24) explicitly excludes judges' participation in the procedures against members of the count's escort.

37. Statute I, 3.

38. It is put into the C Statute Edition (1: 3, 6), which belongs to the period after 1358.

39. We come to such a conclusion because of the fact that in twenty-six compositions of the *Curia maior* from the first half of the fourteenth century we cannot find such a case (see sources cited above and Diversa cancellariae IV and VI). Moreover, in some cases the primarily elected judge was replaced by another person from the same family, which suggests the idea of representation (MR V, 274, 296).

40. Mahnken, *Dubrovački patricijat* I, 356, 358 and II, table 53.

41. Mahnken, *Dubrovački patricijat* I, 174–75.

42. Ibid., 146; for the *cursus honorum*, see especially Irmgard Mahnken, "O dubrovačkim vlastelinskim rodovima i njihovoj političkoj ulozi u XIV veku," *Istoriski glasnik* 2 (1955): 93.

43. Mahnken, *Dubrovački patricijat* I, 432–33; Mahnken, "O dubrovačkim," 96.

44. MR I, 15, 35, 44; and Mahnken, *Dubrovački patricijat* I, 15.

45. Ibid., 374–75.

46. Ibid., 141 and II, tables X/1 and X/2.

47. Mahnken, "O dubrovačkim," 89.

48. Mahnken, *Dubrovački patricijat* I, 410–11.

49. Ibid., I, 264–65.

50. Ibid., I, 397.

51. In a very interesting analysis, Bariša Krekić examined the relationship between the economic and political power of particular noble families, and the tendency of power concentration ("O problemu koncentracije vlasti u Dubrovniku u XIV i XV vijeku," *Zbornik radova Vizantološkog instituta* 24–25 (1986): 397–406; and "Influence politique et pouvoir économique à Dubrovnik (Raguse) du XIIIe au XVIe siècle," in *Gerarchie economiche e gerarchie sociali, secoli XII–XVIII* (Firenze, 1990), 241–58). He measured political power by evaluating the participation of members of particular families in the *Consilium Rogatorum* and *Consilium Minus,* and in fulfilling the functions of a judge and a count. Since his analysis covers whole centuries and puts emphasis on families and not on individuals, the results are useful but not completely appropriate to our needs. However, it may well be pointed out that not all the judges belonged to the politically most powerful patrician families (Sorgo takes the position number two; Gundula, four; Bona, six; Bodaça, ten), while other families are ranked lower (around position number twenty: Petregna, Tedusio, Prodanello, Saraca), and some considerably lower (Çelipa, Tefla, Pabora).

On the other hand, Marinus de Petregna was a judge at least six times, Johannes de Çelipa at least seven, and Martolus de Tudisio at least nine times (the preserved records on judges' elections in the first half of the fourteenth century are published in MR I, 11, 33, 68, 94, 142, 186, 276; MR II 41, 81, 108, 132; MR V 7, 39, 80, 122, 151, 180, 221, 248, 274, 296, 327, 365, 393; we have also used some unpublished data from HAD, DR, Diversa cancellariae, IV and VI). Krekić emphasizes that the individuals' capabilities could play a crucial role in their social position ("Influence," 257), and it seems to be the case particularly with those fulfilling the functions of a judge.

52. In 1320, a yearly salary of seven *perperi* was introduced for judges of the

Curia Minor who took part in civil cases of lesser importance. This decision of the Minor Council forbids taking money from parties, and a modest sum is determined as compensation (*Liber omnium reformationum,* 44). Because of the value limit this court was overloaded with cases, so such a solution seems to be justified.

53. We took into account the time engagement of four judges who worked in the largest number of cases (Petrus de Prodanello: twenty-four, Ursacius de Bodača: twenty-three, Petrus de Pabora: sixteen, Nicola de Sorco: fifteen), and for the longest period of time (from 30 Sept. 1312 to 18 April 1313). During this period of approximately twenty-seven weeks, they sat in about twenty cases.

54. For an overall analysis of the family structures and their economic activities, see Zdenka Janeković-Römer, *Dubrovačke obitelji od XIII do XV stoljeća* (Master's thesis, University of Zagreb, 1990), p. 79 in particular.

55. For example, Martolus de Tudisio was elected a judge at least nine times in the period 1304–1332. We can see that the replacement of counts, who used to be elected for a period of two years (there were ten of them during the same period), did not influence his re-election as a judge (see Bogišić-Jireček, *Liber,* 461–62).

56. Mahnken, "O dubrovačkim," 98.

57. One accused person in the case was questioned "*coram domino comite et suis iudicibus Marino de Petregna et Luce de Bona,*" and the other "*coram domino comite et suis iudicibus Tefla de Tefla et Johannes de Çelipa*" (fol 5).

58. When in 1266 the count tried to arrest the person who was banned, and undertake judicial measures, the citizens attacked him, killed his escort, and threw him out of the city (*Codex diplomaticus Regni Croatiae, Dalmatiae et Slavoniae V,* ed. T. Smičiklas (Zagreb, 1907), 399–400; cited hereafter CD).

59. Compare the cases analyzed further in the text from DC II, 199–202, and Statute VIII, 58–59.

60. *Listine I,* 211.

61. Ibid., 226.

62. A "*socius*" generally had to be a Venetian, and if not so the count had to ask for a special approval (*Listine I,* 258; Makušev-Šufflay, *Isprave,* 10–11). From time to time two assistants are mentioned after 1256 (Ljubić, "Odnošaji," 98; DC II, 131 and *passim;* Makušev-Šufflay, *Isprave,* 11).

63. See his oath in Statute II, 2 and VIII, 1.

64. Statute VIII, 1; *Liber omnium reformationum,* 44.

65. Fols 1, 1v, 2, 11, 11v, 14, 15, 16v, 18v, 19, 23v, 30, 32v, 34, 34v, 35, 41v, 43, 43v, 45v, 46, 46v (that is, in 22–25 percent of eighty-seven initiated procedures). Once he heard a person who could not approach the court. In one case he was only accompanied by the chancellor: "*Iacobus filius Radosclavi de Matessa iacens in lecto pro dicto vulnere suo sacramento dixit coram domino Marco Gradonico socio domini comitis et me cancellario comunis*" (fol 37v); and in one record from the thirteenth century he was accompanied by judges: "*In presencia domini Nicholai, militis nobilis viri domini Michaelis Mauroceni comitis Ragusii et juratorum judicum Vitalis Binçole et Gubessio de Ragnana missorum ad domum filiorum quondam Gregorii de Petragana, et ad domum de Poça per dominum comitem*" (DC II, 126).

66. "*Dominus Marcus abbas socio domini comitis denunciavit domino comiti et dicit*" (fol 6).

67. The court admonition was always pronounced by the count himself, and in this particular case two judges took part as well (fol 2).

68. "*Item coram domino Marino Urso, milite domini comitis, deputato loco ipsius domini comitis, tunc absentis de Ragusio, et juratis judicibus Andrea de Benissa et Janino Deodati*" (DC II, 155). The second time he took over the withdrawn weapons instead of the count who was sleeping (DC II, 148).

69. In the year 1342 he is mentioned as "*filius domini ducis*" (*Listine II*, 158), at the time when B. Gradonicus was the doge. In 1345 Marcus Gradonicus became the count of Dalmatian town Nin (ibid., 247).

70. At the same time Marino Memo *podestà* of the isles of Hvar and Brač, for example, was allowed to take his son for one of his assistants (*Listine I*, 265).

71. DC II, 191.

72. DC II, 133, 155, 191, 213. See the oath of the counts of Šipan, Lopud and Koločep, Statute II, 33.

73. The chancellor is mentioned in the records at fols 24v and 37v as "*cancellarius comunis.*" Only in 1473 was a special chancellor for the criminal court cases introduced: Vinko Foretić, "*Dubrovački arhiv u srednjem vijeku,*" *Anali Historijskog instituta JAZU u Dubrovniku* 6–7 (1957–59): 323.

74. Konstantin Jireček, "Die mittelalterliche Kanzlei der Ragusaner," *Archiv für slavische Philologie* 25 (1904): 501–21; 26 (1904): 161–214.

75. So was Aço de Titullo, for example, active in Dubrovnik for eleven years: 1285–1296 (Jireček, "Die mittelalterliche Kanzlei," 188).

76. MR I, 25; MR V, 99.

77. *Listine I*, 284. He worked in Dubrovnik for four years altogether (1311–1315).

78. As a typical example, we can point out torture, which was still present in the judicial practice of Italian communes in the middle of the thirteenth century, and was elaborated in the doctrine (see Piero Fiorelli, *La tortura giudiziaria nel diritto comune I* (Roma, 1953), especially 67–131). The Dubrovnik regulations mentioned torture at the end of the fourteenth century (*Liber omnium reformationum,* 118), but the register confirms its earlier application in practice. The record does not contain details, but one can clearly recognize "technical terms" and the points the doctrine insisted on. Only "spontaneous confession"—given after torture—was noted; a confession was only valid as evidence if the accused later confirmed his statement with the whole judicial body being present: "*Dictus Fuscus in presencia domini comitis depositus de tormento sua spontanea voluntate dixit et fuit confessus quod. . . . Dictus Fuscus coram domino comite et suis iudicibus. . . . sua spontanea voluntate sine aliquo tormento omnia et singula supradicta coram eo lecta confessus fuit et suo sacramento firmavit ita esse vera ut superius scriptum est, et in dicta confessione perseveravit*" (fols 31v–32). It thus appears that the *ius commune* had an influence on the judicial practice of Dubrovnik.

79. Statute IV, 71–73; *Statuta et leges civitatis Spalati,* ed. Hanel, *Monumenta historico-iuridica Slavorum Meridionalium* 2 (Zagreb, 1878), 4: 30, cited hereafter as Statute Split.

80. Fol 15: "*Et vidit quod dictus Andreas decapilavit dictum Ivanum, dicendo quod eum poterat castigare quia puer suus erat*"; compare a similar *casus* from Trogir (TS I, 150). In a case from 1284, a master undressed his servant and concubine, took her jewelry away, had her nose cut off and chased her away with her

daughter, and the court set all the participants of this case free (DC II, 180–81, 210). For punishment of servants, see also Statute Split, IV, 30.

81. See Michael R. Weisser, *Crime and Punishment in Early Modern Europe* (London, 1979), 10.

82. Statute VIII, 23–24. A collective responsibility of territorial communities existed, for example, in Florence in the fifteenth century: Marvin B. Becker, "Changing Patterns of Violence and Justice in Fourteenth- and Fifteenth-Century Florence," *Comparative Studies in Society and History* 18:3 (1976): 286.

83. This was not out of the ordinary, as similar occurrences are found elsewhere in medieval Europe. See Alfred Soman, "Deviance and Criminal Justice in Western Europe 1300–1800: An Essay in Structure," *Criminal Justice History* 1 (1980): 7.

84. Such a case of out-of-court reconciliation of parties with compensation is recorded in DC II, 128: "*Et hodie ipse uenit ad me et concordauit se mecum. Et ego dedi ei unum pectem et unam infulam.*" About the medieval doctrine of reconciliation and compensation, see Herman Kantorowicz, *Albertus Gandinus und das Strafrecht der Scholastik II* (Berlin-Leipzig, 1926), 185–209. See also Soman, "Deviance," 13–18; Sarah Blanshei Rubin, "Criminal Law and Politics in Medieval Bologna," *Criminal Justice History* 2 (1981): 6; Becker, "Changing Patterns," 282–85; and W. M. Bowsky, "The Medieval Commune and Internal Violence: Police Power and Public Safety in Siena 1287–1355," *American Historical Review* 73:1 (1967–1968): 12–13.

85. We find out about such an agreement because it was not operative: "*et tunc Thomas dixit ei 'turpis ravaiose et vis tu provam mecum et non fiat acusa.' Et tunc apprehenderunt se et inceperunt se percutere et decapillare.*" (fol 6v).

86. Different from Dubrovnik, some medieval communities tolerated revenge if it remained within limits. For Siena and Firenza, see Bowsky, "Medieval Commune," 12; for Bologna, see Blanshei, "Criminal Law," 5.

87. See below.

88. The claim is called "*accusa*" (fol 6v). The most frequently are used *formulae*: "*denunciat et acusat*" and "*conqueritur.*" Sometimes it is mentioned that the accuser would take an oath.

89. Statute VIII, 33 and 36.

90. They were recorded in the "*Liber de securitatibus.*" See DC II, 45–121.

91. Fol 4.

92. Fol 14.

93. Fols 20 and 33.

94. Fol 27v.

95. "*Et duo Vlachi percussi et cruentati lamentarentur coram domino comite, ipse dominus comes volens de dicta rixa inquirere, invenit in hunc modum*" (fol 9v).

96. Fol 20.

97. Fols 21, 23v, 37, and the last incomplete record, again about an injury (fol 46v).

98. Fol 31.

99. Fol 34.

100. Fol 38v. Some records do not say anything about starting a case, recording only the sentence and sometimes warranty clauses (fols 12v, 29v).

101. MR I, 40 and 130. For the medieval doctrine, see Kantorowicz, *Gandinus*, 151–55.

102. For the medieval doctrine standpoints about the possibilities of impostation of the defense, see Kantorowicz, *Gandinus*, 151–55.

103. The regularly used *formulae: "Examinatus ut supra, ad defensionem sui suo sacramento dixit quod."* (fol 1v) or *"suo sacramento dixit ad sui excusationem de dicta acusa quod."* (fol 5).

104. See DC II, 166–67. This principle is stated, for example, by several Dalmatian and Istrian statutes.

105. This will be the case when we do not first have the list of the names of all the proposed witnesses, and then their statements, as it is usually the case (for example, fols 1, 2, 5v, 7, 34v, 35v, 36, 38, 39, 40v).

106. The person who was found with the stolen wax said he had bought it from another person, and brought the porter as a witness: *"quem bastasium ipse Marcus presentavit domino comiti et dictis iudicibus"* (fol 31).

107. See, for example, fols 13v, 16v, 34v, 44.

108. A trusted person in the merchant colony of Brskovo was delegated to hear a witness who was there on commercial business (DC II, 194).

109. Statute VI, 3. See the records at fols 1v, 5v, 6v, 8, 15v, 16v, 17, 20, 23v–24v, 28, 30, 35v, 36v, 37, 39, 43v. Compare also the court practice from Trogir (TS I, 44, 69, 70 *et passim*).

110. Statute VI, 3, addition from 1283. See, for example, the records at fols 27, 29v, 33v, 37, 39; similarly, see the judicial documents from Trogir (TS I, 69).

111. Such are the questions in cases at fols 1v, 2v, 10v, 21–23, 25–25v, 31–32 34.

112. Fols 24, 27v, 37v, 39.

113. For example, the procedure from DC II, 137 was suspended after the presentation of evidence because the accused did not have full delict capacity. His father confirmed under oath that he was only thirteen. The statute allowed persons younger than fourteen to be exceptionally punished for crimes according to the court's evaluation (VI, 19). About the idea of delict capacity and its limits, see Tancredi Gatti, *L'imputabilità, i moventi del reato e la prevenzione criminale negli statuti italiani dei sec. XII-XVI* (Padova, 1933), 82–89.

114. Fol 5v; fols 17v and 26v: *"testes non habet"*; fols 1 and 15v: *"Testis . . . suo sacramento dixit quod de predictis nihil scit."* In one case, a witness said he did not know anything, while the other one did not know anything about the *meritum* (fol 29v). Sometimes those giving testimony were not eyewitnesses of the act itself: *"Interrogatus si vidit quod dictus Margaritus eam percussit, respondit quod non"* (fol 1v), so their statement was not sufficient for a condemnatory sentence (ibid. and fol 8). Once it was recorded: *"non fuit probatum per dictos testes"* (fol 29).

115. Fols 4, 6, 7v, 8v, 12, 16, 18, 19v, 21v, 33, 40, 44v, 45.

116. The latter was created at the beginning of the thirteenth century for the ecclesiastical court, and was characterized by an official initiation and a more active procedural role of the court. The inquisitorial procedure was becoming more and more important, and played a significant role in the development of criminal procedure in continental Europe. See John H. Langbein, *Prosecuting Crime in the Renaissance: England, Germany, France* (Cambridge, Mass., 1974), 136–39.

117. For example, in the case at fol 29v the wrongdoer was accused of jumping into a garden of a convent, walking over the grass, and throwing rocks on the gardener. The court examined the witnesses about whether the accused had hit and insulted the accusor, a fact that changed the context of the act.

118. See fols 17, 33v. The statement is based on the habit of writing the names of the proposed witnesses right after the claim.

119. According to the nature of the case, this frequently happened in the cases of fights and insults (fols 6v, 13v, 18v, 40v). In the case at fol 40v there was a combination of claim and counterclaim.

120. Fols 20, 21, 23v, and 37: "*Cum ad audienciam domini comitis pervenisset quod Misse filius Andree de Vicsi esset vulneratus in spatula et Iacobus filius Radosclavi de Matessa esset vulneratus in cossia, dominus comes volens ex suo regimine et suo officio inquirere de dicto maleficio, sic invenit.*"

121. For example, fol 31: "*Iunius Mathie de Menç coram domino comite conqueritur quod de domo eius furtive fuerunt ei accepti baroloti V de cera et de alia cera cruda. . . . Et dominus comes volens inquirere de dicto furtu invenit in hunc modum.*" Also fol 9v.

122. These were cases of serious thefts (fol 31), injuries (fols 21, 23v, 37), and improper armament of a galley (fol 20).

123. In the case of rape (fol 9) or one case of injury among the members of his armed escort (fol 39).

124. It is difficult to follow some elements from DC II because the record structure is different (for example, the names of the proposed witnesses are not written down).

125. In the court records of Trogir, we even find trials in which the court hypothetically pronounces the sentence, having considered the claim. The result of the trial depends then on the testimony of the accepted witnesses and probably on the oath of the parties. The court does not have to summarize the results of the evidence and bring a precise adjudication (for the example, see TS I, 47). Not being able to go into a deeper analysis, we can still recognize a relic of the type of procedure known to more or less barbarian legal systems and existing in Croatian regions as well: see Lujo Margetić, "Neki aspekti razvoja sudenja u hrvatskim primorskim krajevima u XII i XIII stoljeću," *Historijski zbornik* 29–30 (1976–1977), 92.

126. On the system of rational and irrational evidence, see the review of Raoul C. Caenegem, "La preuve dans le droit du Moyen Age occidental. Rapport de synthèse," in *La Preuve, Recueils Jean Bodin XVII* (Bruxelles, 1965), 709–40.

127. III, 33 and 36. See Statute Split III, 8.

128. VI, 33 and 34.

129. It dates from the times of the count Marinus Bodoarius, meaning that it could have been passed in the period from 1292 to 1305. It is expressly stated that the previous statutory provision ("*anticum statutum*") according to which the testimony of one witness was enough for a criminal case conviction, was thus changed.

130. We understand here the existence of a regulation about how many and what kinds of evidence were needed for an accusatory sentence: See Jean Philippe Lévy, "L'évolution de la preuve, des origines à nos jours. Synthèse générale," in *La Preuve XVII*, 37–44.

131. This evidence maxim is completely in accordance with the assumptions of the legal evidence doctrine. A similar standpoint, that for a more serious crime the

testimony of only one witness was insufficient, can be found in the Trogir judgements as well (TS I, 32).

132. Statute III, 36. Persons who were considered infamous ("*infames*") would lose their credibility already according to Roman and Canon law (see Fiorelli, *Tortura I*, 265–67).

133. "*Tripon fererius, Petrus buteglerius, Ivan capeller—non creduntur*" (fol 28). We do not know what the impediments were with the mentioned persons; their professions obviously were not. It is interesting to observe that in one case the court did not object to hearing a prostitute, since it was trying very hard to clarify a case of murder in which a night watchman and the count's servant were involved, and the court did not want to be deprived of the testimony of any potential witness (fols 22–22v).

According to the court records of Trogir from the end of the thirteenth century, such negative personal characteristics were, for example, sex (TS I, 54); not belonging to the same social community (controversial: TS I, 32, 143); and negative moral qualities (infamy—TS I, 36, bad reputation—TS I, 71, "*mala mulier*"—TS I, 89, "*levis homo*"—TS I, 32, 75).

134. For example, in the Dubrovnik procedures from the thirteenth century, it is recorded that one witness could not be accepted because he was a "*servus*," that is, a servant of limited legal capacity (DC II, 197). Family relationship with the parties and other reasons were taken into consideration so as to avoid the possible testimony in favor, or to the disadvantage, of the accused (see TS I, 37–80).

135. It was proved that the witness had previously threatened the accused that he would do him harm (DC II, 152).

136. Statute VI, 33 and 34.

137. Statute VI, 33 and 34. See fols 22–22v, the testimony of the prostitute Guercia, and of Mila, the widow of Elias Putigna. A similar situation can be found in other court records (DC II, 148, 205).

138. There are some cases that cannot go under the ones foreseen by the statute, as a case of injury committed during the day (three female witnesses—DC II, 207–8), and a fight among women (DC II, 214–15). It is difficult to establish whether treating women as second-rate witnesses had some influence on the height of the pronounced punishment. Because there was always a larger number of persons who testified, we can see no causal connection.

139. The life of plebean women was not so very retiring that the mentioned occurrence could be explained by their not being present in the street events.

140. Thus, for example, the court came to the conclusion that some type of testimony cannot be accepted because it is inconsistent and contradictory: TS I, 39, 70, 79.

141. Torture was one of the procedural institutes often not mentioned in regulations, even when accepted in practice. When some related statutory provisions did exist, they were normally partial and covered only some dubious questions.

142. The five stolen sacks of wax were valued at one hundred *perperi* (fol 31v). According to the Dalmatian statutes, there was often a possibility of applying torture in the cases of theft. In the Venetian court records of the fourteenth century, half of the cases of torture were connected with theft. Stanley Chojnacki, "Crime, Punishment, and the Trecento Italian State," in *Violence and Civil Disorder in Italian Cities 1200–1500*, ed. L. Martines (Berkeley, Los Angeles, London, 1972),

224, n.109. In the legal systems of medieval Europe, torture was often pronounced in cases of theft because the admission of guilt on the part of the accused made it possible not only to establish his or her liability, but also to find and recuperate the stolen goods: see Chojnacki, "Crime," 223. On the court practice of the court of Korčula in the fifteenth century in an application of torture for stealing, see Nella Lonza, "Tortura u Korčulanskom statutu i sudskim zapisima XV. stoljeća," in *Zbornik radova znanstvenog skupa Statut grada i otoka Korčule iz 1214. godine,* ed. Z. Šeparović (Zagreb-Samobor, 1989), 163–76.

143. On the place and role of torture in the system of evidence, see for more details Fiorelli, *Tortura,* I–II (Roma, 1953–54); Lévy, "Evolution," 47–49, and the literature cited there.

144. "*Dictus Fuscus coram domino comite et suis iudicibus. . . . sua spontanea voluntate sine aliquo tormento omnia et singula supradicta coram eo lecta confessus fuit et suo sacramento firmavit ita esse vera ut superius scriptum est, et in dicta confessione perseveravit*" (fol 32). Statutes of Dalmatian towns very often, out of fear of the misuse of this institute, ordered the presence of the whole judicial *collegium.* In the practice of Dubrovnik this was obviously not required. Similar instances can be seen in the examples of Korčula; see Lonza, *Tortura,* 170–76.

145. "*Merinçaca medicus comunis coram domino comite suo sacramento firmavit quod dicti Jacobus et Misce liberati erant et extra omne periculum de dictis feritis et ipsos liberatos dabat*" (fol 37v). The surgeon (*medicus plagarum*) Merinçaca is mentioned in the documents of Dubrovnik of 1301: Jurica Bacić, *Stazama medicine starog Dubrovnika* (Rijeka, 1988), 11.

146. "*Mernuçacha iuratus medicus comunis examinatus ut supra suo sacramento dixit quod nescit quis percussit dictum Gregorium, sed bene vidit vulnus factum ipsi Gregorio in pectore in latere sinistro aliquantulum supra mamullam et dicit quod dictum vulnus mortale erat et quod exempli ipso vulnere dictus Gregorius statim mortuus est et quod ipsum vulnus factum fuerat cum uno cultello sive cum lançeta*" (fol 23).

147. *Liber omnium reformationum,* 33.

148. See Guido Ruggiero, "The Cooperation of Physicians and the State in the Control of Violence in Renaissance Venice," *Journal of the History of Medicine and Allied Sciences* 33 (1978): 156–66.

149. See Jean Philippe Lévy, "La preuve dans les droits savants de Moyen Age," in *La Preuve XVII,* 150–53.

150. Statute III, 33.

151. See fols 21–23. We did not cover those crimes for which the mutilation punishment was prescribed as supplementary.

152. Fols 20 and 29.

153. Fol 27—four eyewitnesses and elements of confession in the statement of the accused; fol 33v—two eyewitnesses and one witness on *indicia;* fol 35v—two eyewitnesses; fol 44—two eyewitnesses and elements of confession.

154. Fols 2, 5, 7, 10v, 13, 14, 18v, 36, 38, 43.

155. For example, fols 23v–24v, 37–37v, 46. It is difficult to find one common denominator for all these cases. In some of them there is only one testimony that contains an *indicium* (fol 46), but in a knifestabbing case, the court disposed of the assertions of the aggrieved, of the defense of the accused denying the deed, of the statement of one witness having seen the fight-but not the stabbing, and of the

statements of two witnesses who saw the accused waving the knife and the victim crying and holding the bleeding wound. To the explicit question of the court, they said they did not see the actual blow (fols 23v–24).

156. Fols 5, 10v, 13, 18v, 43.

157. On the Venetian practice in the fourteenth century of examining all the potential witnesses in murder cases, see Chojnacki, "Crime," 223.

158. For example, in the case of a physical attack, when the witnesses said they did not see the actual deed, the court examined two more persons who could know something about it (fol 8).

159. Fols 34v, 45v (two eyewitnesses).

160. Fols 2, 5, 5v, 18v, 24v, 26, 29, 37v, 40v, 44.

161. E.g., fol 24v.

162. Fol 26.

163. Fols 7, 8, 18v, 26 (*quod verbo vel facto non faciant nec fieri faciant*), 29, 37v, 40v, 44, etc.

164. DC II, 128; DC V, fol 12v—"*die XX. setembris—Priasne de Ranina, Marinus, Paulus fratres eius iuraverunt mandata domini comitis et dominus comes precepit eis et cuilibet eorum quod per se vel per alium modo aliquo vel ingenio, verbo vel facto non faciant nec fieri faciant rixam vel rumorem cum Iohanne de Celipa. Et si scirent quod aliquis alius vellet facere, quod debeant turbare et predicere domino comiti, in pena de pp. C pro quolibet et pro qualibet vice et in pena sacramenti.*"

165. Fol 18v.

166. Fols 2, 7, 24v.

167. DC V, fols 17v, 25, 44v.

168. In the record at fol 18v the accuser is threatened with the penalty of 20 *perperi,* and the other two persons with half as much.

169. *Spisi kancelarije šibenskog kneza Fantina de Cha de Pesaro 1441–1443,* ed. J. Kolanović, *Povijesni spomenici Šibenika i njegova kotara III* (Šibenik, 1989), 200, 201, 207, 208, 211 *et passim.* In contrast to the cases of Dubrovnik, the authorities of Šibenika threatened with pecuniary sanctions for a verbal, and with an arbitrary punishment by the count for a physical attack. Sometimes the penalty of whipping was provided (235).

170. The Statute of Split (IV, 47) provided another type of court admonition that was not accompanied by pecuniary or any other sanction. This involved a warrantor who guaranteed that there would be not further conflicts (" *fideiussores de non offendendo*").

171. The *Liber maleficiorum* from 1284 to 1286 mentions many times the word "*carcer,*" but it is not very clear if it is actually prison or only detention (see DC II 97, 135, 141, 169, 184 *et passim*).

172. The solution of the Statute Split (IV, 5) is logical, according to which detention was used only in cases for which corporal punishment was provided when the penalty was pecuniary, the providing of warrantors was enough to guarantee the execution.

173. The Statute thus foresaw custody until the collection of a fine for a woman who injured someone with a weapon (VI, 3). We can speculate that the court might have used such a measure in other cases as well.

174. "*Dictus Fuscus fugit de carcere et de forcia domini comitis*" (fol 31v).

175. Bariša Krekić, "Slike iz gradske svakodnevnice: prilozi proučavanju života u Dubrovniku u doba humanizma i renesanse," *Anali Zavoda za povijesne znanosti JAZU u Dubrovniku* 26 (1988): 13, n.33.

176. Fols 4, 28. Accessority is pointed out by the fact that the obligation of warranty ceased to exist if the accused has died (DC II, 108). Sometimes the warrantor guaranteed both responding to the court summons as well as the execution of the penalty. For example, DC II, 130 and 195; see also DC V, fols 21, 22v *et passim*. For the medieval doctrine see Kantorowicz, *Gandinus*, 153–55.

177. Statute VI, 29, 1: "*Si contumaciter venire contempserit, pro judicato super ipsa injuria habeatur, et veniens postea super hoc non audiatur*"; See also Statute Split IV, 4.

178. Statute VI, 29, 4.

179. This possibility existed, for instance, in the case of murder, if the defendant became reconciled with the family of the deceased and approached the court to undergo a regular procedure (Statute VI, 29, 3).

180. See fols 20, 23, 39v.

181. On spreading such a practice in Italian towns, see Desiderio Cavalca, *Il bando nella prassi e nella dottrina giuridica medievale* (Milano, 1978), 253.

182. "*Item clamavit quod dominus comes facit omnibus ad memoriam quod dominus Belletus Falletro, tunc comes Ragusii, in sententia quam dedit contra dictum Micham dixit quod si aliquis in Ragusio vel districtu offenderet vel occideret dictum Micham existentem in banno et contumacia processus domini Belleti, nulla pena incurrat.*" (fol 20). The mentioned sentence was pronounced a few years earlier (1305–1307), and the count repeated it in connection with another contumacious procedure against the same offender.

183. Fols 9 and 20—twenty-five *perperi* in addition to fifty; fol 39v—twelve *perperi* in addition to a twenty-five *perperi* fine.

184. With very few exceptions, it was the case in Trogir at the end of the thirteenth century (TS I, *passim*).

185. The forms of corporal punishment that are mentioned likely hark back to the earlier penal system.

186. "*Eamus ad dominum comitem et sciamus ab eo si ipse uult nobis facere iusticiam de presbitero, et non rationem, quia per rationem ipse non potest eum condempnare nisi LXXV yperperis. Et si dominus comes nollet facere iusticiam de hoc facto, ego irem extra districtum Ragusii ad barcam in qua portatur presbiter et inciderem ei nasum et manum.*" (DC II, 200).

187. DC II, 199–202.

188. Statute VI, 2–10; see Statute Split, Statute Korčula, and TS I, 242. There was a similar model in Bologna at the end of the thirteenth century: Blanshei, "Criminal Law," 11. It is important to mention that in the Venetian *Promissio de maleficiis* of 1232 corporal punishment was more common than fines. The forms of mutilation that were provided in the Byzantine legislation were very similar. We should not, however, jump to conclusions, because similar forms can be found in Carolingian provisions (see Benvenuto Cessi, "Il diritto penale in Venezia prima del mille," *Nuovo Archivio veneto*, s. II, 33 (1917): 15).

189. In the record on the quarrel from the end of the thirteenth century, one person said to the other: "*Vos accusastis Cranoe Margarite de Scarico et fecistis ei trahi occulos et incidi manum.*" (DC II, 128). On the punishment of mutilation

from the second half of the fifteenth century, see Ilija Mitić, "Prilog proučavanju kazne sakaćenja na području Dubrovačke Republike i u nekim dalmatinskim gradovima," *Zbornik Pravnog fakulteta u Zagrebu* 32:1–2 (1982): 141–50; and Krekić, "Slike," 13, n. 33.

190. Statute VI, 1. In 1308 the Venetian doge approved an exception, for the sake of reciprocity with the subjects of the Serbian king Uroš. This was done in spite of the expressed norm from the count's instruction that such a crime had to be punished by the death penalty (Statute VI, 1; VIII, 58–59). On the conflict, as to the death penalty, see Bariša Krekić, "An International Controversy over the Death Penalty in the Balkans in the Early Fourteenth Century," *Byzantine Studies* 5 (1978): 171–76.

The dilemma about how to punish murder is more general, and it occurred in the practice of Italian towns because the *ius commune* provided for the death penalty and the statutes very often for a pecuniary fine (see Kantorowicz, *Gandinus,* 361–63). In the course of the thirteenth century in Bologna, Florence, Lucca, and Perugia, there was a trend toward applying the death penalty, although there was a lot of hesitation in the practice: Blanshei, "Criminal Law," 10, 15.

191. Thus, an injury by a weapon was fined with twenty-five *perperi* (fol 39v, see Statute VI, 3), and an injury by a rock with twelve *perperi* (fols 10, 35v; see Statute VI, 3); for strokes without injuries, six *perperi* (fols 2, 7, 12v, 13v, 14, 27, 30, 32v, 33v, 36, 38, 40v, 44, 46, etc; see Statute VI, 3); and for rape, the pronounced sentence was fifty *perperi* (fol 9; Statute VI, 6; identical punishments can be found in DC II).

The fine for theft was a multiple of the value of the stolen object: If the value of the stolen goods was one hundred *perperi,* the ruled fine, with the compensation, was three times as much (fol 32: "*pro uno quatuor*"; see DC II, 194). This corresponds to the sum provided for in the Statute (VI, 4). The fact that the fine is a multiplied value of the stolen object is, according to Inchiostri, the result of barbarian law's influence: Ugo Inchiostri, "Di alcuni aspetti del diritto penale nei documenti e statuti dalmati del medio evo," *Rivista Dalmatica* (1928): 14. This may be true, but we think that it is also the most convenient and logical solution.

192. Statute VI, 28.

193. For example, fols 11, 13, 18v, 43.

194. Fol 28.

195. See, for example, strokes (with no blood): fols 7, 23v–24v, 27, 32v, 33v, 36, 39–39v, 44, 46.

196. By examining punishments for murders and thefts in Venice in the fourteenth century, Chojnacki established that there were no significant differences that would be the result of the social status: Chojnacki, "Crime," 225–26.

197. All the values have been calculated approximately, according to the data given by Bogumil Hrabak, "Tabela kretanja cena žitarica i mahunjina u Dubrovniku (1300–1620)," *Zbornik Filozofskog fakulteta u Prištini* 7 (1970): 126, and Vinaver, "Prilozi," 51–95.

198. Fols 7, 10, 10v, 12, 12v, 14v, 17v, 29v, 30, 32v, 33v, 37v, 38v. Very interesting is the warranty in one Dubrovnik procedure of 1284. The warrantors obliged themselves that they would, in the case of condemnatory sentence, either hand over the accused, or pay the fine (DC II, 195). Such an unusual solution may

be the result of uncertainty about whether a corporal or pecuniary penalty was to be pronounced.

199. *"Pleç et proprius pagator"* (ibidem). In cases from the end of the thirteenth century they were regularly called *"pleçii et solutores,"* and the records tell us about cases when they really paid the pecuniary penalty, e.g., DC II, 224. On the same type of warranty, see Statute Split IV, 67.

200. The Great Council passed in 1465 a regulation according to which a poor person could substitute the fine for an insult (up to six *perperi*) with a prison term. One day of imprisonment would be the equivalent of six *grossi*. Krekić, "Slike," 12.

201. The more recent historiography refutes the mistake of thinking that in continental Europe imprisonment was an eighteenth-century innovation. Some very interesting analyses, particularly by Ruggiero and Scarabello, have shown that prison sentences, beside pecuniary ones, were common in Venice by the thirteenth century. See Giovanni Scarabello, *Carcerati e carceri a Venezia nell'età moderna* (Roma, 1979), 9–10; Guido Ruggiero, *Patrizi e malfattori: la violenza a Venezia nel primo Rinascimento* (Bologna, 1982), 104–8 *et passim;* and Guido Ruggiero, "Law and Punishment in Early Renaissance Venice," *Journal of Criminal Law & Criminology* 69:2 (1978): 247–49. See also John H. Langbein, *Torture and the Law of Proof: Europe and England in the Ancien Regime* (Chicago and London, 1977), 28–29.

202. Leaving at this time the question of the difficulty in order to give the historical definition of crime and its conceptual (non)viability for the premodern era, we have by this term covered all the behaviors that brought on criminal procedures. For a concise review of a discussion on the definition of crime, see Pieter Spierenburg, "Evaluation des conditions et des principaux problèmes de l'apport de la recherche historique à la comprehension de la criminalité et de la justice penale," in *La recherche historique sur la criminalité et la justice penale, Etudes relatives à la recherche criminologique XXII* (Strasbourg, 1985), especially 68–74.

203. Proportions established for other regions also confirm a significant number of corporal attacks (about one-third), although it would be too risky to equate them because the authors used a different methodology and classification. See Giorgetta Bonfiglio Dosio, "Criminalità ed emarginazione a Brescia nel primo Quattrocento." *Archivio Storico Italiano* 136:1–2 (1978): 115 and on p. 135 data cited from research by Verga for Milan at the turn of the fourteenth century.

204. Fols 11, 13, 18v, 43.

205. There are more property delicts in DC II but they are an obvious minority.

206. Fol 15v.

207. Fol 17v.

208. Fol 20.

209. Fol 28.

210. Fol 29.

211. For example, in *casus* at fol 7 a fight started after a guard had objected to singing.

212. For example, fols 25–25v.

213. Fols 23v–24v. The tendency to resort to violence even for insignificant provocations was noticed by Bowsky, "Medieval Commune," 17.

214. See similar widespread violence in Venice noted by Chojnacki, "Crime," 210.

215. Bowsky calls such offenses "nonviolent crimes." Bowsky, "Medieval Commune," 5.

216. VI, 26; See Statute Split IV, 95; Statute Korčula, 18.

217. VI, 20; In one case from our register the penalty of one *perper* was pronounced *"quia erat sine lumine post tertiam campanam"* (fol 23). See for Dubrovnik, Zdenka Janeković-Römer, " 'Post tertiam campanam': dubrovački noćni život u srednjem vijeku," *Otium* 1 (1993): 6–13; for other Dalmatian towns, Tomislav Raukar, "Komunalna društva u Dalmaciji u XIV stoljeću," *Historijski zbornik* 33–34 (1980–1981): 198–99; and for Siena, Bowsky, "Medieval Commune," 6.

218. VI, 24; See Statute Split IV, 43; Statute Korčula, 53; and Raukar, "Komunalna," 199. In the register, because of carrying a sword after the third ringing of the bell, a penalty of five *perperi* was pronounced and the weapon was seized (fol 23).

219. The prohibition against disguise on other days than during the carnival is repeated many times, and it is accompanied by higher and higher penalties. It was obviously difficult to eliminate (MR V, 164–165, 175, 237, 264, 310). The statutory provision of 1349 (VIII, 97) very clearly points to the social danger: *"et sub illa spetie multa mala et enormia fiebant et fieri poterant, propter que risse, discessiones et scandala nascebantur, quod erat displicibile multis et pluribus hodiosum."*

220. Very illustrative is the case at fols 21–23, in which one of the guards was killed after he had intervened because of walking around at night and carrying weapons.

221. Mario Sbriccoli, "Fonti giudiziarie e fonti giuridiche. Riflessioni sulla fase attuale degli studi di storia del crimine e della giustizia criminale," *Studi storici* 29: 2 (1988): 493–94.

222. The expression goes back to Ruggiero, *Patrizi,* 105.

Policing Piedmont: The "Well-Ordered" Italian Police State in the Age of Revolution, 1789–1821

Michael Broers
University of Leeds

The commonplace of nineteenth-century Italian history is the emergence of the subalpine kingdom, Piedmont-Sardinia, as a viable state of major regional importance, able to aspire to the leadership of the rest of Hesperia.[1] The most obviously dynamic phase of this process—a regional *Risorgimento*—was the Cavourian decade, 1849–1859. Indeed, this was the period of swiftest, most fundamental social and economic change. Although there is a growing body of evidence to show that concerted institutional reforms had been under way since the 1830s, as late as 1851, an observant traveller, Count Arthur de Gobineau, was still able to remark on the rustic, semi-feudal character of many rural areas.[2]

The process of modernization in nineteenth-century Italy is subject to severe qualifications within regions as well as between them.[3] As one economic historian has put it, "Every province has its South";[4] in the major regions of the peninsula, even in its most dynamic phases, the process of evolution was relative. This observation has been made in the context of economic development, with the aim of showing the relative advances made in parts of the *Mezzogiorno* and the social and economic diversity of the south. Yet it is equally applicable to the question of social and institutional evolution, and applied in a more negative manner to the problem of law and order. In general, however, the rapid emergence of Piedmont-Savoy to a position of hegemony by midcentury has been regarded as the surest sign of a fairly comprehensive attainment of economic, social, and political modernization that began in earnest in the decade after 1848.

The specific problem of organized banditry was the salient feature of disorder in Piedmontese history throughout the late seventeenth and early eighteenth centuries, and there is a strong body of evidence to suggest that it was intensifying in the last three decades of the eighteenth century.[5] Its resilience, relative to other forms of disorder, emerges with great clarity in the context of the general dislocation suffered by the region during the revolutionary conflagration of 1796–1802.[6] The politically inspired revolts of the *giacobini* and the wave of petty crime and highway robbery that swept the lowland areas proved transient, even ephemeral, by comparison. They evaporated with the end of formal hostilities and the annexation of Piedmont to France in 1802. However, the core of organized banditry based on smuggling remained, with its central place in the life of the border communities greatly enhanced. The resilience of organized banditry readily becomes apparent when compared with the short-lived—if traumatic—convulsions of war and revolution. It is this resilience, finally overcome, that makes the bandits and the policing methods that destroyed them a crucial aspect of the history of the period. The serious problem of banditry, particularly in the provinces along the borders with Lombardy and Liguria, was solved definitively in the first two decades of the nineteenth century. Its disappearance represents one of the major achievements of Napoleonic rule in the region.

The very existence of banditry in Piedmont gives rise, in turn, to three more basic points. Firstly, there is the very fact that the *ancien regime* Savoyard state actually had a serious problem of law and order before the disruption of the French revolutionary wars. Secondly, this problem was first tackled successfully under Napoleonic rule and sustained by the restored monarchy during its most reactionary period, 1814–1831. Finally, there are the wider implications for the rest of Hesperia, together with the regional framework within which the problem of banditry and collective, communal forms of law breaking in general can be set most usefully. These four points also correspond broadly to the chronology of the period.

THE NATURE OF DISORDER IN THE *ANCIEN REGIME* AND THE *EPOCA FRANCESE*

Without doubt, there was a long tradition of banditry based on the smuggling of salt and livestock in the southern provinces of Piedmont,[7] subsequently the Napoleonic departments of Tanaro, Stura, and Marengo. In a penetrating article written in 1970, Giulio Solavaggione, working in a Lombard context, set out useful structural guidelines about the conditions in which banditry tended to flourish in *ancien regime* Italy: Mountain regions and border areas.[8] Mountain regions were physically isolated and therefore remote from centers of state authority. However, perhaps the most important factor in these areas were the coherent, relatively stable peasant communities the mountains produced, dependent on smuggling but independent of all external authority, proprietorial or bureaucratic.[9]

In this context, it is worth drawing attention to the place of *seigneurialism* in the general context of banditry and disorder in this period.[10] The problem of active baronial involvement in disorder is well known in the

Mezzogiorno, for example, but another aspect of the influence of *seigneurialism* on banditry was juridical disengagement. This was very different from the pattern of baronial patronage and participation in the south. It was by far the more important aspect of *seigneurial* involvement in Piedmont, as it was in the Auvergne, parts of the Rhineland, and the Abruzzi. In all these areas, fiefs became virtual havens for bandits and smugglers not through baronial involvement in banditry, but because the *seigneurs* could not afford—or simply chose not—to enforce their judicial duties. Jails and police forces were too expensive to maintain or, at least, to employ against men whose crimes offended the central government rather than their own local interests. The Piedmontese frontier with Liguria abounded with Imperial fiefs, especially in the Langhe, many of whose conditions corresponded to the general problem of judicial neglect and one of which—Narzole, in the possession of the Marchese Faletti di Barolo—was the base of the most resilient and successful band in Piedmont. The existence of fiefs always contributed to the fabric of lawlessness and, for historic reasons, they also tended to cluster along long-established borders, such as that between Piedmont and Liguria, or the frontier of the Papal States and the Kingdom of Naples.

Border areas, the other element in Solavaggione's typology, were the other essential ingredient. Obviously, the confluence of several frontiers offered the facility of easy escape, but what underpinned their importance in the late eighteenth century were the determinedly mercantilist policies of many governments, which made smuggling profitable and feasible. The Savoyard monarchy was unswervingly committed to economic mercantilism, but topography, together with its limitations in the sphere of law and order, made its tariff barriers leak like a sieve, at least along the southern frontier. Here, then, were the kinds of areas where human, physical, and political geography coalesced to favor organized banditry. This was not lost on contemporaries. Carlo Denina, most directly in his *Dell'impiego, delle persone,* castigated the monarchy for its weakness in dealing with the bandits and roundly condemned the role of the *signori* in the whole problem of policing, while a host of Piedmontese commentators—Gianbattista Vasco and Giuseppe Barretti perhaps the most famous among them—testified to the violent and lawless character of the inhabitants of the provinces along the Ligurian border, noble and peasant alike.[11]

The most overt defiance of mercantilism, and of local autonomy, had been crushed by the monarchy in the "Salt War" of 1680. It had been accomplished with great difficulty and even greater ruthlessness, but the following century did not see this consolidated.[12] The monarchy had the ability to crush overt opposition by the use of military intervention, but it failed significantly to establish a permanent police presence in its "trouble spots."[13] In this case, the result was the perpetuation of salt smuggling and of the more lucrative trade in livestock by local carters, usually protected by the bandits at one remove.

Two great bands dominated the Ligurian border at the start of French rule in 1802, both in areas known as permanent centers of banditry under the *ancien regime*. One was led by Giuseppe Mayno in the hills around La Spinetta, between Alessandria and the Imperial fief of Novi, a major town on the main road between Turin and Genoa. The other was under Giovanni Scarzello in the Imperial fief of Narzole at the point where the Langhe hills meet the lowlands of the valleys of the Stura and Tanaro rivers. Once the chaotic tide of the revolutionary wars had subsided, these bands—and the traditions of lawlessness and collective resistance they epitomized—remained like two great rocks upon which French rule in the region often seemed to crash.

In their character and internal structure, these two bands conformed very closely to the model discerned by Eric Hobsbawm.[14] Eight men formed the core of Scarzello's band, all of them from Narzole, all in their twenties, and most of them related. There were seven men in Mayno's band, most of whom were related to him and only one of whom came from outside La Spinetta.[15] They almost always operated in and around their own areas and, despite the fact that they lived side by side, there is no record of the two bands ever having fought with or against each other. Their deep parochial roots were, of course, their greatest strength; they were an important part of the local economy and far from marginal to their communities. Both *capibandi* were small landowners and Mayno married the niece of the parish priest. Both were also of some standing locally, independent of their role as bandits. The bands were a formidable obstacle for the French, but several fundamental conditions had changed with the absorption of Piedmont into the French state. Most of these changes are related to the arrival in northern Italy of a new, more aggressive and ambitious state, determined to achieve a Weberian monopoly of violence, and to translate into reality the concept of the "well-ordered police state" that Piedmontese reformers had come to cherish, if only in theory, by the last decades of the eighteenth century.[16]

THE IMPACT OF NAPOLEONIC RULE, 1802–1814: THE CREATION OF THE "WELL-ORDERED POLICE STATE"

Initially, several aspects of French rule accentuated the problem of disorder in Piedmont, the chief of which was without doubt the imposition of conscription. Particularly in the mountain areas, conscription added another dimension to the same deeply rooted collective resistance to authority that nurtured banditry. Throughout this period, deserters and *refractaires* swelled the ranks of the small, permanent bands, if only at those times of year when the levies were being raised.[17] Smuggling, too, did not diminish, because the fiscal frontiers remained in force, despite direct annexation to France. Not only did the international border remain with the Italian Republic, but so did the internal customs' frontier with France itself, as did that with the ex-Ligurian Republic following its own annexation to France in 1805. In these conditions the salt trade continued as before, but that in livestock seems to have reversed itself. Before the revolutionary wars, Piedmont had been an important—if illicit—exporter of cattle, whereas after the great epidemics of 1800–1801 it became an illegal importer.[18] This is a reasonable indication of the "big money" involved in this aspect of banditry. The *raison d'etre* for contraband was probably given a further incentive by the new regime's ever-increasing attempts to enforce the Continental Blockade. In local terms, Napoleon's attempts to wage global war on Britain and to restructure the economies of western Europe meant better prospects for Mayno and Scarzello.

Contemporary French officials in the Piedmontese departments had few doubts about the "big money" involved in smuggling, and that the involvement of those able to pay high prices for contraband livestock greatly strengthened the position of the bandits. As the commander of the security forces in Piedmont put it in 1806:

C'est là qu'on trouve la cause reelle de l'appui que recoivent les brigands . . . ils font la contrebande pour une infinite d'individus. J'ai fait des recherches soignees sur la fortune de plusieurs familles des cantons environnant Narzole et je me suis convaincu que c'etait la contrebande qui les avait enriches.[19]

In the course of the trial that followed the capture of the Narzole band, the French came very close to uncovering some of the links Scarzello and his men had had with the financial world in Turin. One Torinese banker, Muscetti, was finally jailed for handling their financial affairs, for which he received 40,000 francs from Scarzello.[20]

Nonetheless, the other changes wrought by the French in the period 1802–1814 far outweighed the policing problems some of their own policies created for themselves. The attitude of the Napoleonic state to the question of crime in general—and to banditry, in particular—represents a determined, concerted, and largely successful attempt to extend and advance the limits of state power. It was a decisive change in the means by which the state exercised social control.

The Savoyard monarchy's policing institutions in the countryside—although not in the larger towns—were negligible. Rural property and persons were in the hands of the army and the local militias; in this respect, at least, the instruments of Piedmontese absolutism more closely resembled Georgian England than Bourbon France. The greatest institutional innovation of the Napoleonic regime in this sphere was the introduction of the *gendarmerie* into the ex-Piedmontese departments, a paramilitary police force distributed in six-man brigades throughout the smaller provincial towns, but whose daily patrols were devoted entirely to the countryside.[21] However widely stretched, undermanned, and generally detested the members of this force often were by the Piedmontese, the *gendarmerie* represented a permanent police presence in the countryside. It was concerned equally with the enforcement of conscription and the preservation of public order. This embraced the protection of persons and property, a fact that unquestionably won the *gendarmes* and the regime a significant, if grudging, degree of local support. The intrusion of the state was deeply resented by many communities in most of its aspects. The general desire was normally to be left alone, as had traditionally been the case. What was wanted was less government, not more, with the important exception of policing. It is arguable that this was virtually the only aspect of the "modern," Revolutionary-Napoleonic state that rural communities actually wanted.

In the course of the 1790s, the revolutionary reformers built upon the foundations they had inherited from the police of the *ancien regime*. The central government had evolved two distinct police forces: the political police, who also dealt with most minor, civil matters in the larger towns, and the *marechaussee*, a paramilitary police force that was used to police the countryside.[22] The essence of these models was preserved in the corps created to carry on their duties after the Revolution. The *commissaires de police* were the direct agents of the Ministry of Police, created in 1796; they dealt with political offenses and minor matters in the towns. For most of the period this branch of the police was under the control of Fouche and, at least in the Italian departments of the empire, these posts tended to be the preserve of men with distinctly Jacobin pasts. The *marechaussee* was succeeded by the *gendarmerie* in December 1791. The new force, like the old, was drawn from veterans of the regular army who were usually noncommissioned officers. Both corps underwent considerable reform in the 1790s. By the time Napoleon expanded French control into Italy and western Germany in the first years of the nineteenth century, France had a very well-developed series of policing institutions. France was almost unique in this in western Europe. Those regions newly brought under her control soon saw these structures applied to their own problems. Piedmont was one such area (Figure 1).

Attacks on property, particularly vineyards and orchards that were as vulnerable as they were valuable, were often the results of private or political vendettas. The efforts of the *gendarmerie* to curb and prevent them does seem to have won it the support of a large section of the propertied classes. A fine example of this occurred in April 1812, when the government sent an entire brigade to the small town of La Rochetta di Tanaro in an effort to protect the local landowners from deliberate vandalism of their vines, 800 of which had been destroyed in a private vendetta. The *gendarmes* were supplied and quartered at the expense of the government, not

Figure 1
The Piedmontese Departments of the Napoleonic Empire 1802–1814

the local community, as had been the norm under the *ancien regime*. They caught the vandals.[23]

Contrasts with the absence of such a police presence under the monarchy are obvious. There is no existing incidence of any community that had a brigade stationed in its midst asking for it to be transferred, even though the central government in Paris did offer them this option in several cases where relations between *gendarmes* and the inhabitants had deteriorated seriously, at times into open violence.[24] That said, the individual members of the force were far from popular, due mainly to a combination of their involvement in the work of conscription and the fact that two-thirds of them were French. This step was taken at the outset of French rule in an effort to ensure impartiality, and it was strictly adhered to throughout the *epoca francese*. Many of the French *gendarmes* had, in fact, to be drawn from the ranks of the army of Italy, a force noted for its "jacobinism." Its officers, however, were frequently men who had seen service in the pacification of the Vendee, and they displayed their distrust of the Catholic peasantry and the nobility in the course of their duties.[25] In the light of this background, the support the *gendarmes* received for their more routine duties is all the more remarkable.

The apolitical protection of persons and property was what the French hoped would win them the support of the Piedmontese propertied classes,

Figure 2
The Major Bandit Strongholds of Piedmont

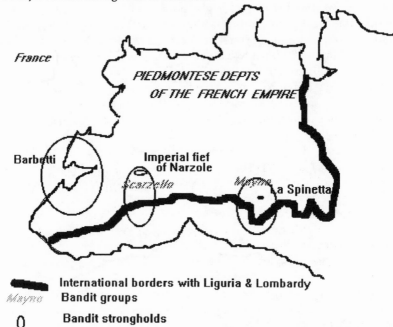

International borders with Liguria & Lombardy
Bandit groups
Bandit strongholds

and it worked to a considerable degree. It is a telling comment on the place of banditry in the life of this region that the same rules did not seem to apply to Mayno and Scarzello until concerted police pressure began to change the behavior of the bandits themselves (Figure 2). That is, it is doubtful if the communities along the Ligurian border saw the bandits as a threat to themselves so long as they confined their activities to the protection of smuggling, raiding traffic along the main highways, and to attacks on the French conscription officers and all things external, if not actually harmful, to the people of the region.

By 1806, this traditional pattern of behavior had begun to change. Smuggling was becoming more difficult following the annexation of Liguria to the French empire in 1805. Although the customs barriers had not disappeared, the political border had, and the *gendarmerie* was now on both sides of it. Two weak states had been replaced by a single, powerful one.

Although the Napoleonic state could not move mountains—or even cross them terribly well, its *gendarmerie* was able to harass the bandits from both sides of them in a series of concerted campaigns, a state of affairs unthinkable under the *ancien regime*. Thus, by 1806 the two once great *capibandi* were sinking to new, unprecedented depths, mainly the kidnapping of local landowners for ransom.[26] In these circumstances, it is no coincidence that they seemed more and more to be living on the fringes of their former strongholds, rather than in the heart of them. Mayno was killed on one of his increasingly rare visits to La Spinetta in April 1806, in a police ambush laid by a spy. His band soon divided between his immediate relatives and his close friends; both factions were destroyed, with considerable local participation, within a few months. Most of Scarzello's band was trapped and captured by local national guards and a few *gendarmes* in March 1807, while they were taking refuge in a barn well outside their traditional stronghold. Scarzello himself was captured in 1808, significantly while trying to enter Narzole, not leaving it.

Essentially, the bands were destroyed because French pressure forced them to change their traditional pattern of behavior, which turned the local population—their own people—against them. When this finally happened, there was a relatively strong and capable police force ready to assist the local community; this was the "new element." *Gendarmes* were invariably experienced soldiers, and their presence at times of crisis seems to have stiffened the resolve of local national guards when confronted by the well-armed, hardened bands. To this extent, the story is fairly straightforward and predictable. What makes it an important turning point is that the bands did not re-emerge; no new leaders came forward to take the place of the slain *capi* in the years that followed. By 1808, a long tradition had been broken. An era had truly come to an end.

In contrast to the regular troops the monarchy would have used in a campaign against the bandits, the *gendarmes* did not withdraw from the old strongholds but stayed on as a permanent presence. In 1814, they were replaced by the *Carabinieri Reale* of the restored monarchy. This new force was one of the few French-inspired institutions that the monarchy chose to retain. It was an exception, but a vital one.[27] The *carabinieri* was modelled directly on its predecessor. Clearly, the *gendarmerie* had given the state a foothold in the countryside from which, even in new and very different hands, it was loath to withdraw. The border, too, did not return and this counted for much. The attitude of the border communities toward banditry and criminality may also have changed during the *epoca francese*. This is difficult to know with precision, but what is tangible is the grip the state had finally acquired on the mountain communities. The southern provinces were now no longer a problem for the government in Turin, and this breakthrough had been made by the French. The greatest importance is that it was a permanent achievement. It was also of much more than regional significance.

THE RESTORATION, 1814–1821: THE CONSOLIDATION OF THE "WELL-ORDERED POLICE STATE" FROM COERCION TO CONSENSUS

The Restoration period offers an interesting contrast to the Napoleonic one, alongside the vital continuity created in these years when the high level of law and order achieved by the French was maintained by the restored monarchy. The contrast is one of methods rather than results. The French had to work very hard to achieve what might best be termed "policing through consensus." This was something they had to earn, and they had to devise their policies with this goal in mind. The restored monarchy could rely on consensus almost from the outset. The fear of annexation to Austria rallied almost all Piedmontese to the dynasty, at least in the years immediately following 1814; almost no one, not even the most committed *giacobini*, seriously challenged its right to rule and, therefore, to exercise police powers. This very basic fact eased its task greatly, enabling policing to continue to be effective in a period of political transition.

The intensely reactionary character of the restored monarchy is almost universally regarded as a major source of weakness. In the sphere of policing, however, there is a strong case for arguing that its Maestrian ideology was actually an asset. There is an emerging body of evidence to suggest that the moralistic intrusions made by the authorities into the realms of family life, marital relations in particular, reflected the real concerns of many propertied families. The existence of a considerable number of private petitions asking the government to involve itself in such matters points to an identity of interests between the state and at least a section of the propertied classes, in an area where the classic liberalism of the Napoleonic regime usually precluded it from entering.[28] This is, inevitably, a "grey area" where firm conclusions are difficult to draw.

Nevertheless, it is undeniable that the committed policy of ideological reaction pursued by the monarchy bound to it many of those sectors of the elite the French had alienated, but who could best provide the indirect, "moral" social control that so eased the task of the police themselves. This was the case with an important section of the aristocracy, but even truer in the case of the Catholic church. The parish clergy were a vital source of information for the *carabinieri* in its daily work, as well as for the political police. Generally, the Church provided a great deal of practical support for the police, as well as moral backing from the pulpit and the confessional, in contrast to its more ambivalent—although not overtly hostile—attitude toward the French.

The end of conscription or, more correctly, of military service outside the kingdom, was an important factor in diminishing disorder after 1814. It must be remembered, however, that Piedmont actually achieved its highest level of law and order during the last years of French rule, between 1809 and 1813, at the very point when the demands of Napoleonic conscription were also at their highest.

When viewed from a wider perspective, it is also clear that the end of conscription was no guarantee in itself that banditry would not return under a weak state. This is obvious from the examples of Spain and the Kingdom of Naples, where the end of the wars left the problem of widespread banditry untouched. In the convulsed years after 1814, it was far from certain that Piedmont would not follow their path. The restored monarchy inherited virtually no armed forces from the French due to its complete absorption into the Napoleonic empire. Finances were strained and chaotic. The policy of reaction excluded all those who had served the French—in practical terms almost everyone with any practical experience of government. The eradication of banditry was very recent in comparison to its long tradition in the life of many parts of the kingdom. Indeed, Piedmont had several marked disadvantages compared to Naples and Spain in these years, as those kingdoms had standing armies and functioning bureaucracies at their disposal from the outset.

That the subalpine kingdom did not follow the path of the other restored Latin monarchies turned on its ability to preserve the legacy of good order left by the French. The *carabinieri* were a crucial factor in this achievement, but they were always undermanned, starved of resources, and underfunded. The reality of their plight was as much a sign of the intrinsic weakness of the restored regime as its commitment to preserving the "well-ordered police state" it had inherited from its more powerful predecessor.[29] They could not have succeeded without a wide consensus of support for their work, especially in view of a series of bad harvests between 1816 and 1818. In the face of this, however, there were only a handful of attempts to practice traditional banditry in these years, mainly in the Astigiani along the main road between Turin and Genoa, and they were dealt with quickly.[30] The *carabinieri* provided the same kind of experienced support for local militias as the *gendarmerie,* probably the most important immediate factor of institutional change in policing.

The available evidence for the first years of the Restoration, 1814–1821, does not permit an analysis of the new force on the detailed lines possible for the Napoleonic period. It has proved impossible to know how much military experience the members of the *carabinieri* actually had, although many of them seem to have been drawn from newly formed Piedmontese provincial regiments and the militia that had been created from Napoleonic veterans.[31] In a few known cases its officers included members of noble families who had kept relatively aloof from the French, such as the Faletti di Barolo, one of whose members became the commander of the Mondovi brigade of the *carabinieri.*[32] This is an isolated case, almost impossible to set in the context of personnel or recruitment, but in the case of this particular noble family, it shows a willingness to become involved in a sphere of public life its members shunned under the French.

Although there is not enough evidence to yield a detailed understanding of the composition of the corps, they can be known by what they did, or more correctly, by what they did not have to do. The records of the years after 1814—like those after 1808—no longer describe *battues generales* against bandits or bands of deserters, but against packs of wolves;[33] the police no longer tracked infamous *capibandi* across the Apennines, but philandering husbands.[34] This kind of work often required the help of authorities in other states. It forms part of a strong body of correspondence for the years 1814–1821 to support the view that the police forces of the various states of Restoration Italy cooperated closely in the pursuit of criminals across their borders.

All of this is not to say, however, that the subalpine kingdom became a model of tranquility. There were still problems of public order, especially in the Ligurian Apennines. The new borders with France and Switzerland threatened, for a time, to become new centers of smuggling. Above all, petty crime—even highway robbery—was rampant during the famine years of 1816–1818.[35] The monarchy's preoccupation with the revival of many of the more archaic, "baroque" aspects of public worship reintroduced older forms of popular disorder that the French had extinguished, along with the ceremonies surrounding them. Many local officials were deeply apprehensive about this. The *Prefetto* of Alba, for example, asked the government to prohibit any *ballo* being held in connection with a revived *festa* of the Madonna of Pilone in the village of Cersole in 1816.[36] And throughout the nineteenth century, until unification and beyond, the Savoyard kingdom continued to have "its own south" in the form of the island of Sardinia, where the royal court-in-exile had fought campaigns against powerful bandits from 1796 to 1814.[37] Nevertheless, in circumstances that could have spelled disaster for the maintenance of law and order, a return to organized banditry was avoided. In this respect, what the records do not report is even more important than what they contain.

What is evident in all of this is that the state, its police, and the public were able to change their attitudes and priorities. The monarchy was confident enough in its social base to concentrate its meager policing resources on problems other than banditry not only because it no longer existed, but because the state did not fear that it would reemerge. The Savoyards drew this confidence from the fact that they could count on the support of the propertied classes and the Catholic church with a degree of assurance the French never really could. Seen in a longer historical perspective, this represents the revival of of a centuries-old consensus. Paradoxically, this consensus was at its strongest during the revolution of 1820–1821, when the rebels themselves renounced any intentions of risking public order by refusing to appeal for a general revolt. If revolution could not be confined to the palace and the barracks, it would not take place.

The Savoyard monarchy also benefitted from a powerful moral and ideological loyalty where it mattered most for public order. Support for the dynasty extended into the popular classes, and thus a much broader base of consensus was established than under the French regime. These residual, almost atavistic loyalties could not be drawn upon by the French, but the restored monarchy used them skillfully to preserve the good order the French had bequeathed to it. This allowed—indeed, willed—a state that was too fragile and potentially weak to survive. It is arguable that the very reactionary ideology that weakened the monarchy in so many respects served to maintain law and order when and where it could so easily have collapsed.

In this climate, the incongruous nature of the restored order emerges in striking form. The quest for a Catholic moral order, a theocracy that included an obsession with the policing of family life (the reality behind the *nomenklatura* of its police, *il buon governo*) was made possible by a thorough, "modernized" mastery of law and order enforced by a truly modern policing system. The "well-ordered police state" was now a prop of a political system dedicated to a neo-Gothic revival. As the liberal nationalist Massimo D'Azeglio termed it, from his own perspective, "the lance of Achilles" was now in "the hand of Tersites."[38] The irony in this is at least twofold: Policing after 1814 worked because it was based on a consensus between the state and its people that was rooted in archaism, while at the same time the good order it perpetuated and fostered had helped to advance those same forces of modernization that would transform subalpine society even further, and destroy the restored order by 1848.

CONCLUSION: THE ITALIAN PERSPECTIVE

The contribution of Napoleonic rule to the process of modernization in Italy has been a central issue in the historiography of the *epoca francese*.[39] In general, discussion has tended to focus on the economic and social aspects of the period, and the influence the Napoleonic regimes had on the land market, the transference of wealth, and the emergence of a politically conscious bourgeoisie. It would far exceed the scope of the present chapter to enter into any of these debates in detail; suffice to say in the present context that they remain deeply debated issues. Nevertheless, the *epoca francese* is generally regarded as a crucial stage for the process of change in modern Italy.

The problem of organized banditry forms a crucial element in the debate over the relationship of Napoleonic rule to the process of modernization. As this chapter has tried to illustrate, there can be little doubt that the French made a fundamental, lasting impact of this problem in the Piedmontese departments. In the period 1802–1814, they transformed the southern departments of the subalpine kingdom from one of the most bandit-infested parts of the peninsula into a relative sea of tranquility. The same was largely true in those other areas of Hesperia that were under their rule long enough to feel the full effects of Napoleonic policing policies, such as Lombardy and the lowland parts of the central duchies. In the course of the early nineteenth century, organized banditry was no longer a major problem outside the *Mezzogiorno* and the Veneto. This was very different from the area when it was inherited by the French.

Prior to French rule, a common pattern of organized banditry had embraced the whole peninsula. It was complex, but discernible. Banditry was charted with respect to the internal character of states and regions—"every region has its south"—based on divisions between mountain and plain and between frontier and highland regions. Henceforth, where the advances made by the French could be maintained, the pattern looked very different. It was based on institutions (on institutional capabilities) and on the relative strengths and weaknesses of the Italian states. Nowhere is this clearer than in Piedmont. The Savoyard monarchy ruled over a much more orderly state than before 1802. It no longer needed to waste its energies against what had, hitherto, been a permanent thorn in its side. A problem once shared with the Papal States and the Kingdom of Naples had now disappeared.

At a structural level, the disappearance of the localized determinants of banditry points toward the emergence of the subalpine kingdom as a truly mature state with a monopoly of violence. Together with Hapsburg Lombardy, Piedmont now formed a block in settenorial Italy where the power of the state had made a lasting advance. At the most basic level, the rulers of northern Italy could now claim to control the countryside. This area coincided exactly with those parts of the peninsula the French had ruled longest and where its policing institutions, the *gendarmerie* in particular, had been able to take root. Specifically, French policing enjoyed its greatest successes where the *gendarmerie* was able to operate as its creators had intended it to: as a sedentary force, scattered in small, permanent brigades across the countryside, usually quartered apart from the population it served, in its own barracks. Once established in this form, the force was better able to win the confidence of the local elites and then, with this precious support behind it, to eradicate organized banditry.

The importance of these factors becomes clearer when compared to the very different way the *gendarmerie* was forced to operate in the Roman departments and the Kingdom of Naples. The force was never able to settle into permanent, stationary brigades in these regions and, as a result, it was incapable of building up a working relationship with the propertied classes. Instead, the *gendarmerie* was used merely as another branch of the army. Most of its time was spent augmenting large *colonnes mobiles,* such as those used by General Manhes in 1810–1811, which covered almost the whole of Calabria in a series of "sweeps" against the bandits of the region. The contrast with the north could not be more striking. The meridional elites and their peasants saw the *gendarmerie* as at best only a transient force for order, and at worst as an army of occupation. In the north, by contrast, the inhabitants of the countryside had come to rely on the presence of a stable police force in their midst. By 1814, it had become a service they expected the state to provide. A clear, decisive point had been reached in the development of the gap between north and south.

Until the processes of industrialization and urbanization began later in the century, law and order in the north—at least west of the Veneto—became a question of common, petty crime and marginalized political subversion, a period of relative tranquility in which the destruction of banditry played a substantial part. The problem of the weak state, like the problem of banditry that is its clearest symptom, was now purely a regional one, however severe it may have been in those particular areas. Perhaps it is in this context that the policing of Napoleonic Piedmont acquires its real significance.

NOTES

1. Much of the work for this article was done in the course of doctoral research, financed by the Carnegie Trust for the Universities of Scotland, and by several Amphlet Martin Bursaries awarded by the Fellows of Worcester College, Oxford. The author wishes to thank both bodies for their generosity. The work on the Restoration period was financed by two British Academy Small Personal Grants in aid of research; again, the author wishes to express his gratitude to that body. The author also wishes to thank Clive Emsley's workshop on Italian policing, particularly Dr. L Riall and Dr. Steven Hughes, for their comments on a paper on which this article is based; to Professors Paul Ginsborg and John Davis for their comments on an earlier version of this article presented as a paper to the ASMI conference in November 1987; and also to Dott. Isabella Massabo'Ricci and Dott. Marco Chirassi, of the Archivio di Stato, Turin, for their help and friendship over the years of my research there, and all the staff of the Archivio.

2. Gobineau to his father, 23 June 1851, cited in Michael Biddiss, *Father of Racist Ideology: The Social and Political Thought of Count Gobineau* (London, 1970), 88–89. The major studies pointing to a significant shift toward reform in Piedmont after 1830 are Nadia Nada, *Dallo stato assoluto all stato costituzionale: Storia del regno di Carlo Alberto dal 1831 al 1848* (Turin, 1980); Gianpaolo Romagnani, *Storiografia e politica culturale nel Piemonte di Carlo Alberto* (Turin, 1985); and idem, *Prospero Balbo, Intellettuale e uomo di stato (1762–1837)* vol. 2 (Turin, 1990), chaps. 7 and 8.

3. The major work in English in a general, European context of the need to examine economic development in regional, rather than national contexts, is Sidney Pollard, *Peaceful Conquest: The Industrialization of Europe, 1760–1970* (Oxford, 1981). For a well-informed, general analysis of the debate on economic modernization in nineteenth-century Italy, see Lucy Riall, *The Risorgimento* (forthcoming), chap. 4. The author is indebted to Dr. Riall for allowing him to consult the manuscript of this work.

4. F. Assante, "Le transformazioni del paesagiio agrario," in Angelo Massafra, *Il mezzogiorno preunitario, Economia, Societa, Istituzioni* (Bari, 1988), cited in Riall, *Risorgimento*.

5. See especially the fundamental recent research of Giusseppe Ricuperati, "Gli strumenti dell'assolutismo sabaudo: segretari di stato e consiglio delle finanze nel xviii secolo," *Rivista Storica Italiana* 102 (1990):796–873. Ricuperati cites the mass of archival evidence for a widespread deterioration of law and order in Piedmont, specifically from the 1770s on, not only in the border areas where banditry was

well entrenched, but in areas close to Turin itself. Between 1776 and 1792, at least 100 communities asked the central government for troops, usually to protect them from thieves and bandits: 798–99.

6. For a general account see Michael Broers, *The Restoration of Order in Napoleonic Piedmont, 1796–1814* (unpublished Oxford D. Phil. thesis, 1986), chaps. 2–4.

7. Its prevalence in the late seventeenth century is well stated in Geoffrey Symcox, *Victor Amadeus II* (London, 1983).

8. Giulio Solavaggione, "Brigantaggio e contrabbando nella campana lombardo del Settecento," *Nuova Rivista Storia* 4 (1970):127–69.

9. O. Raggio, "Social Relations and Control of Resources in an Area of Transit: Eastern Liguria, Sixteenth and Seventeenth Centuries," in Stuart Woolf, *Domestic Strategies: Work and Family in France and Italy, 1600–1800* (Cambridge, 1991): 20–42; and idem, "Parentele, fazioni e banditi: la Val Fontanabuona tra Cinque e Seicento," in G. Ortalli, *Bande armati, banditi banditismo e repressione di giustizia negli stati europei di antico regime* (Rome, 1986), are fine examples of such communities "in action" in a region adjacent to the southern uplands of Piedmont. These areas, dominated by several imperial fiefs, continued to be sources of disorder under Napoleonic rule.

10. For an overview of this in the context of early modern Italy see Karl Oscar von Aretin, "L'ordinamento feudale in Italia nel XVI e XVII secoli e le sue ripurcussioni sulla politica europea," *Annali dell'Istituto storico ital-germanico in Trento* 4 (1978): 51–94. For this problem in the Ligurian and Piedmontese Apennines see Alberto Sisto, *I feudi imperiali del Tortonese (sec. XI–XIX)* (Turin, 1956). For the Abruzzi see Luigi Coppa-Zuccari, *L'Invasione francese negli Abruzzi, 1798–1810*, 4 vols. (Aquila, 1928), specifically 2: 532–47. For the Rhineland see Timothy C.W. Blanning, *The French Revolution in Germany* (Oxford, 1983), 18–59. For Neuchatel see Pierre Henry, *Crime, Justice et Societe dans la Principaute de Neuchatel au xviii siecle (1707–1806)* (Neuchatel, 1984). For the Auvergne see Iain Cameron, *Crime and Repression in the Auvergne and the Guyenne, 1720–1790* (Cambridge, 1981); and Nicole Castan, *Les Criminels du Languedoc* (Toulouse, 1980). On the Perigord see Steven Reinhardt, *Justice in the Sarladais, 1770–1790* (Baton Rouge, 1991).

11. Carlo Denina, *Dell'impiego, delle persone* (Turin, 1803): 96–99. This work met with official disapproval, and was only published at the advent of direct French rule when, significantly, it was regarded as an important justification for their own assault on banditry. For other views similar to Denina's see Giusseppe Barretti, *An Account of the Manners and Custoums of Italy*, 2 vols. (London, 2nd ed., 1769); and Giovanni Marocco, *Gianbattista Vico* (Turin, 1978).

12. Symcox, *Victor Amamdeus II*, 118–33.

13. For a similar pattern in Savoy, a very disturbed border area in the late eighteenth century, see Jean Nicolas, *La Savoie au xviii siecle: noblesse et bourgeois*, 2 vols. (Paris, 1978), 2:1093–1114. Here, too, although the intervention of regular troops was enough to restore order, no permanent presence was established and the troubles continued into the 1790s when the province was annexed to France.

14. This model was set out in Eric Hobsbawn, *Bandits* (London, 1969).

15. The composition of Scarzello's band is outlined fully in Archives Nationales de Paris (ANP) F7 8747, Jugement de la Commission Militaire Extraordinaire de

Turin, 4 Nov. 1808. For Mayno's band, again based on French records, see Michele Ruggiero, *Briganti del Piemonte Napoleonico* (Turin, 1968), 131; and Broers, *Restoration of Order*, 264–70.

16. The classic exposition of the concept of the "well-ordered police state" is Mark Raeff, *The Well Ordered Police State, Social and Institutional Change Through Law in the Germanies and Russia, 1600–1800* (London, 1983). Ricuperati has pointed to a predilection for a concept of the state within the Savoyard bureaucracy, specifically in the second half of the eighteenth century. He finds this outlook strongest among the *nobilta civile* loyal Bogino, and increasingly centered on Prospero Balbo: Ricuperati, "Gli strumenti dell'assolutismo sabaudo," 871–73. This is also a central theme in Romagnani, *Prospero Balbo*, 1. The constant, increasingly urgent advocacy of a wide range of reforms by this group of administrators would seem to be evidence in itself that contemporaries saw much room for improvement at the heart of the Savoyard state; their impassioned advocacy of free internal trade in grain intensified in the last quarter of the eighteenth century, driven in no small part by the growing problem of public order. Romagnani, *Prospero Balbo*, 1:105–41.

17. For the fundamental general study of this problem in the period see Alan Forrest, *Deserteurs et Insoumis sous la Revolution et l'Empire* (Paris, 1988). In a Piedmontese context see Broers, *Restoration of Order*, 247–54.

18. On the epidemics of 1800–1802 and their economic consequences, see Luigi Bulferretti, *Agricoltura, industria e commercio in Piemonte nel secolo xviii* (Turin, 1963), 145.

19. ANP, F7 8747, General Menou to Prefect, dept. de la Sture, 11 Aug. 1806, cited in Broers, *Restoration of Order*, 265: "This is where to find the real cause of the support the brigands receive . . . they smuggle for a countless number of people. I have looked very carefully into the fortunes of many families in the cantons around Narzole and I am convinced they have become rich through smuggling."

20. ANP F7 8747, Jugement de la Commission Militaire Extraordinaire de Turin, 4 Nov. 1808.

21. The organization of the *gendarmerie* in the new Piedmontese departments was carried out by General Wirion, who had fulfilled the same task in the Belgian and Rhenish departments, and also in the Vendee. His original plans were carefully formulated and remained unchanged throughout the period of French rule, then formed the basis for the territorial distribution of the *Carabinieri Reale* after the restoration of the monarchy in 1814. For Wirion's work see Archives de la Guerre (Vincennes) (AG), Xf 150 (Organization, Gendarmerie du Piemont, an. xi/1801). For a general account see Broers, *Restoration of Order*, 213–22.

22. For a good local study of the *marechaussee* in English, see Iain Cameron, *Crime and Repression in the Auvergne and the Guyenne, 1720–1790* (Cambridge, 1981). For a useful overview in English see Clive Emsley, *Policing and Its Context, 1750–1870* (London, 1983), chaps. 2–3.

23. The affair is related in a series of correspondence in ANP F7 8840 (Police Generale, Dept. de la Sture).

24. One of the most infamous of this kind of incident concerned the hamlet of Villanova, near Pinerolo in Dept. Po. In 1803, following attempts at fraternization between the brigade and the local people, the *gendarmes* sacked the town with the

help of another brigade. Following an offer from Paris to relocate the brigade, the local council declined, asking only for the most culpable *gendarmes* to be removed. ANP BB18 635 (Affaires Criminelles, Dept. Po), *Maire* of Villanova to the Minister of Justice, 8 messidor, year xiii/ 1 July 1803.

25. This information is drawn from AG Xf 134, Registre des officiers, Gendarmerie, Dept. de la Sture, 1806, and AG Xf 134 Registre des officiers, Gendarmerie, Dept. Tanaro, 5 brumaire, year xiv/17 Oct. 1805.

26. For Mayno's band: ANP F7 8741, Prefect, Dept. Marengo to the Minister of Police, 3 arrond, 30 fructidor, year xii/ 17 Sept. 1805. For Scarzello's: ANP F7 3690, (4), Prefect, Dept. Stura, to the Minister of the Interior, 22 Oct. 1807. See also Broers, *Restoration of Order*, 270–80.

27. The standard general accounts of the Restoration in Piedmont are Alberto Aspesi, *La Restaurazione in Piemonte* (Turin, 1960); and Aurelio Aquarone, "La politica legislativa della Restaurazione nel Regno di Sardegna," *Bolletino Storico-Bibliografico Subalpino*, 62 (1959): 21–50.

28. This evidence has emerged from several series in the Archivio di Stato, Turin (AST) relating to the period 1814–1821: Materie Giurdiche, Consiglio di Confernza dei Ministri (1817–1819), vols. 1–4; Segretarie degl'Interni: Correspondenza Varie, Registro 212, and Segretarie degli'Interni, Sergretarie al Senato, vols. 24 (1816–1817), 25 (1818) and 26 (1819–1820).

29. See particularly, AST Materie Giurdiche, Consiglio di Conferenze dei Ministri, vol. 1 (1817–19) for the problems of staffing and supplying the *Carabinieri Reale* in its initial phase. In February 1818, the minister responsible for the *Carabinieri Reale* complained that not only had the original target of 2,500 *carabinieri* not been met, but lack of money and recruitment problems had prevented the realization of even the revised target of 2,000. In 1818 it numbered only 1,094, excluding 183 men drawn from the French *gendarmerie* serving in Liguria. AST, Materie Giurdiche, Consiglio di Conferanza dei Ministri, Mazzo I (1817–1819): Sezzione 41, 11 Feb. 1818.

30. The years 1817–1818 seem to have seen the height of such incidents. For the swift repression of banditry in the Astigiani see AST, Segretaria di Stato, Serie I (Giuridico), Lettere al Senato; and Registro Lettere 24 (1816–1817): Segretaria degli'Interni to Avvoccato-Fiscale, prov. Asti, 28 Aug. 1816. As well as the Asti area, there were short-lived bands on the Turin-Suza road—the main route to France—and around Mondovi. AST, Segretaria di Stato, Lettere Ministero, Buon Governo e Polizia (1817–19), IV.

31. This was certainly government policy at the outset of of the Restoration, but it was proving problematic as early as 1815, when new brigades had to be created to police the highway leading over the Grand Simplon into France, following the transfer of Savoy back to Piedmontese rule. Instead, their men were drawn from the provincial regiments—local militias composed mainly of reservists. This represents a clear retreat from the high standards of recruitment originally envisaged. AST, Segretaria di Stato, Lettere, Buon Governo e Polizia (1814–1821), I: Segretaria di Stato to Foreign Minister, 11 April 1815.

32. AST, Reale Patente, 4 Aug. 1815.

33. This problem was especially prevalent in 1816. AST, Segretaria degli'Interni, Serie V (Miscellanea); and Registro II: Lettere ai Govenatori e Commandanti per

affari di Buon Governo e Polizia (1816–1820): Segretaria to Military Commandant, Cuneo, 4 July 1817.

34. There are many such examples scattered throughout the correspondence of the Foreign Ministry in AST. An interesting case combining interstate cooperation with the monarchy's obsession with "moral policing" is that of Domenico Santo Sibilla, a native of Genoa, who abandoned his wife and two sons in the *epoca francese* to contract a civil marriage in Milan, was in 1814 deemed to have been invalid since 1805. By 1818, he had been tracked down and arrested by the police of the two states, seemingly at the request of his sons. AST, Segretaria di Stato, Lettere Ministero, Buon Governo e Polizia (1817–1819), IV: Minister of Police to Foreign Minister, 16 Feb. 1818.

35. This problem seems to have been compounded—at least in the official view—by the frequent escape of criminals from prison, followed by their return to their remote places of origin. The problem was attributed to lack of police personnel and to the "soft" sentences produced by the paternalist attitudes of the monarchy. AST, Materie Giurdiche, Consiglio di Conferenza dei Ministri, Mazzo I (1817–19), Sezzione 41, 11 Feb. 1818.

36. AST, Segretaria degli'Interni, I Serie (Giuridico), Registro 28: Registro Lettere della Segretaria Interni ai Prefetti e Giudici (1816–1820), Segretaria to Prefetto, Alba, 12 Aug. 1816.

37. Giovanni Sotgiu, *Storia della Sardegna Sabauda* (Bari-Rome, 1984): 214–23, 236–37.

38. M. D'Azeglio, *I Miei Ricordi*, 2 vols. (Florence, 1867), 1: 186.

39. See especially Pietro Villani, *Italia napoleonica* (Naples, 1978); Rosabella Davico, *Peuple et Notables* (Paris, 1981); Carlo Capra, "Nobili, notabili, elites: dal modello francese al caso italiano," *Quaderni storici* 37 (1979): 12–42; and idem, *L'eta rivoluzionaria in Italia, 1796–1815* (Turin, 1978); Carlo Zaghi, *Potere, chiesa e societa: Studi e ricerche sull'Italia giacobina e napoleonica* (Naples, 1984); and Raffaele Zangheri, *La proprieta terriera e le origini del Risorgimento nel Bolognese, 1789–1804* (Bologna, 1961). For the best overview in English, see Woolf, *History of Italy*, chaps. 9–10.

Combatting the Sexual Abuse of Children in France, 1825–1913

James M. Donovan

Pennsylvania State University, Mont Alto

INTRODUCTION

Since the 1970s, many Americans have become convinced that the sexual abuse of children and teenagers has reached "epidemic" proportions.[1] Yet there is no real reason to believe that the problem is at present more widespread than in other societies at other times. Not all cultures have condemned or have harshly punished sex between adults and children.[2] Boys were frequently used sexually by older men in ancient Greece and Rome.[3] It has been estimated that one-third of the prostitutes in the French city of Dijon between 1440 and 1540 had sold themselves before the age of fifteen.[4] In early seventeenth-century France, adult servants and courtiers felt little or no guilt about fondling and kissing the genitals of Henri IV's little child, the future Louis XIII.[5] A sharply defined chronological age of consent—set well into adolescence—for sexual relations has been, on the other hand, a feature of Modern Western societies.[6] This presumably owed much to what Philippe Ariès called the "discovery of childhood" by the eighteenth century, with its realization that childhood was a distinct phase of life separate from adulthood, and that children were vulnerable creatures with special needs who needed to be protected from predatory adults.[7]

Nineteenth-century France was one major example of a society that experienced the transition from the old relative tolerance of the sexual abuse of minors to the modern revulsion against pedophilia. France saw a huge rise in prosecutions for sex crimes against children during this period. The increase appears to have been due not to a major rise in the actual number of cases of child sexual abuse, but rather to a growing determination on the part of the law, the courts, and the police to combat pedophilia and the prostitution of minors, which seem to have been recognized as problems

Table 1

Prosecutions for the Rape and Indecent Assault of Minors Under the Age of Fifteen, and for the Same Crimes Against Adults: Total Numbers, Five-Year Annual Average Numbers and Rates per Million Population

	Rape/Indecent Assault of Minors			Rape/Indecent Assault of Adults		
Years	Total Number	Annual Average	Rate	Total Number	Annual Average	Rate
1825-1830	798	133	4.2	1038	173	5.4
1831-1835	781	156	4.8	759	152	4.7
1836-1840	1241	248	7.4	910	182	5.4
1841-1845	1796	359	10.5	1036	207	6.1
1846-1850	2154	431	12.2	1084	217	6.1
1851-1855	3040	608	17.0	1170	234	6.5
1856-1860	3510	702	19.5	1117	223	6.2
1861-1865	3830	766	20.5	1071	214	5.7
1866-1870	3773	755	19.8	765	153	4.0
1871-1875	3740	748	20.7	723	145	4.0
1876-1880	4044	809	21.9	610	122	3.3
1881-1885	3584	717	19.0	516	103	2.7
1886-1890	2957	591	15.5	379	76	2.0
1891-1895	2919	583	15.2	477	95	2.5
1896-1900	2260	452	11.7	349	70	1.8
1901-1905	1746	349	9.0	317	63	1.6
1906-1910	1915	383	9.7	357	71	1.8
1911-1913	1190	397	10.0	173	58	1.5

Sources: Compte général, 1825–1860, Table I, p. 2; 1861–1909, Table I, p. 4; 1910–1913, Table I, p. 6; J.-C. Toutain, La population de la France de 1700 à 1959 (Paris, 1963, 54–55.

in France before they were in other Western societies. This was in turn related to the era's new emphasis on the protection of children.

PROSECUTIONS: AN OVERVIEW

The published judicial statistics contained in the Ministry of Justice's annual *Compte général de l'administration de la justice criminelle* (which appeared every year from 1825),[8] show a tremendous rise in prosecutions for sex crimes against children during the course of the nineteenth century. From 1825 through 1830, an average of 133 persons (or 4.2 per million population) were tried each year for the rape and indecent assault of minors under the age of fifteen. After this, the annual average number increased very sharply, until it reached a maximum of 809 (or 21.9 per million population) from 1876 through 1880. The number of cases then declined significantly during the quarter-century from 1881 through 1905, before rising again (though modestly) from 1906 through 1913. Even with the post-1880 decrease, however, the average annual number of prosecutions during the last two decades of the nineteenth century and the earliest years of the twentieth always exceeded considerably the numbers of cases in the 1820s and 1830s (see Table 1).

Table 2
Number of Persons Prosecuted for the Rape and Indecent Assault of Minors
Under the Age of Fifteen as a Percentage of All Persons Prosecuted for Felonies
in France

Years	Rape/Indecent Assault of Minors	All Felonies
1825-1830	798 (1.9%)	42882
1831-1835	781 (2.1%)	37333
1836-1840	1241 (3.1%)	39424
1841-1845	1796 (5.1%)	35521
1846-1850	2154 (5.8%)	37149
1851-1855	3040 (8.6%)	35520
1856-1860	3510 (13.0%)	26915
1861-1865	3830 (16.8%)	22752
1866-1870	3773 (17.7%)	21376
1871-1875	3740 (14.7%)	25361
1876-1880	4044 (18.5%)	21871
1881-1885	3584 (16.4%)	21908
1886-1890	2957 (14.0%)	21144
1891-1895	2919 (14.5%)	20100
1896-1900	2260 (13.3%)	16997
1901-1905	1746 (11.5%)	15235
1906-1910	1915 (11.7%)	16354
1911-1913	1190 (12.7%)	9361

Source: *Compte général*, 1825–1860, Table I, p. 2 and Table II, p. 3; 1861–1909, Table I, p. 4, and Table II, p. 5; 1910–1913, Table I, p. 6 and Table II, p. 7.

After 1835, cases of child sexual molestation in fact greatly exceeded prosecutions for the rape and indecent assault of adults, and this became increasingly true as the century progressed. From 1831 through 1835 the two figures were nearly even, but after this period the rate of prosecutions for the rape and indecent assault of children drew far ahead of the rate for adults. By the years from 1846 through 1850, the average annual number of persons prosecuted for child molestation (431) was almost double the figure for rape and indecent assault of adults (217). The discrepancy between the two figures became even more marked in subsequent years: From 1876 through 1880 the annual average number of prosecutions for rape and indecent assault of minors (809) was more than six and a half times higher than the figure for such crimes against adults (122). This discrepancy changed little during the following years (see Table 1). Even most of the "adult" victims of rape and indecent assault appear to have been teenagers aged fifteen to twenty.[9]

Persons accused of the rape and indecent assault of minors also accounted for a sharply rising proportion of all persons tried for felonies in France, from only 1.9 percent from 1825 through 1830, to 18.5 percent from 1876 through 1880 (see Table 2). This meant that nearly one of every five defendants by the latter period was charged with raping or in some fashion sexually molesting children under the age of fifteen. Indeed, Benjamin F. Martin has estimated that girl molestation was the second most common offense among accused male felons in France from 1871 to 1931.[10] The crime was so widespread, according to Martin, that it was regarded as "almost banal."[11]

The rise in prosecutions for the rape and indecent assault of children was accompanied by a similar rise in cases of the sexual corruption of minors, which was a misdemeanor under French law, punishable by six months to two years imprisonment, and up to five years when the culprit was the parent or guardian of the child.[12] Most of the persons charged with this crime had apparently been involved in the procuring of teenage prostitutes.[13] From 1826 (the first year the *Compte général* included complete data on the number of misdemeanors) through 1830, an annual average of 162 persons were tried in France for violations of Article 334 of the *Code pénal,* which punished people who had "solicited, favored, or habitually facilitated the debauchery or corruption of youth of either sex under the age of 21"[14] This figure increased significantly thereafter, until it reached its nineteenth-century maximum of 458 from 1861 through 1865. The number of prosecutions declined in a slow and uneven fashion from 1881 through 1900, but then rose significantly again from 1901 on, to reach a peak of 502 per year from 1911 through 1913 (see Table 3).

THE LIMITATIONS OF THE JUDICIAL STATISTICS

Despite these sharp increases, most cases of child molestation and sexual corruption of minors were evidently never reported to the police. The problem of the sexual abuse of minors must have been far greater than the statistics suggest. It is virtually impossible to estimate the real number of such cases in nineteenth-century France. However, in one survey of American college students in the 1950s, about one-third of the respondents of both sexes claimed to have been subjected during childhood or adolescence to some kind of sexual abuse by adults.[15] Only 43 percent of the abused females, and only 16.5 percent of the males, reported the experiences to their parents.[16] No more than one-fourth of the parents whom the girls told ever reported the incidents to the police.[17] Many cases of parent-child incest must have been underreported in nineteenth-century France as in twentieth-century America. In recent years, criminologists and the general public have become increasingly aware that parent-child incest has been far more common than once thought because such cases have seldom been reported. It is not surprising, then, that most reported cases of child molestation in nineteenth-century France appear to have involved perpetrators who were not relatives of the victims, although some instances of incest were recorded.[18]

The evidence suggests that in many cases the sexual assault of young girls was reported only when the victims were afflicted with a venereal

Table 3

Prosecutions for the Soliciting of Minors to Debauchery in France: Total
Numbers, Five-Year Annual Average Numbers and Rates per Million Population

Years	Total Number	Annual Average Number	Rate
1826-1830	808	162	5.1
1831-1835	709	142	4.4
1836-1840	1138	228	6.8
1841-1845	1159	232	6.8
1846-1850	1424	285	8.1
1851-1855	2003	401	11.2
1856-1860	2116	423	11.8
1861-1865	2289.	458	12.2
1866-1870	1724	345	9.1
1871-1875	2222	444	12.3
1876-1880	2137	427	11.6
1881-1885	1707	341	9.1
1886-1890	1807	361	9.5
1891-1895	2028	406	10.6
1896-1900	1521	304	7.9
1901-1905	1849	370	9.5
1906-1910	1710	342	8.7
1911-1913	1507	502	12.7

Sources: Compte général, 1826, Table LXXIV, p. 110; 1827, Table LXXXII, p. 120; 1828,
Table XCI, p. 138; 1829, Table XCII, p. 140; 1830, Table LXVIII, p. 114; 1831, Table
LXV, p. 104; 1832, Table LXVIII, p. 108; 1833, Table LXXIII, p. 116; 1834, Table
LXX, p. 112; 1835-1836, Table LXXVI, p. 118; 1837-1851, Table LXXV, p. 116; 1852,
Table LXXIII, p. 112; 1853, Table LXXII, p. 110; 1854-1857, Table LXXIV, p. 112;
1858-1859, Table LXXII, p. 110; 1860, Table LXX, p. 108; 1861-1863, Table LXX, p.
110; 1864-1869, Table LXVII, p. 108; 1870, Table LXII, p. 100; 1871, Table LX, p.
100; 1872-1873, Table LXIV, p. 106; 1874, Table XXXVIII, p. 86; 1875-1878, Table
XXXV, p. 80; 1879-1885, Table XXXV, p. 84; 1886-1888, Table XXX, p. 60; 1889-
1909, Table XXIX, p. 56; 1910-1913, Table XXIX, p. 58; Toutain, La population de
la France, 54-55.

disease. According to Ambroise Tardieu, a professor of forensic medicine
at the University of Paris and one of the foremost forensic specialists in
France during the second half of the nineteenth century, in the 1870s about
fifty girls under the age of fifteen were admitted each year into the special
venereal hospital of Lourcine (Paris). If the sexual organs of any girl
showed traces of violence, the surgeon, at the time of the child's admission,
was obliged to state this on a certificate addressed to the prefect of police,
who then took the case to justice when he thought the evidence warranted
prosecution, or when the girl's family supplied enough information to arrest the culprit.[19] Indeed, the initiative of the parents must have been crucial
in determining whether child molestation cases were reported to the police.
There seems little reason to believe that many offenses would have been
discovered without the parents alerting the police—a fact that, again,
meant that incest cases must have been especially underreported.

Moreover, many of the cases that were reported apparently never made it to trial. This was often because the physicians charged by the courts with examining the victims could find no physical traces of the sexual abuse, or not enough to come to any significant conclusions.[20] This was especially true in cases of nonviolent indecent assault of children.[21] In the absence of physical evidence, the *juges d'instruction* (examining magistrates who decided whether there was sufficient evidence to take cases to trial) were often left only with the word of the child, which was frequently not believed. According to the estimation of the forensic doctor Paul Brouardel at the turn of the twentieth century, sixty to eighty of every 100 cases were rejected before trial as unfounded.[22]

Persons who violated the law against soliciting minors to debauchery were also often not prosecuted: In both Paris and Marseille during much of the nineteenth century, Article 334 was rarely enforced against the keepers of legal brothels (*maisons de tolérance*), even though they appear to have frequently employed underage prostitutes.[23] The number of trials for this crime certainly understated the real extent of child prostitution, for there seems to have been a large clientele for teenage prostitutes in France by the late nineteenth century. This was true to such an extent that some procuresses allegedly offered to passersby unusually young-looking adult whores dressed as little girls, complete with pigtails, short dresses, and even dolls in their arms.[24]

Further evidence of the popularity of teenage prostitutes among the French "johns" of the period can be seen in the fact that of the 2,582 women arrested in Paris in 1877 for clandestine (i.e., unregistered) prostitution, an actual majority (more than 1,500) were minors under the age of twenty-one, the largest number of whom were fifteen to eighteen years old.[25] In Marseille, of 1,000 clandestine prostitutes brought before the city's *bureau des moeurs* (office of the police morals squad) and released from 1872 to 1882, no less than 366 (or 36.6 percent) were under the age of twenty-one, and of these 140, or 14 percent, were under the age of eighteen.[26] Nor was the frequent prostitution of minors restricted to girls: By the late nineteenth century, boy prostitutes allegedly abounded in Paris.[27]

The judicial statistics are therefore a very unreliable measure of the real extent of child sexual abuse and exploitation. Perhaps the most that can be said about the pervasiveness of the problem is that there is no solid evidence to show that child molestation and prostitution were more common in France than in other Western societies of either the nineteenth or twentieth centuries.[28] Child prostitution was apparently widespread in Victorian England.[29] Furthermore, when the American sociolgist Judson T. Landis had his students at the University of California at Berkeley from 1951 to 1954 fill out a questionnaire on their experiences (or lack thereof) with adult sexual deviates, he discovered that approximately one-third had had such a sexual encounter, in most cases when they were children.[30]

Nor is there any reason to believe that sexual relations between adults and minors were more widespread in France during the mid and late nineteenth century than in earlier periods. It is true that in 1882 a Senate Commission on the Protection of Childhood, in its report to the Parlement, warned of the "growing development, in the great centers, of the public [i.e. legal] and above all clandestine prostitution of minors."[31] However, the commission provided no figures to actually prove that teenage prostitution was more common in the late nineteenth century than in earlier periods. In fact, the prostitution of minors seems to have been more widespread in France in the late eighteenth century than in the nineteenth.[32]

PROSECUTIONS AND THE LAWS ON CHILD SEXUAL ABUSE

It appears, rather, that the principal reason for the sharp rise in prosecutions for crimes involving the sexual abuse and exploitation of children was the French state's growing determination in the course of the nineteenth century to combat pedophilia. This was most pronounced in respect to indecent assaults of minors. The increase in prosecutions for these crimes was due primarily to new laws punishing nonviolent or consensual sexual relations with children. Before 1832, there was no provision in the *Code pénal* against the "statutory" rape and indecent assault of children. The original Napoleonic criminal code of 1810 did punish violent sex crimes against minors more harshly than such crimes against adults. Rape and indecent assault of adults were both punished by *réclusion* (five to twenty years' imprisonment). However, if the victim was under the age of fifteen the penalty was *travaux forces à temps* (five to twenty years of hard labor).[33] But the law applied only to cases where violence or force was used.[34]

During this period, several of the *Cours d'assises* (the trial courts for felonies) tried to punish as guilty of "moral violence" persons who abused the inexperience or weakness of children in order to get their consent to sexual relations. However, the *Cour de cassation* (France's highest court of appeals) interpreted the law against rape and indecent assault literally, and refused to uphold the lower courts' decisions. The law could be applied only against those who used physical force, not against nonviolent molesters who were guilty of "moral violence" because of the young ages of the victims.[35]

This meant that most consensual sexual relations between children and adults were legal. It is true that Articles 356 and 357 of the *Code pénal* of 1810 punished the abduction, without fraud or violence, of a girl under the age of sixteen for the purposes of seduction. But this was not really a crime against morals, but was rather an offense against the authority of a child's parents. It applied only if the girl was taken from her family's home.[36] The number of prosecutions for this crime always remained small.[37] Article 334, the law against habitually soliciting minors to debauchery, was also very restricted in application. The intention of this law was to punish the procurers of underage prostitutes, not persons who merely seduced minors.[38] The key circumstance was *habitude*, which the *Code pénal* did not define, but which left to the courts to determine.[39] The *Cour de cassation* maintained that *habitude* had to be established for Article 334 to apply.[40] In practice this meant that its application was in most instances limited to cases of *proxénétisme* (pimping) of minors.[41] According to Armand Dalloz, an attorney at the *Cour Royale de Paris* (Paris Appeals Court) and an important legal writer of the first half of the nineteenth century, the words "soliciting, favoring or habitually facilitating the debauchery" of minors characterized the *metier* of the *proxénète* (pimp), and not the man who seduces a child for his own sexual gratification.[42]

To be sure, there were cases in the early nineteenth century of persons other than procurers who were prosecuted under Article 334 when they had *habitually* seduced children.[43] Whatever the intent of the law, its literal terms did not make any distinction between the corruptor who habitually acted to procure children for his own pleasure and the pimp who procured minors for the pleasure of others.[44] Between 1810 and 1832, magistrates disturbed by the absence of any law penalizing child seduction as such sought to fill this void by interpreting Article 334 to apply to the seducers as well as to the pimps of minors.[45] In 1830, the *Cour de cassation* upheld a judgment against a man who, "during a fairly long period of time," had habitually solicited and favored the corruption of a fourteen year old girl whom he had received in his home.[46] Before 1832, this interpretation of Article 334 provided the only legal protection for children against nonviolent sexual abuse by adults who acted solely for their personal pleasure.[47] But the *single* seduction of a child (unless it was a girl under the age of sixteen who had been removed or abducted from her parents' home) was not a crime, nor was it punishable to patronize a teenage prostitute.[48] Finally, in 1840, the *Cour de cassation* issued a new ruling stating that Article 334 no longer applied to persons who even habitually seduced minors merely for their own sexual satisfaction.[49] Thereafter, the law against soliciting minors to debauchery could only be enforced against the pimps of underage prostitutes—those who repeatedly engaged in sex acts in the presence of children and thereby provided them with a corrupting example, and those who in some fashion habitually acted in an intermediary role in the debauchery of minors.[50]

The absence of a law against the nonviolent sexual molestation of children in France during the first three decades of the nineteenth century seems to have been due to a number of factors. One was the authorities' apparent relative indifference toward sexual relations between children and adults. This was reflected in the casual approach of the police to underage prostitution. As already shown, Article 334 of the penal code was weakly enforced in this period. Even more symptomatic, perhaps, of the tolerant approach of the police toward the prostitution of minors was their willingness to register teenagers as prostitutes. Prostitution as such was not a crime in France; it was a business regulated by the municipalities. The local ordinances varied somewhat, but they generally required the registration of prostitutes with the police.[51] The only national law concerning the business was the one against soliciting minors to debauchery. Yet the police of the early nineteenth century often registered minors as legal prostitutes, in apparent violation of Article 334. In Paris, an ordinance of 1804 only required that girls be "nubile" at the time of their registration, which the police interpreted in practice to mean age sixteen.[52] But even younger girls were sometimes registered.[53] Although the required age was raised to eighteen in 1823, it was lowered again to sixteen in 1828.[54] According to A.-J.-B. Parent-Duchâtelet, of the 12,550 prostitutes registered by the Paris morals police from 1816 to 1832, 6,264—or half of the total—were under the age of twenty-one at the time of their registration. Of these, 2,043 were inscribed before they were eighteen years old.[55] There were even a few cases of girls who were registered between the ages of ten and fifteen.[56]

The relative indifference of the law and of the law enforcement authorities toward sexual activity between adults and minors was not the only reason for the lack of a statutory rape provision in the penal code. It was also due to the fact that the original Code pénal of 1810 was a sparse document which left unpunished many acts that today are considered crimes. The writers of the code, influenced by the eighteenth-century reformers and the Revolution, reacted against the ancien régime's practice of putting penal law at the service of Christian doctrine, and often ignored infractions regarded as purely moral in nature. They generally contented themselves with penalizing acts that troubled the public order, such as murder, assault, theft, rape, arson, fraud, and political subversion.[57] Therefore, the nonviolent attempts on the morals of children were left unpunished, as was homosexuality (for which the death penalty had been provided under ancien régime law).[58] Even incest, also outlawed in the ancien régime, was no longer penalized.[59] Thus, it is clear that under the original Napoleonic Code pénal children were protected from seduction by adults only in exceptional circumstances. Save in cases of abduction from the parents' home, a single nonviolent sexual encounter between an adult and a child, no matter how young, was legal, even if the child was the abuser's own.

It was not until 1832 that the Code pénal was revised to criminalize all nonviolent sexual encounters with young children under a certain age. In that year, the French Parliament created the new felony (Article 331) of "indecent assault, consummated or attempted without violence on the person of a child of either sex aged less than eleven years." Those found guilty of this offense were to be punished by five to twenty years' imprisonment.[60] If the offender was the parent or guardian of the victim, or in some fashion had authority over him or her, a stiffer penalty of five to twenty years of hard labor was provided (Article 333).[61] The rationale for the new felony was the assumption that in sexual relations between adults and children under the age of eleven violence was always presumed because the victims were too young to have the necessary discernment to give their free consent.[62]

The law covered a broad range of sexual acts. Indecent assault (*attentat à la pudeur*) was "every act performed on a person with a view to offending his sense of decency and of a nature to produce that effect."[63] It included every nonconsensual sex act except rape (*viol*), which in the latter case required vaginal penetration by the penis with force or violence.[64] It ranged from actual or attempted nonviolent intercourse with children under the age of eleven, to all other sex acts with such minors, whether anal or oral, and to the touching of their breasts and genital organs. It extended even to lifting the skirts of young girls to the waist in public.[65] When the victim reached the age of eleven, these acts had to be accompanied by violence to constitute *attentats à la pudeur*, although after 1832 the violent indecent assault of minors between the ages of eleven and fifteen was still more harshly punished than instances of this crime against persons who were older.[66]

In cases of the nonviolent indecent assault of children under the age of eleven, vaginal penetration of the victim was rarely attempted. French forensic doctors of the nineteenth century (and here we must take into account the fact that puberty arrived later during this period than at present) repeatedly stated that the adult male penis cannot enter the vagina of a girl under the age of six, and can do so only in exceptional circumstances when the girl is between this age and the age of ten to thirteen.[67] Most of the cases of the nonviolent indecent assault of children involved the sexual touching, by the perpetrator's fingers or penis, of the victim. According to Alexandre Lacassagne, who in his capacity as a doctor of forensic medicine had examined a number of victims and perpetrators in child molestation cases, the method employed by the majority of the molesters of young children in late nineteenth-century France was the rubbing of the penis against the genital organs of the child, a practice he labelled "external or perineal coitus."[68]

The extremely young ages of some of the victims of these crimes is illustrated by several cases that André Gide recalled from his experience as a juror in Rouen in 1912. In one instance, the accused (whom Gide referred to as "Germain R.") had sexually molested his daughter, who was not yet six years old. The incident occurred while the man's wife was in a hospital. The entire family normally slept together in the same room, on straw, except the father customarily slept in a sack. In the incident that led to his arrest, the accused enticed his daughter to get into the sack with him, and there he molested her. It was alleged that he had made an attempt on the girl at least once before. The jury convicted Germain R.[69] In another case the defendant, a "young day laborer of Maromme," had indecently assaulted a six and a half year old girl whom he had lured into a room by offering her "a little box." He infected her with gonorrhea. The jury also convicted him.[70]

Cases such as these, of course, were covered by the 1832 amendment to the penal code. By Gide's time, however, the law had been extended to protect children closer to the age of puberty. Since the 1832 law punished the nonviolent indecent assault of children only when the victim was no older than the age of ten, it still provided less than adequate protection for minors against sexual molestation by adults. Carnal relations by consent with children aged eleven and older remained legal.[71] Indeed, eleven was an astonishingly young age when one considers that, according to the estimations of Edward Shorter, the average age for the onset of puberty for girls in France was fifteen and a half from 1800 to 1849, and fifteen from 1850 to 1899 (compared with twelve or thirteen by the 1970s).[72]

Later in the century, however, the law was toughened. In 1863 the required age of the victim for a person to be charged with indecent assault without violence of a minor was raised to twelve. Moreover, a perpetrator who was a parent or guardian of the victim could be charged with this offense even if the minor was aged thirteen through twenty, and not yet emancipated by marriage.[73] This law therefore restored the crime of incest for parents who had sexual relations with any of their unmarried minor children.[74] The new age limit of thirteen for nonincest cases remained in effect during the remainder of the nineteenth century and the early years of the twentieth.

The evidence strongly suggests that the new laws of 1832 and 1863 against the nonviolent sexual molestation of children were primarily responsible for the huge rise in prosecutions for felonious sex crimes against minors from the 1830s through the 1870s. Before 1855, the *Compte général*'s statistics did not distinguish between the nonviolent indecent assault of children under the age of eleven and the rape and violent indecent assault of persons under the age of fifteen. Nonetheless, the statistics show that from 1825 through 1831, before the enactment of the law of 1832 on nonviolent child molestation, an average of fewer than 129 persons were tried each year for felonious sex crimes against minors. However, after the new law went into effect the figure rose sharply to an annual average of 213 from 1832 through 1840, a number that continued to increase dramatically thereafter.

The law of 1863 caused another sharp rise. From 1855 through 1862, an average of 325 cases of nonviolent indecent assault of children were tried each year, slightly less than the average of 370 for the rape and violent indecent assault of minors. However, from 1863—when the required age of the victim for a charge of nonviolent indecent assault of a minor was

Table 4
Prosecutions for the Nonviolent Indecent Assault of Children Under the Age of Eleven (Thirteen from 1863), and of Rape and the Violent Indecent Assault of Minors Under the Age of Fifteen: Total Numbers and Annual Average Numbers, by Period

| | Nonviolent Indecent Assault | | Rape/Violent Indecent Assault [1] | |
	Total Number	Annual Average	Total Number	Annual Average
Years				
1825-1831	----	---	901	129
1832-1840	----	---	1919	213
1841-1845	----	---	1796	359
1846-1850	----	---	2154	431
1851-1854	----	---	2446	612
1855-1862	2600	325	2956	370
1863-1870	3570	466	2581	323
1871-1875	2313	463	1427	285
1876-1880	2480	496	1564	313
1881-1885	2435	487	1149	230
1886-1890	1975	395	982	196
1891-1895	1914	383	1005	201
1896-1900	1512	302	748	150
1901-1905	1151	230	595	119
1906-1910	1230	246	685	137
1911-1913	742	247	448	149

1. Includes all felonious sex crimes against children before 1855.

Source: Compte général, 1855–1860, Table I, p. 2; 1861–1909, Table I, p. 4; 1910–1913, Table I, p. 6.

raised to twelve—through 1870, the average annual number of persons accused of this crime rose sharply to 446, which was now well above the figure of 323 for the rape and violent indecent assault of minors under the age of fifteen. The nonviolent cases continued to rise until they reached a maximum average of 496 per year from 1876 through 1880, while the number of violent cases actually declined. In fact, from 1863 through 1913 the number of prosecutions for the nonviolent indecent assault of children always greatly exceeded the violent offenses, though from 1881 to 1905 the numbers for both types of crimes decreased significantly (see Table 4). Contemporaries—including the Ministry of Justice itself—were very much aware of the importance of the 1863 law in raising the number of prosecutions for sex crimes against minors in the 1860s and 1870s.[75]

SEX CRIMES AND THE FINDINGS OF JURIES

The authorities' increasingly vigorous repression of child sexual molestation was endorsed apparently to some extent by the juries which tried cases in the Cours d'assises, the courts with jurisdiction over felonies, and the only tribunals in France to use juries.[76] Contemporaries often claimed that French jurymen frequently reflected public opinion in rendering their ver-

Table 5
Convictions and Acquittals For Rape/Indecent Assault of Children Under the Age
of Fifteen, for Rape/Indecent Assault of Adults, and for All Felonies, by Period

	Rape/Indecent Assault Of Children		Rape/Indedcent Assault of Adults		All Felonies	
	Convicted	Acquitted	Convicted	Acquitted	Convicted	Acquitted
Years						
1825-1831	564 (62.6%)	337 (37.4%)	551 (47.8%)	602 (52.2%)	30432 (60.3%)	20056 (39.7%)
1832-1862	10826 (78.0)	3045 (22.0%)	3707 (57.5%)	2735 (42.5%)	143379 (67.0%)	70680 (33.0%)
1863-1880	11384 (81.7%)	2551 (18.3%)	1859 (69.2%)	829 (30.8%)	63143 (77.4%)	18414 (22.6%)
1881-1913	11960 (72.2%)	4611 (27.8%)	1648 (64.2%)	920 (35.8%)	84024 (69.4%)	37075 (30.6%)

Source: Compte général, 1825–1860, Tables I and II, pp. 2–3; 1861–1909, Tables I and II,
    pp. 4–5; 1910–1913, Tables I and II, pp. 6–7.

dicts, a propensity that allegedly led to many instances of biased justice.[77]
It is perhaps more accurate to say that they reflected *bourgeois* opinion;
because of laws excluding manual workers and domestics from jury duty
before 1908, most jurymen belonged to the upper and middle classes.[78]
This was significant in that the nineteenth century's new emphasis on children's welfare and well-being was presumably most evident among the
bourgeoisie.[79] Such an orientation suggests that the jurymen were inclined
to come down hard on child molesters. This was made easier by the fact
that (except during 1831–1835 and 1848–1853, periods when the number
of jurors needed to convict an accused person was raised to eight) only a
simple majority of seven out of twelve jurors was necessary to render a
guilty verdict.[80]
    The judicial statistics show that the juries were certainly more inclined
to convict child molesters than was the case with persons accused of the
rape and indecent assault of adults. Throughout the period 1825–1913, the
conviction rate of persons charged with the rape and indecent assault of
minors was slightly above the conviction rate for all felonies, and significantly higher than the rate for sexual assaults of adults (see Table 5). There
was also a correspondence between the proclivity to convict child molesters
and the degree of repression exerted against such persons by the authorities.
From 1825 through 1831, when the number of child molestation cases
prosecuted in the *Cours d'assises* was rather small and did not yet include
nonviolent indecent assault, the conviction rate was 62.6 percent. But the

CRIMINAL JUSTICE HISTORY

Table 6
Grants of Extenuating Circumstances for Persons Convicted of Felonious Sex
Crimes Against Children, by Period

Years	Nonviolent Indecent Assault		Rape/ Violent Indecent Assault		Total	
	Con- Victed	Exten- uating Circumstances	Con- Victed	Exten- uating Circumstances	Con- victed	Exten- uating Circumstances
1833-1854	----	----	----	----	6063	3892 (64.2%)
1855-1862	2131	1818 (85.3%)	2511	1176 (46.8%)	4642	2994 (64.5%)
1863-1880	6624	5825 (87.9%)	4760	2154 (45.3%)	11384	7979 (70.1%)
1881-1913	7523	6956 (92.5%)	4437	1917 (43.2%)	11960	8873 (74.2%)

Source: Compte général, 1833–1848, Table I, p. 2 and Table IV, p. 6; 1849–1860, Table I,
p. 2 and Table VII, pp. 14–15; 1861–1870, Table I, p. 4 and Table VII, pp. 16–17; 1871–
1873, Table I, p. 4 and Table VII, pp. 18–19; 1874–1885, Table I, p. 4 and Table VIII,
pp. 26–27; 1886–1909, Table I, p. 4 and Table III, pp. 20–21; 1910–1913, Table I, p. 6
and Table VIII, pp. 22–23.

figure rose significantly to 78.0 percent from 1832 through 1862, under
the new law against nonviolent molestation, when the total number of cases
rose sharply.

Some of the rise in the conviction rate must also have been due to another
new law of 1832, which allowed juries to determine whether extenuating
circumstances existed for the criminals they convicted. Since a ruling of
extenuating circumstances meant an automatic reduction in the penalty
below the minimum prescribed by the penal code, the Ministry of Justice
claimed that juries in criminal cases in general became more willing to
convict, because they knew that they could avoid the very harsh punishments of the Code pénal by convicting with extenuating circumstances
rather than by acquitting altogether.[81] In fact, juries did find extenuating
circumstances in a substantial majority of those they convicted of sex
crimes against children (see Table 6).

The law on extenuating circumstances was not the only cause of the
rising conviction rate for the rape and indecent assault of minors. The rate
continued to increase long after 1832, reaching a high of 81.7 percent from
1863 through 1880. This followed the passage of the law raising to twelve
the age for which the statute against felonious nonviolent molestation of a
child could apply, and was during a period when the average annual numbers of child sexual assault cases peaked. The rate of convictions dropped

Table 7

Convictions and Acquittals for the Nonviolent Indecent Assault of Children
Under the Age of Eleven (Thirteen from 1863), and for the Rape/Violent
Indecent Assault of Minors Under the Age of Fifteen, by Period

	Nonviolent Indecent Assault of Children		Rape/Violent Indecent Assault of Minors	
	Convicted	Acquitted	Convicted	Acquitted
Years				
1855-1862	2131(82.0%)	469(18.0%)	2511(84.9%)	445(15.1%)
1863-1880	6624(79.2%)	1739(20.8%)	4760(85.4%)	812(14.6%)
1881-1913	7523(68.6%)	3436(31.4%)	4437(79.1%)	1175(20.9%)

Source: Compte général, 1855–1860, Table I, p. 2; 1861–1909, Table I, p. 4; 1910–1913,
Table I, p. 6.

somewhat, to 72.2 percent, from 1881 through 1913, during the same
period in which the *procureurs* (district attorneys) were taking fewer cases
of child sexual molestation to the courts.

There was, however, one major exception to the juries' severity: They
were much more lenient toward nonviolent sex crimes against children than
they were toward the violent cases. The jurors seem to have balked at the
punishments provided in the penal code for the nonviolent indecent assault
of children. This does not mean that they did not take such cases seriously.
Most of the nonviolent molesters were convicted, and from 1855 through
1880, at least, the conviction rate for the indecent assault of children without violence was only slightly below the rate for the violent cases (see Table
7). Yet the juries were far more willing to grant extenuating circumstances
to the nonviolent molesters than to the violent ones. From 1855 through
1913 fewer than half of the persons convicted of the rape and violent indecent assault of minors were granted extenuating circumstances, but this
favor was accorded to approximately nine of ten persons convicted of nonviolent indecent assault of children. In fact, after 1863 (when the statutory
rape and indecent assault age was raised to just under thirteen), grants of
extenuating circumstances for nonviolent molestation increased slightly
while the grants for the violent sex crimes against minors actually declined
by a small margin (see Table 6).

It is impossible to know just why the juries so often granted extenuating
circumstances to the persons they convicted of nonviolent indecent assault
of minors. Juries, in their verdicts, did not have to explain their reasons for
finding extenuating circumstances.[82] Nor have the records of jury deliber-
ations from nineteenth-century France been preserved.[83] Certainly there
must have been genuine mitigating circumstances in some of the cases.

However, the fact that the juries granted extenuating circumstances to such an overwhelming majority of the persons they convicted of nonviolent child molestation suggests that they regarded the punishment prescribed by the penal code (at least five years' imprisonment when no extenuating circumstances were found) as too harsh for most cases. In fact, some contemporaries asserted that, in respect to felonies in general, juries frequently granted extenuating circumstances to the persons they found guilty in order to circumvent the stern punishments provided by the *Code pénal*.[84]

The relative leniency of the juries toward nonviolent child molesters does not, however, negate the thesis that the repression of the sexual abuse of minors increased in France during the nineteenth century. Even though most of the convicted nonviolent offenders received lesser penalties than had been prescribed by the law, they were still being punished for acts that before 1832 or 1863 they would not have been punished for at all. To this, of course, can be added the facts that from the 1830s through the 1870s the district attorneys were bringing more and more cases of felonious child sexual molestation to trial, and in an increasing number of instances they were able to secure convictions.

THE REPRESSION OF TEENAGE PROSTITUTION

The crackdown on the sexual molestation of minors was accompanied by a similar crackdown on child prostitution. This was not caused by changes in the law (the text of Article 334 on the soliciting of minors to debauchery was not altered from 1810 to 1903).[85] However, just as the juries became progressively more severe toward child molesters (at least in respect to convictions) from the 1830s through the 1870s, the magistrates of the *Tribunaux correctionnels* (the courts with jurisdiction over *délits*, or misdemeanors, which used only three-judge panels without juries)[86] became progressively more severe toward persons accused of violations of Article 334. The conviction rate for this offense rose from 75.5 percent from 1826 through 1831 to 92.4 percent from 1863 through 1880 (see Table 8). Moreover, there is evidence that, beginning in the 1830s, the police in Paris and in other municipalities began to take the problem of child prostitution more seriously than before, and to enforce Article 334 with greater vigor. This is suggested, of course, by the huge increase in prosecutions of persons for soliciting minors to debauchery, which suddenly rose significantly from the annual average of 142 from 1831 through 1835 to 228 from 1836 through 1840, and thereafter continued to rise until it reached its peak (for the nineteenth century) of 458 from 1861 through 1865. As already shown, the figure dropped slowly throughout the late nineteenth century. But it still remained well above what it had been from the late 1820s through the 1840s (see Table 3).

The rise in such prosecutions was accompanied by a growing reluctance

Table 8

Convictions and Acquittals for the Soliciting of Minors to Debauchery

	Convicted	Acquitted
Years		
1826-1831	725 (75.5%)	235 (24.5%)
1832-1862	7846 (83.7%)	1530 (16.3%)
1863-1880	6834 (92.4%)	559 (7.6%)
1881-1913	10964 (90.4%)	1165 (9.6%)

Source: Compte général, 1826, Table LXXIV, p. 110; 1827, Table LXXXII, p. 120; 1828, Table XCI, p. 138; 1829, Table XCII, p. 140; 1830, Table LXVIII, p. 108; 1831, Table LXV, p. 104; 1832, Table LXVIII, p. 108; 1833, Table LXXIII, p. 116; 1834, Table LXX, p. 112; 1835–1836, Table LXXVI, p. 118; 1837–1851, Table LXXV, p. 116; 1852, Table LXXXIII, p. 112; 1853, Table LXXII, p. 111; 1854–1857, Table LXXIV, p. 113; 1858–1859, Table LXXII, p. 111; 1860, Table LXX, p. 109; 1861–1863, Table LXX, p. 111; 1864–1869, Table LXVII, p. 109; 1870, Table LXII, p. 101; 1871, Table LX, p. 101; 1874, Table XXXVIII, p. 87; 1875–1878, Table XXXV, p. 81; 1879–1885, Table XXXV, p. 85; 1886–1888, Table XXX, p. 61; 1889–1909, Table XXIX, p. 57; 1910–1913, Table XXIX, p. 59.

on the part of the police to register teenage prostitutes.[87] According to data compiled by C.J. Lecour in 1870, 2,217 (or 34.6 percent) of the 6,407 prostitutes registered in Paris from 1855 through 1869 were under the age of twenty-one.[88] This proportion was well below the figure of 49.9 percent given by A.-J.-B. Parent-Duchâtelet for the period 1816–1832. The decline in registrations was especially sharp for girls under the age of eighteen: The figure of 16.3 percent recorded by Parent-Duchâtelet for 1816–1832 was halved to only 8 percent (or 513 of the total number of inscribed prostitutes) for the period 1855–1869.[89] Only in exceptional cases were girls registered at age sixteen.[90] In France as a whole, it appears that by the early 1880s girls under the age of seventeen were rarely registered as prostitutes by the police.[91]

The authorities of many municipalities also placed increasingly stringent conditions on which underage girls and women could be inscribed. In Marseille, for instance, a new Règlement général du service des moeurs of 1878 forbade the madams of the maisons de tolérance to employ any minors as prostitutes.[92] Article 6 of the règlement placed strict new limits on which minors could be registered.[93] The authorities justified registration as a last resort; if a minor persisted in being a prostitute, it was preferable that she be a legal one who had to submit to medical inspections for venereal diseases.[94] By the early 1880s, police in other municipalities in France also generally registered underage prostitutes only if they were incorrigible, and if their continued clandestine status threatened the public health.[95]

Explanations for the Crackdown

The evidence in respect to both child molestation and rape, and teenage prostitution, suggests a major crackdown on the part of the law and the police against sexual relations between adults and minors in France in the nineteenth century, even though many cases were still not reported. There were several explanations for this trend. One was that the problem of the sexual abuse of children was apparently recognized in France earlier than in other major modern Western countries. In the second half of the nineteenth century, a considerable literature on child sexual molestation developed in France, in which a number of forensic doctors and criminologists openly—and often graphically—described the problem. The first published work to concern itself with the sexual abuse of children was *Étude médico-légale sur les attentats aux moeurs* (A Forensic Study of Assaults on Decency), originally published in 1857, and written by Ambroise Tardieu.[96] This book inspired a whole new body of literature on sexual assaults on children. Alexandre Lacassagne, as a professor of forensic medicine at the University of Lyon, in the 1880s urged his students to write about the sexual abuse of children.[97] Other works besides that of Tardieu (which went through no less than seven editions between 1857 and 1878), devoted wholly or in part to the sexual abuse of children, appeared in France during the late nineteenth and early twentieth centuries.[98] Even that most taboo of subjects—incest between children and their parents—was openly discussed by Tardieu and his fellow forensic specialist Paul Brouardel.[99]

The relatively early recognition in France of the reality of the sexual abuse of children was in rather strong contrast to the situation in other Western countries of the nineteenth century, where the phenomenon was ignored or was considered taboo. In England, there was little concern with the problem of child prostitution before the 1880s, despite the fact that it was apparently quite common in the nation's larger cities.[100] Girls could also be legally seduced as young as the age of twelve. Even cases of the seduction of girls under this age were rarely prosecuted.[101] It was not until the 1880s that an organized movement against child prostitution became a major crusade in England.[102] This agitation resulted in Parliament's passage of the Criminal Law Amendment Act of 1885, which raised the age of consent for sexual intercourse to sixteen.[103]

In Austria, child sexual abuse—especially when it involved incest—appears to have been a taboo subject down through the end of the nineteenth century and well into the next. According to Jeffrey Moussaieff Masson, Sigmund Freud—who studied in Paris in the 1880s and was familiar with the French literature of the period on the sexual abuse of children—originally believed that his hysterical patients suffered from the suppressed memories of actual childhood seduction, including incest.[104] But after he announced this discovery in a paper ("The Aetiology of Hysteria") delivered before the Society for Psychiatry and Neurology at Vienna in 1896, he met with antagonism and ostracism from his fellow Viennese psychiatrists.[105] It was then that Freud abandoned his original insight concerning the reality of child sexual abuse, and advanced instead his theory that his patients' stories were fantasies induced by the "Oedipus complex."[106] In fact, the concept of child abuse was not recognized in Austria at this time, and it was rare for child abusers of any kind to be prosecuted there.[107]

In the United States, it was not until the 1970s that much attention was paid to the sexual abuse of children and to the prostitution of teenagers.[108] Naturally enough, when people become aware of the problem there is a greater propensity to report cases of child molestation.[109] Benjamin F. Martin may very well be correct, then, in assuming that one reason why the sexual molestation of children was (relatively) so often prosecuted in late nineteenth-century France was that people in that country were more willing than in others to recognize the reality and pervasiveness of this crime and report cases to the police.[110] Therefore, the growing awareness in France of the existence of child molestation and the prostitution of minors must have contributed to the rise in prosecutions for sex crimes against children.

The increase in prosecutions for sexual offenses involving children appears to have also been related to political developments. Such cases reached their maximum in the period between 1850 and 1880 (see Tables 1 through 3). During almost this entire era, France was governed by the conservative regimes of the Second Empire (1852–1870) and early Third Republic government of "moral order" (1870–1879). The conservatives and clericals who dominated these regimes were especially concerned with child prostitution and with the need to protect minors from this scourge.[111] In such an atmosphere, the *procureurs* (who were political appointees without security of tenure and were therefore responsive to the political imperatives of the governments that appointed them)[112] must have felt increased pressure to bring cases of child molestation and the exploitation of teenage prostitutes to justice. Indeed, this era was characterized by major increases in prosecutions for crimes against morals in general (public indecency, pornography, adultery, and abortion, as well as child molestation and soliciting minors to debauchery).[113]

Perhaps the most important reason for the crackdown on child sexual molestation and teenage prostitution was the growing movement toward the protection of minors from exploitation and abuse. In the nineteenth century, the government in France, as elsewhere in Europe, increasingly concerned itself with the welfare of children—now seen as helpless and vulnerable beings with special needs rather than as miniature adults.[114] The state now "assumed the guise of the great Mother, or the great Father."[115] This was reflected in the enactment of child labor laws in France and other European countries.[116]

The movement toward the protection of minors accelerated from the middle of the century, especially after the appearance in France in the 1860s of societies concerned with child welfare.[117] Rachel Ginnis Fuchs has noted a significant rise in prosecutions for nonsexual crimes against children (such as infanticide and the homicide of minors) during the middle of the nineteenth century. According to her analysis, this large increase was caused not so much by an actual rise in such offenses, but in part by the public officials' new concern with the victimization of minors and their need for state protection.[118] This became especially evident from the 1870s, when politicians and officials moved even further away from their old indifference to the neglect and abuse of minors, which had been manifested in such activities as the use of mercenary wet-nurses, child abandonment, and violence and cruelty toward children.[119] The result was the enactment of a number of child protection laws.[120] It was only natural that in this atmosphere the authorities should have cracked down harder on child molesters and on the exploiters of teenage prostitutes. In fact, Fuchs' figures show that the number of prosecutions for nonsexual crimes against children rose sharply during roughly the same period (from the 1830s to the 1860s)[121] as did the sexual cases.

After 1880—A Relaxation of Repression?

One problem, however, in tying the rise in prosecutions for sex crimes against children to the state's increasing concern for the welfare of minors is the apparent slackening of the repression against child sexual abuse after 1880. This was manifested in prosecutions, convictions, and punishments. As already shown, prosecutions for felonious sex crimes against minors dropped significantly between 1881 and 1905 (see Table 1). These figures suggest at least a temporary retreat in the movement to protect children from sexual abuse. It is possible that this decline reflected in part a real decrease in cases of sex crimes against children. Perhaps the stricter repression of indecent assault and rape of children had finally had some deterrent effect. But this was by no means certain. Paul Brouardel considered the possibility that the decline in cases of the rape and indecent assault of minors in the last decades of the nineteenth century was more apparent than real, caused perhaps by a loss of zeal on the part of the district attorneys for prosecuting these crimes.[122] In fact, the decline in prosecutions in the *Cours d'assises* may have been due simply to changes in judicial practice. The *juges d'instruction,* who had to investigate criminal cases before trial, sometimes decided to drop original felony charges of *attentat à la pudeur* and prosecute the culprits instead (if possible) for *outrage public à la pudeur* (public indecency), a misdemeanor. This was done to increase the chances of conviction, since the judges of the *Tribunaux correctionnels* were more inclined to convict accused persons than were the

Table 9
Punishments of Persons Convicted of the Rape and Violent Indecent Assault of
Children Under the Age of Fifteen

Years	Hard Labor	5+ Years Prison	1-5 Years Prison	1 Year or Less Prison	Minors[1]	Total
1855-1862	812(32.3%)	876(34.95)	746(29.7%)	74(2.9%)	3(0.1%)	2511
1863-1880	1443(30.3%)	1534(32.2%)	1614(33.9%)	161(3.4%)	8(3.4%)	4760
1881-1913	1101(24.8%)	1247(28.1%)	1810(40.8%)	265(6.0%)	14(0.3%)	4437

1. Children under the age of sixteen who were convicted of crimes were
ordinarily sent to Houses of Correction.

Source: Compte général, 1855–1860, Table I, p. 2; 1861–1909, Table I, p. 4; 1910–1913,
   Table I, p. 6.

juries of the Cours d'assises.[123] It is impossible to tell from the statistics
how many cases were thus affected, but the correctionnalisation of many
felonies became common in the late nineteenth century.[124]

Whether it was due to fewer arrests, or to correctionnalisation, sex
crimes against children accounted for a decreasing percentage of felony
prosecutions. The total number of prosecutions for felonies declined in
France during the late nineteenth century.[125] However, after 1880 prosecutions for the rape and indecent assault of children dropped proportion-
ately more sharply than prosecutions for felonies in general. Hence, sex
crimes against minors as a percentage of all cases tried by the Cours
d'assises decreased from a high of 18.5 percent from 1876 through 1880
to only 11.5 percent from 1901 through 1905 (see Table 2).

Not only were the district attorneys bringing fewer child molesters to
trial in the Cours d'assises, but a declining percentage of those who were
prosecuted were being convicted. As already stated, the conviction rate for
the rape and indecent assault of minors dropped from a high of 81.7 percent in 1863 through 1880, to 72.2 percent in 1881 through 1913. The
decline was sharper for the nonviolent cases than for the violent ones: The
conviction rate for the nonviolent indecent assault of minors dropped from
79.2 percent in 1863 through 1880, to 68.6 percent in 1881 through 1913;
the figure for the violent cases decreased less significantly from 85.4 to 79.1
percent (see Table 5).

It was not only the juries that became more lenient toward child molesters after 1880; the same was true of the magistrates, if one is to judge
by the sentences they handed out. Persons convicted of the rape and violent
indecent assault of minors were now more often sentenced to prison terms
of five years or less, and fewer were condemned to the maximum punishment of hard labor (see Table 9). More dramatic yet were the decreasing
penalties meted out to those persons convicted of the nonviolent indecent
assault of children. The proportion of these culprits who were punished by

Table 10
Punishments of Persons Convicted of the Nonviolent Indecent Assault of Children

Years	5+ Years Prison	1-5 Years Prison	1 Year or Less Prison	Minors	Total
1855-1862	602(28.2%)	1352(63.4%)	176(8.3%)	1(0.05%)	2131
1863-1880	1521(23.0%)	4377(66.1%)	720(10.9%)	6 (0.1%)	6624
1881-1913	1364(18.1%)	4370(58.1%)	1768(23.5%)	21(0.3%)	7523

Source: Compte général, 1855-1860, Table I, p. 2; 1861-1909, Table I, p. 4; 1910-1913, Table I, p. 6.

the maximum penalty of more than five years' imprisonment dropped only rather slightly from 1863-1880 to 1881-1913, but the percentage sentenced to prison terms of up to one year more than doubled from 10.9 to 23.5 percent (see Table 10).

This decline in the repression of child molestation cases after 1880 was paralled by a similar relaxation of the enforcement of the law against soliciting minors to debauchery, at least until just after 1900. As already noted, the number of prosecutions decreased. The average annual number of persons prosecuted for violations of Article 334 dropped from 427 in 1876-1880, to 341 in 1881-1885. The number continued to decline slightly thereafter, until it reached 304 in 1896-1900. The figure then rose to 370 for 1901-1905, and to 502 during 1911-1913. This renewed rise appears to have been due to a heightened concern in France in the period around 1900 with the prostitution of minors—especially with the "white slave" traffic in girls—[126] which resulted in the strengthening of Article 334 in 1903 to prevent the sale of children in brothels, and to crack down harder on souteneurs (pimps) for practicing their trade.[127]

But the new law of 1903 did not reverse the decline in punishments, which was even more marked for the soliciting of minors to debauchery than for the indecent assault of children. The conviction rate for the former crime scarcely changed after 1880 from what it had been in the preceding period (see Table 8), and it was also much higher than the conviction rates for both the violent and nonviolent indecent assault of minors: The magistrates of the Tribunaux correctionnels had a reputation for greater severity than the juries of the Cours d'assises when it came to convicting people.[128]

Nevertheless, those same magistrates became over time much more lenient in the punishments they handed out. From 1832 through 1862, 42 percent of the persons convicted of violating Article 334 were sentenced to more than a year in prison, and 54.4 percent were sentenced to a year or less. The former figure dropped somewhat to 31.2 percent from 1863 through 1880, and the latter rose to 62.5 percent during those same years.

Table 11
Punishments and Grants of Extenuating Circumstances for Persons Convicted of
the Soliciting of Minors to Debauchery[1]

	Year or More Prison	Less than Year Prison	Fine Only	Minors	Total	Granted Extenuating Circumstances
Years						
1826-1831	375(51.7%)	335(46.2%)	11(1.5%)	4(0.6%)	725	64(8.8%)
1832-1862	3297(42.0%)	4272(54.4%)	182(2.3%)	95(1.2%)	7846	2508(32.0%)
1863-1880	2130(31.2%)	4268(62.5%)	261(3.8%)	175(2.6%)	6834	3417(50.0%)
1881-1902	829(12.0%)	5558(80.3%)	491(7.1%)	44(0.6%)	6922	4658(67.3%)
1903-1913	362(9.0%)	3244(80.3%)	408(10.1%)	28(0.7%)	4042	2444(60.5%)

1. A law of 1824 granted to magistrates (but not yet the juries of the
Cours d'assises) the authority to rule on extenuating circumstances in certain
cases (Patricia Moulin, "Extenuating Circumstances," in I, Pierre Riviere,
Having Slaughtered My Mother, My Sister, and My Brother..., ed. Michel Foucault
(New York, 1975), 213.). This probably explains why data on grants of
extenuating circumstances for persons convicted of delits were available in the
Compte general from 1826 on, but not for persons convicted of crimes (who from
1832 could only be granted extenuating circumstances by the juries and not by
the judges) until 1833.

Source: Compte général, 1826, Table LXXIV, p. 110; 1827, Table LXXXII, p. 120; 1828,
Table XCI, p. 138; 1829, Table XCII, p. 140; 1830, Table LXVIII, p. 114; 1831, Table
LXV, p. 104; 1832, Table LXVIII, p. 108; 1833, Table LXXIII, p. 116; 1834, Table
LXX, p. 112; 1835–1836, Table LXXVI, p. 118; 1837–1851, Table LXXV, p. 116; 1852,
Table LXXIII, p. 112; 1853, Table LXXII, p. 111; 1854–1857, Table LXXIV, p. 113;
1858–1859, Table LXXII, p. 111; 1860, Table LXX, p. 109; 1861–1863, Table LXX, p.
111; 1864–1869, Table LXVII, p. 109; 1870, Table LXII, p. 101; 1871, Table LX, p.
101; 1872–1873, Table LXIV, p. 107; 1874, Table XXXVIII, p. 87; 1875–1878, Table
XXXV, p. 81; 1879–1885, Table XXXV, p. 85; 1886–1888, Table XXX, p. 61; 1889–
1909, Table XXIX, p. 57; 1910–1913, Table XXIX, p. 59.

But by far the most dramatic decline in penalties occurred after 1880: From
1881 through 1902 only 12 percent of the persons convicted for soliciting
minors to debauchery were sentenced to more than a year in prison, and
80.3 percent were sentenced to a year or less. Furthermore, even though
the new law of 1903 raised the maximum penalty for violations of Article
334 to three years' imprisonment,[129] the proportion of offenders sentenced
to more than a year in prison continued to decline, to only 9 percent from
1903 through 1913, while the figure for those condemned to a year or less
in jail remained the same as in the preceding period. The growing leniency
of the judges went even further than this: The proportion of convicts punished merely with fines rose from 2.3 percent in 1832 through 1862 to 10.1
percent in 1903 through 1913 (see Table 11).

    The decline in penalties meted out to persons convicted of soliciting mi-
nors to debauchery must have been due in large part to the increased proclivity of the judges to grant extenuating circumstances to those they found

guilty of this crime. The magistrates of the *Tribunaux correctionnels* ruled in favor of extenuating circumstances for violations of Article 334 in a smaller proportion of cases than did the juries for those they convicted of felonious sex crimes against children. Even so, the percentage of persons convicted of soliciting minors to debauchery who were granted extenuating circumstances rose from 32 percent in 1832–1862, to 50 percent in 1863–1880, and 67.3 percent in 1881–1902, before declining somewhat to 60.5 percent in 1903–1913 (see Table 11).

Although the statistics suggest that after 1880 the authorities relaxed their repression of the sexual abuse of minors, this did not mean a reversion to the old lack of concern with child sexual molestation and exploitation. By the opening of the twentieth century, prosecutions for sex crimes against children were still far more numerous than in the 1820s and 1830s, and far exceeded prosecutions for sex crimes against adults. Also lessening the significance of the decrease in indictments for child molesting was the fact that the decline in prosecutions for sex crimes against children was part of a relaxation in the repression of sex crimes in general: The drop in cases of rape and indecent assault of children was paralleled by a drop in cases of rape and indecent assault of adults (see Table 1).

THE POST-1880 CAMPAIGN AGAINST POLICE REGISTRATION OF UNDERAGE PROSTITUTES

The continuing concern of the authorities with the sexual abuse of minors after 1880 was reflected in one area (the traces of which largely escape the *Compte général*'s statistics) where they actually got tougher. This was the movement to abolish the police registration of teenagers as prostitutes, culminating in an act of 1908 that outlawed the practice.

As late as the years around 1880, the police—albeit with increased reluctance—still registered a significant number of minors as prostitutes. Of 3,584 prostitutes registered by the morals bureau in Marseille from 1872 to 1882, 374 (or 10.4 percent) were under the age of twenty-one. Of these, 104 (or 2.9 percent of the total) were under the age of eighteen. One of the registered prostitutes was only fourteen years old, and twelve were age fifteen.[130] Similarly in Paris between 1878 and 1887, no less than 1,868 minors were inscribed in the city's police register of prostitutes.[131] In France as a whole, the 1882 Senate Commission on the Protection of Childhood compiled figures that showed that, in the fifty-seven departments that responded to the commission's questionnaire on teenage prostitution, 1,338 minors were registered as prostitutes in the preceding year, including 300 in Lyon, 187 in Paris, 98 in Bordeaux, and 26 in Marseille.[132]

Soon thereafter, however, the police registration of teenage prostitutes came under increasing attack, and by the time of World War I the practice had been prohibited. The post-1880 crusade against underage prostitution and its sanctioning by the police was an outgrowth of several trends. These included the Third Republic's growing solicitude for the welfare of children, the rise of a vocal crusade to abolish the system of regulated prostitution, followed by the emergence of a "neoregulationist" movement that sought to defend the system of police regulation by reforming it (which meant, among other things, ending the registration of minors), the establishment of new moral reform organizations, and heightened publicity about the "white slave traffic" in young girls in the years around 1900.

In respect to the first trend, the advocates of child welfare expressed a growing tendency to view underage prostitutes not as delinquents, but as victims of society who were in need of the state's protection.[133] This was related to the Third Republic's increased concern for the welfare of children. As Rachel Ginnis Fuchs has demonstrated, under the Third Republic the movement for child protection intensified. This was reflected on a number of levels. Abandoned children, regarded as wards of the state, sent to foundling hospitals and then to foster families under state supervision, now received better medical attention than formerly, and the foster parents were more closely supervised by state officials in order to prevent the abuse and neglect of their young charges.[134] In 1874, the Roussel Law was passed to regulate the wet nursing business.[135] Legislation for compulsory education was passed in 1882.[136] This was followed by a law of 1889 for the protection of the *moralement abandonnés,* which allowed the government to remove children from the authority of parents who were drunken, criminal, immoral, or abusive, and make them wards of the state.[137] Yet another law was passed in 1898 which, for the first time, imposed criminal penalties for parents who abused, starved, or mistreated their children.[138]

In the same vein, the proponents of child welfare called for the end of police sanctioning of teenage prostitution. Senator Theophile Roussel, the foremost champion of child welfare in France in the 1870s and 1880s (and the sponsor of the 1874 Roussel Law), crusaded against the prostitution of minors. In 1881 he proposed that prostitutes aged sixteen and under be taken to a *juge de paix* (Justice of the Peace), who would then (if it was proven that the minor was a prostitute) place the child under the care of either the Bureau of Public Assistance, or an authorized private institution or person who would act as guardian for the minor until she reached the age of majority.[139] In 1888, in a speech before the Academy of Medicine, Roussel strengthened his proposal by adding that it should apply not only to minors of sixteen and under, but to *all* minors (that is, to persons up to the age of twenty-one) caught in an *état habituel* of prostitution.[140]

The movement to eliminate teenage prostitution was also encouraged by the crusade, begun in the 1870s, of feminists, moralists, and civil libertarians to abolish the system of regulated prostitution.[141] The abolitionists criticized the registration and medical inspection of prostitutes for several reasons: It institutionalized the "double standard" of sexual morality by setting aside certain women for premarital and extramarital sexual use by men,[142] the practices of the morals squads often violated the rights of prostitutes, and the police were giving their sanction to immorality.[143] To the abolitionists, the police, by registering some minors as prostitutes, were "white slavers."[144] The abolitionists supported legislation to suppress the prostitution of minors,[145] and so did the feminists.[146]

The rise of the "neoregulationist" movement of the 1880s and after added to the efforts of those who wanted to end the registration of minors as prostitutes. The neoregulationists sought to reform rather than abolish the system of police regulation of prostitution.[147] In this fashion, they outflanked the abolitionists by ridding the regulatory system of its worst abuses.[148] One of the criticized abuses was, of course, the registration of underage prostitutes, and the neoregulationists agreed with the abolitionists that the practice should be stopped.[149] In fact, according to Alain Corbin, the neoregulationists cited the need to suppress the corruption of minors in order to convince more of the public to support the continuation of the regulatory system, rather than its abolition.[150]

The abolitionist and neoregulationist efforts to combat teenage prostitution were supplemented by (and were not always clearly distinct from) the rise of a vigorous moral reform movement in France in the 1890s, which, among other things, sought to protect the sexual morals of the young.[151] This caused the movement to agitate against the prostitution of minors. The *Ligue de la Moralité Publique,* formed in 1895, was very much concerned with the issue of underage prostitution.[152] The organization was represented in the Senate by René Bérenger, a neoregulationist and strong opponent of teenage prostitution.[153]

Therefore, by the opening of the twentieth century there was a growing concern on the part of all the factions in the prostitution debate with the prostitution of minors,[154] and they arrived at a consensus on the need to enact laws to protect teenagers from the business.[155] This consensus first bore fruit in the form of legislation to combat the "white slave traffic" in young girls. As already mentioned, the issue of white slavery received a lot of attention in the years around 1900. The victims of this trade were often perceived as virgins scarcely above childhood.[156] A number of international conferences on the transnational trade in young prostitutes were held at the turn of the century.[157] Particularly influential in France was the conference held at Paris in 1902. The French Parlement responded to the meeting a year later by passing an act strengthening Article 334 by raising the penalty for its violation from two to three years' imprisonment (except for parents and guardians of the minors, who were still punished by a maximum of five years), and adding new provisions aimed at combatting the "white slave" traffic.[158]

This was followed by legislation outlawing the police registration of teenage prostitutes. In 1895, Senator René Bérenger introduced a bill reforming the system of regulation which, among other provisions, would end the registration of minors as prostitutes.[159] This bill failed.[160] However, an Extraparliamentary Commission on the Moral Regime, which met from 1904 to 1906, endorsed Bérenger's proposal.[161] This became the basis for a comprehensive act dealing with the prostitution of minors, which was finally enacted into law by the French Parlement in 1908. Under this law, prostitutes aged eighteen and under were no longer to be registered by the police.[162] Rather, the police were obliged to take the minor to the district attorney, who was required take the case to the *Tribunal civil,* which would then decide whether the youngster should be put into the custody of her parents or be sent to a special public or private reform institution for her "moral reform" until she reached her majority or marriage.[163] One interesting feature of the new law was that it did not make any distinction between underage prostitutes based on gender. It referred to "tout mineur" (any minor), and thus took into account the existence of boy as well as girl prostitution.[164] The law of 1908 also reflected the new concept that child prostitutes (like children generally) must be protected by the state, and their welfare looked after. The lawyer Eugene Prevost, commenting on the 1908 law, wrote that it embodied the "idea that the state surely has a duty towards very young prostitutes, a duty to which, henceforth, it can no longer close its eyes."[165]

CONCLUSIONS

Prevost's statement indeed reflected the new attitude of concern the French state had gradually adopted, in the course of the nineteenth century, toward the sexual abuse and exploitation of children. To be sure, there remained limitations to this concern. As late as the eve of World War I, it was still legal to seduce a thirteen year old, provided she was not one's own child, and she had not been abducted from her parent's home. The number of child molestation cases actually prosecuted must still have been only a tiny fraction of the real number. Yet during the preceding century the progress in the fight against child sexual abuse had been considerable. In the first decades of the nineteenth century, the state had in fact closed its eyes to the problem, or did not recognize its existence. The original *Code pénal* of 1810 provided children with almost no protection from sexual abuse, save in cases of abduction, violent assault, or *habitude.*

This indifference was hardly surprising. In early nineteenth-century France, adults felt quite free to abuse and exploit children in many ways. There were, after all, no laws against child labor until 1841.[166] Similarly, there were no criminal sanctions against the physical abuse of children until almost the end of the century. And France was very much a patriarchal society. Women and children gained some new rights (such as divorce by mutual consent and lower ages for majority) during the Revolution, but Napoleon's Civil Code of 1804 restored firmly the *ancien régime*'s principle of almost unlimited paternal authority.[167] The father could do virtually as he pleased with his children, even to use them sexually for his own enjoyment.[168] The relative tolerance of the sexual abuse of children must be seen in this context. There was a recognition that the nonviolent sexual abuser of children was a morally reprehensible individual; this was implied by the efforts (though unsuccessful) of some of the *Cours d'assises* before 1832 to punish nonviolent child molesters for "moral violence," and the rather more successful attempts of the *Tribunaux correctionnels* to interpret Article 334 so that it might apply to the habitual seducers of children. But the courts were inhibited by the fact that the *Code pénal* was concerned with order, not morality. Even incest was not a crime. This was a heritage of the secular, laissez-faire legal notions of the French Revolution. Under the Napoleonic code, child sexual abuse was not a crime with a victim; it was a purely moral matter outside the scope of the law.

French law and the French state slowly began to concern itself with protecting children from abuse and exploitation on a number of levels toward the middle of the nineteenth century. This included new laws enacted against child molestation, in particular those of 1832 and 1863, and prosecutions for sex crimes against minors soared. Even after prosecutions began to decline in the 1880s, an accelerated campaign against the prostitution of minors got underway, culminating in the law of 1908 that completely banned the registration of children under the age of nineteen as prostitutes. The new attitude was also undoubtedly helped along by the fact that the French had come to recognize the existence and scope of child sexual abuse, even incest, well before the British, the Austrians, and the Americans had done so.

NOTES

1. The increased concern of Americans with the sexual abuse of children and adolescents has been reflected in recent years by a proliferation of books and articles (not to mention interviews on television talk shows) on the subject. Some of the better known works are: Louise Armstrong, *Kiss Daddy Goodnight: A Speak-Out on Incest* (New York, 1978); Florence Rush, *The Best Kept Secret: Sexual Abuse of Children* (New York, 1980); D. Kelly Weisberg, *Children of the Night: A Study of Adolescent Prostitution* (Lexington, Mass., 1985).

2. Donal E. J. MacNamara and Eduard Sagarin, *Sex, Crime and the Law* (New York, 1977), 65–66.

3. Lloyd deMause, "The Evolution of Childhood," in *The History of Childhood*, ed. Lloyd deMause (New York, 1974), 43.

4. Jacques Rossiaud, *Medieval Prostitution*, trans, Lydia G. Cochrane (New York, 1988), 32.

5. David Hunt, *Parents and Children in History: The Psychology of Family Life in Early Modern France* (New York, 1970), 162.

6. MacNamara and Sagarin, *Sex, Crime and the Law*, 65, 94.

7. Philippe Ariès, *Centuries of Childhood: A Social History of Family Life*, trans. Robert Baldick (New York, 1962).

8. Ministère de la Justice, *Compte général de l'administration de la justice criminelle*, 1825–1913 (Paris, 1827–1915), hereafter referred to as *Compte général*.

9. The *Compte général* does not include information on the specific ages of the victims of rape and indecent assault other than to state whether they were under the ages of eleven, thirteen (from 1863), or fifteen, or were fifteen and over. However, of the 632 cases of rape and indecent assault examined by the notable Paris forensic doctor Ambroise Tardieu by 1878, 525 were children under the age of fifteen, and only ninety-three were fifteen or older. Of the latter ninety-three, most (eighty-four) were fifteen to twenty years old, and only nine were over twenty. In fourteen other cases, the ages of the victims were not indicated. Ambroise Tardieu, *Étude médico-légale sur les attentats aux moeurs* (Paris, 1878), 23.

10. Benjamin F. Martin, *Crime and Criminal Justice Under the Third Republic: The Shame of Marianne* (Baton Rouge, La., 1990), 12.

11. Ibid., 37.

12. J. B. Duvergier, *Code pénal annoté* (Paris, 1833), 54.

13. There are no nationwide data available to indicate what proportion of persons accused of "the solicitation of minors to debauchery" were involved in the prostitution of minors in the nineteenth century. However, a statistical analysis of the 259 persons convicted of this crime by the Correctional Court of Marseille from 1825 to 1850 and from 1870 to 1885 shows that at least 221 (or 85.3 percent) were prosecuted because they in some way facilitated, or profited from, the prostitution of children or adolescents. James M. Donovan, "Justice and Sexuality in Victorian Marseille 1825–1885," *Journal of Social History* 21 (1987): 258n.

14. Duvergier, *Code pénal*, 54.

15. Judson T. Landis, "Experiences of 500 Children with Adult Sexual Deviation," *Psychiatric Quarterly, Supplement* 30 (1956): 93–94.

16. Ibid., 99.

17. Ibid., 100.

18. The official statistics in the *Compte général* did not mention the relationship between the perpetrators and the victims in sex crimes, or in any others. However, Paul Brouardel, a professor of forensic medicine at the Faculty of Medicine of the University of Paris, did do so in his analysis of the 232 cases of rape and indecent assault he had examined as a forensic doctor in the years before 1909. In nineteen cases the father of the victim was the perpetrator. In another four cases it was the stepfather, and in six instances it was an uncle. P. Brouardel, *Les attentats aux moeurs* (Paris, 1909), 8. Moreover, the writer André Gide, who served on a jury in Rouen in 1912, recalled that of the four cases of rape and indecent assault of minors tried by the panel when he sat on it, in two instances the accused was the father of the girl. André Gide, *Recollections of the Assize Court*, trans. Philip A. Wilkins (London, n.d.), 22–23, 38, 51–53, 62–63.

19. Tardieu, *Étude médico-légale*, 39.

20. Alexandre Lacassagne, "Attentats à la pudeur sur les petites filles," *Archives d'anthropologie criminelle et des sciences pénales* 1 (1886): 60.

21. Adolphe Toulmouche, "Des attentats à la pudeur et du viol," *Annales d'hygiène publique et du médecine légale* 6 (1856): 102–3.

22. Brouardel, *Les attentats aux moeurs*, 52. The *Compte général* did include figures on the numbers of reported rapes and indecent assaults that were left unprosecuted, but in its tables on the abandoned accusations (unlike in the tables on the prosecuted cases) it did not distinguish between these crimes against adults and the cases of child molestation.

23. Jill Harsin, *Policing Prostitution in Nineteenth Century Paris* (Princeton, N.J., 1985), xix–xx; Donovan, "Justice and Sexuality," 258n.

24. Alain Corbin, *Women for Hire: Prostitution and Sexuality in France After 1850,* trans. Alan Sheridan (Cambridge, Mass., 1990), 320.

25. [Gabriel Paul Othenin de Cleron] Le Vicomte d'Haussonville, *L'Enfance a Paris* (Paris, 1879), 246.

26. Dr. H. Mireur, *La prostitution à Marselle: histoire, administration, et police hygiène* (Paris, 1882), 218.

27. Eugene Prevost, *De la prostitution des enfants: Étude juridique et sociale (Loi du 11 avril 1908)* (Paris, 1909), 48–50; Tardieu, *Étude médico-légale,* 200, 204.

28. Martin, *Crime and Criminal Justice,* 35–37.

29. Ronald Pearsall, *The Worm in the Bud: The World of Victorian Sexuality* (London, 1969), 289–94.

30. Landis, "Experiences of 500 Children," 92–93.

31. France, *Assemblée Nationale: Senat. Commission relative à la protection de l'enfance. Rapport fait au nom de la Commission chargée d'examiner* (Theophile Roussel, Secretaire et Rapporteur de la Commission), hereafter referred to as *Commission relative à la protection de l'enfance* (Paris, 1882), 1: 35.

32. According to A.-J.-B. Parent-Duchâtelet, for instance, when the registration of prostitutes began in Paris in 1796, a great number of the inscribed prostitutes were girls of ten, twelve, fourteen, fifteen, and sixteen years old. Their extreme youth was no obstacle to their registration, and teenage prostitutes abounded in Paris at this time. *De la prostitution dans la ville de Paris, considerée sous la rapport de l'hygiène publique, de la morale et de l'administration* (Bruxelles, 1836), 223.

33. Duvergier, *Code pénal,* 464n.

34. Edouard Dalloz, et al., *Code pénal annoté et explique d'apres la jurisprudence et la doctrine* (Paris, 1881), 507.

35. Ibid.; E. Garçon, *Code pénal annoté* (Paris, 1901–1911), 1: 844.

36. Garçon, *Code pénal,* 1: 981.

37. In the entire period 1825–1913, only 1,103 persons were tried for the *enlevement et détournement des mineurs* (the abduction and seduction of minors). An average of twelve persons were tried for this offense each year. The actual yearly figure oscillated between a maximum of twenty-seven (in 1825 and 1850) and a minimum of three (in 1902, 1904 and 1906). *Compte général,* 1825–1860, Table I, p. 2; 1861–1909, Table I, p. 4; 1910–1913, Table I, p. 6.

38. Armand Dalloz, *Dictionnaire général et raisonné de legislation, de doctrine et de jurisprudence en matière civile, commerciale, criminelle, administrative et de droit public. Partie supplementaire. Periode de 1834 à 1842* (Paris, December 1841), 5: 90–91.

39. Ibid., 5: 90.

40. Ibid., 5: 91.

41. Ibid., 5: 90.

42. Ibid., 5: 91.

43. In 1830, for instance, the *Cour de cassation* upheld the conviction of a man prosecuted for violating Article 334 because he had "habitually, for a fairly long period of time, solicited and favored the corruption of a fourteen year old girl, who he had received in his home.": Armand Dalloz, *Dictionnaire général et raisonné de legislation, de doctrine et de jurisprudence en matière civile, commerciale, criminelle, administrative et de droit public* [nouvelle edition] [Paris, 1844], 1: 234. At least four pederasts were prosecuted under Article 334 in Marseille 1825 to 1832. Donovan, "Justice and Sexuality," 232.

44. Edouard Dalloz, et al., *Code pénal*, 519–20.

45. Garçon, *Code pénal*, 1, 875.

46. Duvergier, *Code pénal*, 54n.

47. Edouard Dalloz, et al., *Code pénal*, 520.

48. Ibid., 523.

49. Ibid., 520.

50. Ibid., 521; Garçon, *Code pénal*, 1: 870–74.

51. Corbin, *Women for Hire*, 30–33.

52. C. J. Lecour, *La prostitution à Paris et à Londres 1789–1870* (Paris, 1870), 165.

53. Harsin, *Policing Prostitution*, 26.

54. Lecour, *La prostitution*, 165.

55. Parent-Duchâtelet, *De la prostitution*, 225.

56. Ibid., 60.

57. A. Corbes, "La Cour d'assises des Côtes-du-Nord de 1811 à 1832," *Annales de Bretagne* 56 (1959): 326.

58. Ibid., 325; Garçon, *Code pénal*, 1: 875.

59. Edouard Dalloz, et al., *Code pénal*, 502; Garçon, *Code pénal*, 1: 852.

60. Duvergier, *Code pénal*, 53.

61. Ibid.

62. R. Garraud and P. Bernard, "Des attentats à la pudeur et des viols sur les enfants (legislation-statistique)," *Archives d'anthropologie criminelle et des sciences pénales* 1 (1886): 402.

63. L. Thoinot, *Medicolegal Aspects of Moral Offenses*, trans. Arthur W. Weysse (Philadelphia, 1920), 7.

64. Garraud and Bernard, "Des attentats à la pudeur," 399–400; Tardieu, *Étude médico-légale*, 17.

65. Thoinot, *Medicolegal Aspects*, 7; Garçon, *Code pénal*, 1, 849, 852.

66. Duvergier, *Code pénal*, 53.

67. Dr. Paul Bernard, *Des attentats à la pudeur sur les petites filles* (Paris, 1886), 78–79; Brouardel, *Les attentats aux moeurs*, 129; Tardieu, *Étude médico-légale*, 36; Toulmouche, "Des attentats à la pudeur et du viol," 100.

68. Lacassagne, "Attentats à la pudeur," 63–64.

69. Gide, *Recollections*, 51–53.

70. Ibid., 62–63.

71. Bernard, *Des attentats à la pudeur*, 26.

72. Edward Shorter, "L'age des premières réglés en France, 1750–1950," *Annales: Économies, Sociétés, Civilisations* 36 (1981): 497.

73. *Compte général*, 1880, p. XI.

74. Garçon, *Code pénal*, 1: 852.

75. *Compte général*, 1880, p. XI; Garraud and Bernard, "Des attentats à la pudeur," 403.

76. Howard C. Payne, *The Police State of Louis Napoleon Bonaparte 1851–1860* (Seattle, 1966), 23.

77. James M. Donovan, "Justice Unblind: The Juries and the Criminal Classes in France, 1825–1914," *Journal of Social History* 15 (1981): 90–100.

78. Ibid., 92, 94.

79. Edward Shorter, *The Making of the Modern Family* (New York, 1975), 191–92; Peter N. Stearns, *European Society in Upheaval: Social History Since 1750* (New York, 1975), 140.

80. A. Esmein, *A History of Continental Criminal Procedure, with Special Reference to France*, trans. John Simpson (New York, 1968), 532–33.

81. *Compte général*, 1860, XXXVIII–XXXIX.

82. James W. Garner, "Criminal Procedure in France," *Yale Law Journal* 25 (1916): 280.

83. Dominique Vallaud, "Le crime d'infanticide et l'indulgence des cours d'assises en France au XIX siècle," *Social Science Information* 21 (1982): 492n.

84. Gabriel Tarde, *Penal Philosophy*, trans. Rapelje Howell (Boston, 1912), 460–61; Garner, "Criminal Procedure in France," 274.

85. Garçon, *Code pénal*, 1: 868–70.

86. Frederic R. Coudert, "French Criminal Procedure," *Yale Law Journal* 19 (1910): 331, 337.

87. Corbin, *Women for Hire*, 320–21; Vern L. Bullough, *The History of Prostitution* (New Hyde Park, N.Y., 1964), 167.

88. Lecour, *La prostitution à Paris et à Londres*, 125.

89. Ibid.

90. Ibid., 165.

91. *Commission relative à la protection de l'enfance*, II: CXXXIX–CXL.

92. Mireur, *La prostitution à Marseille*, 135.

93. Ibid., 132.

94. *Commission relative à la protection de l'enfance*, II: 88.

95. Ibid., II: CXXXIX.

96. Jeffrey Moussaieff Masson, *The Assault on Truth: Freud's Suppression of the Seduction Theory* (New York, 1984), 23.

97. Ibid., 25.

98. Besides Tardieu's book, other works devoted wholly or in part to child sexual abuse and underage prostitution published in France during the late nineteenth and early twentieth centuries that have already been cited include Bernard (1886), Garraud and Bernard (1886), Lacassagne (1886), Brouardel (1909), Prevost (1909), and Thoinot (1920). See also A. Toulmouche, "Des attentats à la pudeur: des tentatives de viol sur des enfants ou des filles a peines nubiles et sur des adultes, et des grossesses simulées ou réelles suivies ou non d'infanticides," *Annales d'hygiène publique et de médecine légale* 22 (1864): 333–83; Marc Reveille, *La pros-*

titution des mineures selon la loi pénale (Paris, 1896); Felix Lohse, *La prostitution des mineures en France avant et après la loi du 11 avril 1908* (Paris, 1913).

99. Brouardel, *Les attentats aux moeurs,* 8; Tardieu, *Étude médico-légale,* 62.
100. Pearsall, *The Worm in the Bud,* 290–91.
101. Bullough, *The History of Prostitution,* 175.
102. Deborah Gorham, "The 'Maiden Tribute of Modern Babylon' Re-Examined: Child Prostitution and the Idea of Childhood in Late-Victorian England," *Victorian Studies* 53 (1978): 354–59.
103. Ibid., 362.
104. Masson, *The Assault on Truth,* xxii–xxiii, 3, 14–15, 38, 40, 53.
105. Ibid., 136, 191. The text of Freud's "The Aetiology of Hysteria" is on pp. 251–82 of the Appendix to Masson's book.
106. Ibid., 11–12, 110, 112–14, 144, 188–90.
107. Larry Wolff, *Postcards from the End of the World: Child Abuse in Freud's Vienna* (New York, 1988), 60–61.
108. U.S. Department of Health, Education, and Welfare, National Center on Child Abuse and Neglect, *Child Sexual Abuse: Incest, Assault, and Sexual Exploitation* (Washington, D.C., 1978), i, 3; Weisberg, *Children of the Night,* 1.
109. It is difficult, however, to know to what extent this has been true in the United States in recent years, for data on the number of child molestation cases on the national level are apparently not available. The FBI, in its annual *Uniform Crime Reports,* lists the numbers of arrests for rape, sex offenses and prostitution, but does not distinguish between adult and minor victims. Federal Bureau of Investigation, *Uniform Crime Reports for the United States,* 1990 (Washington, D.C., 1991), 175–76.
110. Martin, *Crime and Criminal Justice,* 37.
111. Corbin, *Women for Hire,* 320.
112. Payne, *The Police State,* 23–24; Martin, *Crime and Criminal Justice,* 146.
113. Donovan, "Justice and Sexuality," 246; James M. Donovan, "Abortion, the Law, and the Juries in France, 1825–1913," *Criminal Justice History: An International Annual* 9 (1988): 159.
114. Priscilla Robertson, "Home As a Nest: Middle Class Childhood in Nineteenth-Century Europe," in deMause, ed., *The History of Childhood,* 426–28.
115. Ibid., 426.
116. Laws were passed in France in 1841 and 1874 limiting the hours children could work and regulating the circumstances under which they could be employed. Colin Heywood, *Childhood in Nineteenth-Century France: Work, Health and Education Among the 'Classes Populaires'* (Cambridge, 1988), 229, 264–65. In England, the movement to protect child workers began with the first Factory Act in 1802, which was applied to orphan apprentices who were wards of the state. Robertson, "Home As a Nest," 427.
117. Jacques Donzelot, *The Policing of Families,* trans. Robert Hurley (New York, 1979), 30.
118. Rachel Ginnis Fuchs, "Crimes Against Children in Nineteenth Century France," *Law and Human Behavior* 6 (1982): 239–40.
119. Ibid., 253–54.
120. Ibid., 254–56.
121. Ibid., 239.

122. Brouardel, *Les attentats aux moeurs,* 7.

123. André Toulemon, *La question du jury* (Paris, 1930), 34.

124. Jean Cruppi, *La Cour d'assises* (Paris, 1898), 3–4.

125. The total number of persons prosecuted for felonies in France declined from 7,071 in 1851 to 4,184 in 1885, and to 3,279 in 1900: André Davidovitch, "Criminialité et répression in France depuis un siècle (1851–1852)," *Revue française de sociologie* 2 (1961): 47.

126. Corbin, *Women for Hire,* 275–98.

127. Harsin, *Policing Prostitution,* 348.

128. According to the calculations of statistician Maurice Yvernes, from 1881 to 1900 the acquittal rate for all persons tried by the *Cours d'assises* varied from a low of twenty-four per 100 in the years 1881–1885 to a high of twenty-seven per 100 in 1896–1900. However, the acquittal rate in the *Tribunaux correctionnels* varied from only about seven per 100 accusations to about eight per 100 throughout the period. Maurice Yvernes, "La justice en France de 1881 à 1900," *Journal de la Société de Statistique de Paris* 44 (1903): 303, 312.

129. Garçon, *Code pénal,* 1: 890.

130. Mireur, *La prostitution à Marseille,* 158.

131. Elisabeth Anne Weston, *Prostitution in Paris in the Later Nineteenth Century: A Study of Political and Social Ideology* (Ph.D. Dissertation, State University of New York at Buffalo, 1979), 61.

132. *Commission relative à la protection de l'enfance,* II: CXXXVI–CXXXVII.

133. Weston, *Prostitution in Paris,* 159–61, 177.

134. Rachel Ginnis Fuchs, *Abandoned Children: Foundlings and Child Welfare in Nineteenth Century France* (New York, 1984), 47–48, 57, 280–81.

135. George D. Sussman, "The End of the Wet-Nursing Business in France, 1874–1914," in *Family and Sexuality in French History,* ed. Robert Wheaton and Tamara K. Hareven (Philadelphia, 1980), 230–31.

136. Fuchs, "Crimes Against Children," 254.

137. Fuchs, *Abandoned Children,* 58.

138. Fuchs, "Crimes Against Children," 254–55.

139. Prevost, *De la prostitution des enfants,* 15.

140. Ibid., 15–16.

141. Weston, *Prostitution in Paris,* 72.

142. Harsin, *Policing Prostitution,* 355.

143. Corbin, *Women for Hire,* 214–34.

144. Weston, *Prostitution in Paris,* 62.

145. Ibid., 188.

146. Ibid., 98.

147. Ibid., 126; Harsin, *Policing Prostitution,* 335.

148. Harsin, *Policing Prostitution,* 334–36, 347.

149. Ibid., 355; Weston, *Prostitution in Paris,* 140–42, 144, 153–54, 162.

150. Corbin, *Women for Hire,* 297.

151. Weston, *Prostitution in Paris,* 159.

152. Ibid.

153. Ibid.; Corbin, *Women for Hire,* 258.

154. Weston, *Prostitution in Paris,* 159.

155. Ibid., 162.

156. Corbin, *Women for Hire*, 291.

157. Ibid., 278–79, 294–95.

158. Ibid., 294–95; Garçon, *Code pénal*, 1: 866–70.

159. Weston, *Prostitution in Paris*, 160.

160. Ibid., 161.

161. Ibid., 177.

162. Prevost, *De la prostitution des enfants*, 108, 136.

163. Ibid., 46.

164. Ibid., 47–48.

165. Ibid., 43.

166. Heywood, *Childhood in Nineteenth-Century France*, 229.

167. Robert A. Nye, *Masculinity and Male Codes of Honor in Modern France* (New York, 1993), 55–56.

168. Napoleon's Civil Code stated that the father was the authority in the family, and he was even allowed to have his minor children jailed without government approval. Robert B. Holtman, *The Napoleonic Revolution* (Philadelphia, 1967), 90.

The Constabulary and the Criminal Justice System in Nineteenth-Century Ireland

Ian Bridgeman
Luton University

Recently, legal historian John F. McEldowney noted that "the research effort on policing in Ireland to date has tended to obscure the criminal trial and prosecution system while concentrating exclusively on the organization of the police, the personnel, and the problems of agrarian crime."[1] McEldowney's essay addresses "the central issue of police involvement with the criminal law," raising a series of questions related to the role of the Irish police in the nineteenth-century system of Irish criminal prosecution. He asks, "How important was the criminal law in the work of the police?" Further, since this central question raises others related to police procedures in reporting offenses, gathering evidence, and prosecuting offenders, McEldowney identifies three key areas requiring investigation: Were all offenders prosecuted? Were alternative sanctions available? How were cases prepared for trial and what was the police role?[2] This chapter will address these questions, and in essence build upon the work of McEldowney. In addition, the magnitude of the special political operations of the police will be considered in order to place in perspective this key intelligence role with regard to the "ordinary" investigation of "ordinary" crime. Since the roots of the constabulary were in the prevention and detection of political and agrarian offenses, if it can be shown that in practical terms the amount of resources allocated to the political aspect of police work in relation to the overall effort made within the ordinary criminal justice system were minimal, then the contention that the constabulary was much more than simply a "political police" is advanced.

PUBLIC PROSECUTIONS IN IRELAND

At the end of British rule in Ireland, the Irish system of criminal justice was very different from that of England and Wales. The Irish system owes its origins to English common law and a prosecution system based firmly upon the principle of private prosecution. By the end of the eighteenth century, however, the system of private prosecution began to break down in Ireland. The prime cause of the breakdown was the inability of the state to find prosecutors, witnesses, and jurors who would convict in cases of agrarian crime.[3] In the face of intimidation, and the lack of consensus over the enforcement of the law when the law came into conflict with agrarian mores, the system of private prosecution collapsed. This collapse paralyzed the courts, which were the main weapon of the state in dealing with agrarian disturbances. To resolve the problem following the Act of Union, there evolved a system of state prosecution. But in order to be successful in prosecution, the state needed to protect witnesses and jurors from intimidation. The task of protecting witnesses fell to the police. As a result, the growth of public prosecutions increased the requirement for a reliable police, and the existence of a reliable police improved the efficiency of public prosecutions. Major George Warburton gave evidence to a select committee[4] that witnesses in agrarian prosecutions were either lodged with the police or kept in jail, and that at the court crown witnesses were brought either in the custody of the police or the jailer. He added that those offended against would frequently not wish to prosecute through fear of reprisal and would "not come forward" as witnesses. Even when witnesses were bound by a recognizance to give evidence in court, they were often prepared to forfeit their recognizance by not giving evidence, and since they could not pay the money fine, they chose to "pay in their persons" by being sent to jail.[5]

At the heart of the system were solicitors employed by the state who gathered evidence from witnesses and prepared a brief for counsel acting on behalf of the crown. The date of the appointment of crown solicitors for each of the six Irish assize circuits is uncertain, but the earliest records are dated 1801.[6] From about 1830, the attorney general "began to direct a solicitor in each county, who was called a Sessional Crown Solicitor, to conduct prosecutions at Quarter Sessions,"[7] and from 1842 the crown solicitors were also appointed on a county basis. The two offices were amalgamated at the end of the nineteenth century.[8] Thus, prosecutions for virtually all offenses brought to trial at assize and quarter sessions were undertaken by the state, and had been processed by a comprehensive prosecution system.

The extent of the involvement of the state solicitors in the gathering of evidence is unclear. They certainly prepared the indictment, gathered all the necessary papers to form a brief, and instructed a barrister to conduct the prosecution for the crown.[9] However, it would appear that certain individual state solicitors in preparing documents of evidence took an active and much more wide-ranging role. Leonard Dobbin considered that it was necessary for the state solicitor to be resident in the county, where he could facilitate it [the system of prosecutions] greatly by being resident there previously to the Assize, examining the witnesses, when it became necessary to send for witnesses, and investigating the case previously and coolly before . . . the Assize.[10]

He also considered that local knowledge would be an advantage to the state solicitor, for

if challenges for jurors became necessary, he would be perfectly acquainted with the character of the jurors of his county, and would be able to give important advice to the Crown lawyers in challenging.[11]

Equally important was the resident state solicitor's ability to instruct crown counsel on the character of witnesses. The implication of Dobbin's evidence was that part of the duties of local crown solicitors was to establish effective lines of communication with local police and resident and local magistrates, in order to obtain prior knowledge of the likely prejudices and intentions of witnesses, jurors, defendants, and all who were brought before court. Although Dobbin felt that the crown solicitor could give active assistance to magistrates in "cases of great importance," as a general rule "legal men" should not conduct investigations in the "first instance," because

the truth comes better out in a preliminary inquiry before magistrates or country gentlemen, in which they determine merely whether the man is to be put on his trial or sent into confinement, or whether the question is to be investigated before a jury.[12]

But when a complex case occurred, he considered "the assistance of professional persons may be necessary."

Such a difficult case occurred in 1838 when the chief constable of County Meath arrested a man for burglary and took him before a local magistrate for examination. In the course of the investigation, the accused gave information concerning the local Catholic Ribbon Society, which led to the arrest of a number of men. The decision to prosecute the Ribbon men was not made at the local level. Instead, the evidence was forwarded to the constabulary inspector general at Dublin castle, who passed the file to the attorney general's office. The decision to prosecute was made after examination of the available evidence,[13] and instructions were sent to the Meath crown solicitor to prepare a prosecution for the next assize at Drogheda. Meanwhile, the accused, who had been held in Drogheda jail, were released on bail to appear at the next assize. The men, however, failed to appear, and the crown was unable to call in their recognizance because of a "blunder" by either the Meath head police office or crown solicitor in not sending the bail bonds to the clerk of the crown. Eventually the chief constable, Hatton, arrested one of the men in the street and took him directly to the crown solicitor's office.[14]

The motive behind Hatton's action is uncertain. Whether he intended to question the man further, or to arrange for his committal to jail by magistrates, or more probably a combination of the two, is not made clear by the evidence given to the select committee. But what is certain is that Hatton's actions in taking a prisoner to the crown solicitor, for whatever reason, did not surprise the committee, and therefore by implication it would seem that in some cases crown solicitors were active rather than reactive in the conduct of criminal investigations.

This close investigative cooperation between crown solicitors and the police seems to have been a permanent feature of criminal investigation and prosecution. For example, during investigation of the Maamtrasna murders in 1882, John Charles Gardiner, the resident magistrate, examined prisoners and witnesses and worked closely with the crown solicitor, George Bolton.[15] This is not to suggest that crown solicitors undertook "police work" as a routine, but in sensitive and difficult cases they were able to offer direct legal advice to those investigating the crime and maintained close links with all the agents of state prosecutions.

The administrative staff attached to the criminal courts of limited jurisdiction, the assize, quarter, and petty sessions, were the clerks of the crown, clerks of the peace, and petty sessions clerks.[16] The clerk of the crown was responsible for the routine functioning of the assize court and kept the court's records.[17] He was also responsible, with the county treasurer, for the presentments made to the grand jury at assize in order to agree to a rate and raise revenue for local services. The clerk's role was to keep the fiscal records and provide the treasurer with a list of the money to be raised.[18] The assize judges had the power to approve the grand jury's presentments, and assent seems to have been a formality.[19] Following the inquiry of the select committee on the county assessments in 1836, much of the initial financial work was carried out by the grand jury at an annual presentment session. The jurors were selected by the county high sheriff, who was in turn appointed annually by the government. Thus, in theory, the government could control local authority through appointment to the grand jury. But in practice, the government exercised little local control over the grand juries except to supervise their more important functions.[20]

This curious system of local government lasted until 1898, when the grand jury ceased to exist as an administrative body[21] and local administration passed into the hands of elected councils.[22] The clerk of the crown was a government appointment and usually a local practicing solicitor. The workload was considerable, and the clerk often employed a deputy and a small staff.[23] In criminal cases, the framing of the indictment was done by the state solicitor, and forwarded together with copies of statements to the crown clerk. The clerk then copied the indictment into the crown book, issued any summons, held the recognizance bonds, and arranged for the prisoner to be brought to trial. It was also possible for a complainant to bypass the state solicitor and have the crown clerk draw up an indictment for a fee.[24] The duties of the clerk of the peace for quarter sessions were similar to those of the crown clerk except for the fiscal administration. The clerk of the peace, however, was appointed by the custos rotulorum—the magistrates—of the county. It was not uncommon for both appointments to be held by the same man,[25] and because of the similarity between the two offices it was often suggested that they should be amalgamated. In 1877 legislation was enacted that enabled the amalgamation to be accomplished.[26] From 1827, magistrates meeting in petty sessions could appoint a clerk for the district who would be paid from the fees received. By 1858 the clerk was a salaried official with precise duties and qualifications. By the middle of the nineteenth century there were 600 petty session districts in Ireland.[27]

THE MAGISTRACY

An essential element of any judicial system are the magistrates who preside in petty sessions and sit in judgment on the bulk of offenses brought before the courts. In Ireland, the small size of the county gentry meant that the number of men available for duty was limited. Further, it was considered by the government that the limited choice had led to a number of unsuitable men being appointed.[28] It has been shown that one of the main concerns of government in attempting to suppress disorder was to improve the efficiency of the country magistrates. This policy was pursued by providing the county magistrates with the assistance of professional police and stipendiary magistrates, and by undertaking a series of reforms and purges of the magistracy. This simple policy was complicated by the issue of who was to control the police and stipendiary magistrates. Naturally, the amateur, unpaid county magistrates were unwilling to give up the powers they enjoyed—and in particular the control of local police—and place themselves under the direction of a stipendiary magistrate. But agrarian disorder dictated the response of government, and county magistrates found themselves increasingly drawn into a centralized structure that determined the policy they were to implement. The reform of the magistracy was not achieved easily or quickly, but came about over an extended period as an integral part of the police reform process.

Thus, the first major revisions of the magistracy in the nineteenth century were part of the police reforms that brought about the formation of the county constabulary in 1822. A number of concessions that gave the county magistrates considerable influence over the operation of the police were made with regard to three factors. First, the government was determined not to repeat the mistake of making the constabulary as unpopular as the Peace Preservation Force had been with the rate payers. Second, the Peace Preservation Act would not be repealed by the new legislation, therefore leaving the government in control of a centrally directed police should circumstances require. Third, the long-awaited reform of the magistracy was contemplated. Broeker suggested that

no one in government circles questioned the worth of the venerable institution of the magistracy; rather the criticism was directed at its unworthy members. If the institution could be purged of the timid, the inefficient, and the corrupt there was no reason that the Constabulary should not be placed in the hands of a "reformed" magistracy.[29]

During the autumn of 1822, all existing commissions were cancelled and a revised list issued. Old, unfit men, magistrates of questionable loyalty, activity, or ethics, absentee gentlemen, army officers, constables made magistrates during the 1820–1821 disturbances, and dead men were to be removed from the roll. Broeker was uncertain how far-reaching the reform was, and how many men were removed from the position of magistrate. He wrote that out of fifty Meath magistrates only four were removed.[30] The evidence of Richard Willocks, however, suggests that the reform was more extensive. In Cork, eighty out of 300 recorded magistrates were excluded, being mainly "a large portion of the clergy, all the military, and such gentlemen as are connected with the revenue." Limerick lost thirty-four magistrates and Tipperary "two dozen."[31] The revision had substantial effects, as Wellesley wrote to Peel: "the mere knowledge of . . . revision had produced salutary consequences by increasing the diligence, accuracy and careful conduct of the magistrates."[32]

Allied to the revision of the magistracy was strong government pressure on magistrates to conduct their business at "petty sessions" with two or more magistrates sitting in public, thus eliminating the possibility of arbitrary action by a single magistrate. From 1822, the holding of country petty sessions became more common, and in 1827 the Petty Sessions Act, which provided for a clerk, fixed fees, records, and proscribed times, "formalised a growing practice."[33]

The power the government had to impose a stipendiary magistrate on a locality without first consulting local magistrates was an area of considerable contention. This power was not necessarily used, but on this issue the threat of government was plain. If local magistrates failed to do their duty as the administration perceived it, then a paid government magistrate would do it for them.

Prior to 1836, the relationship between the resident stipendiary magistrate and the local magistracy was sufficiently ill-defined in practical terms to avoid the worst of the friction in all but a few instances. Despite available legislation to the contrary, the government was always keen to stress the police function of the stipendiary and so shift the emphasis toward aid for the local magistracy rather than outright replacement. It appeared that under the provisions of the 1836 Constabulary Act, the resident magistrates were evidently intended to be subject to the jurisdiction of the inspector general of the constabulary. This measure was intended to reassure the magistracy by emphasizing the police function of stipendiaries in aid of the local magistrates. However, no sooner was the bill safely through Parliament, than the Irish administration began to exercise its authority over the "combined constabularies" and removed the resident magistrates from the control of the inspector general and placed them directly under the responsibility of the under-secretary.[34] The move was strongly opposed by the first inspector general, Shaw-Kennedy, who saw government interference as an encroachment on his independent judgment in matters of appointment and promotion. Senior constabulary officers saw the resident magistracy as a natural avenue of advancement, and any alterations in recruitment would work to their disadvantage. It was also judged that the government would make the appointments on "political considerations" without due regard to the efficiency of the system. The row rumbled on for some months before Shaw-Kennedy resigned in mid-1836.[35] Thus, effective day-to-day management of the resident magistrates was firmly in the hands of the under-secretary, and increasingly directed at rectifying the perceived inactivity of the local magistrates.[36] Over the next decades, resident magistrates began to assume an increasingly prominent position in the policing of the countryside, and in the formation and operation of petty sessions.

Naturally, jealousy arose as resident magistrates began to extend their function into "civil" areas that had once been performed by local magistrates free of charge.

It is only natural that the local Justices should feel a certain degree of jealousy of the paid Magistrates, and their more exclusive connections with the Constabulary. Formerly the Constabulary were under the local justices as a County Force, and they no doubt feel themselves superseded.[37]

Lord Carlisle, with a considerable degree of understatement, noted that many of the complaints emanating from the "old Ascendancy party (in parliament) may not be altogether free from some political bias."[38] The under-secretary, Thomas Larcom,[39] supported Carlisle's view and attributed much of the general feelings against the stipendiaries to political maneuvering. "I am bound to say that I do not think the feeling is by any means general, or that it prevails to any serious or injurious extent."[40] Both Carlisle and Larcom were probably correct to attribute the complaints to a small political base, but rather misjudged the situation when they considered the opinion not to be representative of the condition of the magistracy and indicative of the slide into obscurity of the Ascendancy.

The great failing of the Irish magistracy was that at certain times when personal risk was high the magistrate failed in his duty, while during less risky times he was happy to accept the title of justice of the peace. In human terms, the failings of the magistrates were quite understandable: Sanctions used against zealous magistrates were extreme. In places where hostility existed between the stipendiary and local magistrates, Larcom felt that it might be due to the feeling of being superseded by a paid man. But often the situation was entirely the fault of the gentry.

I think the feeling as far as it exists, is to be traced to the circumstances that the local magistrates devolve the unpleasant part of their duty on the Stipendiary Magistrate and thereby lose much of their own influence.[41]

In addition, in the period of calm that followed the famine, more magistrates were willing to act, but because there was less for them to do in a period of magisterial surfeit, conflicts of interest quickly arose.

The attitude of the administration was one of essentially avoiding further antagonism while continuing a policy of extending its influence into local justice and government. Larcom wrote:

Before paid magistrates were established, we had a dominant class from which the magistrates were chosen, but the relation between them and the people was that of master and serf—not protector and dependent. . . . They [the gentry] are not what magistrates are in England and what they once were. But the former state of things has passed away, and the present condition of the magistracy and the Constabulary is an incident of the change.[42]

Larcom recognized that the relationship between landowner and tenant, and the moral rights and obligations that each owed the other, had failed to establish themselves in Ireland. The "planted" gentry had generated nothing but hostility and suspicion. "So long as the state of society is such that the gentry mistrust the people, and the people mistrust the gentry, the necessity for a stipendiary magistrate will continue."[43]

Chief Secretary Robert Peel, however, recognized that the resident magistrates and the constabulary had roused strong feelings against them, and he was prepared to give serious consideration as to "whether the dissatisfaction which appears so generally to prevail are justified in fact, and if so what steps should be taken with the view to remedy existing defects."[44]

Even though he acknowledged the discontent of the magistracy and was generally sympathetic, he was adamant that radical change would not occur, and the office of stipendiary magistrate would remain as an arm of government. Peel continued:

There are those who . . . recommend total abolition . . . and think its duties might . . . be advantageously transferred to the experienced magistrate, county gentlemen, clergy . . . as in England. I am not in favour of so radical a change—neither do I imagine it would be judicious under the present circumstances of the country.[45]

In order to calm local feelings, Peel brought about some changes in an attempt to improve the relationship between the stipendiaries and the magistracy, but most of his efforts were cosmetic and made in defense of the system. In the last analysis, Peel's modest reforms strengthened the position of the resident magistrate in Ireland by making the office more efficient and the men more accountable.

Peel considered that much of the bad feeling against the resident magistrates was caused by the constabulary procedures for reporting crime, which insisted that a constable report directly to the resident magistrate of the district.

No doubt the Constabulary almost entirely ignore the County Justices, as may be particularly instanced in the case of any serious outrage . . . when the constable in charge is . . . to communicate with the nearest stipendiary magistrate . . . who may be resident some 10 miles distant and not with the local justice.[46]

The requirement for good intelligence without delay, or the gross embellishments that had so plagued the reporting of the magistracy in the past, had necessitated this procedure. But the removal of the justices from early involvement in an important aspect of local police work had naturally eroded local prestige and effectiveness.

By design, the phraseology of the Constabulary Code tended to reinforce the exclusion of the local magistrate. Regulation 207 stated:

It is further enjoined that on the occurrence of any serious outrage, especially where life has been taken or attempted, the officer, head or other constable in charge nearest to the scene will make the point of sending, without a moments loss of time, an intimation thereof to the nearest Resident Magistrate.

The only ambiguity within the regulation lay in the interpretation of "a serious outrage." To avoid criticism, every "outrage" would be deemed "serious" and be reported to the stipendiary. Only after making the report to the stipendiary would a report be made to the local justices, and the necessary procedure was outlined by regulations 77 and 206 of the Code.

Regulation 77. He [the constable or officer in charge] is to report to the nearest magistrate whether local or stipendiary, every outrage or other matter seriously affecting the peace of the district, acting in such a case as in enjoined in section 206 of the present regulation.

Regulation 206. With this view it is strictly directed that every outrage, or apprehended outrage, should be reported with the least possible delay by the officer or constable of a station, if within a reasonable distance, that the officer or Head Constable attending Petty Sessions shall present, for the information of the bench a summary of all outrages or other remarkable occurrences.[47]

In order to follow regulation 77 and not fall foul of regulation 207, every outrage would be considered serious and reported to the resident magistrate. Having done so, the responsibility of informing the local magistrates was passed to the district head constable or inspector and, according to regulation 206, this might be done at the next petty sessions. If the relations between police, stipendiary, and county justices were strained in any one area, by the application and working of these regulations the local magistracy might be totally excluded from the investigation of crime. Under these circumstances, the knowledge of the commission of an outrage might only reach a local magistrate by way of gossip, with the corresponding loss of dignity and importance. Thus, in the formulation of the regulations of the Constabulary Code to achieve rapid and accurate intelligence of conditions in the countryside, the potential to exclude county justices from the investigative process was an integral part of the framework. The extent of the exclusion was probably more accidental than intended, although the thrust of the regulations was intended to distance the county magistrates from direct influence over the police and limit their involvement to that of advisors rather than controllers. In any event, the exclusion of the magistrates led to a perceived loss of dignity and status in the districts and was translated into a general hostility toward the stipendiaries.

The government felt inclined to take some action as criticism mounted, and attempted to improve relations between the stipendiaries and the county justices. Peel was convinced that the procedures excluded the local magistrates to too great an extent, and that their earlier involvement would not only deflect criticism away from government but also improve the detection rate. He felt that the local magistrate "would 9 times out of 10 do his duty" just as efficiently as the stipendiary, and by his local knowledge and experience be able "to facilitate a more rapid detection of offenders than the official returns at present testify."[48] Peel's sympathies with the local magistrate were evident, and he was also conscious of the criticism of the constabulary made at assizes over the poor detection rates. He attributed the poor performance of the police in areas of serious crime to the lack of informed local direction by the stipendiaries, and considered that this could be improved by closer involvement of the magistracy. "The stipendiaries of the county . . . do not respect . . . the obligations towards the justices in matters affecting the public peace."[49] In other words, Peel felt that the resident magistrates were failing to provide one the main elements of their duties—local leadership. In Peel's view, the ideal stipendiary would act as the civil fulcrum of his district; he would actively involve and enlist the aid of the county justices in providing intelligence and active service, and so provide the stimulus that the government felt the magistracy needed. In areas where Peel saw the resident magistrates fulfilling their role and actively involving the county justices in the policing process, criticism was deflected away from the government, and the improved flow of information improved detection rates and silenced the assize judges.

Peel recommended a thorough revision of the list of resident magistrates and the discharge of at least twenty he found to be inadequate and incapable. "Its abolition . . . is out of the question and our only course is to keep it as efficient as possible."[50] Out of the seventy-two resident magistrates in 1862, thirty-eight were over the age of fifty, and nineteen over the age of sixty. The backgrounds of the stipendiaries was also surprising: Thirty had been county justices, twenty-one had military backgrounds, twelve had served in the constabulary, and only four were barristers with any legal training. Considering the odium that the administration sometimes held the magistracy, the 42 percent of ex-county magistrates was high. It appears that government had been either content to recruit the best of the magistracy or had used the post of resident magistrate as a political reward. Since the system of stipendiaries was not a complete success, it does suggest that the government did not simply recruit the best available county justices, and instead caused most of its own problems by jobbing (giving positions for political rewards). In any event, why pay a man when he is doing good voluntary service? If jobbing were at the heart of the problem, it does explain the lack of activity on the part of some of the stipendiaries that caused so much of the discontent with the unpaid county justices, and also would introduce an element of individual and personal jealousy that would exacerbate local bad feelings.[51] Four of the previous occupations of the resident magistrates do suggest that patronage and reward for meritorious service was the reason for appointment and that great activity was unlikely to be entertained.[52]

The level of local leadership required to police a crisis necessitated the appointment of active, committed, and determined men. The government had diluted the resident magistrates by allowing some of the posts to become tied to political rewards. Ten years before Peel's recommendations, Sir Duncan McGregor,[53] in order to restore the commitment of the stipendiaries, had urged the government that the appointment of resident magistrates should be made from the ranks of the constabulary and that it should remain under the control of the inspector general. The stipendiaries would then be subject to constabulary discipline, and more "cordial cooperation between the two bodies secured, and a greater unity given to all police proceedings." McGregor continued:

The advancement of officers to the important situation of stipendiary magistrate
was not to be by seniority alone (but by) other considerations, in order that the
most eligible County Inspector should be detached for the vacant office . . . however
low his name might stand in the Constabulary List.

McGregor's willingness to risk the discontent of his officers by disregarding the revered constabulary list shows how much he was willing to
venture in order to gain control of the appointments of the resident magistrates, and how much he disliked the present system of appointments. He
concluded that if his system were considered inadvisable, "I earnestly trust
that the present system of our establishment will not be disturbed by any
further connexion with the 'gentlemen in question.' "[54]

The appointment of the stipendiaries was too great a prize for the government to relinquish, but the need for some revision of the system and the
infusion of professional men meant that some concessions were necessary.
McGregor's urgings prompted a ruling that every third vacancy in the resident magistracy might be filled from the ranks of the county inspectors on
the recommendation of the inspector general. By the 1860s, the position
and potential influence of the local magistrates, while noisy, was effectively
so weak that the government could now relax the almost total embargo of
local influence over the constabulary. In doing so, critics would be silenced,
and probably the effectiveness of the police improved. An infusion of constabulary county Inspectors into the profession of stipendiary magistrate
had restored commitment and provided a degree of standardization across
the country.

The concessions that the government made to the local magistrates were
marginal, and in one sense simply strengthened the constabulary system by
incorporating local magistrates into it, rather that by devolving authority
to local magistrates. In the last analysis, the government's attempt to restore
some dignity to local magistrates weakened their position further. Thus, by
the late 1860s the process begun in the late eighteenth century of removing
from local gentlemen the control of the functions of local justice and placing it into the hands of impartial government servants was almost complete.
The process was so advanced that now even local magistrates operated
through a structure organized and administered by the state.

THE ROLE OF THE CONSTABULARY

The Constabulary were an integral and necessary part of this centralized
system. At the lowest level of the petty sessions courts, the police provided
the necessary information to the petty session clerk for the preparation of
a summons and prosecuted the case in court. It would appear from the
sparse evidence available that the decision to prosecute in a minor offense—
a road nuisance for example—was taken at a local level by either the head

constable or the sub or district Inspector. The patrolling policeman, on discovering an offense and deciding on this occasion to prosecute, would forward a written report to the head constable of the police district. If he was satisfied that there was a case to answer, a copy of the report would be sent to the clerk of the petty sessions district where the offense occurred and would form the basis of the summons information. The summons would be prepared, signed by a magistrate, and forwarded to the police for service on the defendant. The prosecution would be conducted in court by the head constable, and the prosecuting policemen would be a witness.[55]

The police acted as gatherers of information on crime and criminal activities, and through the office of the county inspectors clerk passed evidence, in the form of depositions and witness statements taken before magistrates, to headquarters in Dublin castle. If there was a suspect in the case, the reports would be passed on to the Irish attorney general—with whom ultimate responsibility for prosecution rested, and to the crown solicitor of the county.

At the heart of the Irish judicial system was the principal of trial by jury. However, the problem with jury trials in Ireland was that for certain offenses the law did not receive general acceptance, and consequently the state was not able to convict where the sympathies of the jurors lay with the accused. In order to make jury trial more efficient, the state had devised a system of state prosecution. But these reforms were insufficient in themselves, because when brought to trial, jurors were sometimes unwilling to consider evidence from the crown and acquitted the accused. What was required was a steady flow of information from the police on potential jurors, and in locating jurors who were free from prejudice and intimidation. The information gathered would be used by the crown to challenge and "stand by" suspect jurors. Since the crown had the unlimited right to "stand by" jurors, and was in charge of compilation of jury lists, it was hoped that by these two processes a jury that was not hostile to the crown would be found. The success of the system rested on information provided by the police, and their success depended on payments to informants and the infiltration of organizations hostile to the crown by paid spies.

Another essential ingredient in the information-gathering process were the paid stipendiary magistrates, more commonly known as resident magistrates. As Derek Sheills has pointed out, the humourous fictional stories by Somerville and Ross

portray the pursuit of local justice as a none too serious contest between the quick witted Irish and the ponderous Major Yeates who has been characterized as "well meaning," but only "vaguely comprehending," of the people and events around him.[56]

In fact, Sheills's research has shown that the real Major Yates in all probability was not as amiable as his fictional counterpart. He was disciplined and his file was marked with an unfavorable record for striking a Mr. Ellis in 1889. Major Yates was seventy-one at the time, an ex-army officer whose career spanned from 1867 to 1891. Resident magistrates (RMs) were rather like policemen, in that they could be posted and transferred to any part of Ireland that the administration saw fit. Yates served in Donegal, Louth, Galway, and Leitrim during his twenty-five years of service. One RM served in twelve places in seventeen years. Under the provisions of the 1836 Constabulary Act, the government could appoint up to 142 RMs, but in practice appointed around seventy. In 1884, slightly under half of the RMs were ex-army officers, with one-third ex-RIC officers. The Crimes Act of 1887 required that RMs have legal experience and legal knowledge to the satisfaction of the attorney general. This requirement changed the recruitment pattern, and by 1912 half of the RMs were either barristers or solicitors and one-third were ex-RIC. These police magistrates knew their localities well, and became reliable sources of information on conspiracies, potential jurors, and the reliability of local appointments. They "occupied a fine space between ordinary and exceptional law and coercive law,"[57] and were the lynchpin of police operations against agrarian disturbance.

Another aspect of the Irish criminal justice system was a whole package of extensive powers, such as, the prohibition of arms, the prohibition of jury trial for certain scheduled offenses, powers to proclaim districts, summon witnesses, arrest strangers, and a whole range of measures to suppress disorder. This complex system, developed to deal with agrarian crime, shaped the administration of justice and the roles of the police, magistrates, and government departments, but has also shaped the perceptions of historians who have looked at the mechanism of the criminal justice system and have drawn conclusions critical of its fairness and legitimacy based wholly upon the structure of the system. The nature of the system was, however, rather different, and if the overall usage of the system—the totals—are considered, a different picture begins to emerge. In fact, the bulk of offenses committed in Ireland were prosecuted by the constabulary in petty sessions before local magistrates. At this point there seems little evidence of the legitimacy of the law being at risk. This is not to deny the existence of a secret side to the system of spies, informers, and police agents. It is, however, the extent of the secret side's infiltration and influence on the ordinary functions of the criminal justice system that is of critical importance in establishing whether the legitimacy of the *ordinary* law was affected by the *secret* part of the system.

THE SECRET SIDE

To maintain order and political control in Ireland, the British government and Irish administrations had to overcome the "problem of obtaining, organizing and evaluating intelligence."[58] The task of intelligence gathering was principally undertaken by both the constabulary and the Dublin Metropolitan Police. For instance, within the police's detective unit, the G division, a number of men specialized in political work. The structure of the constabulary's intelligence gathering was rather different, primarily due to the dispersed nature of policing the whole country. The constabulary established a central special crimes office in Dublin castle staffed by a county inspector, a district inspector, and a small number of clerks. Its function was to organize the gathering of intelligence on political crime, and to evaluate and disseminate it. Liaison between this office and the Dublin Metropolitan Police's detective unit, both housed in Dublin castle, appears to have been close. For example, information of use to Dublin detectives was ordered to be sent directly to the police from constabulary detectives.[59] Insofar as close cooperation between the two detective branches was an essential ingredient in successful intelligence gathering, the operation would fail if the gathered information was not passed on to the appropriate authority by an efficient administrative office. Given the importance of intelligence dissemination, the role of the administrative structure will be considered before an analysis of the role of the intelligence gatherers, because it would appear that the administrative structure determined the methods, type, and quality of the intelligence gathered.

The Irish government had long experimented with the analysis and dissemination of intelligence, and by 1914 a system was in place that attempted to resolve the system of distribution. Both the inspector general and the commissioner of the Metropolitan Police stated at the Royal Commission of 1916 that they passed their information on to the undersecretary, who was the effective day-to-day head of the civil executive in Ireland.[60] This bland assertion masks the fact that *at the time* the two police forces reported to the administration of the chief secretary's office, and, more specifically, to one of its divisions, the Judicial Division, which was given the prime role in the preparation of intelligence notes. The division was intimately concerned "with all matters relating to the preservation of order in the country." And any "questions arising in connection with the magistracy and police" were referred directly to this division.[61] However, a large part of the business of the division was to receive the day-to-day reports from the police. Naturally the bulk of these reports concerned fairly mundane matters requiring the decision of the attorney general's office on whether to institute prosecutions. Any orders made by the attorney general after consideration were issued to the police and crown solicitors by officials of the Judicial Division. The division was also concerned with the control, discipline, and distribution of both the constabulary and the Metropolitan Police. Due to the extensive duties of the division it proved necessary to separate the intelligence analysis from day-to-day matters to prevent vital information from being swamped by daily trivia. Thus, within the Judicial Division, a Crime Branch Special was established. The branch received intelligence reports from three other agencies: the Crime Branch Special within the constabulary, the Crime Branch Special Dublin Metropolitan Police, and the transfer of reports from the Crime Branch Special at the Home Office in London. This structure had evolved over decades as a matter of trial, error, and economy as governments had tried to gauge the depth of political feeling.

The genesis of the system can be traced back to the Fenian Rising of 1867 when an experienced crown solicitor, Samuel Lee Anderson, was based at Dublin castle to deal exclusively with Fenian matters and, later, agrarian and political crime. When the chief secretary's office was reorganized in 1876, the opportunity was missed to enhance the efficiency of intelligence gathering by creating a separate department with responsibility for crime and outrage. During the early 1880s, the increased levels of agrarian crime caused the office to be inundated with reports to such an extent that the staff was unable to cope with the additional police work. Thus the permanent under-secretary, T. H. Burke, wrote to the chief secretary, W. E. Forster:

After an experience of more than five years of the scheme therein proposed, I have arrived at the conclusion that it was a mistake not to have established in addition to the Financial and Administrative Divisions, a Crime Division, to deal with the reports of the Resident and local magistrates, and Constabulary relating to crime and outrage.[62]

Burke recommended the establishment of a Crime Division, which would deal "with all matters of detail" and submit all important papers to the under-secretary. A year later, following the Phoenix Park murders in May 1882, a separate division was established; Samuel Lee Anderson "and his assistants" were transferred to the new unit. By August 1882 the level of police work was significantly above the expected norm, and an additional post of assistant under-secretary for police and crime was needed to ease the burden of work. Edward G. Jenkinson was appointed to the new post. However, levels of crime rapidly declined to the expected norm, and Jenkinson's post was allowed to lapse in 1885. Further economy measures were taken by having the police and crime administration transferred to the inspector general of the RIC. This arrangement commenced in October 1885, and the inspector general was to be responsible for the administration of the crime branches both "special and ordinary" and with the custody of its records.[63] An essential part of the duties of the administration of the Crime Branch Special's Judicial Division was the preparation of a series of intelligence notes from the analysis of police reports, and a daily abstract of newspaper reports. The notes were forwarded for the information of the chief secretary on a regular basis, and thus were a key element in the formulation of government policy and attitude toward crime, outrage, and the perception of agrarian discontent.[64]

The arrangement whereby the inspector general was responsible for both crime branches was not successful. By 1887 it was seen that despite cooperation between the constabulary and the Metropolitan Police at an organizational and operational level—for example, the shadowing of suspects, when it came to the preparation of intelligence reports there was unnecessary duplication.[65] Shortly after A. J. Balfour's appointment as chief secretary in March 1887, the administration of the intelligence work began to be transferred away from the RIC, and by 1890 the process was complete and became part of the administrative division of the secretary's office. During this period, a specific department within the secretary's office was established to collect, classify, and index information in order to supply accurate estimates and memoranda on political activity. In November 1891, the amalgamation process was complete when the two branches of the Crime Department, together with the intelligence department and the various intelligence activities carried out by the RIC, were brought together under the administration of James H. Davies in the chief secretary's office. The mundane collectivist nature of the work is partially illustrated by Davies's previous career as an archivist.[66] The two branches of the Crime Division dealt with (1) ordinary crime, and (2) special crime—"the working of secret societies and political crime, domestic and foreign, its papers [now] being separately registered."[67] These tended under previous administrations to merge together but were now separate and distinct. Finally, in July 1904 all the administration of police and crime, which had been performed by the Police and Crime Division of the chief secretary's office, was transferred to the new Judicial Division.[68] This division remained in charge of police and crime until 1918.

The intelligence gatherers were almost exclusively policemen. Although the general officer commanding-in-chief had a Special Intelligence Department that dealt with political matters, the information gained by this branch "is chiefly obtained from the police," and only supplemented by information from the military censors and the Military Intelligence Department.[69] The Dublin Metropolitan Police's G division dealt with the investigation of crime, and a number of "selected men from this division are employed on work connected with political crime and intelligence."[70] Due to the devolved nature of policing the countryside, the constabulary had two distinct offices dealing with crime. The first, the RIC Crimes Branch, dealt with ordinary crime and was to a great extent a record office staffed by civilians. The actual police work connected with ordinary crime was dealt with by the local police. On the other hand, the RIC Crime Branch Special was staffed by policemen, since the branch was responsible for intelligence gathering as well as the preliminary analysis and indexing of material. In charge of the branch was a county inspector, assisted by a

district inspector with a "few sergeants and constables" as clerks.[71] The
police work, however, was performed by specific sergeants and constables
in each county. The manpower resources the constabulary allocated to the
intelligence-gathering operation were not large. The divisional lists of "Special" men attached to the Crime Department, Special Branch (see Appendix
A), reveal that only forty-two men were employed throughout the country
in 1890.[72] These men made their reports to the Dublin Special Branch
through the local county inspector, and it was only the inspector who had
the authority to apply for money from the Secret Service fund. Although
the Special Branch men were attached to a barracks, in theory, their activities were meant to be secret and they were to remain unknown to the
ordinary policemen. However, some years earlier in January 1881, Inspector General Hillier felt it necessary to remind officers of the force that

the employment of detectives is secret and should be known to no member of the
force unless it is absolutely necessary to inform him of it. Every recommendation
or communication made relative to the employment of detectives must be made a
separate entry. No copy is to be kept of it, and the name of every person aware of
the employment or contemplated employment of the detectives is to be given on
paper.

Given the barrack structure of constabulary life, with its gossip and insu-
larity, it was more than likely that the identities of the county branch men
were well known.

The work of the Special Branch detectives has been recorded in the vo-
luminous Police and Crime Records 1887–1917, Crime Branch Special,
deposited in the State Paper Office, Dublin castle. Most of the archive reveals just how mundane and routine the work actually was. The county
inspector's monthly confidential report was based upon the intelligence
gathered by the county's Special Branch men, and these reports were syn-
thesized into the inspector general's monthly confidential report made to
the chief secretary. The inspector general and the metropolitan police commissioner also prepared a precis of Special Branch monthly reports on secret societies. Most of these reports give the impression of conforming to
a precise administrative pattern, and contain very little that would alarm
or threaten the government, at least in the period prior to 1916. However,
more important to the intelligence operation than the synthesis of rumor
was the concentration on known suspects. Complete files with the life history and photographs were prepared on individuals believed to pose a
threat.[73]

The central element of this style of intelligence gathering and the way
that "facts" were made known came to be known as "shadowing," or the
constant following of the suspect. During the 1880s, the Crime Branch
Special devised a system of constant observation of suspected persons by

compiling a list of suspects active in nationalist politics, and then placing the suspects into three categories depending on the threat each posed. List A contained the names of the top nationalists, and their movements were constantly shadowed by Special Branch policemen in each country. The suspects on List B were active nationalists who were to be monitored by "cyphering." This system noted the destination of nationalists when they left their normal district and forwarded the information by telegraph to the Special Branch in Dublin. The suspect's destination office was forewarned and observation could begin on the nationalist's arrival. The third category, List C, was reserved for nationalists who travelled less frequently, and simply noted their activity in and around their district. The classification system was revised and updated monthly.[74] It is difficult to gauge the success of the shadowing policy. Certainly it was useful in gathering evidence to convict those involved in boycotting, and in Dublin, when the Land League was proscribed, it enabled the leaders to be arrested rapidly.[75] However, those arrested made little attempt to evade arrest or conceal "guilt" and in such circumstances other more conventional means of evidence gathering would have been just as successful. Where shadowing probably gave the greatest return during the period up to World War I was in providing the government with a "blank" return—a reliable source of information that confirmed what it already suspected. And during this period, the government suspected that it had very little to fear from any sudden popular physical force movement.

While individuals active in the nationalist movement were targeted for surveillance, the organizations they belonged to were subject to scrutiny by the classic method of spies and paid informants. The spies used by the Special Branch fall into three categories: the ethically motivated, the professional spy, and the occasional paid informant. The first, and considered to be the best informants, were those who gave their information freely and without reward.[76] These informants, however, were not under any control, and if it suited their purpose would "decline to follow up a matter and give further information." The second class "may in return for what they receive be looked upon as Secret Agents and may be expected to follow up matters and clear up points on which information required, when directed."[77]

Throughout Ireland around 1890, the Special branch employed 150 spies "who can be said to be regularly employed," and it would appear that they were under the control of the Special Branch detectives posted to the counties. These spies were able to respond to direction and provide specific information. An exceptional spy employed in the South-Eastern Division was known by the code of "Inventor" and had a regular stipend of £100 per annum, and during 1889 he had been paid an additional £100 for information. More typical were Cassidy, Fall, Ross, and Parker of the Eastern Division, who were described as "old hands" and were paid sums between £3 and £17 for information described as "important and trustworthy information about Ribbon Societys," "important information about Irish Ribbon Society (I.R.B.) organizations," and "about movements of organizers, visits of suspects and meetings of the I.R.B." In the Western Division, the information reflected the turbulent politics and greater levels of agrarian crime experienced in the west of Ireland during the late 1880s. The informant "Coo" was paid £19 for "trustworthy information on state of the district, plots to assassinate, and contemplated outrages," and "Joe," a member of the Galway West Riding I.R.B. inner circle, gave information as to the "secret societies organization in his district." There is no doubt that a well-placed spy was effective in disrupting the nationalist activities in a district. For example, Mary Sullivan had been an active spy since October 1886, and during 1889 was paid £60, since it was

chiefly through this informant's help that the Plan of Campaign on Kenmore Estate was successfully combated, and O'Brien thwarted. She enabled us to break up a boycotting conspiracy started by Mick Flemming (convicted and sentenced to 6 months imprisonment). She enabled us to check the "Castle Manifesto" Conspiracy and arrest 3 of the conspirators.[78]

Not all informers provided such valuable and regular intelligence, but if their potential as spies warranted they were given small sums to maintain links. "Almanac," a prominent member of the I.R.B. who had given information since 1882, was "paid £1 to keep him in hands." According to the return, £898 had been paid to informers during 1889. A few large sums had been paid, but the majority were small amounts of less than £5. Payments were usually made after the information was provided, and the system operated whereby "money is distributed for information . . . , we pay by results. On the information being tested, a sum is given which we consider equivalent."[79] Thus, by paying in arrears, the possibility of fraudulent and misleading information being accepted was minimized.

The third group were the undisclosed number of informers "who receive something from time to time for anything of value." The return does not disclose how many informers were involved or how much money was paid to them. Maintaining links with occasional informers could, however, prove of value if the informer moved into a position whereby he had regular access to intelligence. For example, "Salt" had only been giving regular information since October 1889, but he had provided information about the I.R.B. in the past and was thought "a new man likely to prove useful."[80]

In making an assessment of the intelligence-gathering operation it is necessary first to try to understand what the government hoped to achieve. It would seem that it had two objectives: first, to gain political intelligence on the nationalists' objectives and the methods that nationalist politicians would employ to gain those objectives, and second, to gain evidence to sustain a criminal prosecution against those who promoted and conducted agrarian crime. It is also clear that a distinction between political and criminal intelligence was blurred in the minds of the Special Branch administrators who referred to the narrow divide between criminal and political crime in Ireland.[81] With regard to the political intelligence, it can be said that the Special Branch were reasonably successful in providing government with accurate assessments of the goals of nationalist politicians and the methods they were prepared to use to attain them. The possibility of armed insurrection prior to 1914 was never thought to be strong, although Special Branch administrators continued to direct detectives and informants to search for evidence of it. On the other hand, despite limited local success, the Special Branch and the constabulary were unable to make any significant impact on levels of agrarian crime. In overall terms, the impact of the Special Branch operations in the Irish countryside was probably insignificant. The methods they used, informants and following suspects, were always a key part of successful detective policing whether the objective was political or criminal. The question remains, however, of just how deeply the constabulary was influenced by the presence of a Special Branch. To begin to answer the question it is necessary to examine the role of the Criminal Investigation Department (CID) in investigating "ordinary" crime, and assess the impact of the methods involved in investigating "political" crime on other criminal prosecutions and the criminal prosecution system.

THE CONSTABULARY C.I.D.

The constabulary did not have a specific department responsible for the investigation of crime such as the G division of the Dublin Metropolitan Police. The Constabulary Crimes Branch at Dublin castle was in fact a record office mostly staffed by civilians. Instead, the county structure of the constabulary dictated that crime was investigated at the local level by local policemen, and the number of policemen employed on detective work was in keeping with the level of crime. Because the level of crime in the counties was low, most counties only allocated two or three experienced policemen to work in plain clothes as and when circumstances required. These men were known by the less threatening title of "disposable men," a title that reflected their ability to be put to some other use when called upon.[82] On the other hand, counties with large urban populations—Limerick, Cork, and particularly Belfast—maintained considerable detective establishments. In the countryside, the rarity of serious criminal incidents meant that investigation could be conducted by a combination of local police, the resident magistrate, and the crown solicitor. For example, in the Trillick murder of 1902, the investigation of the rape and murder of forty year old

Anne McConn was carried out by District Inspector Wall and Sergeant Ladly.[83]

In that murder case, three suspects were arrested and questioned by the resident magistrate, James Brien. The first was a tramp, John Burnett, who was unfortunate enough to have been in the area at the time of the murder. The second was a local man, Joseph Woods, who was arrested after being seen outside the barracks with scratch marks on his face. The third suspect, Joseph Moon, was arrested following inquiries that showed he had been seen in the same area as McConn shortly before her murder. Blood stains on his trousers and pocket knife, which after analysis proved to be human, sealed his fate and he was convicted at the Belfast Winter Assize of 1903 and executed in Londonderry Jail on Tuesday, 5 January 1904. Moon was only convicted after three retrials. The first was at the 1903 Omagh Spring Sessions when eight jurors were for conviction, the second at the Omagh Summer Sessions when eleven jurors were for conviction, and finally the crown managed to secure a conviction only after the trial was moved to the Belfast Winter Assize of 1903.

This curious case raises some interesting questions. Why was it so difficult for the crown to convict given the apparent strength of the evidence, and only then by moving the trial away from the locality? The motive for the murder was sexual, far removed from politics. Perhaps Moon was known to some members of the jury and thus looked to them for protection. Certainly, when the trial was moved away from local influence, the weight of evidence alone secured a conviction. If Moon was protected by certain jurors, then the crown failed to use its powers to stand by jurors effectively, and further, their intelligence on the jurors was defective.[84] This suggests that although the crown had considerable powers, the powers were not always applied effectively or efficiently. To return to the events of the investigation, the fact that Moon was arrested following information given to the police suggests that the police were assisted by public cooperation. Without this cooperation it was unlikely that the police would have been able to make a speedy arrest with the blood stains still evident on Moon's trousers. The inexperience of the police in investigating serious crime is shown by the slightly panicky ten-page telegram outlining every detail of the case to the Crimes Branch in Dublin. The inspector general, ever aware of costs, rebuked District Inspector Wall for sending an "unnecessarily full" telegram.[85]

In Belfast, however, the level of serious crime was considerably above that of country districts, and it was necessary to have a considerable force of plainclothes policemen and detectives. Prior to 1902, a system of detective policing had developed that reflected the emphasis the constabulary placed on the district and local plainclothesmen. Throughout the various districts of Belfast there were seventy-one plainclothes policemen selected by and under the direction of the local district inspector. Thus, to a large extent the level of criminal activity in the districts determined how many men the inspectors allocated to plainclothes duties. To supplement the work of the district plainclothesmen there were thirty-one specially selected men who were employed as full-time detectives. These detectives were under the immediate command of a detective director, who held the rank of district inspector, and a head constable. The distinction between these two branches had grown out of the long practice of policing Belfast, and the requirement of a central pool of detectives to supplement the work of local plainclothesmen. The nature of plainclothes work was such that men moved into detective work and back to beat work at the direction of their district inspector. It was felt by the Belfast commissioner in 1902 that the system of plainclothesmen and detectives had grown unwieldy, and that the system would be made more rational and efficient by implementing a system of district detectives. The central detective staff was increased to thirty-five, and twenty-five detectives were allocated to the districts. As a result of abolishing the district plainclothesmen, forty-two policemen were returned to beat duties. The system of using full-time detectives was obviously successful, and in 1904 a further decentralization was carried out, leaving a central staff of nine. However, this reorganization resulted in a considerable loss of coordination. While, "the general principle of the efficiency and necessity for district detectives as compared with Plain Clothes men is supported," it was considered in 1907 that a central staff of twenty-four were necessary to be able to marshal and concentrate detectives on a particular task. Furthermore, "the Detective Director would be in charge of all the detectives, both central and district," and should he require it he would be able to withdraw the divisional detectives for exceptional duties. Normally, however, the divisional detectives would operate under the orders of their district inspector.[86]

Thus, over the years, Belfast developed a detective department that by its origins and structure matched the requirements of ordinary and not political crime. Certainly there was a secret side to policing Belfast, but in comparison to the effort spent on ordinary crime, the secret side remained a necessary but marginal activity. Further, there was no suggestion that the secret activities influenced the criminal justice procedures in or outside Belfast. In fact, it would appear that "good detective practice"—the use of informers and the surveillance of suspects—had grown out of the requirements of ordinary policing rather that the influence of political policing. After all, the Special Branch detectives had been recruited from the ordinary detective police, and had learned detective practice in towns such as Belfast while investigating ordinary crime.

THE IRISH CRIMINAL JUSTICE SYSTEM IN CONCLUSION

The criminal justice system in England and Wales had by the end of the nineteenth century evolved into a "professional machine which had replaced amateur hand labour."[87] The durability of amateurs in England partly reflects their determination to continue to participate in, and their success in maintaining a commitment to, the rule of law. By way of contrast, in Ireland the "amateur hand labour"—a system of local justice administered by magistrates—had long proved unable to cope with agrarian crime, and had largely been replaced by a professional system. This professional system developed as part of the centralized administration of Ireland in the first four decades after the Act of Union, and an essential part of the criminal justice system was the Irish constabulary. It has been argued that the constabulary was developed and structured in such a way as to preserve British rule in Ireland, and that once it was established and placed within the criminal justice system it began to function as an ordinary police force. The main concern of an ordinary police force was with the criminal law. Cornish and Clarke have pointed out that during the Victorian period most of those in charge of the system shared a common outlook that crime must at all costs be stamped out.[88] This outlook was just as appropriate in Ireland, with the added ingredient of concern for the preservation of British rule. Evidence from a variety of inquiries into the workings of the constabulary suggests that the criminal law occupied a central place in the day-to-day activities of the police.[89] The policemen were expected to learn new criminal legislation, and promotion could be accelerated by success in detecting crime. Even in country areas, the police enforced a range of minor laws in the absence of any serious crime. Thus, in answer to the first question posed at the beginning of this chapter of "how important was the criminal law in the work of the police," it can be said with conviction that both qualitatively—in the status given to the "clearing up" of ordinary crime, and quantitatively—in the amount of time and resources taken up by ordinary crime, that the day-to-day emphasis of the constabulary was on ordinary crime and the criminal law.

With regard to the subsidiary questions raised—whether all offenders were prosecuted, whether alternative sanctions were available, and how cases were prepared and what the role of the constabulary was—it has been shown that the constabulary was a part of a centrally administered state system of professional magistrates, solicitors, and police that was designed to ensure that, at the very least, the state would not be at a disadvantage in a criminal trial. The first two questions, however, cannot be answered with the certainty of the third. It was quite unlikely that all offenders were prosecuted. More likely, there were an unknown and unquantifiable number of offenders who were subject to various levels of police discretion. This discretion could operate through all levels of the constabulary from the individual policeman choosing to warn (or ignore) an offender following the commission of an offense for a variety of personal reasons, to the government giving an instruction to the inspector general to concentrate his force on a particular offense. A whole range of alternative sanctions—from the local drunk cleaning the barrack yard and tidying the magistrate's garden—were available, but due to their dubious legality, documentary evidence of quasi-official sanctions do not appear in official accounts. Further, it has been argued that the police and the judicial system were themselves a part of a rural system of sanctions that used the official system as a stage in the settling of disputes.[90]

In practical terms, the special political operations of the constabulary remained an adjunct to the criminal policing of Ireland. Further, the low levels of crime in the countryside did not warrant the maintenance of a substantial detective department, and only the major towns of Ireland had levels of crime that justified investigation by detectives. It was from these detectives, and with their methods of investigation, that the Special Branch detectives were recruited. Thus it can be said that the ordinary detective policing of Ireland influenced the methods used by the Special Branch, rather that those of the branch influencing the policing of Ireland.

In the last analysis, the constabulary occupied a dual role in policing Ireland: to maintain public tranquility *and* to perform the many functions that are associated with a police force. If there existed a conflict between these aims, that conflict was highlighted during specific periods of political tension. During such a crisis, the decision concerning the priorities of the constabulary were intractably political.[91] It would be wrong, therefore, to draw specific conclusions as to the function of the constabulary in the judicial system based simply upon the policing during a crisis. A more accurate estimation of the role of the constabulary would be gained by an analysis of the policing of the peace. The exact levels of crime, both nationally and locally, and the impact of the police in preventing crime, will be the subject of further research.

APPENDIX A: SPECIAL BRANCH DIVISIONAL LIST, 1890

Northern Division.

Rank and Name	App to SB	Station
Sgt McBarron, R	23-1-84	Dundalk
Act Sgt Kilcourse, M	30-1-84	Newry
Sgt Oakley, T	1-12-85	L'Derry
Sgt Christal, T	13-1-86	Enniskellen
Sgt Kearney, D	13-6-88	Letterkenny
Act Sgt McLoughlin, P	26-12-88	Monaghan

Midland Division

Rank	Name	App to SB	Station
Sgt Sullivan, J		6-7-85	Cavan
Sgt Rowan, J		15-4-89	Naas
Act Sgt McKenna, P		1-9-88	Tullamore
Sgt Carroll, P		23-9-82	Carrick on Shannon
Con Lyden, W.H		21-1-90	Carrick on Shannon
Sgt Ryan, O		11-9-84	Longford
Sgt Doolan, I		16-5-87	Trim
Sgt Phillips, J		1-9-87	Sligo
Sgt Clarke, J		20-11-88	Mullingar

Western Division

Rank	Name	App to SB	Station
Sgt McGlenen, I		1-7-85	Loughrea
Sgt Doonan, T.L		1-3-88	Ballinasloe
Hd Con Preston, J		9-10-82	Westport
Sgt Mullen, R		1-1-89	Ballyhournis
Sgt Gleeson, M		17-4-90	Galway
Sgt Devney, J		24-4-90	Boyle
Sgt Doyle, J.S		12-5-90	Athlone

South Western Division

Rank Name	App to SB	Station
Hd Con Brennan, E.J	15-10-88	Cork City
Act Sgt Corry, M	13-1-90	Cork City
Sgt Drohan, T	1-11-84	Mallow
Sgt Brady, J	1-9-87	Millstreet
Sgt Morrow, J	1-1-88	Limerick City
Sgt Sullivan, J	1-3-90	Newcastle
Sgt McNulty, F	15-12-87	Banteen

South Eastern Division

Rank Name	App to SB	Station
Sgt Clarke, P	6-10-82	Clonmel
Sgt Collins, J	1-5-85	Enniscarthy
Sgt Hennessy, J	1-9-86	John St, Kilkenny
Sgt Carthy, J	1-9-86	Thurles
Sgt Hourican, I	1-12-90	Maryboro
Con Mullone, D	1-10-84	Carlow
Sgt Wilson, J	23-12-82	Ladylane, Waterford
Sgt Sullivan, P	15-5-90	Limerick Junction

Kerry and Clare Division

Rank Name	App to SB	Station
Sgt Duggan, J	4-12-88	Killarney
Sgt Brien, C	9-7-87	Tralee
Hd Con O'Halloran	(No date)	Ennis

City of Belfast

Rank Name	App to SB	Station
Hd Con Hussey, W.H	1-12-89	Gt Victoria St
Sgt Stewey, J	5-11-85	Gt Victoria St

1. R.I.C. Crime Department, Special Branch, Divisional List 29 April 1890 in Police and Crime Records 1887-1917, Crime Branch Special 501/239/5, State Paper Office, Dublin Castle.

NOTES

1. John F. McEldowney, "Policing and the Administration of Justice in Nineteenth-Century Ireland," in *Policing Western Europe: Politics, Professionalism, and Public Order, 1850–1940,* ed. Clive Emsley and Barbara Weinberger (London, 1991), 18–35.

2. McEldowney, "Policing and the Administration of Justice," 18–19.

3. Defined as "crimes arising out of disputes as to occupation of land or arising out of political or religious antagonism and aggravated assaults." *Report from the Select Committee of the House of Lords appointed to enquire into the operation of the Irish Jury Laws,* House of Lords Parliamentary Papers 1881 XI.I., quoted in McEldowney, "Policing and the Administration of Justice," 29.

4. *Select Committee of the House of Lords on the State of Ireland in respect of Crime,* House of Lords Parliamentary Papers 1839 (20) XX. Major George Warburton was appointed a chief magistrate with the Peace Preservation Force in 1816, and provincial inspector for Connaught on the formation of the county constabulary in 1822. He was deputy inspector general of the Irish Constabulary from 1836 and for the month June 1838 was caretaker inspector general. He retired in July 1838. Q566–573, 25 April 1839.

5. *Select Committee of the House of Lords in respect of Crime,* 1839, Warburton, Q1106–7, 26 April 1839, and Q1290–94, 29 April 1839.

6. McEldowney, "Policing and the Administration of Justice," 22.

7. V.T.H. Delvaney, *The Administration of Justice in Ireland* (Dublin, 1962), 47.

8. McEldowney, "Policing and the Administration of Justice," 23.

9. *Select Committee of the House of Commons on the County Cess, Ireland, 1836, Minutes of Evidence,* House of Commons Parliamentary Papers 1836 (527) XII. Evidence of Leonard Dobbin, clerk of the crown for the County of Armagh, 17 May 1836.

10. *Select Committee on the County Cess, 1836,* evidence of Leonard Dobbin, Q1020.

11. *Select Committee on the County Cess, 1836,* evidence of Leonard Dobbin, Q1019.

12. *Select Committee on the County Cess, 1836,* evidence of Leonard Dobbin, Q1023.

13. Although the final responsibility rested with the attorney general, it was likely that the decision was made by a member of the office, or in the office of the law adviser. The duties of the law adviser were never defined but he was a member of the bar who gave assistance to the attorney and solicitor general. Magistrates at petty sessions also sought his advice. From 1849 a salary was provided and the office was discontinued in 1883. See R. B. McDowell, *The Irish Administration 1801–1914* (London, 1964), 120–21.

14. *Select Committee of the House of Lords in respect of Crime,* 1839, Evidence of John H. Hatton, Chief Constable County Meath 1838, Q2804–22.

15. Maamtrasna Massacre File, CRF 1902 J13 4328A, State Paper Office, Dublin. See also an excellent account of the murders in Jarlath Waldron, *Maamtrasna: The Murders and the Mystery* (Dublin, 1992), 31 for the role of the RMs and the crown solicitor.

16. For the "legal administrative service" and the administration of courts of a wider jurisdiction see McDowell, *The Irish Administration,* 122–32.

17. McDowell, *The Irish Administration,* 132.

18. *Select Committee on the County Cess, 1836,* evidence of Daniel Kelly, Q1400.

19. McDowell, *The Irish Administration,* 164.

20. For government supervision of local authorities see McDowell, *The Irish Administration,* 165.

21. The grand jury retained its judicial function until 1924 when the Courts of Justice Act abolished the grand jury. See Delvaney, *The Administration of Justice,* 47.

22. The Local Government Act of 1898, 61 and 62 Vict., cap 37.

23. *Select Committee on the County Cess, 1836,* evidence of Leonard Dobbin, Q965, 966, 973.

24. *Select Committee on the County Cess, 1836,* evidence of Rice Hussey, crown clerk for Donegal, Q1577–81.

25. *Select Committee on the County Cess, 1836,* evidence of Leonard Dobbin, Q952, 953.

26. County Offices and Courts (Ireland) Act 1877, 40 and 41 Vict., cap 56; and McDowell, *The Irish Administration,* 133.

27. McDowell, *The Irish Administration,* 134.

28. Stanley Palmer, *Police and Protest in England and Ireland 1780–1850* (Cambridge, 1988), 210.

29. Galen Broeker, *Rural Disorder and Police Reform in Ireland, 1812–36* (London, 1970), 149–50.

30. Broeker, *Rural Disorder and Police Reform,* 151.

31. *Lords' Select Committee appointed to examine the nature and extent of the Disturbances . . . in Ireland,* House of Lords Parliamentary papers 1825 (200) VII, Evidence of Richard Willocks 55–77.

32. HO 100/208/31. Wellesley to Peel, 29 January 1823; and Broeker, *Rural Disorder and Police Reform,* 151. Palmer, *Police and Protest,* 246 agrees that the revision was substantial.

33. Broeker, *Rural Disorder and Police Reform,* 152; and Palmer, *Police and Protest,* 246.

34. The Whig government also instituted another reform of the magistracy at this time, and over the next few years over a third of the existing JPs were removed. See Oliver Macdonagh, "Ideas and Institutions, 1830–1845" in *A New History of Ireland, Vol. 5, Ireland Under the Union 1801–70,* ed. W. E. Vaughan (Oxford, 1989), 214.

35. Gregory J. Fulham, "James Shaw-Kennedy and the Reformation of the Irish Constabulary, 1836–1838," in *Eire-Ireland,* Vol. 16 (1981); and Evidence of Colonel J. S. Kennedy, in *Minutes of Evidence Before Select Committee of the House of Lords appointed to inquire into the state of Ireland since 1835 in respect to Crime and Outrage,* House of Lords Parliamentary Papers 1839 (423) XI–XII, for full details of Shaw-Kennedy's resignation.

36. Larcom Papers, Manuscript Series 7618, National Library of Ireland, Dublin, Inspector-General Duncan McGregor to Lord Naas, 14 October 1852, for McGregor's opinion of the control of the Stipendiary Magistrates.

37. Larcom Papers, MS 7618, N.L.I., Dublin, Thomas Larcom's memo on Sir Robert Peel's letter of 20 May 1862.

38. Larcom Papers, MS 7619, N.L.I., Dublin, Lord Carlisle to Lord Grey, 26 March 1864.

39. Sir Thomas Larcom was permanent under-secretary at Dublin castle from 1853 to 1868.

40. Larcom Papers, MS 7618, N.L.I., Dublin, Thomas Larcom's memo.

41. Larcom Papers, MS 7618, N.L.I., Dublin, Thomas Larcom's memo.

42. Larcom Papers, MS 7618, N.L.I., Dublin, Thomas Larcom's memo.

43. Larcom Papers, MS 7618, N.L.I., Dublin, Thomas Larcom's memo.

44. Larcom Papers, MS 7618, N.L.I., Dublin, Sir Robert Peel to Lord Carlisle, 20 May 1862.

45. Larcom Papers, MS 7618, N.L.I., Dublin, Peel to Carlisle.

46. Larcom Papers, MS 7618, N.L.I., Dublin, Peel to Carlisle.

47. Larcom Papers, MS 7618, N.L.I., Dublin, Constabulary Code Regulation 77, 206, 207.

48. Larcom Papers, MS 7618, N.L.I., Dublin, Peel to Carlisle.

49. Larcom Papers, MS 7618, N.L.I., Dublin, Peel to Carlisle.

50. Larcom Papers, MS 7618, N.L.I., Dublin, Peel to Carlisle.

51. It would seem that from the 1860s a more professional attitude was expected from RMs, and the number of ex-military and ex-RIC appointments to RMs increased significantly. See later for the changes that occurred in the 1880s and 1910s.

52. *Evening Mail*, 28 May 1862. The four appointments were: (1) Commissioner of Public Institutions; (2) Member of the Relief Commission of 1847; (3) An Agent for H. M. Crown Lands; and (4) Superintendent of Kildare Training School.

53. Sir Duncan McGregor was inspector general from 1836 to 1858.

54. Larcom Papers, MS 7618 N.L.I., Dublin, Sir Duncan McGregor to Lord Naas, 14 October 1852.

55. *Select Committee of the House of Lords appointed to consider the consequences of extending the functions of the Constabulary in Ireland to the suppression of illicit distillation*, House of Lords Parliamentary Papers, 1854 (53) X, evidence of W. S. Tracey R. M. Q1318; and *Civil Service (In Ireland) Inquiry Commission, 1872*, House of Commons Parliamentary Papers, 1873 (831) XXII, report 141 and evidence of County Inspector Arthur W. Stafford Q1350.

56. Derek Sheills, "The Resident Magistracy in Ireland 1860–1922", in *IAHCCJ Bulletin No. 15 February 1992*, Paris 1992, 39–53; quote at 39.

57. Sheills, "The Resident Magistracy," 53.

58. Eunan O'Halpin, "British Intelligence in Ireland, 1914–1921," in *The Missing Dimension: Governments and Intelligence Communities in the Twentieth Century*, ed. Christopher Andrew and David Dilks (London, 1984). See also an excellent article by Richard Hawkins, "Government Versus Secret Societies: The Parnell Era," in *The Irish Struggle, 1916–1926* (Dublin 1972), for a commentary on the development of the Irish intelligence network.

59. RIC Circular No. 155, 8 November 1883, Irish Crimes Records, RIC Circulars 1880–1884 VIIIB W.P.2 II, State Paper Office, Dublin Castle.

60. *Royal Commission of Inquiry into the 1916 Rebellion*, 1916, (8279) XI, 171, 185.

61. *Royal Commission on the Civil Service, Fourth Report,* Second Appendix, House of Commons Parliamentary Papers 1914, XVI, 545.

62. T. H. Burke to W. E. Forster, 7 June 1881, Chief Secretary's Office Registered Papers 8452/1898, State Paper Office, Dublin Castle.

63. R. G. C. Hamilton to Treasury, 11 March 1886, Chief Secretary's Office, Government Letter Book, State Paper Office, Dublin Castle, 163.

64. Memorandum as to the Organization and Staff of the C.S.O., and other Departments connected with the Irish Government, February 1913.

65. W. S. B. Kaye to Treasury, 10 August 1887, Chief Secretary's Office, Government Letter Book, State Paper Office, Dublin Castle, 412.

66. Davies was employed in the Public Record Office from 1872 until 1878, and on his transfer to the C.S.O. he acted as private secretary to three under-secretaries in the period 1883–1891. J. W. Ridgeway to Treasury, 7 December 1891, Chief Secretary's Office, Government Letter Book, State Paper Office, Dublin Castle, 466.

67. A. J. Balfour to Treasury, 7 November 1891, T1/18063/1891, Public Record Office, Kew.

68. A. P. MacDonald to Treasury, 26 June 1904, Chief Secretary's Office, Government Letter Book, State Paper Office, Dublin Castle, 7A.

69. Brig. Joseph A. Byrne, Inspector General R.I.C., "The Organization of the C.I.D. in Ireland", C.A.B. 37/151/1, Public Record Office, Kew. In 1920 the composition of this department was supplemented by the secondment of a County Inspector, Major Price, and two constabulary officials from the Crimes Special Branch. Also, due to the failure of police intelligence, "four or five military intelligence officers have now been appointed for work in the country districts."

70. Byrne, "The Organization of the C.I.D. in Ireland", C.A.B. 37/151/1, PRO Kew.

71. Byrne, "The Organization of the C.I.D. in Ireland", C.A.B. 37/151/1, PRO Kew.

72. R.I.C. Crime Department, Special Branch, Divisional List, 29 April 1890 in Police and Crime Records 1887–1917, Crime Branch Special 501/239/5, State Paper Office, Dublin Castle.

73. Police and Crime Records 1887–1917, Crime Branch Special, State Paper Office, Dublin Castle. For example, file 501S/1181 19, August 1890, gives the history of Edward Harrington M.P.

74. See "Return of Persons on the General 'A' List," 501S/1221, and "Memo on Shadowing," Inspector General Andrew Reed, 27 June 1890, 501/783S, for the mechanics, and *Irish Times,* 20 June 1890, for the Parliamentary debate on shadowing and the exchange between A. J. Balfour and the nationalist MPs Healy and Dillon. The antecedents of the shadowing practice are described in a "Memorandum to the Chief Secretary," 20 June 1890, 501/783S, State Paper Office, Dublin Castle.

75. Divisional Commissioners and D.M.P. reports on Shadowing, 26 June 1890, Crime Branch Special, 501/730S, State Paper Office, Dublin Castle.

76. Memorandum to Under-Secretary, "Payment for Information," 1890, Crime Branch Special, 501/1416S, State Paper Office, Dublin Castle.

77. Memorandum, "Payment for Information," 501/1416S, S.P.O., Dublin.

78. Memorandum, "Payment for Information," 501/1416S, S.P.O., Dublin.

79. Memorandum, "Payment for Information," 501/1416S, S.P.O., Dublin.

80. Memorandum, "Payment for Information," 501/1416S, S.P.O., Dublin.

81. Brig. Joseph A. Byrne, Inspector General RIC, wrote "The dividing line between political crime and ordinary crime in Ireland is often a very narrow one." In "The Organization of the C.I.D. in Ireland," C.A.B. 37/151/1, Public Record Office, Kew.

82. Elizabeth Malcolm is at present working on the composition and role of the RIC detectives.

83. Trillick Murder File 1902, State Paper Office, Dublin Castle.

84. Unfortunately, research has so far failed to trace the trial documents.

85. Trillick Murder File, S.P.O., Dublin.

86. N. Chamberlain to Under-Secretary, "Re-organization of the Detective Department in Belfast," 13 March 1907, Chief Secretary's Office Registered Papers 7720 filed in 1919 C.S.O.R.P. 26565.

87. W. R. Cornish and G. de N. Clarke, *Law and Society in England 1750–1950* (London, 1989), 613.

88. Cornish and Clarke, *Law and Society in England*, 613.

89. Select Committee of the House of Lords Appointed to consider the consequences of extending the functions of the Constabulary in Ireland to the suppression of illicit distillation, House of Lords Parliamentary Papers, 1854 (53) X; *Commission Directed by the Treasury to Inquire into the state of the Constabulary Force in Ireland,* House of Commons Parliamentary Papers, 1866 (3658) XXXIV; Civil Service (In Ireland) Enquiry Commission 1872, House of Commons Parliamentary Papers, 1873 (831) XXII; and Royal Irish Constabulary Inquiry 1882, House of Commons Parliamentary Papers, 1883 (3576) XXXII.

90. See Ian Bridgeman, "Policing Rural Ireland: A Study of the Origins, Development and Role of the Irish Constabulary, and its Impact on Crime Prevention and Detection in the Nineteenth Century," PhD. Thesis, Open University, 1993, for a full account of the points raised here.

91. Laurence Lustgarten, *The Governance of Police* (London, 1986), especially Chapter Five, 68–73.

Anti-Irish Violence in Victorian England: Some Perspectives

Roger Swift
Chester College

During the past decade, the study of crime and disorder has merited a relatively low profile within the burgeoning historiography of the experiences of Irish immigrants in Victorian England. There have been some studies of aspects of Irish criminality during the Victorian period,[1] but there is ample scope for further research in this area and the first doctoral thesis on the subject has yet to be produced. Likewise, the study of criminal violence against the Irish has received scant attention, but for one recent analysis.[2] This is surprising in view of the fact that during the nineteenth century some contemporary observers, including Irish nationalists,[3] claimed that anti-Irish violence was but one manifestation of the sustained hostility, rooted in English prejudice, that was directed toward Irish immigrants in Victorian England. Indeed, *The Nation,* a Dublin weekly newspaper, was moved to comment on 6 June 1868 that "Nowhere in England can our countrymen consider themselves safe from English mob violence."[4] This theme has been developed further during the twentieth century by some historians of the Irish in Britain who have pointed to large-scale public disorders, small-scale disturbances, violence in the workplace, and individual attacks on Irish people as evidence of English hostility to Irish immigrants throughout the Victorian period.[5] This chapter seeks to examine this assertion by analysing aspects of anti-Irish violence in the broader context of the recent historiography of the experiences of Irish immigrants in Victorian England.

THE CONTEXT OF ANTI-IRISH VIOLENCE

Clearly, any examination of anti-Irish violence in Victorian England needs to be placed in the broader context of English attitudes toward the Irish, which had a long and complex history.[6] Although hostility to the Irish had ancient roots in England, the growth of anti-Hibernian sentiment during the early and mid-Victorian years was a consequence of the economic, social, political, and religious currents of the period and was intimately linked to the enormous influx of refugees from Ireland during the Great Famine of 1845–1851.[7] The increase in the Irish-born population of England and Wales from 289,404 in 1841 to a peak of 601,634 in 1861 exacerbated hostility to the Irish poor by raising the profile of "the Condition of England Question," notably in regard to the issues of poverty, public health, and crime, for which the Irish emerged as convenient scapegoats.[8]

English antipathy to the largely Catholic Irish was heightened by the restoration of the Catholic hierarchy in England and Wales in 1850, and over the next twenty years both public and government went through a phase of anti-Catholicism in response to "Papal aggression." Indeed, most anti-Irish disorders belong to this period, notably in South Lancashire.[9] The activities of the Orange Order compounded this situation,[10] as did the activities of anti-Catholic lecturers such as William Murphy.[11] Political factors also fanned the flames of anti-Irish behavior, particularly between 1865 and 1868, when Fenian activities on the mainland brought a sense of fear of Irish nationalist violence to the host population. The dramatic events of 1867, which witnessed the abortive Fenian raid on Chester Castle, the case of the "Manchester Martyrs," and the Clerkenwell bombing,[12] all served to raise Anglo-Irish tensions, albeit temporarily. It has also been argued that economic competition between English and Irish workers exacerbated native reactions to the newcomers because the Irish threatened to undercut wage levels and were prepared to work as strike-breakers.[13] However, there is some evidence to suggest that the Irish impact on wage rates has been exaggerated, that competition between English and Irish workers was essentially a product of the pre-Famine period,[14] that there was relative harmony and some political and trade unionist cooperation between English and Irish workers,[15] and that Irish and English cotton operatives sometimes acted in unison during moments of industrial militancy.[16] Nevertheless, there is a considerable body of evidence to suggest that poor, working-class Irish Catholic immigrants were in some respects the "outcasts" of mid-Victorian English society on the grounds of their poverty, ethnicity, religion, and politics,[17] although this view is more difficult to substantiate for the late-Victorian period.[18]

TYPES OF ANTI-IRISH VIOLENCE

Anti-Irish violence, and particularly anti-Irish disorder, was essentially multicausal and came in various shapes and sizes. It operated on both intracommunal and intercommunal levels within specific communities, revealing different types of behaviour according to time and place.

First, there were intracommunal disorders, consisting largely of drunken brawls, quarrels between neighbors, and domestic disputes that were confined to Irish districts. Much of this violence was between and among rather than against Irish people. There was, for example, a good deal of factional fighting in rural Ireland, and a tradition of hostility between men from rival counties and provinces; as James Handley has observed, "Connacht men disapproved of the men from Ulster; Tyrone men frowned on the natives of Antrim, and Monaghan men scowled at immigrants from Donegal."[19] These rivalries were sustained in English cities, notably Liverpool and Manchester, and in London, where it was noted as early as 1817 that that the Irish in Calmel Buildings "give each other pitched battles, every Saturday night, when heroes and heroines show their prowess at fisticuffs"; while in neighboring St. Giles "early on the Sunday morning you will see Irishmen quite drunk and fighting with their shelelas; at times three or four hundred will collect together."[20] Indeed, the drunkenness, noise, and casual violence associated with Saturday night saturnalia in the public houses, beershops, and lodging-houses of the "Little Irelands" of English towns—not to mention the celebration of weddings, wakes, and St. Patrick's Day—made the Irish more visible, reinforcing the popular perception of the Irish predeliction for drunkenness and disorderly behavior, and sometimes inviting attention from the police. Yet these Irish disorders, commonly described by the provincial press as "Irish rows," which so horrified "respectable" opinion, rarely reflected English prejudice against the Irish and were of little interest to the police or magistrates unless they spilled over into the public domain.

In contrast, violence bred of sectarian rivalries often spilled over into the public domain. Ulster immigrants of the Orange Order introduced their fratricidal strife with Irish Catholics into a number of English cities during the early decades of the nineteenth century,[21] most notably in Liverpool, where sectarian competition for jobs in a weakly unionized economy polarized local politics between the Orange and the Green.[22] Yet Liverpool appears to have been the only English city where sectarian violence was both ingrained and continuous throughout the nineteenth century.[23] This was due in part to the strength of the Protestant-Tory political machine. Sectarian violence appears to have been atypical of the experiences of Irish communities in nineteenth-century Britain as a whole, confined as it was to Merseyside and Clydeside. Moreover, Liverpool apart, there was no comparable wave of sectarian violence after the 1860s to that which had characterised the mid-Victorian years. Significantly, the next major outbreak of religious rioting focused not on Catholics but on the Salvation Army in 1882.[24]

Second, there were intercommunal disorders that involved attacks on Irish people by the non-Irish. Clashes between the Irish and the police had a character of their own. There is a wealth of evidence to suggest that the attempts of provincial police forces after 1835 to monitor more closely the working-class districts of English towns and cities made Irish districts particularly vulnerable to police surveillance. Police attempts to quell intra-communal disorders, enforce the licensing laws (notably the Beer Act of 1848, which regulated the sale of beer and other liquors on the Sabbath), trace illegal stills, regulate lodging-houses (which were regarded by the police as nurseries of crime and havens for criminals), and apprehend suspicious characters in Irish districts, were perceived by the Irish as examples of police violence and often led to serious and more generalized disorders. At this point the distinction between "intracommunal" and "intercommunal" violence becomes blurred. For example, the deputy-constable of Manchester noted in 1839:

In Angel Meadow, or Little Ireland, if a legal execution of any kind is to be made, either for rent, for debt, or for taxes, the officer who serves the process almost always applies to me for assistance to protect him; in affording that protection my officers are often maltreated by brickbats and other missiles.[25]

In the meantime, the superintendent of the night watch observed:

It repeatedly happens that, in order to apprehend one Irishman in the Irish parts of the town, we are forced to take from ten or twenty, or even more, watchmen. The whole neighbourhood will turn out with weapons, even women, half-naked, carrying brickbats and stones for the men to throw. A man will resist, fighting and struggling, in order to gain time till his friends collect for a rescue, so that he has scarcely a rag left upon him when he is brought to the lock-up.[26]

Similarly, in 1849, the chief constable of Wolverhampton reported that it was necessary to remove policemen from other parts of the town in order to contain disturbances in the Irish district, noting:

Whenever a disturbance takes place, these overcrowded lodging-houses pour forth their inmates in almost incredible numbers, attacking a single policeman or two with great ferocity and savageness, but being equally expert in beating a retreat when faced by a sufficient force to repel their lawless proceedings.[27]

In short, whole Irish communities often stood shoulder to shoulder in face of what was popularly held to be police harassment. The overrepresentation of Irish people in statistics pertaining to assaults on the police, which often occurred during the kind of disorders already described, could be seen in part as an index of Irish hostility to police interference, even though there were also disproportionate numbers of Irishmen in the police. W. J. Lowe has shown, for example, that 33 percent of all people arrested for assaults on the police in Liverpool and Manchester between 1841 and 1871 were Irish.[28] In Birmingham, the Irish represented on average 20 percent of all arrests for assaults on the police during the period 1862–1877, although they comprised only 4 percent of the local population.[29]

It is not always easy to lay exclusive blame on either side during some of these intercommunal disorders. There were, for example, some famous battles between Irish and English railway navvies during the 1830s and 1840s, which were in part rooted in the harshness of that kind of life. These included a pitched battle between navvies working on the North Union Railway near Preston in 1838, as a result of which Preston Council reviewed policing arrangements in the town; three days of fierce fighting between 300 Irish navvies and 250 English railway laborers engaged on the line of the Chester and Birkenhead Railway at Childer Thornton in 1839, which was only ended by the use of troops from Chester and Liverpool; and the serious clashes between English and Irish navvies on the Lancaster and Carlisle line at Penrith and Kendal in 1846.[30] Navvy riots were multicausal. In some instances they involved violence by the Irish as a protest against their exploitation by contractors and gangers; in others they may be ascribed to English xenophobia, which resulted in violence against the Irish. There were, too, instances of navvy violence being manipulated by rival railway companies in order to establish control over disputed tracts of land. This was reflected in a riot that occurred near Wolverhampton in 1850, when Irish navvies employed, respectively, by the London and North-Western Railway and the Shrewsbury and Birmingham Railway, fought a pitched battle that was only ended by the deployment of police armed with cutlasses, and troops with bayonets fixed.[31] However, such disorders were largely confined to the 1830s and 1840s. Moreover, they suggest, contrary to popular belief, that the Irish did not have a monopoly of navvy violence. Indeed, about one-third of navvies were Irish, one-third English, and one-third Scottish. Because of this potentially combustible mixture, navvy gangs were often segregated.[32]

In contrast, intercommunal disorders that, on the surface at least, were rooted in religious differences between the Irish and the host society were frequently the product of violence directed against the Irish as Roman Catholics and often provoked a violent Irish Catholic response. This was particularly evident during the mid-Victorian period, when the resurgence of popular Protestantism in the wake of the Tractarian controversy and the re-establishment of the Roman Catholic hierarchy provided an additional cutting-edge to Anglo-Irish tensions and contributed to a number of serious anti-Catholic and anti-Irish disorders. These included the infamous Stockport riots of 1852,[33] the Oldham disorders of 1861,[34] and the more widespread Murphy riots, which witnessed ugly clashes between the English and Irish in a number of industrial towns in South Lancashire, the Potteries, and the West Midlands between 1867 and 1871.[35] Yet even these disorders were, at root, multicausal. Indeed, the Stockport riots offer a useful illustration of the extent to which the interplay of a variety of factors influenced violence against the Irish. For example, the riots may have arisen from the underlying antagonism between Irish immigrants and the hard-pressed English cotton workers who resented the incursion of cheap Irish labor into the mills. Although this in itself was insufficient to cause the initial violence, the actual occasion was the restoration of the Catholic hierarchy, fanned to a flame by local Anglican clergymen and electorally vulnerable Tory politicians who played the Irish card in a bid for political power.[36] Indeed, what is clear from disturbances that were superficially the product of religious tensions is that more often than not they were the reflection of deeper ethnic, economic, and political strains within local communities.[37]

PROBLEMS OF INTERPRETATION

The study of anti-Irish violence in Victorian England remains problematic, and three particular issues are deserving of closer scrutiny. First, we know much more about those serious anti-Irish riots that achieved national notoriety during the period than we do about the less-serious, "B" class disturbances, including "Irish rows." In the context of the former, the systematic analysis of the crowd through the study of Home Office correspondence, contemporary newspapers, police reports, and criminal statistics has enabled us to establish who participated in these disorders and to offer some explanations for their participation. In the context of the latter, however, our understanding of the causes, character, and frequency of such disorders beyond South Lancashire and the West Midlands is at best patchy. There is, indeed ample scope for the systematic and diachronic study of these less serious anti-Irish disorders, particularly in those towns and regions whose immigrant Irish populations have not, thus far, received a great deal of attention from historians.

For example, Frank Neal has shown the value of such an approach in a recent study of English-Irish conflict in the northeast of England—a region where it was long held that the English and the Irish lived and worked in relative harmony.[38] Neal has traced a dozen serious disorders and numerous less serious disturbances in the towns and pit villages of Northumberland and Durham between 1847 and 1877. Seven of the major clashes, in Durham (1856), Jarrow (1869), Hebburn (1873), and Consett (1868, 1870, 1871, and 1877), appear to have arisen largely from the activities of the Orange Order. In contrast, three disturbances—in Newcastle (1847), Shotley Bridge (1847), and Durham (1858)—involved clashes between English and Irish workers and were motivated primarily by local economic factors. The less-serious disorders had a range of causes, but cultural differences caused most of the resentment. The Irish were considered different on account of accent, clothing, politics, and religion. These cultural differences, suggests Neal, were collectively and wrongly described as "race."

Yet Neal's study also shows that some of the factors that apparently contributed to Anglo-Irish conflict in other parts of England were largely absent in the northeast. The regional economy, based on coal, iron, and shipbuilding, expanded during the period, and there is no evidence that the Irish had an adverse effect on real wages. The scale of Irish immigration simply was not big enough. In addition, the vitriolic anti-Catholicism of South Lancashire was almost totally absent, and press concern over the alleged financial burden of the Irish poor was relatively muted. Nevertheless, Neal's examination of the local newspapers reveals a lengthy catalogue of ugly clashes between the English and Irish—sometimes instigated by the former, sometimes by the latter—which resulted in eleven deaths and six capital convictions for murder during the period.[39]

Second, our knowledge of anti-Irish violence, including popular disorders, has been based largely on qualitative evidence (dramatic but often impressionistic) rather than quantitative, and it could be argued that this imbalance has distorted our understanding of the realities of communal relations in those towns where the Irish settled. Indeed, systematic studies of the statistics of anti-Irish violence during the Victorian period as a whole have yet to be undertaken on national, regional, or local levels. Yet, while an aggregate study of the statistics of anti-Irish violence might well be an immense, if not almost impossible task, local studies of the criminal statistics are clearly both possible and practical. Of course, statistical evidence has its limitations. In this context, it would only provide information about recorded acts of violence against the Irish at a time when much anti-Irish violence, notably violence in the workplace and individual attacks on Irish people, probably went unreported. Moreover, while it is relatively easy to trace Irish-born persons in the statistics, if second- and third-generation Irish men, women, and juveniles, born in England of Irish parents but retaining an Irish identity, are brought into the equation, the task is much more difficult. Indeed, this reflects a definitional and methodological conundrum that has to some extent bedevilled the study of the Irish immigrant experience during the nineteenth century, and particularly during the late-Victorian period.[40]

Third, while it is clear that the incidence of anti-Irish disorders was neither as widespread nor prolonged as some historians have suggested, varying as it did in time and place, the reasons for this still remain unclear. Indeed, further local research can only serve to enhance our understanding of the reasons why intercommunal violence was particularly marked in some towns and regions, but appears to have operated at a far lower level— if at all—in others. For example, we know a great deal about communal relations in the industrial towns of Victorian Lancashire,[41] but we need to know much more about communal relations in other regions where there was significant Irish settlement—notably Yorkshire, the East Midlands, and the Southwest. We also need to know much more about the Irish experience in those smaller towns, such as Stafford,[42] whose development and character during the Victorian period were very different from those of great cities such as Liverpool and Manchester. Indeed, a recent study by Kristina Jeffes of communal violence in Chester between 1841 and 1851 has illustrated the value of such an approach. There was, for example, a small but relatively clearly delineated Irish-born population in Chester in 1841 which expanded considerably during the subsequent decade, due largely to Irish immigration during the famine years. Yet it appears that the Chester Irish lived in relative harmony with their neighbors, and the Chester newspapers reported only three minor "Irish rows" during the period.[43]

THE DECLINE OF ANTI-IRISH VIOLENCE

In attempting to assess the extent to which anti-Irish violence declined during the late Victorian period, and the reasons for the decline, it should be emphasized that relatively little is known about the Irish experience in late Victorian England, certainly in comparison with the more detailed and at times dramatic picture that emerges during the mid-Victorian years.[44] However, qualitative evidence would seem to suggest that anti-Irish violence, including public disorders, was relatively scarce after 1870. Indeed, arguably the most serious outburst of violence against the Irish during the period took place not in England but in South Wales, at Tredegar in July 1882. Here, economic rivalries between Irish and Welsh workers, exacerbated by the activities of local Salvationists and compounded by the anti-Irish feeling that had been aroused by the Phoenix Park murders in Dublin in May, resulted in several days of rioting which culminated in the eviction of some 400 Irish men, women, and children.[45] Nevertheless, if anti-Irish violence did decline in England during the period—and this still awaits statistical confirmation, a number of possible explanations for this decline may be advanced.

First, the decline of anti-Irish violence needs to be placed in the broader context of the general decline of violence and the emergence of a more orderly society in late Victorian England, within which improved policing and improved techniques of riot control played their part.[46]

Second, the decline in popular violence against the Irish was a reflection of the changing face of protest in the context of the growth of more organized and institutional procedures for expressing working-class grievances, the impact of political and social reform, and the distinctive cultural influences that shaped English society during the late nineteenth century. Indeed, by the 1880s and 1890s, working-class Irish men and women were making an important contribution to a growing labor movement, most notably in the context of the "new unionism."[47]

Third, it has been generally assumed that just as the sudden increase in anti-Irish violence was a consequence of the famine influx coupled with mid-Victorian fears of Catholicism, a subsequent decrease in Irish immigration, newcomers, and hosts enabled an accommodation as the Catholic church became less of a threat and more a part of the religious fabric of the nation. Thus, Irish immigration and its consequences were no longer a contentious issue, and the Irish were integrated into the institutions and social life of the areas in which they lived, with a pattern of development that had been interrupted by the famine immigration and the revival of anti-Catholic feeling. This thesis fits the chronology, shows hosts and new-comers as adaptable, and explains the persistence of violence in cities such as Liverpool. However, as Alan O'Day has observed, it is important to recognize that anti-Catholicism did not fade around 1870: Witness the per-sistence of the denominational education issue after 1870, and the revival of the Liberal Nonconformist cry of "Rome on the Rates" in the aftermath of the 1902 Education Act.[48]

Fourth, it is possible that economic growth in the second half of the nineteenth century may have helped to reduce ethnic rivalries.[49] Yet the late Victorian economy did not necessarily offer grounds for a softening of racial conflict in England. The economy was contracting as anti-Irish vio-lence declined: Industrial expansion slowed, agriculture was depressed, and emigration rose. Indeed, the Irish could well have been perceived as a greater economic threat during this period, but, significantly, immigration from Ireland was declining. Ironically, the perceived threat in the 1880s and 1890s came not from the Irish, but from the thousands of poor Jewish immigrants fleeing from persecution in Eastern Europe. These Jewish im-migrants received a reception from the English that was as hostile as that accorded to the Irish forty years earlier.[50] As David Englander has shown, Jewish immigrants appear to have been far more quiescent and much more determined to keep to themselves than the Irish, although communal ten-sions sometimes ran high in those East London streets colonized by both Jewish and Irish immigrants.[51]

Fifth, there were influences within Irish communities that may well have contributed to a decline in anti-Irish violence. For example, the vast ma-jority of the Irish in England sought to avoid brutal confrontations and were often quick to assert their loyalty to the crown, as their response to the Clerkenwell bombings indicates. Although some retained a sympathy for Irish nationalist aspirations, this was tempered by an absence of support for Fenian violence, which was an embarrassment to the Irish in England. Moreover, although Ireland's grievances were at the center of British pol-itics after 1870, the Irish in England were reluctant to get involved with Irish Nationalist groups and were gradually absorbed into mainstream Brit-ish politics, supporting the Liberal Party after Gladstone's conversion to Home Rule in 1886.[52] The Roman Catholic clergy also worked to soften intracommunal relations during the late nineteenth and early twentieth cen-turies, and helped to prevent a polarization in British society that might otherwise have fostered the temptation to single out the Irish as targets.[53]

Finally, the tendency for the Irish to disperse both between and within English cities (as many of the "Little Irelands" of early Victorian England disappeared), and to integrate and disappear into English society over time (as a dynamic rather than static group), reduced their exposure to riots and other expressions of ethnic hate. Thus it could be argued that the Irish became an increasingly evasive target for physical assaults,[54] although the extent of this would have varied from place to place. Indeed, Steven Fielding has illustrated recently how a distinctive Irish Catholic ethnic consciousness—and the communal tensions that accompanied it—was able to survive in Manchester up to and beyond World War II.[55]

CONCLUSION

Explanations for the gradual and relative decline in the incidence of anti-Irish violence in Victorian England remain tentative. While the number of recorded incidents against Irish people during the period may well have been relatively few and heavily concentrated in certain towns, notably in Lancashire, it is possible that anti-Irish sentiment was expressed in more subtle and less public ways within working-class communities.[56] Thus Alan O'Day has suggested that psychological terror, small-scale brawls, attacks on individuals, and a routine diet of discrimination rather than regularized mob violence were the more usual weapons by which the natives vented their aggressions on the Irish,[57] although these await scholarly analysis. Indeed, it is important to recognize that anti-Irish feeling continued throughout the late nineteenth and twentieth centuries, particularly at moments of crisis in Anglo-Irish political relations. The extent to which this was translated into acts of violence against Irish people will remain problematic until substantial research has been conducted. Such studies are crucial to our understanding of the causes and nature of prejudice in the broader context of the experiences of immigrants and minorities in Victorian society.

NOTES

This chapter is a revised version of a paper prepared for the Social History Society Conference on "Crime, the Law and Criminal Justice," which was held at the University of Luton in January 1994. I am particularly grateful to Clive Emsley and Alan O'Day for their advice and assistance.

1. See, for example, Roger Swift, "Crime and the Irish in Nineteenth-Century Britain," in *The Irish in Britain, 1815–1939*, ed. Roger Swift and Sheridan Gilley (London, 1989), 163–82; Frank Neal, "A Criminal Profile of the Liverpool Irish," *Transactions of the Historic Society of Lancashire and Cheshire* 140 (1991):161–99.

2. Alan O'Day, "Varieties of Anti-Irish Behaviour in Britain, 1846–1922," in

Racial Violence in Britain, 1840–1950, ed. Panikos Panayi (Leicester and London, 1993), 26–43.

3. See, for example, John Denvir, *The Irish in Britain* (London, 1892), 157–59, 460–62.

4. *The Nation,* 6 June 1868.

5. See, for example, J. E. Handley, *The Irish in Scotland, 1798–1845* (Cork, 1945), 141–68; J. E. Handley, *The Irish in Modern Scotland* (Cork, 1947), 93–121; J. A. Jackson, *The Irish in Britain* (London, 1963), 40–51.

6. Sheridan Gilley, "English Attitudes to the Irish in England, 1780–1900," in *Immigrants and Minorities in British Society,* ed. Colin Holmes (London, 1978), 81–110.

7. O'Day, "Varieties of Anti-Irish Behaviour," 26.

8. Graham Davis, "Little Irelands," in Swift and Gilley, *The Irish in Britain,* 104–33.

9. See, for example, Neville Kirk, "Ethnicity, Class and Popular Toryism, 1850–1870," in *Hosts, Immigrants and Minorities,* ed. Kenneth Lunn (Folkestone, 1980), 64–106.

10. See, for example, Tom Gallagher, "A Tale of Two Cities: Communal Strife in Glasgow and Liverpool Before 1914," in *The Irish in the Victorian City,* ed. Roger Swift and Sheridan Gilley (London, 1985), 106–29; Frank Neal, *Sectarian Violence: The Liverpool Experience 1819–1914* (Manchester, 1988), 37–79, 151–75; Frank Neal, "Manchester Origins of the English Orange Order," *Manchester Region History Review* (Autumn, 1990), 12–24.

11. See especially W. L. Arnstein, "The Murphy Riots: A Victorian Dilemma," *Victorian Studies* 19 (1975): 55–71; Donald Richter, *Riotous Victorians* (London, 1970), 35–50; Roger Swift, "Anti-Catholicism and Irish Disturbances: Public Order in Mid-Victorian Wolverhampton," *Midland History* 9 (1984):87–108.

12. W. J. Lowe, "Lancashire Fenianism, 1864–71," *Transactions of the Historic Society of Lancashire and Cheshire* 121 (1977):156–85; Patrick Quinlivan and Paul Rose, *The Fenians in England, 1865–72* (London, 1982), 43–94.

13. Arthur Redford, *Labour Migration in England, 1800–1850* (London, 1926; rev. ed. Manchester, 1964), 159–64.

14. Jeffrey G. Williamson, "The Impact of the Irish on British Labour Markets During the Industrial Revolution," *Journal of Economic History* 46 (Sept. 1986), 693–721.

15. E. P. Thompson, *The Making of the English Working Class* (London, 1963), 469–85; J. Foster, *Class Struggle and the Industrial Revolution* (London, 1974), 333.

16. Kirk, "Ethnicity, Class and Popular Toryism," 64–106.

17. Swift and Gilley, *The Irish in the Victorian City,* 1–12.

18. Swift and Gilley, *The Irish in Britain,* 1–9; see also Brenda Collins, "The Irish in Britain, 1780–1921," in *An Historical Geography of Ireland,* ed. B. J. Graham and L. J. Proudfoot (London, 1993), 366–98.

19. Handley, *The Irish in Scotland,* 260–61.

20. "Report of the Select Committee on the Police of the Metropolis," *Parliamentary Papers* (1817), 151.

21. For further details of the growth of the Orange Order, see especially H. Senior, *Orangeism in Ireland and Britain, 1795–1835* (London, 1966).

22. Gallagher, "A Tale of Two Cities," 106–29.

23. Neal, *Sectarian Violence,* 196–249; see also the essays by Anne Bryson, "Riotous Liverpool, 1815–1860," and John Bohstedt, "More than One Working Class: Protestant and Catholic Riots in Edwardian Liverpool," in *Popular Politics, Riot and Labour: Essays in Liverpool History 1790–1940,* ed. John Belchem (Liverpool, 1992), 98–134, 173–216.

24. See especially Victor Bailey, "Salvation Army Riots, the 'Skeleton Army' and Legal Authority in the Provincial Town," in *Social Control in Nineteenth Century Britain,* ed. A. P. Donajgrodzki (London, 1977), 231–53; Norman H. Murdoch, "From Militancy to Social Mission: The Salvation Army and Street Disturbances in Liverpool, 1879–1887," in Belchem, *Popular Politics, Riot and Labour,* 160–72.

25. "Report of the Royal Commission to Inquire into the Best Means of Establishing an Efficient Constabulary Force in the Counties of England and Wales," *Parliamentary Papers* (1839), 169, xix, 87.

26. Ibid., 88.

27. "Report to the Board of Health on the Sanitary Condition of Wolverhampton," *Parliamentary Papers* (1849), 28.

28. W. J. Lowe, *The Irish in Mid-Victorian Lancashire* (New York, 1989), 102.

29. B. Weinburger, "The Police and the Public in Mid-Nineteenth Century Warwickshire," in *Policing and Punishment in Nineteenth Century Britain,* ed. Victor Bailey (London, 1982), 69–71.

30. Terry Coleman, *The Railway Navvies* (London, 1965), 83–90.

31. Roger Swift, "Another Stafford Street Row: Law, Order and the Irish Presence in Mid-Victorian Wolverhampton," *Immigrants and Minorities* 3 (1984): 5–29.

32. Coleman, *The Railway Navvies,* 84.

33. See especially Pauline Millward, "The Stockport Riots of 1852: A Study of Anti-Catholic and Anti-Irish Sentiment," in Swift and Gilley, *The Irish in the Victorian City,* 207–24.

34. Foster, *Class Struggle and the Industrial Revolution,* 343–46.

35. Richter, *Riotous Victorians,* 35–50.

36. Millward, "The Stockport Riots of 1852," 217–20.

37. Swift, "Anti-Catholicism and Irish Disturbances," 87.

38. See, for example, R. J. Cooter, "The Irish in County Durham and Newcastle, 1840–1880" (M.A. thesis, University of Durham, 1973).

39. Frank Neal, "English-Irish Conflict in the North-East of England," in *The Irish in British Labour History,* ed. Patrick Buckland and John Belchem (Liverpool, 1993), 59–85.

40. Roger Swift, "The Historiography of the Irish in Nineteenth-Century Britain: Some Perspectives," in Buckland and Belchem, *The Irish in British Labour History,* 11–18.

41. Lowe, *The Irish in Mid-Victorian Lancashire,* 145–78.

42. John Herson, "Irish Migration and Settlement in Victorian England: A Small-Town Perspective," in Swift and Gilley, *The Irish in Britain,* 84–103.

43. Kristina Jeffes, "The Irish in Chester, 1841 to 1851: An Outcast Community?" (B.A. thesis, University of Manchester, 1991), Ch. 3, "Crime, Disorder and Communal Violence: Aspects of Irish alienation," 44–68.

44. Roger Swift, "The Historiography of the Irish in Nineteenth-Century Britain," in *The Irish World Wide, Vol. 2., The Irish in the New Communities,* ed. Patrick O'Sullivan (London, 1992), 52–81.

45. Jon Parry, "The Tredegar Anti-Irish Riots of 1882," *Llafur* 3 (1983): 20–23; see also Denvir, *The Irish in Britain,* 294–312.

46. John Stevenson, *Popular Disturbances in England 1700–1870* (London, 1979) 316–23; Clive Emsley, *Policing and its Context, 1750–1870* (London, 1983), 132–47.

47. Roger Swift, *The Irish in Britain 1815–1914: Perspectives and Sources* (London, 1990), 16.

48. O'Day, "Varieties of Anti-Irish Behaviour," 37.

49. E. H. Hunt, *British Labour History, 1815–1914* (London, 1981), 164–75.

50. See, for example, Chaim Bermant, *London's East End: Point of Arrival* (London, 1974), 138–63; James Walvin, *Passage to Britain: Immigration in British History and Politics* (London, 1984), 61–75; Colin Holmes, *John Bull's Island: Immigration and British Society, 1871–1971* (London, 1988), 56–83; V. D. Lipman, *A History of the Jews in Britain Since 1858* (Leicester, 1990), 43–88.

51. David Englander, "Booth's Jews: The Presentation of Jews and Judaism in *Life and Labour of the People in London,*" *Victorian Studies* 32 (1988–1989): 551–71.

52. See especially Alan O'Day, "Irish Influence on Parliamentary Elections in London, 1885–1914: A Simple Test," in Swift and Gilley, *The Irish in the Victorian City,* 98–105; and Alan O'Day, "The Political Organisation of the Irish in Britain, 1867–90," in Swift and Gilley, *The Irish in Britain,* 183–211.

53. O'Day, "Varieties of Anti-Irish Behaviour," 39.

54. Ibid., 40.

55. Steven Fielding, *Class and Ethnicity: Irish Catholics in England, 1880–1939* (Buckingham, 1993), 79–126.

56. See, for example, Robert Roberts, *The Classic Slum: Salford Life in the First Quarter of the Century* (London, 1971), 6–7, 84–85.

57. O'Day, "Varieties of Anti-Irish Behaviour," 26.

Minorities Policing Minorities as a Strategy of Social Control: A Historical Analysis of Tribal Police in the United States

David E. Barlow
University of Wisconsin, Milwaukee

INTRODUCTION

While on a campaign to apprehend a "hostile" band of Apache in the Arizona Indian Territory, a cavalry officer stated that using standard tactics there was "like chasing deer with a brass band."[1] A recognition of the clumsy and awkward inefficiency of traditional white culture techniques of investigation, travel, and conflict in this alien land led the army to employ Native Americans as U.S. Army scouts. David Roberts explains that "the Army's success in pacifying most of [the Apache] depended on enlisting warriors from one band to track and fight against those of another."[2] It is within this context that the first tribal police began to emerge.[3] The purpose of this chapter is to explore the development of tribal police in the United States, and to consider tribal police as an example of minorities policing minorities as a strategy for social control.

When an alien culture attempts to repress the activities of another, it is not surprising if the social control agents of the repressive culture feel as if they are "chasing deer with a brass band." If the social control agents are not a part of the culture that they are attempting to suppress, they typically lack an understanding of the people. Therefore, they cannot anticipate their actions or predict their movements. Communication is hindered because the agents of social control lack an understanding of the people's language, customs, and values. This leads to inaccurate information, poor cooperation, confusion, frustration, and ultimately unnecessary violence and the use of force.[4] The lack of legitimacy that inheres in the control of one culture by another, together with the strategic difficulties involved in controlling a truly alien culture, necessitate rule by force. That force is typically crude and awkward because the agents of control are ignorant with regard to the people they are policing.

HISTORY OF TRIBAL POLICE

The War Department

According to William T. Hagan, before the last quarter of the nineteenth century, Indian reservations were largely regulated by federal troops.[5] This observation is supported by the official domination of the War Department over Indian affairs until 1849. The Office of Superintendent of Indian Trade was established in the War Department in 1806. The secretary of war, John C. Calhoun, created the Bureau of Indian Affairs within the Department of War. Even after the department lost its official status as supervisor of Indian affairs in 1849, for all practical purposes it continued to dominate the day-to-day operations on reservations, especially those on the Western plains and in the Southwest.[6]

Although federal troops were the primary agents of social control on Indian reservations, soon after the birth of this nation's government the U.S. Congress sought to "civilize" the American Indian by bringing Western law to Indian Country. Vine Deloria, Jr. and Clifford M. Lytle identify the Indian Interstate Act of 1790 as the first federal legislation designed for this purpose.[7] The act dealt with crimes committed by non-Indians against Indians. If the Indians could catch a suspect and bring the offender to the U.S. Federal or Territorial Court, and if the defendant was convicted by an all-white jury, then the non-Indian would receive the same punishment as would be applied when a victim was a non-Indian. In 1796, punishment was established for Indians who crossed state and territorial lines and committed any of various offenses. Inciting Indians against the United States became a crime in 1800. In the War of 1812's Treaty of Ghent, Congress placed Indian tribes in the United States under federal jurisdiction, and in 1817 Congress established a new system of criminal justice applicable to both Indians and non-Indians within Indian country. Both came under federal jurisdiction and were deemed to receive the same punishment as any other offender within federal jurisdiction. The only exceptions were offenses involving Indians against another Indian. This act, therefore, recognized the internal sovereignty of the tribe.[8]

William T. Hagan explained that the Indian Intercourse Act of 1790 and its amendments led to the placement of Anglo-Saxon-style federal judges and marshals in charge of enforcing the federal law on Indian reservations.[9] Although the "Courts of Federal Regulation" hung many people, they had little impact on social control. Indian country was very dangerous and life was cheap. Many infamous outlaws, including Bob Dalton, Belle Starr, Bill Cook, Smokey Mankiller, and Blue Duck, found Indian country a safe haven from justice. The military, as the primary enforcer of law and order, was equally incapable of protecting the Indians on the reservation.[10] Hagan further suggested that not only did Indians have to endure being victimized by the outlaws, but when one of their own was arrested they experienced a new form of victimization.[11] When Indians were arrested by the federal marshals they were thrust into a foreign criminal justice system that left them lost and confused. They were frequently transported to courts hundreds of miles away, and expected to mount a defense in a language and culture they did not understand.

Although the Eastern reservations, largely populated by the so-called "civilized" tribes, greatly resented the intrusion of federal marshals into their nation, they adjusted much more easily to the process than the nomadic and militaristic Plains and Southwestern tribes.[12] The first pieces of legislation were directed toward the Eastern reservations. As the United States' sphere of influence and domination spread westward, these same policies were transferred to the Western reservations, but not without great difficulty.

The Thirsty Indian and Trade and Intercourse Act of 1834 and its amendments attempted to confront the vast and diverse frontier. These acts shied away from domestic law and eventually removed from federal jurisdiction "offenses committed by Indians against non-Indians in Indian Country who had 'been punished by the local law of the tribe.' "[13] Two exceptions were arson and assault with intent to kill or maim. The idea was that if Indians and non-Indians were not able to burn or kill each other, peace would come to the frontier.[14]

The Department of the Interior

In 1849 the Bureau of Indian Affairs was moved from the War Department and placed in the newly formed Department of the Interior. A shift in public opinion was taking place, at least in Washington and on the East Coast, toward peace and away from militaristic solutions. As the Indian wars became more distant to those in the East, sympathy toward Indians grew, as did the desire to assimilate them into the American way of life.[15] Wilcomb E. Washburn identified another reason for this shift in focus—land acquisition.[16] As separate nations, the tribes retained valuable land that the new nation wanted. As tribe members became assimilated land owners, this land could be opened for settlement and exploited.

From the beginning, early efforts to force an Anglo-Saxon judicial system upon the Indians were rooted in an attempt to Christianize, civilize, and assimilate the indigenous populations into white European culture.[17] In 1806, President Thomas Jefferson articulated this grand design in a speech to a delegation of Indians:

When once you have property, you will want laws and magistrates to protect your property and persons. . . . You will find that our laws are good for this purpose.

. . . You will unite yourselves with us . . . form one people with us, and we shall all be Americans.[18]

This speech also foreshadowed the government's efforts, through allotment, to force tribes to embrace the value of private property over their deeply rooted culture of communal life. In sum, the process of privatizing the land meant breaking the Indians' communal monopolistic control over the land within the reservation and creating new opportunities for land acquisition by white Americans.[19]

Although the Bureau of Indian Affairs was removed from the direct, official control of the War Department in 1849, for all practical purposes the military remained the primary enforcer of law and order on the reservation. With no mode of enforcement other than the military available to the Indian agents, they were often puppets of the local federal troops. The War Department was not pleased with the loss of the Bureau of Indian Affairs and continued to lobby for its return. Opposition to the military's supervision of Indian affairs, however, became more intense following the end of the Civil War. The general public was war-weary from the four-year ordeal and the military was downsizing rapidly. As the last of the Indian Wars were underway in the West, the people of the United States were forming a "revulsion against the seemingly endless bloodletting on the Plains."[20] In addition, the conflicting policies in Washington, D.C. perpetuated the confusion that existed in the Bureau of Indian Affairs. At the same time, the bureau was confronted with a series of revelations about graft and corruption in the administration of reservations.[21]

The culmination of these events "led to the re-examination of our basic approach to the Indian problem."[22] The first such effort was the 1865 Congressional committee investigation, which concluded that Indians were on the road to extinction. This investigation led to an 1867 commission to eliminate the causes of Plains warfare in three ways: (1) concentrating the Indian populations within reservations, (2) extending the federal government's control over Indians on reservations, and (3) utilizing missionaries and teachers to assist in the civilization of Indians.[23] In 1868, the Peace Commission met in Chicago and presented the president and the Congress with a set of resolutions to feed, clothe, and protect Indians living on reservations.[24] The people and the press in the East were seriously dissatisfied with the role of the military in Indian affairs. "General George Cook, Commander of the Department of Arizona, was pursuing a policy which appeared to the East to be brutally harsh."[25] These people were also concerned about the demoralizing impact the troops were having on the process of civilizing Indians.[26]

The Society of Friends was a major actor in the construction of President Ulysses S. Grant's new "peace policy." Upon President Grant's election, it was anticipated that he would return the Bureau of Indian Affairs to the

War Department. The Quakers, however, successfully lobbied the president and Congress to keep the bureau from under the control of the War Department. The Quakers wanted to "civilize" American Indians while the army wanted to eliminate them or, at least, keep them secure as prisoners of war. The Quakers envisioned self-government as the key to civilization and eventual assimilation. In 1869, the Society of Friends was able to convince President Grant to develop a new approach, often referred to as Grant's Quaker or Peace Policy. An essential part of this policy included the agreement that the president's administration would seek recommendations from church groups for appointments to Indian service. In addition, the Civilian Board of Indian Affairs was established to advise the government on Indian affairs, and to exercise joint control with the secretary of the interior to administer funds. Even with all these major events, the most significant factor in the physical removal of federal troops from the day-to-day regulation of Indian country is probably the phenomenal success of tribal police and courts.[27]

The Origin and Success of Tribal Police

According to William T. Hagan, the development of tribal police served two purposes.[28] The first goal of those who sought to establish tribal police was to secure peace on the reservation by settling disputes, enforcing federal regulations, tracking and capturing fugitives, and making sure that tribes stayed on the reservation. The tribal police were the eyes and ears of the Indian agents responsible for the maintenance of the reservation. Another major role of the tribal police was to expel white intruders who cut timber, gathered nuts, fished, hunted, stole horses, and grazed cattle on Native American land.[29]

The goal of maintaining order on the reservation is clearly reflected in the early efforts to appoint tribal members responsible for "policing" the reservation. In 1874, Indian Agent John P. Clum came to the San Carlos Indian Agency in the Arizona Territory to administer the Apache reservations. He was placed in charge of a rough, mountainous area about the size of Connecticut. The reservation was in a state of disorder, with continual rebellion and violence. The military had a continual presence and dictated to the former agents. Clum transformed this situation by pushing for self-government. He appointed a handful of Apache to serve as social control agents, or "tribal police," and hired a white man, Clay Beuford, to serve as the Apache Tribal Police Chief.

These newly created tribal police were extremely successful. Clum's records suggest that in approximately two years he and his small group of tribal police (never more than twenty-five) captured or killed 159 "renegades," including Geronimo and his fifty followers. According to Hagan, Clum reported that "our little squad of Indian Police [has] done more effective scouting . . . than General Kautz has done with all his troops and four companies of Indian Scouts."[30] When General August V. Kautz complained to the secretary of the interior about Clum, the secretary sent an inspector to investigate. The inspector "alleged that Clum had been subjected to 'persistent and bitter opposition from military authorities,' but, 'by the aid of his Indian Police force accomplished far more than [Kautz] with his two regiments of regulation soldiers to assist.'"[31]

The phenomenal success of the San Carlos Tribal Police led to the virtual elimination of the military presence on the reservation in three months. Their continual success staved off repeated efforts by the U.S. Cavalry to discredit Clum and move back in. During the 1870s, tribal police were established by Indian reservation agents on the reservations of the Pawnee, Klamoth, Madoc, Navajo, Apache, Blackfeet, Chippewa, and Sioux. The creation of Indian police forces was officially authorized in 1878. By 1880 two-thirds of the Indian reservation agencies had Indian police. Even though they were poorly paid, tribal police had to provide their own mounts and were often not supplied guns or ammunition.[32]

The second goal in the establishment of tribal police was to expedite assimilation of the aboriginal people to the white European culture of the dominant society. Hagan explains that the purpose for establishing tribal police was to "civilize" the Indians by undermining the power of tribal chiefs and weakening traditional lines of self-government.[33] As the two cultures clashed, Native Americans were forced to conform to Western, Anglo standards of conduct. Tribal police were often used to curtail recreational activities (such as horse stealing and gambling) that were viewed as criminal by the dominant white culture. They were also responsible for suppressing their own tribal religion by opposing the influence of medicine men, confronting witches, and stopping unwanted activities such as the old "heathen" dances (e.g., the Sundance and the Scalpdance). In addition, tribal police were instructed to force the tribe's children to attend the Indian boarding schools.[34]

Hagan explained that these enforcement activities were especially difficult, both morally and physically, for the tribal police.[35] Not only did their efforts to break long-held traditions turn many former friends and family members into enemies, their actions often directly conflicted with their own religious beliefs. In addition, the extremely high mortality rate of those children who attended the Indian boarding schools, combined with the numerous violent confrontations associated with forcing the children to attend, made this duty especially morally and physically challenging. These schools were notorious for beating the Indian language and culture out of the children. Many police resigned because they could not enforce the rules that specifically confronted their religious beliefs and killed their children. However, in case after case, the tribal police showed tremendous courage and loyalty to the Indian agents. Although they were involved in numerous shoot-outs and controversial enforcement policies, their actions helped prevent massacres. As a result, the use of troops declined.[36]

One may question why the tribal police were so successful for the Indian agents. First, they were carefully recruited. The agents selected those tribal members who were considered progressives; that is, those who displayed a willingness to adapt to the ways of the whites. The more traditional or conservative members, those who resisted assimilation, were rejected. Second, the agents gave high preference to ex-U.S. Scouts because they had military experience and had been exposed to Western European discipline. In addition, agents tried to select representatives from each clan within the tribe.[37] Finally, Wilcomb E. Washburn suggests that the

prestige and power, the right to bear arms among fellow warriors deprived of their arms, the privilege of wearing formal uniforms expressing that authority, and the frequent scouting and teaching missions against renegades, gave back to the Indian something he thought he had lost forever.[38]

In other words, tribal police officers could envision themselves as the last of the warriors.[39]

Self-Determination v. Social Control

Washburn expresses the dual purpose of the tribal police and courts in the following passage:

The origin of Indian police and Indian courts derives not, as might be thought, from an attempt to allow or give a measure of self-government to the Indians. The reverse is true. Indian police and courts were created in large measure for the purpose of controlling the Indian and breaking up tribal leadership and tribal government.[40]

Although the establishment of tribal police was authorized in 1878, no specific provisions had been made for the trial and punishment of offenders until 1883, with the creation of the first formal Courts of Indian Offenses by Secretary of the Interior H. M. Teller. The contradictory goals of self-government and social control continued to be reflected in this effort to formulate tribal governments. According to Washburn, the secretary established the courts because he wanted "to eradicate 'certain of the old heathenish dances; such as the sundance, scalp-dance, & C.' as well as to attack the institution of polygamy, the power of medicine men, and other Indian customs."[41] The tribal judges were appointed by, and served at the pleasure of, the Indian agent.[42]

The lack of real commitment to true self-government by Native American tribal nations is reflected in the passage of the Major Crimes Act of 1885, which was a reaction to the U.S. Supreme Court decision in *Ex Parte Crow Dog* (109 U.S. 556, 1883). On the Rosebud Reservation in the territory of Dakota, a very popular Brule Sioux chief was killed by a Sioux Indian named Crow Dog. Vine Deloria, Jr. and Clifford M. Lytle explained that "Spotted Tail had been a pliant and peaceful chief who acted as a buffer between the United States and the more aggressive Sioux leaders, such as Red Cloud, Sitting Bull, and Crazy Horse."[43] Spotted Tail was well rewarded by the federal government for his progovernment position and peace counseling. Many of the other chiefs were resentful of the favoritism, special privileges, power to select tribal police officers, and two-story house that the federal government had bestowed upon Spotted Tail.[44] Captain Crow Dog of the Indian police became the leader of a rival faction that wanted to challenge Spotted Tail's authority.[45] When Spotted Tail began to take up with the other chiefs' wives, Crow Dog resigned from the tribal police force and shot and killed him at point-blank range.[46]

Much like other communal societies, many American Indian tribes including the Sioux traditionally have social equilibrium as the ultimate goal in resolving transgressions. Western jurisprudence, with its emphasis on retribution, was often met with complete confusion by these tribes. Many stories exist involving interactions between whites and Indians where each party tried to resolve transgressions against each other within their own traditional ways, and the opposite culture interpreted the techniques of resolution by the other culture as shockingly barbaric.[47] Historically, whites have misinterpreted the role of the Indian chief as similar to the rulers found in the European experience, such as kings. For example, Europeans continuously sought out "the" chief of a particular Indian tribe to make agreements and treaties for the entire tribe. On the contrary, the members of one tribe may have shared a common language and ancestry, but they were often very fragmented and organized under clans and representative chiefs. This situation was especially true among the nomadic tribes. In addition, such chiefs acted primarily as mediators of conflict, striving to maintain social cohesion and equilibrium. The chief sought to create satisfaction among all parties rather than to establish guilt or innocence. It was not uncommon for chiefs to pay restitution to an injured party from their own property in order to keep peace.[48]

In keeping with this tradition, the two families of Crow Dog and Spotted Tail met in order to resolve the murder of Spotted Tail. His relatives eagerly accepted the proposed compensation offered by Crow Dog's family for the purpose of preventing a continuing feud. When the white public and the federal government officials who had befriended Spotted Tail discovered that not only was Crow Dog not going to be executed, but he was not even going to appear before the tribal court, protests erupted and the federal government arrested Crow Dog. Crow Dog was tried, convicted, and sentenced to hang in the federal territorial court in Deadwood, Dakota

Territory. To the shock of many, the federal marshall agreed to release Crow Dog so that he could settle his affairs at home. Although many people wagered that Crow Dog would never return, he struggled through a snow storm to arrive at the appointed time. As a result, Crow Dog became a hero in the eyes of the public. Viewing him as a noble and honorable man, newspapers and attorneys volunteered to take a writ of habeas corpus to the U.S. Supreme Court, and eventually the Congress voted to pay his legal expenses. Citing an exception in the legislation of 1817, the Thirsty Indian and Trade and Intercourse Act of 1834, and the General Crimes Act of 1854, the Supreme Court ruled that Congress had clearly established tribal jurisdiction over crimes involving an Indian against another Indian while in Indian Country. Crow Dog was granted his writ and released.[49]

Although the white public may have been relieved that this noble and honorable "savage" was released, they continued to view the failure of the tribal justice system to execute Crow Dog as a sign that Indian justice was savage and primitive, and in need of greater efforts to Christianize and civilize the justice process. Public pressure on Congress led to the Major Crimes Act of 1885.[50] With no hearings or expressions of Indian opinions, extensive federal intrusion into tribal self-government occurred. Congress transferred jurisdiction to the federal government for seven major crimes when committed by an Indian in Indian country. These crimes were murder, manslaughter, rape, assault with the intent to kill, arson, burglary, and larceny. The reservations in Oklahoma that held the Five Civilized Tribes (Cherokee, Choctaw, Creek, Chickasaw, and Seminole) were exempt because their tribal justice system had already developed an Anglo-American system of government by the 1860s. The list of applicable crimes was expanded in 1909, and several more times throughout the twentieth century. Washburn suggested that the "Seven Major Crimes Act of 1885 . . . illustrated the persistent congressional effort to eliminate by legislation the legal distinctions between the Indian and the non-Indian population in the United States."[51]

The desire to remove Indians from special legal status was further advanced by the General Allotment or Dawes Severalty Act of 1887, which dealt tribal police, courts, and governments a crippling blow. So-called "friends" of the Indians, such as Massachusetts Senator Henry Dawes, agreed with the comments of people like President Thomas Jefferson, who felt that private property was the key to "civilizing" the Indian and ultimately assimilating them into white European America. "Private property [federal officials] believed, had mystical magical qualities about it that led people directly to a 'civilized' state."[52] The expressed feeling was that teaching the Indian the value of private property and individualism was an essential step toward integration.[53] A convergence of ideologies occurred as the "enemies" of the Indians also supported this act because they envisioned the opportunity to obtain valuable land that had been protected by the communal property status of the reservations. White land-grabbers sought to acquire cheap land from the Indians by thrusting them into the world of competition and individualism. The only people who did not like this new piece of legislation were the Indians.[54]

The Dawes Act was the result of a massive drive toward "severalty" or "allotment."[55] This act was an effort to destroy the tribal customs of communal ownership of land. It empowered the president to take segments of reservation land away from the tribes and give it to individual tribe members.[56] Hagan noted that those who received allotments would be given preference for tribal police appointments.[57] Twenty-five years after initially receiving an allotment of land, the title to the land was given to the respective Indian, free of restrictions against sale. Once an Indian received title, citizenship was granted and the Indian was placed under the civil and criminal jurisdiction of the state or territory. As the white land-grabbers became impatient, however, the Burk Act of 1906 was passed to accelerate the allotment process. The act led to many of the allotments of land being sold to whites.[58] It should also be noted that "surplus land" that was not allotted to tribal members was sold directly to whites by the federal government. The effects of this program were devastating to tribal sovereignty, as tribal landholdings dropped from 138 million acres in 1887 to 48 million in 1934. Twenty million of the remaining 48 million acres "were desert or semiarid and virtually useless for any kind of annual farming ventures."[59]

American Indian Policy: 1887–1978

The federal policy toward Indian affairs between 1887 and 1934 centered on the assimilation of individual Indians, the systematic dismantling of traditional tribal cohesion, and the continued intrusion of the federal government. The land within the southwestern desert reservations, on the other hand, was not as desirable as that of most other reservations; thus there was less white interest in allotment for these reservations.[60] In 1924, all Indians were granted U.S. citizenship. A 1928 report by the Institute for Government Research, the Meriam Survey, stated that the "economic base of traditional Indian culture had been destroyed by the encroachment of white civilization."[61]

Even though federal efforts to weaken tribal sovereignty greatly diminished the size and power of tribal police, small pockets of tribal police remained and played an important role in identifying heirs, making up payrolls, acting as handymen, and assisting other law enforcement agencies as informants and trackers. Tribal courts were hit even harder than the police, as many were lost between 1887 and 1934. Most of the tribal courts that remained merely served to record vital statistics and to hold preliminary hearings for off-reservation courts.[62] Washburn explained that, despite federal efforts to destroy communal relationships, degrade chiefs, and eliminate the need for separate tribal governments, many tribes managed to maintain traditional forms of government almost until the passage of the Reorganization Act of 1934.[63]

According to Vine Deloria, Jr. and Clifford M. Lytle, the Indian Reorganization Act of 1934 formally ended the government's policy of allotment as it re-established formal tribal governments.[64] As part of President Franklin D. Roosevelt's New Deal, this act not only admitted the failure of the severalty policy and reversed the Curtis Act, it returned to tribal ownership the surplus Indian lands previously open to sale and acquired additional lands for the reservations. Also known as the Wheeler-Howard Act, it reorganized and encouraged tribal organization by authorizing the establishment of tribal governments and the fostering of tribal economic enterprises. The act enabled tribes to organize for the common welfare and adopt federally approved constitutions and bylaws.[65] Traditional Native Americans criticized these newly formed tribal governments because the constitutions were based on Anglo-American culture and values. Within this act, the tribal justice system was officially ensured jurisdiction over Native Americans who committed misdemeanor offenses on the reservation. The federal government claimed jurisdiction over Native Americans who committed felonies on the reservation and non-Indians who committed any crime against a Native American on the reservation. The states were given jurisdiction over non-Indians who committed crimes against other non-Indians.[66] According to Lawrence French, state governments, for the most part, do not have jurisdiction over matters involving Indian tribes or Indian people in Indian country unless there is a federal statute granting them jurisdiction.[67]

The jurisdiction of the tribal police was also severely restricted due to the U.S. Supreme Court case *Oliphant v. Suquamish* (435 U.S. 1978), which ruled that tribal courts do not have inherent criminal jurisdiction to try non-Indians without specific congressional authorization.[68] As a matter of fact, "no offenses over which Indian tribal courts have jurisdiction carry a penalty of more than six months in jail."[69] The role of tribal police and courts may have been similar to that of the Anglo-American Justice of the Peace, except for the tribal justice system's very limited jurisdiction based on race. The tribal police continue to play an important role in resolving criminal cases on reservations. They are usually the ones who discover the crime, conduct initial interviews, know the personalities and circumstances involved, and provide continued assistance throughout the case. Their recommendations are well respected by the federal government.[70]

AFRICAN-AMERICANS AND NATIVE AMERICANS AS POLICE

The History of African-American Police Officers in the United States

The historical development of local police departments in the United States and the history of African-Americans are closely linked. For example, the earliest recorded police departments are found not in New York or Boston, but in the South. Although the creation of the municipal police department is often attributed to urbanization and industrialization, the first modern-style police department was established in Charleston, South Carolina, in the 1740s. Each of the Southern states soon followed suit. The stated mission of these police agencies was to catch runaway slaves and to maintain discipline and order through the regulation of the routine activities of slaves. They had the power to break into slave homes, punish those traveling without passes, and whip slaves who were not properly obedient. From their inception in this country, police departments were racially segregated in terms of those who could enforce the law and those who were the targets of law enforcement.[71]

Black slavery was a great asset for Southern landowners in that it provided cheap labor. But it was also a liability because Africans did not simply acquiesce to bondage. "African slaves had to be systematically coerced to accept their abasement. . . . White policing of black populations became an integral component of each stage of white racial domination of blacks."[72] Certain slave laws, or "black codes," were enacted to regulate the activities of African-Americans and to protect the social structure from black rebellions. For example, slaves had to have a pass to travel off the plantation. Originally, the enforcement of these slaves codes was largely left to individual white people who wished to confront suspicious blacks. The early police departments or slave patrols were established to coordinate the aggressive enforcement of these regulations. By the 1800s, however, the regulation of free blacks, such as requiring them to carry mandatory freedom papers and register with the mayor upon moving, was also enforced by these patrols. For example, "in 1838 the constable of Raleigh was required to check the entire city and its suburbs no less than two Sundays a month and search any suspect house as a preventive measure against strange blacks moving into town."[73] Although the North did not have slave populations to regulate, many Northern cities did enact laws specifically designed to regulate black populations. This "policing" of the black community, however, was very selective. The police were acutely interested in maintaining order, but were not concerned with enforcing the law with respect to black-on-black crime.[74]

After slavery came to an end following the Civil War, new problems

emerged, particularly in the South. Two fundamental questions that sur-
faced were: (1) how to control this large population of newly freed blacks,
and (2) how to obtain cheap labor to work the plantations and rebuild the
South. The police, along with the entire justice system, sought to solve both
these problems simultaneously. Christopher Adamson explained that the
South adopted a system that had been effective in supplying factory labor
in the North, that is, imprisonment with hard labor combined with a convict lease system.[75] The Southern states, however, directed this new approach more systematically toward freed blacks.[76] Following the Civil War,
the Southern states enacted laws which made it a crime for a black person
to be without written proof of employment. Many of the newly freed blacks
were rounded up under such legislation and placed in prisons that had
developed an elaborate convict-lease system designed to provide cheap convict labor to the plantations.[77] In addition, black orphans, or children who
the court determined could not be supported by their parents, could be
bound over to white employers in apprenticeships. These children could be
forced to provide free labor against the will of their parents and the white
employers could use corporal punishment to discipline them. Essentially,
old forms of slavery were replaced with new ones. Many freed slaves mi-
grated to Northern cities only to be confronted with resentful immigrants
and white police officers enforcing racist laws and policies. For example,
Jim Crow laws were a Northern creation and were only transferred to the
South after slavery ended.[78] Hubert Williams and Patrick Murphy note
that, while traveling through the United States in 1830, Alexis de Tocqueville observed more racism in the North than in the South.[79]

A historical review of policing in the United States reveals that not only
did the police fail to protect African-Americans from slavery, segregation,
and discrimination, they aggressively enforced the laws designed to preserve
this caste system.[80] This fundamental function of the police to maintain the
status quo of current power relations is the source of continued conflict
between police and African-Americans in the United States. For example,
in the race riots of 1917 and 1919, when massive numbers of whites de-
scended upon black townships looting, burning, and killing, the police not
only failed to protect the black residents, they actively assisted the assailants
by disarming blacks. Again, throughout the civil rights movement of the
1960s, police officers again aggressively sought to control blacks and preserve segregation, discrimination, and current power relations.[81]

African-American Police Officers

The historical development of African-American police in the United States
reflects a racial caste-like system. The circumstances of the initial entry of
African-Americans into local police departments differed between North
and South. In the Southern states, just as Republicans during Reconstruc-

tion assisted in the election of black representatives and mayors, they supported the introduction of black police officers in an effort to expedite freedom of Southern blacks and to humiliate the defeated rebels. In the 1860s and early 1870s, several Southern police departments, especially those in cities with Republicans in office and with large black populations, hired African-American police officers (e.g., in Selma, Houston, New Orleans, and Jackson, Mississippi). The decline of the Southern African-American police officer began in 1877 with the end of Reconstruction. Williams and Murphy explain that "the effects were quickly seen in police departments. In department after department, blacks lost their jobs either by dismissal or by being forced to resign."[82] For example, the number of African-American New Orleans police officers decreased from 177 in 1870 to zero in 1910. Black police officers were virtually eliminated from Southern policing shortly after the turn of the century.[83]

The Northern states experienced a similar phenomenon. The actual origin of the African-American police officer is somewhat in doubt. Peggy S. Sullivan suggests that the first was in Washington, D.C. in 1861,[84] while Williams and Murphy suggest that the first Northern African-American police officer was in Chicago in 1872.[85] An important aspect of these conflicting statements rests on defining what is a police officer. President Abraham Lincoln was known to have used black troops to protect the Capitol and maintain order in the city of Washington during the Civil War. These soldiers could be viewed as having police powers. The number of African-American police officers then grew steadily as many Northern cities (e.g., Chicago, Washington, D.C., Indianapolis, Cleveland, and Boston) began to hire African-American police officers. As was the case in the South, however, most of these black police officers were nearly eliminated by 1910. Most of them were hired to work in large cities, and their numbers peaked by 1900 to a level of 2.7 percent of the total number of police officers. By 1910, they made up less than 0.1 percent of the police workforce.[86] Much of this decline can be attributed to the massive reorganization of public municipal police departments from 1877 to the early 1900s. During this period, the police underwent a radical transformation, especially in the area of civil service.[87] The new qualifications and racially biased civil service testing stopped the flow of blacks into police work. The goal of professionalization, along with civil service testing and evaluation, led to the nearly systematic exclusion of African-Americans as future police officers.[88]

The segregation and second-class citizenship of African-Americans in the field of police work was demonstrated in the Northern police departments where they remained. In Philadelphia, black police officers worked in plainclothes so as not to offend white sensibilities. They were assigned to black neighborhoods and were usually prohibited from arresting white people. Some cities went as far as establishing different designations, such as "patrol officer" for blacks and "police officer" for whites. Riots ensued on more than one occasion when a black officer attempted to override his authority by arresting a white suspect.[89] Sullivan explains that "often black police officers were hired to patrol black areas and were allowed only to arrest other black citizens."[90]

The segmentation of black and white officers continued throughout the twentieth century. Black officers were assigned to work areas that were almost exclusively black, and if a white person committed a crime in the black community, the black officer usually had to call for a white officer to come to the scene and arrest the white offender. Thus, the number of African-American police officers steadily and slowly grew, especially after World War II.[91] A 1961 study by the President's Commission on Law Enforcement and Administration of Justice found that "31 percent of the departments surveyed restricted the right of blacks to make felony arrests; the power of black officers to make misdemeanor arrests was even more limited."[92] Sullivan describes the recollection of the former executive director of the National Organization of Black Law Enforcement Executives of growing up in a small Louisiana town where black police officers rode in cars marked "Colored Police," and were allowed only to arrest "colored people."[93] A 1968 *Ebony* magazine study found that twenty-eight departments restricted the arrest powers of black officers. In addition, they were often denied desired assignments, especially in high profile areas such as honor guards.[94] Blacks were often excluded from promotion and, when they were promoted, they were not usually given the same command powers as a comparable white supervisor. Not until the late 1960s and early 1970s did African-American police officers throughout the country receive full jurisdiction and arrest powers.[95]

Comparative Observations

The similarities between the development of self-government on Indian reservations and the empowerment of African-American communities in the United States are abundant. One of the most obvious similarities is the historical use of white social control agents in each of these "alien" communities. "To the Black community, white policemen represented nothing less than a hostile occupation army,"[96] just as the military control of the reservation was greatly resented by Native Americans.[97] A second similarity is that while both these sets of residents were concerned about being "overpoliced," they were also concerned that they were not receiving equal protection from these agents of social control.[98] A third similarity is that forced assimilation occurred in varying degrees in both communities. Just as the military and the tribal police participated in the suppression of tribal traditions on Indian reservations, Ellis Cashmore explains how law enforcement agencies played a critical role in repressing the distinctively ethnic orientation of African-American culture.[99] The process of integration and assimilation for black citizens has led to the systematic deterioration of many traditional black institutions. In addition, the internal movement among black people to regain an African identity and to empower the African-American community is similar to the movement among Native Americans to achieve full sovereignty and to revitalize tribal traditions.

Fourth, one aspect of the empowerment process for both groups has been the establishment of African-American and Native American police officers to work in the African-American community and on the reservation respectively. Through continual struggle, these groups have worked to remove the "occupying army" and to create more responsive policing through the hiring of people from their own ethnic group.[100]

Fifth, the key motivation of the white dominant power structure for recruiting African-American police officers[101] and for establishing tribal police departments was to increase the effectiveness of social control.[102] As Harry W. More and W. Fred Wegener explain:

[It] is very difficult for minorities who feel discriminated against to view law enforcement as being responsive to their needs, unbiased and generally interested in justice if they do not see members of their group represented on the department's personnel roster.[103]

White police officers working in minority communities frequently describe their difficulties in terms that are very similar to those of the cavalry officer who said that it was "like chasing deer with a brass band."[104] The differences between their own culture and that of the minority community limit their effectiveness as agents of social control. Therefore, despite the rhetoric of responsiveness to the community and the efforts of grassroots organizations to develop a representative police force, results are best characterized in terms of increases in the effectiveness of social control.

The continuation of white dominance is clearly reflected in the limited nature of jurisdiction granted to minority police officers. For example, early African-American police officers in the United States were frequently only allowed to arrest members of their own race.[105] The jurisdiction of tribal police also was restricted to members of their own race.[106] However, a significant difference between these two groups is that African-American police officers were able to obtain equal jurisdiction in the 1960s. The tribal police, on the other hand, still lack equal jurisdiction with white officers, even though they receive training equal to or greater than that of their white counterparts in similar size departments. According to Deloria and Lytle, this limitation is a serious source of frustration for tribal police officers attempting to enforce the law on Indian reservations.[107]

Explanations

The similarities in the legal restrictions placed upon tribal police and black police, and the heavy-handed control of Native Americans and African-Americans in a class society dominated by white European-Americans, are easier to explain than the differences that appear around issues of jurisdiction between tribal and black police. Because of the official government policies of genocide against Native Americans and the slavery of Africans in this society, no other minority group has been oppressed more severely or more blatantly than these two. At the same time, precisely because of these extreme and obvious oppressions, as well as their lasting repercussions, these two groups have historically represented the greatest potential threats to the current power relations. Therefore, it makes sense that those who have benefitted most from current power relations (powerful and influential decision makers) would be eager to construct mechanisms of social control that directly regulate the activities of these two groups. When the policies of genocide and slavery were no longer effective methods of social control, largely because they had lost popular support, new methods were created. One such method was the application of Western jurisprudence administered by white enforcers. By criminalizing the activities of those deemed subversive and threatening within each of these two groups, white authorities justified continued coercive control.

The blatant exercise of coercive control through criminal justice administered by white enforcers had its limits as it elicited open resistance from both Native American and African-American populations. A major shortcoming in the use of force to control people is that it exposes inequalities and angers those being repressed. Therefore, a useful strategy is to instill legitimacy within the apparatus of social control.[108] Nowhere is the practice of cloaking oppression in a mantle of legitimacy better exemplified than in the practice of utilizing members of oppressed group to "police" themselves. It is well documented that Nazi Germany used concentration camp prisoners to regulate other prisoners. South Africa has systematically placed key black Africans in uniform to maintain order in the black townships. Not only do these social control agents serve as a buffer between the oppressed and the oppressors, they are often much more effective in communication, information gathering, and locating insurgents than are members of the oppressing group. Therefore, the use of tribal police and African-American police as agents of social control makes imminent sense within the context of developments in U.S. society, and the fundamental race and class divisions in its structure. Again, the more difficult challenge is to explain the differential developments in jurisdiction between these two policing entities.

Both African-American police and tribal police were initially granted very limited jurisdiction, but African-Americans have obtained enforcement powers equal to their white counterparts. Although American Indian tribes have long sought sovereignty for their reservations, since the end of the Indian Wars they have not had the power to demand this right. As a group, American Indians have not been able to exercise the political and economic power that African-Americans have been able to invoke. African-Americans as a racially defined population in the 1960s were able to mobilize their combined economic power through boycotts to strike down some forms of segregation, their political power to achieve civil rights and eventually equal law enforcement powers for African-American police officers. The second critical difference between tribal police and black police concerns the structural conditions within which individual officers were able to act. African-American police have only been allowed to enforce laws based on Western jurisprudence within police agencies that are constructed by white European-Americans. African-Americans have never had the opportunity to incorporate aspects of African culture into their actions. Even as they have moved into executive positions, they merely administer the law, policies, and procedures of white European-American jurisprudence. Therefore, granting African-Americans police powers did not fundamentally change police procedures or place any white people in jeopardy of serious racial discrimination. If Native Americans chose to leave the reservation and work within the structural confinements of a typical U.S. police department, they also could achieve enforcement powers equal to those of their white counterparts. A key difference between the experiences of these two groups is that the reservation is legally defined while the black ghetto is economically defined. The legal status of the reservation allows the tribes to have more direct control over how they are policed. Although tribal police departments were constructed on a foundation based on Western jurisprudence, American Indians have continuously struggled to retain as much of their own culture and tradition within tribal police operations as possible. Within the very limited jurisdiction in which tribal police have been allowed to exercise their police powers, American Indians have struggled to incorporate tribal laws and procedures. Dominant white authorities are reluctant to allow Indian police agencies to have power over their own when whites do not control the laws and procedures of that agency.

CONCLUSION

The fundamental role of police is to maintain social order, and it is within this function that the use of racial and ethnic minorities as police officers can be best explained. The hiring of minority police officers is often presented as a progressive reform designed to reduce racism within the enforcement of law and to empower minorities by granting them the power to dispense justice. Not only do police administrators and government officials use the growth in the number of minority police officers, chiefs, judges, and legislators as a barometer for measuring the decline in the significance of race in criminal justice, but many minority community organizers and leaders focus on these numbers as a guide for determining the level of racism within government agencies or institutions. Increasing the proportion of minorities in these institutions can have a significant impact on government's responsiveness to minority communities and the level of individual racist acts by government representatives. Yet, it is critical that analyses of police officers recognize the significance of minority police for the social control of minority populations.

The analysis presented here conceives of the origin and development of Native American tribal police as an example of the use of minorities policing minorities as a strategy of social control. The key to explaining tribal police is to explore the dialectic nature of this phenomenon. First, contradictory policies were pursued simultaneously with the same program. Tribal police were supported by some because such a policy encouraged self-determination, and by others because it assisted assimilation and control. Second, the creation of tribal police enhanced social control at both an ideological and a material level. Materially, the use of tribal police increased the effectiveness of investigating agencies by using officers who understood the language and customs of the people being controlled. Ideologically, the use of tribal police helped social control agencies achieve greater legitimacy among those being policed, to whom it appeared that their race was taking part in the dispensing of justice. It is much easier and more effective to restrict a community's freedom with a recognized and legitimate authority, than through the use of force and violence.

Applying these observations about tribal police to the use of racial and ethnic minority police officers throughout the United States leads to several interesting conclusions about criminal justice reform. First, criminal justice researchers, as well as social reformers, should not place too much emphasis on the number of minority police officers within police departments as a gauge of progress toward greater equality in the realm of law enforcement. Focusing on this adjustment to the system may distract attention from more substantial issues, such as institutional racism, class bias within law, and economic class power. Second, the historical analysis presented here provides further evidence for the dialectical nature of reform. Reforms such as hiring minority police officers are often presented as humanitarian efforts to improve the criminal justice system. Placing this reform within the context of historical developments in class and race relations of power suggests that it is best understood as a method for achieving more effective control of subordinate populations. Therefore, criminal justice reforms should be analyzed in relation to whether and how they increase the system's effectiveness. Often effectiveness is enhanced at the ideological level as adjustments to the system are made under a banner of progress and humanitarianism that tends to mask institutional racism and class relations. Even if some promoters of such reforms have good intentions, the structural conditions in which reforms are implemented tend to mold them in a way that makes the reforms more effective social control mechanisms.[109]

Finally, this historical investigation of tribal police demonstrates that race is an important consideration in criminal justice history separate from class. In many areas of criminology the explanatory value of race and racism in the U.S. criminal justice system has been challenged. The criminal justice system and particularly the police represent the repressive apparatus of the state, which is primarily designed to maintain order and preserve current power relations by regulating the activities of the lower class. Without denying the critical impact of class, and the foundation of class relations supporting racism in U.S. society, the history of tribal police and African-American police, particularly regarding jurisdiction and police power restrictions, demonstrate that racism is an important dynamic in the exercise of social control.

NOTES

An earlier version of this article was presented to the American Society of Criminology, Annual Meeting, New Orleans, November 1992. I wish to thank the Menominee Nation and their tribal police for inspiring this historical investigation. I also wish to thank Melissa Hickman Barlow for her comments and suggestions on earlier versions of this article.

1. David Roberts, "Geronimo," *National Geographic* 182: no. 4 (October, 1992): 58.

2. Roberts, "Geronimo," 52.

3. William T. Hagan, *Indian Police and Judges: Experiments in Acculturation and Control* (New Haven, 1966).

4. Roger Solomon and Ron McCarthy, *Fear: It Kills. A Training Guide for Law Enforcement in the 1990s* (Arlington, 1989).

5. Hagan, *Indian Police and Judges.*

6. Ibid.

7. Vine Deloria, Jr. and Clifford M. Lytle, *American Indians; American Justice* (Austin, 1983).

8. Deloria and Lytle, *American Indians, American Justice.*

9. Hagan, *Indian Police and Judges.*

10. Deloria and Lytle, *American Indians, American Justice.*

11. Hagan, *Indian Police and Judges.*

12. Deloria and Lytle, *American Indians, American Justice.*

13. Ibid., 167.

14. Deloria and Lytle, *American Indians, American Justice.*

15. Hagan, *Indian Police and Judges.*

16. Wilcomb E. Washburn, *Red Man's Land/White Man's Law: A Study of the Past and Present Status of the American Indians* (New York, 1971).

17. Hagan, *Indian Police and Judges;* Deloria and Lytle, *American Indians, American Justice;* Washburn, *Red Man's Land/White Man's Law.*

18. Washburn, *Red Man's Land/White Man's Law,* 61.

19. Washburn, *Red Man's Land/White Man's Law.*

20. Hagan, *Indian Police and Judges,* 1.

21. Hagan, *Indian Police and Judges.*

22. Ibid., 1.

23. Hagan, *Indian Police and Judges.*

24. Washburn, *Red Man's Land/White Man's Law.*

25. Ibid., 28–29.

26. Hagan, *Indian Police and Judges.*

27. Washburn, *Red Man's Land/White Man's Law;* Hagan, *Indian Police and Judges.*

28. Hagan, *Indian Police and Judges.*

29. Ibid.

30. Ibid., 37.

31. Ibid., 38.

32. Hagan, *Indian Police and Judges.*

33. Ibid.

34. Ibid.; Washburn, *Red Man's Land/White Man's Law.*

35. Hagan, *Indian Police and Judges.*

36. Ibid.

37. Ibid.

38. Washburn, *Red Man's Land/White Man's Law,* 171.

39. Washburn, *Red Man's Land/White Man's Law.*

40. Ibid., 168.

41. Ibid., 169–70.

42. Deloria and Lytle, *American Indians, American Justice.*

43. Ibid., 168.

44. Deloria and Lytle, *American Indians, American Justice.*

45. Hagan, *Indian Police and Judges.*

46. Deloria and Lytle, *American Indians, American Justice.*

47. Ibid.

48. Ibid.

49. Hagan, *Indian Police and Judges;* Washburn, *Red Man's Land/White Man's Law;* Deloria and Lytle, *American Indians, American Justice.*

50. Deloria and Lytle, *American Indians, American Justice.*

51. Washburn, *Red Man's Land/White Man's Law,* 173.

52. Deloria and Lytle, *Red Man's Land/White Man's Law,* 9.

53. Deloria and Lytle, *American Indians, American Justice;* Washburn, *Red Man's Land/White Man's Law.*

54. Washburn, *Red Man's Land/White Man's Law.*

55. Ibid.

56. Deloria and Lytle, *American Indians, American Justice.*

57. Hagan, *Indian Police and Judges.*

58. Deloria and Lytle, *American Indians, American Justice.*

59. Hagan, *Indian Police and Judges,* 10.

60. Washburn, *Red Man's Land/White Man's Law.*

61. Ibid., 76.

62. Hagan, *Indian Police and Judges.*

63. Washburn, *Red Man's Land/White Man's Law.*

64. Deloria and Lytle, *Red Man's Land/White Man's Law.*

65. Washburn, *Red Man's Land/White Man's Law.*

66. Deloria and Lytle, *Red Man's Land/White Man's Law.*

67. Lawrence French, ed., *Indians and Criminal Justice* (New Jersey, 1982).

68. David Wachtel, "Indian Law Enforcement," in French, *Indians and Criminal Justice.*

69. Washburn, *Red Man's Land/White Man's Law,* 175.

70. Deloria and Lytle, *American Indians, American Justice.*

71. Samuel Walker, *Popular Justice: The History of American Criminal Justice* (New York, 1980); Hubert Williams and Patrick V. Murphy, "The Evolving Strategy of Police: A Minority View," in *Perspectives on Policing* (Washington, D.C., 1990).

72. Homer Hawkins and Richard Thomas, "White Policing of Black Populations: A History of Race and Social Control in America," in *Out of Order: Policing Black People,* ed. Ellis Cashmore and Eugene McLaughlin (New York, 1991), 66–67.

73. Hawkins and Thomas, "White Policing," 71.

74. Ibid.

75. Christopher Adamson, "Punishment After Slavery: Southern State Penal Systems, 1865–1890," *Social Problems* 30, no. 5 (1984): 555–69.

76. Adamson, "Punishment After Slavery"; Hawkins and Thomas, "White Policing."

77. Adamson, "Punishment After Slavery."

78. Williams and Murphy, "The Evolving Strategy of Police."

79. Ibid.

80. Ibid.

81. Fred R. Harris and Tom Wicker, eds., *The Kerner Report: The 1968 Report of the National Advisory Commission on Civil Disorders* (New York, 1988); Walker, *Popular Justice.*

82. Williams and Murphy, "The Evolving Strategy of Police," 9.

83. Williams and Murphy, "The Evolving Strategy of Police."

84. Peggy S. Sullivan, "Minority Officers: Current Issues," in *Critical Issues in Policing: Contemporary Readings,* ed. Roger G. Dunham and Geoffrey P. Alpert (Prospect Heights, IL, 1989).

85. Williams and Murphy, "The Evolving Strategy of Police."

86. Ibid.

87. Sidney L. Harring, *Policing a Class Society: The Experience of American Cities, 1865–1915* (New Brunswick, NJ, 1983).

88. Williams and Murphy, "The Evolving Strategy of Police."

89. Ibid.

90. Sullivan, "Minority Officers," 332.

91. Sullivan, "Minority Officers."

92. Williams and Murphy, "The Evolving Strategy of Police," 8.

93. Sullivan, "Minority Officers," 331.

94. Sullivan, "Minority Officers."

95. Williams and Murphy, "The Evolving Strategy of Police."

96. Hawkins and Thomas, "White Policing," 65.

97. Hagan, *Indian Police and Judges.*

98. Ibid.; French, *Indians and Criminal Justice;* Hawkins and Thomas, "White Policing."

99. Ellis Cashmore, "Black Cops Inc.," in *Out of Order: Policing Black People,* ed. Ellis Cashmore and Eugene McLaughlin (New York, 1991).

100. Stephen Leinen, *Black Police, White Society* (New York, 1984); Deloria and Lytle, *American Indians, American Justice.*

101. Harry W. More and W. Fred Wegener, *Effective Police Supervision* (Cincinnati, 1990).

102. Washburn, *Red Man's Land/White Man's Law;* Hagan, *Indian Police and Judges.*

103. More and Wegener, *Effective Police Supervision,* 389.

104. Leinen, *Black Police, White Society.*

105. Ibid.; Cashmore, "Black Cops Inc."

106. Deloria and Lytle, *American Indians, American Justice.*

107. Ibid.

108. Quintin Hoare and Geoffrey Nowell Smith, eds., *Selections from the Prison Notebooks of Antonio Gramsci* (New York, 1971).

109. For historical examples of this co-optation process see David E. Barlow and Melissa Hickman Barlow, "Cultural Diversity Training in Criminal Justice: A Progressive or Conservative Reform?" *Social Justice* (forthcoming); and David E. Barlow, Melissa Hickman Barlow, and Theodore G. Chiricos, "Long Economic Cycles and the Criminal Justice System in the U.S.," *Crime, Law and Social Change* 19 (1993).

The Technology of Professionalism: The Identification of Criminals in Early Twentieth-Century Canada

Greg Marquis
Halifax, Nova Scotia

The police have been central to modern state formation, a process based on regulation, social welfare, and information. State surveillance in European nations and colonies such as Ireland and India reflected official fears of independence movements, intrigues among refugee communities, and working-class radicalism. Twentieth-century British political policing, for example, grew out of Scotland Yard's Special Branch, concerned with Irish nationalist terrorism in the 1880s.[1] The U.S. Federal Bureau of Investigation had the fingerprints of millions of Americans, 40 million of whom had never been charged with a criminal offense. In collecting and exchanging information on suspicious individuals and organizations, twentieth-century police agencies have not always separated criminal offenses from suspect political behavior. Yet interpretations that view the growth of the "vigilant state" in North America primarily in terms of intelligence gathering on political radicals and labor organizations ignore a far larger segment of the population—criminals—whose "creation" as a national class represented a profound shift in state power.

Although police definitions of criminality were problematic, the police began to document and monitor, on a national basis, a class of offenders. Improved documentation and identification procedures produced, over time, evidence of frequent recidivism among prison and penitentiary inmates. As Michel Foucault explains of the French criminal justice system, "Police surveillance provides the prison with offenders, which prison transforms into delinquents, the target and auxiliaries of police supervision, which regularly send back a certain number of them to prison."[2] The fingerprint movement had a far broader mandate than control of the political left. Criminal identification for police purposes in early twentieth-century Canada was primarily an exercise in crime control and police professionalization. The latter hinged on the increasing association of police work with "science."

ANTHROPOMETRY AND CRIMINALISTICS

Criminal identification, by the 1890s, was one of the great issues of North American law enforcement, at least inside the profession. In civilian circles, issues such as prohibition loomed larger.[3] The police shared no uniform theory of criminality, yet police officials were concerned by recidivism. Crime experts suggested that if recidivists were scientifically identified, and the information shared among police departments, the rate of crime would fall markedly. Most police work was of a peacekeeping or social service nature, with few resources devoted to combatting or investigating crime. The fact that the drunk and disorderly constituted the majority of arrests did little to build a reputation of police professionalism. Criminal identification, with its technological and crime-fighting associations, was a potential solution to this problem. There were more prosaic applications as well. The emergence of criminal investigation specialists or detectives (and, in larger departments, detective squads) reflected the increasing specialization and bureaucratization of the municipal police. Detectives were concerned not with drunks, Saturday night brawlers, or street arabs, but "serious" criminals—principally thieves, robbers, fraud artists, fences, and, depending on the local moral reform climate, gamblers, bootleggers, prostitutes, madames, pimps, and drug addicts. Intelligence on the local underworld became more important as urban centers became larger and more heterogeneous. The exchange of intelligence among police departments, initially through circulars and photographs, increased with railway travel. Thus, the Ohio-based *National Detective,* a pioneering police journal, began publicizing information on well-known American and Canadian criminals in the early 1880s.[4]

In 1897, the Toronto Board of Commissioners of Police instructed William Stark, one of Canada's eminent detectives, to report on identification methods in New York and Chicago. Stark subsequently advised the adoption of the Bertillon system of anthropometric identification. A number of American penal institutions and police departments had instituted the Bertillon "signalment" method, based on metric measurements of the individual's head, body, and limbs. The system's French originator, Alphonse Bertillon, argued that although a criminal's appearance may change over the years, basic physical characteristics, such as the size and shape of the head, remained. Bertillon added standardized "mug shots" or photographs as well as a *portrait parle,* a detailed written description of wanted persons, noting scars, tattoos, and birthmarks. Mug shots were standardized frontal and side views of the prisoner, recorded on a fixed scale with a special camera. The very photographing and elaborate measurement of criminals, it was felt, would have a positive moral effect. Although the system's accuracy was open to human error, two decades after its adoption by the Paris Prefecture of Police in 1879 it "functioned as the universal language for the identification of recidivists."[5] "Bertillonage" was endorsed by the National Association of Chiefs of Police (NACP) and the American Prison Wardens' Association and supported by a number of Canadian police chiefs. The NACP sponsored an identification bureau, based in Chicago, to which participating police agencies contributed a small fee. The association also lobbied the U.S. Congress to support a national identification office centered in Washington.[6]

Promoters of Bertillonage operated on the premise that the police and penal authorities had to monitor and control a distinct criminal class thought to be largely beyond rehabilitation. Bertillon's methods appealed to the same popular prejudices that supported eugenics and biological determinism.[7] Police definitions of criminality, like doctors' perceptions of mental illness, were subjective and changed over time.[8] Turn-of-the century statistics indicate that most persons convicted for indictable offenses in Canada were first-time offenders.[9] The police, nonetheless, were convinced that a small number of recidivists were responsible for a large volume of "professional" crime, principally theft. Toronto and other departments had started "rogues' galleries," photographic records of recidivists, in recognition of this belief. A similar policy was followed by Ontario's Central Prison.

In his appearance before the 1890 Royal Commission on the Prison and Reformatory System of Ontario, Stark, who was already investigating Bertillon's methods, identified Ontario's true criminals not as vagrants or drunks (two categories of offenders who dominated the jails), but a small, mobile, and troublesome class of professional thieves. Members of this class were known as much for "the criminal habit" as for actual offenses or the value of articles stolen. Stark's 1897 report suggested that Bertillon measurements of Canada's convict population would provide "the signalments of a very large proportion of the criminal population of the country."[10] Stark rejected the notion of a biological or physical criminal type, yet as a supporter of Bertillon identification he also challenged classical penology by assuming that penitentiary inmates would return to crime after completing their sentences. The exchange of Bertillonage information among police and penal authorities in North America never lived up to its potential, but the movement was a further elaboration on Bentham's panopticism. The latter facilitated the surveillance of prisoners; body measurements and photographs would make inmates (and other offenders) visible outside of prison walls.[11]

Bertillonage, by linking physical characteristics to behavior, strengthened the hereditarian or French school of the emerging pseudo-science of criminology. Although environmentalists were in the vanguard of social reform efforts, biological determinism won converts. Many North American police and corrections officials were attracted to the theory that criminality was the result of moral or even genetic failure, particularly among the lower classes or certain racial and ethnic types.[12] Like English-Canadian social workers, doctors, and public health officials who were attracted to eugenics with its emphasis on inherited mental and physical weaknesses, criminal justice officials were not always social environmentalists. The first Dominion parole officer, W. P. Archibald, although promoting the rehabilitation of deserving convicts, subscribed to theories of criminal heredity to the extent of urging the regulation of marriage among the mentally and morally weak. John Wilson Murray, Ontario's "Great Detective," believed that the criminal was a "bad type," the offspring of defective stock: "Crime is a disease. It is hereditary, just as consumption is hereditary." A Montreal detective stated in 1907 that habitual criminality was a type of insanity.[13]

The anthropometric file enjoyed a certain acceptance in police circles. Yet faith in Bertillon's theories was of secondary importance; it was possible to reject the pseudo-science of anthropometry on the one hand but reap its practical benefits on the other. Identification reformers were not proclaiming the existence of a physical criminal type à la Lombroso; they were interested in tracking a criminal cadre. For North American police officials, the criminal class was known by its lifestyle, associates, and activities, not by its biological makeup.[14] As explained by George Porteous, the superintendent of the NACP Bureau of Criminal Identification, the exchange of uniform information would enable police departments to identify and root out likely troublemakers. Theories of criminal causation, for police officers, were best left to "do-gooders." Bertillonage, nonetheless, was a potentially powerful crime-prevention strategy. Its success depended on the growth of records and their exchange among jurisdictions through a centralized authority, something that the American and Canadian systems of government did not encourage. The NACP's push for a coordinated criminal records effort represented a narrowing of function in that it "focused on crime control, to the exclusion of the myriad other duties which the uniformed police had begun life earlier in the nineteenth century."[15]

Bertillonage was adopted slowly in North America, partly because of the decentralized state system. Neither the United States nor Canada had a national police. In Canada only Toronto contributed regularly to the NACP's Central Bureau of Identification, organized in 1899. The Toronto department had a complete set of Bertillon equipment, including, by 1897, "a small delicate instrument for measurement of scars and birthmarks." The NACP, tired of legislative inaction on a government-financed and-administered identification system, had taken matters into its own hands. Its service collected photographs and Bertillon information and attempted to verify the identity of offenders. By 1904, fewer that seventy municipal departments were subscribing. In 1905, Montreal became the second Canadian city to participate.[16] Corrections officials were equally slow in adopting anthropometry. The International Prison Congress of 1895, reflecting French practice, recommended that vagrants and professional thieves be subjected to Bertillon classification. Canadian penal authorities, judging by Ontario's 1891 royal commission, were aware of the system but appear to have done little to secure its implementation.[17]

Canada's federal system was a major obstacle to police cooperation in the area of criminal records. Law enforcement, under the British North America Act, was a provincial and municipal responsibility, although Parliament was involved framing criminal law such as the 1892 Criminal Code. The federal government's largest law enforcement agency, the North-West Mounted Police, as of 1900 was confined to the unorganized territories of the West and the Yukon. Ottawa's older constabulary, the Dominion Police, although smaller in size, was a more likely instrument of police cooperation. The immediate responsibilities of the Dominion Police, which reported to the minister of justice, were guarding Parliament, other government buildings, and naval dockyards, and enforcing a number of federal statutes. Its commissioner, Percy Sherwood, had important Ottawa connections and was in touch with chief constables across Canada. As of 1899 his agency became involved in administering the Ticket-of-Leave Act, which increased ties with the penitentiaries. Sherwood, who was active in the National Association of Chiefs of Police, also maintained American and British contacts.

Sherwood had interested the Conservative minister of justice in the Bertillon system in 1896, but had been frustrated by a change in government. The best he could manage was to have Bertillon equipment sent to the federal penitentiary at Dorchester, New Brunswick.[18] A Dominion Police memorandum, influenced by Stark, detailed Sherwood's strategy of federal coordination. The memo explained that Bertillonage was regarded by detective departments throughout the world as the most effective identification system. It also revealed the police opinion that most ex-convicts were likely to return to crime. Sherwood wanted the Bertillon process applied to all federal inmates and the information centralized by the Department of Justice.[19]

IDENTIFICATION OF CRIMINALS ACT

In 1898, Sherwood's efforts were rewarded when the Liberal government secured the Identification of Criminals Act, which, with its amendments, remains the core of Canada's criminal identification system to this day. The path had been smoothed by support from the Toronto police and a meeting of penitentiary wardens who agreed on the utility of an identification bureau under the Dominion Police. The law authorized the taking of Bertillon measurements for persons "in lawful custody" charged with indictable offenses. This limitation proved fundamental to the evolution of Canada's identification system. In keeping with contemporary penology, the aim was to better monitor recidivists. Force, if necessary, was allowed and officers were absolved from all civil and criminal liabilities. Justice Minister David Mills explained that the measure would assist police "to trace parties who have been confined in prisons and penitentiaries after they are discharged, and have no difficulty in identifying them notwithstanding any change of name they might adopt."[20] The wording of the legislation was somewhat open-ended in that it authorized not only the Bertillon signaletic system, but also "any measurements, processes or operations sanctioned by the Governor in Council having the like object in view." Furthermore, the law allowed the "publication" of identification results for the "purpose of affording information to officers and others engaged in the execution or administration of the law."[21]

Although the legislation and subsequent amendments limited procedures to indictable offenses, it did allow the police to identify all persons *charged* with these offenses. Thus, a long-standing police belief that convictions alone were a conservative measure of criminality was institutionalized. Police officials, or at least big-city detectives, insisted that they possessed a professional ability to determine whether specific individuals were serious criminals virtually on sight. The case of five American pickpockets arrested by Montreal detectives in April 1913 illustrates this belief. The alleged pickpockets, three from New York and two from Chicago, were arrested in the financial district. The suspects were fingerprinted, measured, and photographed, then remanded for a week to allow detectives to learn more about their records. The *Montreal Gazette* reported that "there is no doubt as to the five being pickpockets," but admitted that "it might be difficult to secure their conviction, as they were not caught with the goods." In the end, the Americans were released, but in the eyes of both the police and the *Gazette* they were criminals all the same. Their Bertillon measurements, photographs, and fingerprints would have been exchanged with other police departments.[22] Evidence of prior criminality, or even a contact with the police, confirmed through fingerprints and photographs, became another weapon in the police arsenal for not simply solving crime, but disciplining marginal elements.[23]

Despite the "signaletic" system's legal authorization in 1898, government parsimony and a lack of coordination delayed immediate progress. Ottawa provided no funds for the operation of a central records bureau. Sherwood, whose entire establishment was smaller than that of many municipal departments, managed to secure a modest storeroom and to distribute measuring equipment and material to federal penitentiaries. By 1901, however, budgetary restraints had prevented the appointment of an identification officer. In a letter to the warden of the Illinois State Penitentiary, the commissioner complained of "non-believers."[24] Although equipment had been obtained, Bertillonage, as Sherwood explained to the deputy minister of justice in 1902, had languished because "it was found difficult to get anyone interested in the institutions [penitentiaries] to take energetic hold of it without extra remuneration." Two years later the assistant commissioner of the Royal North-West Mounted Police urged Commissioner Aylesworth Bowen-Perry to establish a Bertillon bureau within the RNWMP. The RNWMP comptroller, Fred White, believed that such a responsibility rested with the Dominion Police, which although smaller in terms of personnel, was more of a national institution and headquartered in Ottawa.[25]

FINGERPRINTS AND CRIME CONTROL

As North American police departments adopted Bertillon's methods in the late 1890s, anthropometry was challenged by another technique, fingerprinting. The use of finger and thumb prints for identification was not a new discovery, but a refinement of ancient Asian practices. During the second half of the century European students of dactylography established that an individual's unique fingerprint patterns remained unchanged from infancy to death. At mid-century William Herschell, a British magistrate in India, had experimented with fingerprints to identify "natives" in court. A generation later, fingerprints attracted the attention of British scientist Sir Francis Galton, a cousin of Charles Darwin. Galton, known for his writings on heredity and eugenics, published three books on dactylography. E. R. Henry, later chief commissioner of New Scotland Yard, by the late 1890s had improved on the work of earlier experts and secured fingerprinting as the official identification method in Bengal. The system soon was adopted in Britain, where the Home Office decided to discontinue Bertillonage. The International Association of Chiefs of Police (IACP, whose name had been changed from NACP in the midst of an international panic over Anarchists) remained committed to anthropometric measurements, descriptions, and photographs, yet its members were interested in the new British system. Many acknowledged that anthropometric measurements were outmoded, but believed that photography, not dactylography, was the way of the future. In 1904 an IACP committee sided with Alphonse Bertillon, who argued that fingerprints were useful for verifying his method, but insufficient in themselves.[26]

In addition to the identification of known offenders, fingerprints offered investigators the possibility of securing evidence in the form of latent prints left on objects. Such "scene of the crime" investigation techniques, associated with the fiction detective, exercised a more powerful hold on the public imagination than did routine identification procedures. On both accounts, fingerprinting was a definite boost to police professionalism. Unlike Bertillonage, fingerprinting had few connections with theories of a criminal type. But like Bertillonage, it could assist the authorities in tracking repeat offenders. Sherwood began gathering information on fingerprinting in 1903, corresponding with the Criminal Investigation Division of New Scotland Yard.[27]

North American events were the catalyst to both Canada's criminal identification system and the formation of the Chief Constables' Association. Sherwood and a handful of Canadian municipal chief constables had been involved with the International Association of Chiefs of Police since the mid-1890s. In 1904 the IACP, whose second vice-president was Chief Henry J. Grasett of Toronto, held its convention in conjunction with the World's Fair at St. Louis, Missouri. At the fair, Dominion Police Constable Edward Foster, assigned to guard a Canadian exhibit, made the acquaintance of Detective J. K. Ferrier of New Scotland Yard. Ferrier was an expert in fingerprinting, which had officially been adopted by English constabularies. Ferrier explained to IACP delegates that fingerprinting was cheaper, simpler, and faster than the anthropometric system and, better still, virtually infallible. Fingerprinting also encouraged the centralization of records, as more skill was required in classifying prints than in their recording. The Henry method coded common characteristics to allow for easy retrieval in a collection of thousands of fingerprint cards. With the approval of his superior, Foster studied fingerprinting with the British detective for several months and returned to Ottawa a convert. His faith in the British approach was confirmed by further studies of Bertillonage in New York. By 1905, fingerprinting had been adopted by the Winnipeg Police and had engaged the interest of the Royal North-West Mounted Police as well as the warden of the Kingston Penitentiary.[28]

After circularizing a number of police chiefs, Sherwood, with the assistance of William Stark and Henry J. Grasett, convened the organizational meeting of the Chief Constables' Association of Canada (CCAC) at Toronto in 1905. This was not the first Canadian association of its kind. Ontario police chiefs and high constables had organized on the county and provincial level in the late nineteenth century. The Ontario Provincial Constabulary Association, whose 1896 meeting was attended by police chiefs, high constables, and rural constables, had been interested in improving rural policing. The Ontario association, which favored a provincial identification bureau based on "the French system," was moribund by the late 1890s.[29] The IACP, Sherwood explained to Joseph Rogers, Ontario provincial detective, proved the value of personal acquaintances in dealings between police agencies. A Canadian organization, the delegates of 1905 believed, could examine specific Canadian concerns and counteract localism and regionalism. The charter members elected Henry Grasett president and Chief Oliver Campeau of Montreal vice-president. Joining Sir Percy Sherwood on the executive committee were the police chiefs of Winnipeg, Guelph, Westmount, and Quebec. Most of the original fifty members represented Ontario departments, establishing the province's historic domination of the association. Nine Quebec police officials attended. Also present was Philip Holland of Chicago, publisher of *The Detective,* the unofficial organ of the IACP.[30] William Stark was elected secretary-treasurer of the CCAC, whose first lobbying activity was to form a committee to secure a national fingerprint bureau. Foster, impressed by the IACP, had suggested to Sherwood that a Canadian organization could act as a vehicle for establishing a workable national identification system.[31]

While the Dominion Police spread the gospel of dactylography among the municipal police, CCAC members continued to press Ottawa for a proper identification facility. The Minister of Justice decided that Bertillonage, still practised in the United States, should not be abandoned altogether. Foster fingerprinted a portion of the inmates at the Kingston Penitentiary, but a plan to fingerprint and photograph prisoners in all five federal penal institutions stalled. In 1908, Sherwood's lobbying resulted in PC 1614, a Cabinet order sanctioning the use of fingerprinting in connection with the Identification of Criminals Act. Bertillonage in Canada had been superseded by the preferred identification method of Scotland Yard without recourse to parliamentary debate. Yet permissive legislation did not create a national criminal records office. In 1910 the sensational escape of a prisoner convicted for murdering an Ontario constable jolted the minister of justice into action. Edward Foster was elevated to inspector and placed in charge of a new Criminal Identification Bureau (CCIB) in Ottawa. The Dominion Police photographed and fingerprinted all federal penitentiary inmates and arranged for the regular fingerprinting of new convicts in these institutions. Because of uncertainty surrounding the legality of photographing persons charged with or convicted of indictable offenses, Sherwood secured a second Order-in-Council to clarify the matter in 1911. PC 559 authorized "the process or operation of photography as an additional means of identification for the purposes of the Criminal Identification Act."[32]

Through the 1910s the CCAC encouraged municipal departments, who were under no legislative obligation whatsoever, to forward copies of prints, photographs, and records to the Dominion Police bureau. The CCIB in turn was able to send inquiring departments the complete criminal records of individuals in custody. Although not all police departments participated immediately or in a consistent manner, a major goal of the Chief Constables' Association had been achieved by World War I. Canada had the rudiments of a national criminal identification system based on submissions from the penitentiaries, provincial prisons, and jails, and the municipal police. The RNWMP, stationed in rural detachments, began to contribute. Records also arrived from the United States and Great Britain. Not all police departments, however, were convinced of the system's efficiency or utility. Western chief constables throughout the 1920s complained that the machinery of CCIB in distant Ottawa moved too slowly.

On the local level, police departments concentrated on building their own criminal files and cooperated regionally; these efforts both complemented and competed with the work of the CCIB. Foster opposed regional and provincial identification bureaus, believing they would undermine the efficiency of the Dominion Police collection. British Columbia's natural criminal information conduit, with the exception of neighboring Alberta, was the Pacific coast. As of 1916, the Victoria police, which claimed to employ the only "lady fingerprint expert" in Canada, had amassed 20,000 sets of prints and 40,000 photographs, many of them from the western states. The department's fingerprint cards multiplied to 60,000 by 1928. The Vancouver police developed an extensive criminal records office, which for a number of years operated as a de facto regional bureau. By the late 1930s, the Vancouver department was making several thousand identifications yearly through its own fingerprints and photographs and those sent from Ottawa, Victoria, and other exchange bureaus. In 1938 and 1939, Vancouver also sent several thousand updated criminal records to the RCMP in Ottawa and the FBI in Washington, D.C.[33]

The CCAC also turned to the provincially operated jails, reformatories, and prisons that held prisoners sentenced to terms of under two years. Only one in ten offenders incarcerated on indictable charges went to penitentiary; the remainder ended up in provincial institutions. By voluntarily contributing sets of prints and photographs to the CCIB, provincial governments assisted the police in identifying a new class. The criminal class, like recidivism, was very much a "statistical creation."[34] The Ontario Central Prison installed a system of fingerprinting and photography in 1911. Saskatchewan and Manitoba prisons followed in 1912 and 1913, New Brunswick and Quebec in 1914 and 1915. British Columbia prisons began to participate in the national program in 1918. These efforts helped produce more centralized and systematic criminal records for the use of police, the courts, and corrections officials. Evidence of previous criminality had an impact on bail practices, sentencing, and parole. Identification was also promoted to assist in tracking parole violators, who constituted a tiny minority of the over 21,000 prisoners released on Ticket of Leave, or parole from federal and provincial institutions, in the period 1899–1930.[35]

In the 1920s, it proved easier to coordinate the exchange of records in British Columbia because Provincial Police Superintendent J. H. McMullan doubled as Inspector of Prisons. The British Columbia Provincial Police (BCPP) formed its own criminal identification bureau at Victoria in 1924, starting with records from the Oakalla Prison Farm and the provincial jail at Nelson. It also pioneered the use of telegraph to transmit fingerprint classifications through code. By the late 1920s, the BCPP reported, the Ottawa bureau was able to communicate identification information by wire within twenty-four hours of receiving a request for a set of records. By 1939, the BCPP had classified the prints of over 25,000 offenders, including American convicts.[36]

Other provinces also maintained, at various times, rural constabularies to enforce prohibition and other provincial statutes. The provincial police in Alberta and Saskatchewan formed in 1917 exchanged records with the CCIB and with other police agencies. As part of its first major expansion, the Royal Canadian Mounted Police (RCMP) absorbed the Prairie and Maritime provincial police in the years 1928 to 1932, also taking over their records. The Ontario Provincial Police, officially organized in 1909, established a full-fledged provincial identification bureau at a relatively late date. The Ottawa Provincial Police (OPP) began a separate identification unit within its Criminal Investigation Branch in 1946 to aid detachments and municipal departments. In 1950, the OPP obtained over 12,000 identification forms from provincial jails and "reform institutions," which, together with thousands of records from field units, produced a large provincial criminal intelligence collection.[37]

IDENTIFICATION AND POLICE PROFESSIONALISM

Finger and thumbprints detected on weapons, glass, blood, soap, painted surfaces, and other scene-of-the-crime materials assisted police and prosecutors and helped boost the police image as crime fighters. Such cases figured prominently in the published reports of the RCMP and the municipal and provincial police. Soon after the establishment of the CCIB, Inspector Edward Foster appeared as an expert witness in an American murder trial in which the prosecution's case hinged on latent fingerprints. The accused was found guilty and executed. Breaking and entering investigations were the typical Canadian cases involving the use of latent prints. The key piece of evidence in one Ottawa conviction was a print found on a cigarette package wrapper. As the courts came to accept latent prints as opinion evidence, it became possible to secure convictions on the basis of fingerprints alone. Individual cases built on latent fingerprint evidence, such as the 1950 murder of two Langton, Ontario, residents who had been pursuing bank robbers, matched the exploits of dime novel and motion picture detectives. Yet in terms of total prosecutions for murder, manslaughter, robbery, and burglary, the use of fingerprints as forensic evidence was not crucial.[38]

In the wake of the 1919 Winnipeg General Strike, the federal government reorganized and expanded the RNWMP, assigning it responsibility for security and intelligence. The new Royal Canadian Mounted Police absorbed over 150 Dominion Police employees and became the nation's leading police organization. With headquarters now in Ottawa, the RCMP assumed control of Ticket-of-Leave coordination and the operation of the Canadian Criminal Identification Bureau. From 1911 until early 1920, the Dominion Police had received and classified over 70,000 sets of prints and over 10,000 photographs, resulting in over 5,000 identifications, the discharge of seventy-three parole violators, and the location of forty-four escapees.[39] The number of identifications made, compared to the total volume of indictable arrests and convictions, was relatively insignificant; from 1910 until the end of 1919 Canada's courts registered over 170,000 indictable offense convictions. More important is the fact that Canada had established a national identification bureau more than a decade before the United States. (The U.S. Department of Justice merged its identification collection, held at the Leavenworth Penitentiary, with that of the IACP in 1924. The system's custodian was the FBI.) Despite the proprietorial attitude of the RCMP, the Dominion Police and the Chief Constables' Association had served as midwives for police cooperation on the national level.[40]

The commissioner of the RCMP reported in 1920 that although the work of the identification bureau was a national service "entirely in the interests of the provinces," it had not reached its full potential owing to inconsistent participation by local police departments. As late as 1922, for example, the Montreal police were not sending records to Ottawa. Montreal instead operated an informal regional bureau for surrounding municipalities. Quebec City also was negligent, as were the provincial police and jails following the election of Quebec's Union Nationale government in 1936. From 1920 to the end of 1929 the CCIB received over 202,000 records and confirmed 24,000 identifications. Indictable offense convictions for this period totalled only 184,325, suggesting the importance of foreign contributions, records of persons arrested but not convicted, and a backlog effect. As time went on, some municipal and provincial officials, although appreciative of the CCIB, began to view the service as a possible instrument of police centralization. Even when this fear was absent, not all agencies participated with equal vigor nor updated records following additional arrests or convictions. The identification bureau, however, kept municipal departments in contact with the RCMP and one another. It also brought RCMP officials to the annual conventions of the Chief Constables' Association. By 1932, the year Foster retired, the RCMP had acquired over 300,000 sets of prints. Follow-up procedures gradually improved. According to the 1934 report, the fingerprint section did not file new prints in cases where charges were withdrawn or dismissed, but other evidence indicates that the RCMP retained all records received.[41]

Local police departments were selective not only in the records forwarded to Ottawa, but also in prints and photographs taken for their own purposes. Bertillonage had been a rarity among Canadian police departments; fingerprinting and photography, by comparison, became routine but not universal. Fingerprints were preferred to more expensive and time-consuming photography. The Dominion Bureau of Statistics began recording municipal police identification activity in 1920. Canada's numerous small police departments were less likely to use identification procedures than those of large towns and cities. From 1920 to the end of 1929, during which over 184,000 indictable offense convictions were registered, the municipal police recorded over 220,000 sets of prints and took over 50,000 mug shots. This effort established over 45,000 identifications, an incidence of 20 percent. These totals did not include records produced by the RCMP, several provincial constabularies, and the railway police. During the 1930s, indictable convictions doubled in comparison to the previous decade to over 354,000. In this same period, municipal police recorded over 230,000 sets of prints and over 180,000 photographs, while the RCMP bureau obtained nearly 410,000 fingerprint records. Part of the difference between the municipal totals and the latter figure can be explained by contributions from the British Columbia, Ontario, and Quebec provincial police. The RCMP Fingerprint Section's rate of positive identification in the 1930s was 16 percent.[42]

During the 1930s, the RCMP expanded identification efforts as part of its national police services. Three criminal intelligence innovations were promoted: the single fingerprint file, a *modus operandi* (MO, methods of operation) registry, and a national police circular. The Batley system of single print classification adopted by North American police in the 1920s and 1930s had been designed to assist New Scotland Yard in identifying the latent prints of burglars. The BCPP reported a "dactylscopic collection" of 4,500 single prints by 1935. The RCMP Fingerprint Section started with the single prints of incarcerated individuals. By the end of World War II, the new unit amassed over 220,000 single prints of burglars, automobile thieves, and other known criminals. This amassing of tens of thousands of fingerprint/photograph files appears excessive, yet it was perfectly in keeping with contemporary police administration and penology.[43]

Modus operandi records also were copied from British police practice, where detectives developed profiles on the patterns and habits of known offenders such as check artists or safe crackers, and of the perpetrators of unsolved crimes. As CCAC convention delegates were informed during the 1920s, MO files allowed police departments to organize their growing and unsystematic collection of circulars and special bulletins. By the mid 1930s, the BCPP had MO files on 1,700 individuals classified on the basis of sixteen types of crimes. The RCMP, in addition to its *modus operandi* or crime index section, organized a photographic section (1932) and a handguns registry (1935), the latter to coordinate Canada's first registration of revolvers and pistols. These collections, although sorted manually like the regular fingerprint, photograph, and arrest/conviction records, represented a greater centralization of criminal justice information.[44]

The *RCMP Gazette* was a weekly bulletin first issued to Western RCMP detachments, municipal departments, and the Canadian Pacific Railway and Canadian National Railways Departments of Investigation in 1937. Supported by the Chief Constables' Association, the RCMP expanded the *Gazette* in 1938 to cover the entire country with a distribution of roughly

1,000. It published photographs and descriptions of wanted persons, detailed legal cases, and reported on policing issues. Other police forces instituted circulars for both internal and cooperative use. The BCPP, for example, produced detailed photographic reference books of all prisoners released from provincial and federal institutions in British Columbia. By the late 1930s, the force's divisions and detachments were also sent the photographs of "suspicious characters," and detailed information on the automobiles used by "known criminals." The RCMP recognized the professional thirst for information on the criminal class. Superior resources and a national, centralized administration, together with custody of the identification bureau, allowed the RCMP publication to assume a role originally envisioned for the CCAC's *Canadian Police Bulletin.* The *RCMP Gazette,* not the Chief Constables' journal, quickly became the Canadian version of the FBI's *Law Enforcement Bulletin.*[45]

During the 1920s and 1930s, police chiefs, police commissions, civic officials, and lobby groups periodically called for the extension of the provisions of the Identification of Criminals Act—the creation of an even larger "criminal class." The act did not cover summary conviction offenses associated with habitual criminals such as frequenting a bawdy house, vagrancy, and bootlegging (keeping a bawdy house and living off the avails of prostitution were indictable offenses). Juvenile offenders also were exempt. Summary conviction offenses, which also included breaches of the peace, municipal by-law violations, and drunkenness, were more typical of police work. In the period 1900–1940, nonindictable convictions outnumbered the indictable by roughly ten to one. Nonindictable convictions, where the option of a fine was the norm, were far less likely to result in incarceration. Yet chief constables and detectives, in describing the local underworld in cities such as Vancouver, Winnipeg, Toronto, and Montreal, seldom differentiated between indictable and summary conviction offenses.[46] They were not implying that all persons convicted of summary offenses were criminals in the police understanding of the term. But crime control advocates contended that the ranks of summary conviction offenders included many "lifestyle" criminals who under current legislation could not be added to the criminal identification network.

The supposed crime wave of the 1920s and 1930s, together with the antiradical ideology of the RCMP, provincial constabularies, municipal police departments, and the railway police (all represented in the CCAC) lent legitimacy to the police demand for expanded identification. A number of police officials supported fingerprinting taxi drivers, who held licenses courtesy of police commissions or other civic authorities. By 1940, the Vancouver police were fingerprinting several hundred cab drivers each year; a similar plan on the part of the Toronto Board of Police Commissioners in 1930 proved too controversial. Vancouver City Solicitor J. B. Williams attempted to interest the attorney general in the benefits of fingerprinting bootleggers upon their second offense, a measure supported by Ontario police chiefs.[47] Evidence from the annual conventions of the Chief Constables' Association suggests that a number of police forces, either through ignorance or design, violated the Identification of Criminals Act by fingerprinting summary offenders. One example was the fingerprinting of vagrants, who were then remanded pending a response from the RCMP Fingerprint Section. Another abuse was holding suspects without charge in order to search for their true identity and record. Vancouver police, according to prisoners' record books for 1898–1917, ignored the letter of the law and photographed and fingerprinted individuals charged as vagrants and prostitutes.[48]

The chief social question discussed by the interwar CCAC was unemployment, which placed considerable strains on local government. Chief constables, whose municipalities bore the brunt of the relief burden and law enforcement, wanted the Dominion authorities to register the unemployed. Police officials also demanded expanded identification powers over summary offenses in order to uncover the incidence of prior criminality among the jobless. (Such a policy would be implemented by the American Works Progress Administration during Roosevelt's New Deal.)[49] In 1927, the superintendent of the BCPP advocated fingerprinting vagrants and hoboes who violated the Railway Act by hitching rides on freight trains. RCMP Commissioner Cortlandt Starnes, speaking to the CCAC convention that same year, supported the creation of a "much larger criminal class" through fingerprinting the unemployed. Yet not all CCAC members supported this proposal. During the Depression, the Chief Constables' Association lobbied without success to enlarge the scope of the Identification of Criminals Act. In 1936, the CCAC discussed the merits of fingerprinting all persons in lawful custody, including drunks and vagrants. This measure, which amounted to a demand to increase the criminal class tenfold, was supported by Chief Dennis Draper of Toronto, A. G. Shute of Edmonton, and George Shea, director of the Canadian National Railways Department of Investigation. The RCMP superintendent in charge of the Fingerprint Section repeated this suggestion in 1940. This demand for a wider use of identification procedures clashed with the due process sensibilities of legislators and the press, whose constitutionalism would not tolerate the subjection of occasional and petty offenders to the stigma of criminal identification.[50]

Immigration control was another potential area for the extension of fingerprinting and photography. In the 1920s and 1930s police chiefs, convinced that "foreigners" were clogging the lock-ups, magistrates' courts and jails, were leading voices in immigration restriction. The CCAC appointed a committee to look into the possibility of fingerprinting foreigners in the late 1920s. On one occasion, the commissioner of the RCMP chastised municipal and provincial police administrators for fanning the flames of intolerance. The RCMP was involved in investigating not only intelligence and security matters, but also the character of naturalization applicants and in exchanging information with the American Immigration Service. In the early 1930s, RCMP Commissioner James MacBrien advocated fingerprinting all applicants for naturalization. Duplicate fingerprint and photographic records, he suggested, could be sent to the police authorities in the country of origin. MacBrien also supported the fingerprinting of all "suspicious" immigrants, following American practice, in order to facilitate the deportation of undesirables. The police were not alone. In 1931, the Senate discussed a draft "Identification of Aliens Bill," which did not survive the legislative process.[51]

Under the Immigration Act of 1919, only certain classes of non-naturalized offenders were liable for deportation: those convicted of crimes involving moral turpitude, prostitutes, pimps living off the avails of prostitution, professional beggars or vagrants, and political offenders—those advocating violent political change or affiliated with subversive groups. Almost one-third of those deported from Canada in the period 1903–1929 were removed for "criminality." Most were deported back to Britain and the United States.[52] The CCAC linked crime and Communism to the mistakes of past immigration policy. Yet the association reached no consensus from 1927 to 1939 as to exactly which immigrant groups should be fingerprinted. Some chief constables suggested registering all immigrants; others were more specific: Americans, Jews, and Europeans. It was clearly fear of political radicalism, not crime, that prompted the majority to submit to the determination of Chief Draper of Toronto to send a delegation to Ottawa in 1938. This effort achieved little other than adverse publicity, but indicated the dangers that police professional goals could pose to civil liberties.[53]

Criminal intelligence as practiced by the RCMP, the provincial constabularies, and the larger municipal police departments was closely associated with political intelligence. In the early 1930s, for example, RCMP E Division (British Columbia) reorganized its Criminal Investigation Bureau to include a revolutionary organizations section. Although most chief constables had little personal involvement with Communists, all concluded that Communism was a crime against the state and applauded Ontario's 1931 prosecution of Communist Party leaders. Members of the early CCAC had entertained similar views on Anarchism. In keeping with their approach to certain summary offenders, the police found it tempting to fingerprint or photograph "agitators" in order to discover their true names, places of birth, and criminal records. Technically this was illegal. The CCAC's 1931 request of the minister of justice for legislative authority to fingerprint and photograph vagrants was aimed largely at controlling Communist organization of the unemployed. An equally unsuccessful request for greater powers over public parades and demonstrations was similarly motivated.[54]

Universal fingerprinting had strong support within North American police circles. In the 1920s, Edward Foster had publicized the benefits of registering citizens' fingerprints with the police. Cases of amnesia and sudden death by accident, Foster argued, could be cleared up through "personal" or noncriminal fingerprinting. It was ironic that Canada, with a political culture supposedly less devoted to individual rights, offered so little support for voluntary fingerprinting as promoted by the FBI in the 1930s and 1940s. J. Edgar Hoover utilized his immense prestige to encourage mass voluntary fingerprinting as proof of patriotism. The CCAC, in contrast, sensed popular hostility and wisely made no public statement on the question. Expressions of support outside of police circles for universal identification were rare and usually reflected short-term panics over crime, drugs, and radicalism. (In 1925 a Vancouver grand jury recommended the compulsory fingerprinting of the entire population as a crime control measure.) Quebec officials, influenced by procedures on the Continent, advocated citizen identification cards and forwarded the fingerprints of provincial civil servants to the Ottawa bureau's noncriminal collection, which experienced modest growth during the 1930s. For most Canadians, however, to be fingerprinted or photographed by the police was to be made a criminal.[55]

Neither the Mackenzie King government nor the more repressive Bennett regime of 1930–1935 appears to have considered seriously the extention of police identification powers. World War II produced little public enthusiasm for voluntary fingerprinting. National security concerns, however, allowed the RCMP to greatly expand its fingerprint collection. Much of this was accomplished under the Defense of Canada Regulations or simply by administrative fiat in conjunction with wartime industries. Enemy aliens, Royal Canadian Air Force personnel, and the civilian employees of munitions plants and other wartime industries contributed prints in the hundreds of thousands, resulting in an explosion of noncriminal records at RCMP headquarters. RCMP officials informed CCAC delegates that the RCAF-Civil Security records, covering over 800,000 individuals, were not part of the regular criminal collection. During the 1940s, the exchange of criminal records between Canadian police agencies and the FBI increased; American-Canadian defense and economic cooperation was mirrored in the law enforcement sphere, although FBI "cooperation" was notoriously one-sided.[56]

Prior to the 1960s, few people appear to have publicly questioned the police practice of retaining fingerprints and mug shots of persons exonerated in court or released upon expiry of their sentence. During the 1920s and the 1930s the torch of Canadian civil liberties was carried by organized labor and the political left. The Communist-organized Canadian Labor Defense League signed up thousands of members. Academics, lawyers, church groups and social service organizations joined in to condemn specific policies aimed at trade unionists, Communists, and unemployed demonstrations. Progressive opinion criticized Section 98 of the Criminal Code (sedition), police responses to the organized unemployed in Vancouver and Regina and to socialists in Toronto, and the enforcement of Quebec's 1937 Padlock law. Trade unions and labor councils protested the policing of strikes. Yet police powers over the common offender were all but ignored. There were individual protests. In 1916, a commissioner appointed to investigate Manitoba jails had questioned the legality of the Identification of Criminals Act. Vancouver police commission records reveal complaints by arrested persons and their counsel that identification procedures violated "British justice." In 1904, one individual complained that the Vancouver police "put me in the stocks, took my height, the colour of my hair, my general dimensions, in fact treated me like a convict or criminal"—a reference to Bertillonage.[57]

An important exception was the 1938 Report of Royal Commission on the Penal System of Canada (Archambault Report), which recommended granting trial judges the authority to order the destruction of fingerprint records in cases where the accused were found not guilty. Allowing the local police and the RCMP to retain the photographs and prints of acquitted persons, the commissioners believed, subjected the innocent to "lifelong indignity." Canadians were victims of malicious arrest in many cases. Yet the members of the Archambault commission were not willing to make this policy universal, agreeing with the police that "dangerous characters" often went unpunished by the courts and should be monitored through identification. The report, although reformist in tone, reflected the law enforcement maxim that crime statistics based on convictions told only part of the story.[58] Canada's flexible rules of evidence did not force police to be overly careful as to the legal formalities of fingerprinting. Nor did the common law position that seemed to allow the fingerprinting of persons charged with an indictable offense or any offense tried by way of summary conviction, a situation that continued into the 1950s and 1960s.[59]

Privacy, human rights, and access-to-information legislation caused no small amount of anxiety in police circles during the 1970s. Bail reform, effective in 1972, placed minor restrictions on police identification practices. Yet the basic structure of criminal identification survived. Five decades after the Archambault Report, in a landmark ruling for police and crown prosecutors, the Supreme Court of Canada decided that the Identification of Criminals Act was constitutional. An appeal launched following a successful criminal prosecution had argued that fingerprinting an individual prior to conviction was a violation of the Charter of Rights and Freedoms. Most notable in the 1987 Supreme Court case was the intervention of the Canadian Association of Chiefs of Police, which argued that identification law was absolutely essential to police investigations, cooperation, and the integrity of criminal records. The court, in a unanimous decision, agreed.[60]

CONCLUSION

Identification, although involving minimal resources, was important to police professionalism in the decades following the organization of the CCAC. The media associated fingerprinting with scientific crime fighting—a glamorous image that was encouraged by police officials. The reality of criminal identification, however, was more subtle and far more significant. The real authority of the police is derived not from law, but from "the control of information."[61] The power of the police within the state apparatus stemmed in no little measure from their ability to trace the movements of repeat—and potential—offenders. For all its practical application to police work, criminal identification has served as a means of ordering elements of the population. The police never fully embraced the biological determinism of the 1890s, perhaps because it removed "individual, conscious responsibility for crime" in favor of impersonal "scientific" explanations.[62] The identification system and the national police network obviously benefited RCMP surveillance of the political left. Antiradical applications of criminal intelligence and identification, however useful for the RCMP security branch, were of secondary importance to the larger police community. The police derived their legitimacy from crime fighting, not red baiting. The question of whether crime was a hereditary taint or the product of environmental influences was, for the police, of minor concern. Crime-fighting ideology could produce an open-ended definition of the criminal class, one that included any person who had been arrested for an indictable offense. According to this detective mentality, a police record justified long-term surveillance. Therefore, prison and penitentiary recidivism rates confirmed, for the police, the utility of coordinated, centralized criminal records. The extent of the local and national criminal intelligence efforts suggest that the police, despite their public reassurances, remained deeply suspicious of rehabilitative measures such as parole.[63]

At the municipal, provincial, and national levels the police, judging by their extensive collections of fingerprint cards, mug shots, MO files, circulars, and other records, pioneered state surveillance in Canada. The key forces behind the development of the vigilant state in Canada were the Chief Constables' Association, the Dominion Police, and the Royal Canadian Mounted Police. Thirty-five years after the formation of the CCAC, national and international cooperation among police and prison officials had created a national criminal class of considerable proportions, in defiance of the constitutional division of powers between the national and provincial governments.[64] This was more of an administrative reality than an actual homogeneous, self-conscious class. Yet such a classification had not existed beyond the local level in 1900, in spite of the Identification of Criminals Act. Politicians, by refusing to broaden the legislation of 1897, 1908, and 1911, limited the size of the identification collection, a constraint often ignored by local police, particularly when it came to status offenses (vagrancy). But thousands of Canadians who were never convicted of indictable offenses became criminals in an administrative sense. As Foucault notes, by the mid–twentieth century the police record had replaced the convict's passport of the previous century. In time, with the growth of the welfare state and corporate capitalism, police records would be surpassed in volume by those of the civil bureaucracy and the private sector. Yet rarely was this information as sensitive as that held by the police, or its possession so power-enhancing. The RCMP Identification Branch made records available to the Department of Immigration, the Department of National Health and Welfare, and parole officers. Prior to the legal and administrative reforms of the 1970s and 1980s, only financial constraint, police discretion, and political culture kept criminal identification efforts from taking on even greater dimensions.[65]

NOTES

An earlier version of this paper was presented to the Canadian Historical Association, Annual Meeting, Charlottetown, P.E.I., 30 May 1992.

1. Bernard Porter, *The Origins of the Vigilant State: The London Metropolitan Police Special Branch Before the First World War* (London, 1987); David Arnold, *Police Power and Colonial Rule: Madras 1859–1947* (Bombay, 1986).

2. Michel Foucault, *Discipline and Punish: The Birth of the Prison* (London, 1977), 282.

3. Greg Marquis, "The Canadian Police and Prohibition, 1890–1930," unpublished paper, 1990.

4. David Johnson, *American Law Enforcement: A History* (St. Louis, 1981), 110–13; *Saint John Daily Evening News,* 12 May 1882.

5. Henri Souchon, "Alphonse Bertillon Criminalistics," in *Pioneers of Policing,* ed. Philip John Stead (Montclair, 1977), 122.

6. NACP (1895), 38, from *Proceedings of the Annual Convention of the International Association of Chiefs of Police, 1893–1905* (New York, 1971).

7. Canada, House of Commons, *Debates* (1892), 2784; for the nineteenth-century criminal class, see Hans Gros, *Criminal Investigation: A Practical Handbook for Magistrates, Police Officers and Lawyers* (Madras, 1916), 265–76; David Garland, *Punishment and Welfare: A History of Penal Strategies* (Aldershot, 1985), 105–6; J.A. Sharpe, "The History of Crime in England, c. 1300–1914", in *A History of British Criminology,* ed. Paul Rock (Oxford, 1988), 129.

8. Sanders L. Gilman, *Disease and Representation: Images of Illness from Madness to AIDS* (Ithaca, 1988), 230.

9. *Canada Year Book 1906* (Ottawa, 1907), 478. For a discussion of research on criminal classes, see Clive Emsley, *Crime and Society in England, 1750–1900* (New York, 1987), 129–36.

10. Marjorie Freeman Campbell, *A Century of Crime: The Development of Crime Detection Methods in Canada* (Toronto, 1970), 125; *Report of the Com-*

mission to Inquire into the Prison and Reformatory System of Ontario (Toronto, 1891), 718–22; R. F. Quinton, *Crime and Criminals, 1876–1910* (London, 1910), 161.

11. Foucault, *Discipline and Punish*, 195–228.

12. Others agreed with Alan Pinkerton's theory that criminals were motivated by greed or passion, traits found in all layers of society. *Professional Thieves and the Detectives* (New York, 1880), v–vi.

13. Angus MacLaren, *Our Own Master Race: Eugenics in Canada, 1885–1945* (Toronto, 1990); *Report of the Minister of Justice as to the Penitentiaries of Canada 1910* (Ottawa, 1911), 15–17; *Memoirs of a Great Canadian Detective: Incidents in the Life of John Wilson Murray* (1904) (Toronto, 1977), 24; *Canadian Municipal Journal (CMJ)*, (1907), 427–28. See also Alfred E. Lavell, *The Convicted Criminal and His Re-Establishment as a Citizen* (Toronto, 1926), 11–12.

14. Criminal anthropology, which searched for personal, biological causes of criminality, was popular at this time but represented only one school of thought. It had parallels, but no direct connections, to anthropometry. See Stephen Jay Gould, *The Mismeasure of Man* (New York, 1981), 122–42.

15. IACP, *Proceedings* (1898), 25–37; Eric H. Monkkonen, *Police In Urban America, 1860–1920* (New York, 1981), 156.

16. *Toronto Mail and Empire*, 3 Dec. 1897; IACP, *Proceedings* (1897), 21. Only a fraction of American police agencies contributed to the bureau.

17. *Report of the Commission to Inquire into the Prison System*, 662–63.

18. Public Archives of Canada, RG18 E (Royal Canadian Mounted Police), Dominion Police Records (DPR), vol. 3104, A. P. Sherwood to Warden of Dorchester Penitentiary, 5 July 1897.

19. DPR, vol. 3102, Memorandum, 29 Dec. 1897. See also, vol. 3101, Sherwood to James Massie, Oct. 1896.

20. *Report of the Minister of Justice as to Penitentiaries*, 1898, xvi–xvii; Canada, Senate, *Debates* (1898), 855. Indictable offenses included aggravated assault, murder, manslaughter, assault and battery, assault on a law officer, and property crimes such as forgery, embezzlement, fraud, receiving stolen goods, burglary, and robbery. At the turn of the century, the largest category of indictable crime was larceny, which amounted to 56 percent of convicted offenders. Indictable offenders were largely male, Canadian born, white, and under forty years of age. Most in the period 1901–1905 were first-time offenders. See *Canada Year Book 1906*, 478. The majority of indictable offenses that went to court were tried summarily.

21. Chap. 54, "An Act Respecting the Identification of Criminals," *Statutes of Canada* (1898), 229. In a 1959 law digest, W. J. Tremeear noted that the Identification of Criminals Act was passed to extend, not minimize, the common-law right to fingerprint. This view was based on a 1943 British Columbia Supreme Court decision, *Canadian Encyclopedic Digest (Western) Criminal Law*, Vol. 17 (Calgary, 1959), 271.

22. *Montreal Gazette*, 7 April 1913.

23. Richard Ericson, *Reproducing Order: A Study of Police Patrol Work* (Toronto, 1982), ch. 6.

24. DPR, vol. 3103, Memo for the Minister of Justice, 21 April 1899; Sherwood to Major R. W. McClaughry, 13 Jan. 1899; vol. 3108, Sherwood to Sam Hughes, 21 June 1901.

25. DPR, vol. 3108, Sherwood to Deputy Minister of Justice, 18 March 1902; Gary Saunders, "75th Anniversary of Fingerprinting in Canada," *RCMP Gazette* 48 (1986): 4.

26. IACP, *Proceedings* (1904), 20; "Sir Francis Galton," *Encyclopedia Britannica* 11, 11th ed. (Cambridge, 1910), 427–28; John Cronin, "The Fingerprinters: Identification as the Basic Police Science", in Stead, *Pioneers of Policing*, 159–73. In 1896, Argentina became the first Western Hemisphere nation to adopt fingerprinting for police purposes.

27. DPR, vol. 3112, Sherwood to C. E. Collins, 9 Oct. 1903.

28. IACP, *Proceedings* (1904), 91–96; Royal Canadian Mounted Police, Edward Foster Scrapbook; *Toronto Star Weekly*, 5 Nov. 1927; Robert Hutchinson, *A Century of Service: A History of the Winnipeg Police Department* (Winnipeg, 1974), 25.

29. DPR, vol. 3116, Sherwood to Bowen-Perry, 3 August 1905; *Report of the Proceedings of the Second Annual Meeting of the Ontario Provincial Constabulary Association* (Ridgetown, 1896), 3–10.

30. IACP, *Proceedings* (1905), 47; DPR, vol. 3116, Sherwood to Rogers, 12 June 1905; *CMJ* (1906), 387–89.

31. "50 Years of Fingerprinting," *RCMP Quarterly* 26 (1961), 156. The other major activity of the CCAC was suggesting amendments to the Criminal Code. See Greg Marquis, "Canadian Police Chiefs and Law Reform: The Historical Perspective," *Canadian Journal of Criminology* 14 (July–Oct. 1991), 385–406.

32. RCMP Headquarters, Edward Foster Scrapbook; Saunders, "75th Anniversary," 4–6; *Canada Gazette*, 7 April 1911, 3484. At the turn of the century, many local police departments depended on the services of commercial photographers for mug shots. See Gerald Wallace, William Higgins, and Peter McGahan, *The Saint John Police Story: The Clark Years, 1890–1915* (Fredericton, 1991), 83.

33. "Report of the Chief of Police," *Report of the Corporation of the City of Victoria, British Columbia for the Year Ending December 31, 1916* (Victoria, 1917), 86; "Report of the Chief of Police" (1928), 82; *Report of the Vancouver Police Department 1940–41* (Vancouver, 1940–1941).

34. Patricia O'Brien, *The Promise of Punishment: Prisons in Nineteenth Century France* (Princeton, 1982), 289.

35. DBS, *Criminal and Other Statistics*, 1942 (Ottawa, 1943), App., Table 1; Campbell, *A Century of Crime*, 171–72; Donald G. Wetherall, "To Discipline and Train: Adult Rehabilitation Programmes in Ontario Prisons, 1874–1900," in *Lawful Authority: Readings on the History of Criminal Justice in Canada*, ed. R. C. Macleod (Toronto, 1988), 259; *Canadian Annual Review* 1930–31 (Toronto, 1931), 91.

36. British Columbia, *Report of the Superintendent of the Provincial Police* 1924–39 (Victoria, 1925–1940).

37. *Annual Report of the Commissioner of the OPP, 1950* (Toronto, 1950); Dahn D. Higley, *OPP: The History of the Ontario Provincial Police Force* (Toronto, 1984), 354.

38. *Canadian Encyclopedic Digest*, Vol. 17, p. 271; "*Rex v. DeGeorgio*" [1934], *Digest of British Columbia Reports* Vols. 45–63 (1953), 302; *Report of the Commissioner of the RCMP* (1938), (Ottawa, 1938), 159; *Annual Report of the OPP* (1950), 15–16. The 1950 OPP investigation of the Langton murders sent Arthur

Bank, an army veteran, to the gallows. Fingerprint evidence was essential to the case.

39. *Report of the Commissioner of the RCMP* (1920), 29.

40. *Criminal and Other Statistics* (1942), App., Tables 1–2.

41. *RCMP Report* (1920), 29; (1929); (1933); (1934); CCAC, *Proceedings of the Annual Convention of the Chief Constables' Association of Canada* (1912), 19–25; (1922), 113–14; Foster Scrapbook; *Criminal and Other Statistics* (1942), App., Table 1. An interview with a twenty-year veteran of the RCMP Identification branch revealed that few records were sent back. The RCMP, furthermore, eventually subdivided its major collection on the basis of confirmed convictions and nonconvictions. Interview with RCMP veteran, 12 Feb. 1992.

42. DBS, "Police Statistics," *Criminal and Other Statistics* (1920–1949); *Criminal and Other Statistics* (1942), App., Table 1; *RCMP Report* (1940–1949). From 1940 to 1949, the municipal police recorded 336,637 fingerprint sets and 192,696 mug shots. Most pre-1950s police statistics should be approached with caution. The DBS had major problems in obtaining uniform statistics from Canada's hundreds of police departments.

43. *Report of the Superintendent of Provincial Police* (hereafter, *BCPP Report*) (1935), 18; *RCMP Report* (1935), 119. The single print collection consisted primarily of separate cards for the ten finger and thumbprints of each individual; 1,000 individuals would produce 10,000 records. It also housed a "Scenes of the Crime Sub-Collection," photographic records of impressions on objects sent to the RCMP.

44. CCAC, *Proceedings* (1925–1928); *BCPP Report* (1936).

45. *RCMP Report* (1939), 38; *BCPP Report* (1937–1938). During the 1930s the RCMP instituted two regional fingerprint bureaus, in Winnipeg and Edmonton, reflecting the geographic disposition of the force.

46. *Criminal and Other Offenses* (1942), App., Tables 1–3. The Vancouver police department's 1928 list of "undesirable characters" included bootleggers, pimps, and keepers of disorderly houses, some of whom had no criminal record. See RG 75 (B), 6, File 9, Undesirable Characters, 14 Nov. 1928.

47. *Report of the Vancouver Police Department, 1940,* 17; VCA, RG 75(B) 6, File 11, Williams to Vancouver Board of Police Commissioners, 8 June 1925; M. G. Marquis, "The Early Twentieth Century Toronto Police Institution" (Ph.D. Thesis, Queen's University, 1987), 43.

48. Norman Borins, "Police Investigation and the Rights of the Accused," Law Society of Upper Canada, *Special Lectures of the Law Society of Upper Canada* Part 4 (Toronto, 1963), 72–73; VCA, RG 37 C8-8; RG 75 C2; RG 116 E1 (1898–1917).

49. Sanford Unger, *FBI* (Toronto, 1976), 55.

50. *BCPP Report* (1924), 12–13; CCAC, *Proceedings* (1927); (1936); *RCMP Report* (1940), 197.

51. *RCMP Report* (1935), 33; (1936), 38; Senate, *Debates* (1931), 242–46; 403; 429; 451–53.

52. W. G. Smith, *A Study in Canadian Immigration* (Toronto, 1920), 353–56; *Canada Year Book* (1930), 173. The Opium and Narcotic Drug Act allowed the police to fingerprint and photograph persons charged. Records of offenders under the act were sent to the immigration authorities in case of the possibility of deportation.

53. CCAC, *Proceedings* (1938–1939).

54. CCAC, *Proceedings* (1931); Pierre Berton, *The Great Depression, 1929–1939* (Toronto, 1990), 534.

55. VCA, RG 75 (B) 6, File 6, Extract, Grand Jury Presentment, Fall Assizes, 1925; *RCMP Report* (1937).

56. *RCMP Report* (1941); CCAC, *Proceedings* (1942–1944).

57. "Report of the Special Commissioner Appointed to Investigate into the Management and Supervision of the Gaol and Prison Farm of the Eastern Judicial District of Manitoba," Manitoba, *Sessional Papers* (1916), 1132–33; VCA, RG 75 (A) 4 File 7, W. B. Ross to Board of Police Commissioners, 11 Feb. 1904.

58. *Report of the Royal Commission to Investigate the Penal System of Canada* (Ottawa, 1938), 170.

59. Borins, "Police Investigation," 75.

60. William and Nora Kelly, *Policing in Canada* (Toronto, 1976); CACP, *Canadian Police Chief*, Jan. 1988. The 1972 reform, which encouraged police to release suspects prior to fingerprinting, echoed recommendations found in Martin Friedland's *Detention Before Trial* (Toronto, 1965), 30–32.

61. Ericson, *Reproducing Order*, 199.

62. James B. Gilbert, "Anthropometrics in the United States Bureau of Education: The Case of Arthur MacDonald's Laboratory," in *Crime and Justice in America 5*, ed. Eric Monkkonen (New York, 1992), 214.

63. By the late 1950s, 80 percent of male penitentiary inmates previously had been confined to a reformatory, jail, or penitentiary. See A. M. Kirkpatrick, "Correcting Corrections," *Criminal Law Quarterly* 4 (Feb. 1960), 421.

64. From 1910 to the end of 1939, the Ottawa bureau received fingerprint records for roughly 781,000 individuals. From 1920 to 1939, municipal police recorded roughly 450,000 sets of prints.

65. Foucault, *Discipline and Punish*, 272; Canada, House of Commons, *Proceedings of the Standing Committee on Justice and Legal Affairs*, April 1970, 5–13. By 1970, fingerprints were only expunged upon death or an individual reaching the age of seventy-four.

War, Delinquency, and Society in Bordeaux, 1914–1918

Philippe Chassaigne
University of Orléans

Bordeaux in 1914 was by its size—260,000 inhabitants—the fourth largest city in France. The urban network had spread unevenly on both sides of the Garonne River. As the city had grown essentially on the left bank, settlers were still scarce on the right bank where they were amalgamated in small villages, except for some important ones (such as Lormont) located on top of the nearby plateau of *l'Entre-Deux-Mers* (see Fig. 1). World-renowned for its wines, the city's economic activities were somewhat more versatile, encompassing cod fishing as well as the trade in colonial produce.

Though southwestern France was far remote from the war front, Bordeaux had been more than once directly involved in the war. The French government settled in Bordeaux for the last four months of 1914, as Paris was endangered by the sudden rush of the German army. Once ministers and members of Parlement had reintegrated Paris, refugees and prisoners of war remained in Bordeaux to keep its people directly in touch with the state of activities. Finally, it was in Bordeaux, along with a few other Atlantic ports, that American troops were landed and quartered in 1917.

The general purpose of this chapter is to describe how law-breaking had been affected by the state of war. Different patterns of crime required different measures to maintain public order, such as controlling politically suspect persons (anarchists, defeatists, or other pacifists), or the local repercussions of the crisis of 1917 when war-weary soldiers mutinied in the trenches and workers went on strike in the factories. In addition, the chapter will examine the disruptive effects on local society of the massive arrival of refugees, prisoners of war, and American troops: Did they bring, or induce, new unlawful behaviors, and how did the people of Bordeaux react when confronted with these people?

Many sources were available for this study. The most helpful proved to be the archives of the *Préfecture*, which include the daily reports from the

Figure 1
The Bordeaux Conurbation and the War Front, 1914–1918

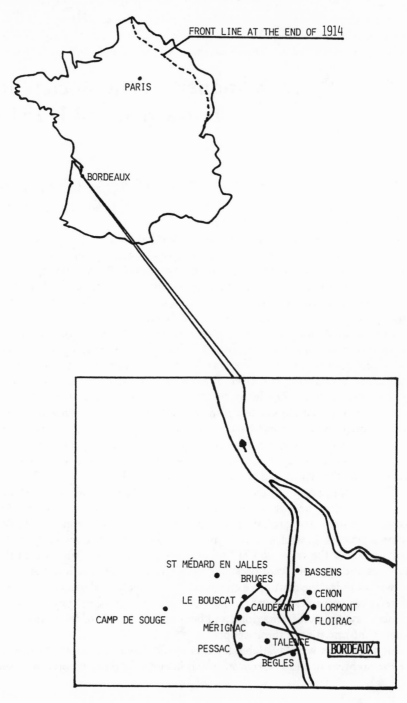

chief superintendent to the *Préfet;*[1] the weekly reports from the *Préfet* to the Home Minister, which describe the state of mind of the population;[2] and reports on "suspect" persons—i.e. peace activists,[3] on refugees[4] and foreigners,[5] as well as American troops.[6] In addition, the minutes of evidence of the court of first instance[7] can be used to check some of the assertions of those official reports. Since a lot of criminal offenses had been reduced to misdemeanors, those courts were trying many more cases than the Assizes, and therefore are of greater assistance in gauging the actual level of law-breaking. At last, and in spite of the censorship, the local press can be used as a secondary source,[8] reflecting the concerns of the local population.

THE STATE OF WAR AND ITS CONSEQUENCES ON LAW-BREAKING

It is widely held that war causes noticeable changes in patterns of criminality and delinquency. In a first step, all the turmoil surrounding the declaration of war is seen as favoring law-breaking, and the number of offenses committed tends to rise. This is a short-lived phenomenon. Young males are the first to be concerned by the mobilization order, an act that drastically diminishes the proportion of criminal characters in society. Consequently, the period of war usually witnesses a sharp decrease in delinquency until the end of the conflict, when demobilization brings back into the circuit the same suspicious characters, leading to a new increase in the figures of recorded crime.

Bordeaux seems to have provided no exception to the rule. The chief superintendent reports and those from the *Préfet* agreed on the low level of law-breaking and on how public order was maintained: "public order is not troubled, the minds are indifferent to the war";[9] "public security: all quiet in Bordeaux";[10] and in 1915, public security was still described as "satisfactory"[11] by the chief superintendent, who explained it as such: "The court is trying half as many cases as in peacetime. This is due to the departure of a lot of habitual criminals to the army, but as well to the special and as yet unusual severity of the court."[12]

Other sources corroborate this. In the local press, *La Petite Gironde* heralded the occasional misdemeanors, yet most of these were the deeds of pickpockets operating in the busy downtown streets, and contenting themselves with small items such as linen, jewelry, and sometimes a few coins. But such activity hardly made the headlines, nor did it contribute to any editorial comment about insecurity.

Judgments rendered by the court of first instance give a quantitative account of delinquency (see Table 1). At first glance, the figures seem to confirm this evolution. For the second half of 1914, the total number of cases tried dropped from 367 in July to only 162 in December, a decline

CRIMINAL JUSTICE HISTORY

Table 1
Delinquency in Bordeaux, July–December 1914

OFFENCES	JULY 1914		AUGUST 1914		SEPT. 1914		OCT. 1914		NOV. 1914		DEC. 1914	
TOTAL	367		120		95		220		144		162	
INCLUDING:												
*ASSAULTS	40		12		6		38		23		31	
*MANSLAUGHTER	3		1		-		1		1		-	
*INDECENT EXPOSURE	2	14.9%	2	13.3%	1	7.3%	2	19.5%	2	18.7%	-	20.9%
*INSULTS ETC.	10		1		-		2		1		3	
*THEFT	51		25		29		43		40		51	
*BURGLARY	5		2		-		1		4		2	
*EMBEZZLEMENT	16	23.9%	3	25%	7	37.8%	8	35.9%	8	41.6%	13	45.1%
*FRAUD	16		-		-		27		8		7	
*VAGRANCY, BEGGARY	31		51		27		25		14		13	
*INSULTING BEHAVIOR	29	19.6%	14	55%	15	44.2%	26	32.7%	26	34%	24	25.9%
*SMUGGLING	10		1		-		1		7		4	
*1893 LAW ON TRANSPORT	2		-		-		20		2		1	
	215	58.5%	112	93.3%	85	89.4%	194	88.1%	136	94.4%	149	91.9%

Source: Minutes of Evidence of the Court of First Instance, A.D.G., U 3486–3548.

of 55 percent. The range of the offenses, however, became restricted. The twelve offenses that have been selected for analysis amounted to 58.5 percent of all the cases tried in July 1914. At the end of the year, this proportion had soared to 92 percent. A wide range of minor offenses—such as those pertaining to the forest or unlawful fishing—had disappeared.

Trials for vagrancy were less frequent after peaking in August 1914. This is not really surprising. At the beginning of the war, the initial setbacks of the French and the German invasion in the north of France were likely to get people on the road. After a while, fewer and fewer people were found guilty of vagrancy. It coincided with the government and the Parlement being settled in Bordeaux, and we can assume that vagrants were carefully avoiding a city likely to be swarming with policemen. The daily reports from the superintendent mentioned police raids in various "hot" places. On 19 August, forty-four vagrants were arrested; thirteen were arrested ten days later, but only three on 15 September. For the whole of October, the police did not arrest more than four or five of them per night.[13]

The rapid and important decrease in the number of offenses against the person is worth noting, as well. (Assaults formed the bulk of such offenses.) This can be seen as confirming the superintendent's analysis quoted above. He explained the decrease in delinquency by the recruitment in the army of the most troublesome characters of the city, yet without giving any precise estimate of how many of them had cleared the way.

This is only a partial analysis. A closer look at the figures will lead one to be more cautious about the consequences of war on law-breaking. Indeed, the offenses against the person increased again as soon as October 1914, rising from 7.3 percent of all cases heard the month before to roughly one-fifth, or 19.5 percent. This level remained basically unchanged for the two following months, and it was higher than before the war (14.9 percent) in July. As expected, assaults were the particular offense responsible for this increase, a sign that the usual troublemakers were far from being liable for every crime.[14] The situation is the same when we take into account all of the violent offenses, such as assaults, manslaughters, breaking and entering, and menaces or insulting behavior. If they are summed up month after month, they account for 23.7 percent of all cases in July 1914, 25 percent in August, 27 percent in September, 30.9 percent in October, 38.1 percent in November, and 37.1 percent in December.[15]

This can be explained by the excitement of these months. Agonizing news was coming in abundance—the retreat of the French troops, the evacuation of Paris, and even the incapacity of marching forward after the Marne victory. Police reports mentioned rather frequently the outbreaks of violence that occurred in the city. "The people are distinctively edgy, the cause being all the contradictory news they are beset with," read a report dated from August 25;[16] on 1 October, a man fired at two soldiers in the cours Victor Hugo, one of the busiest thoroughfares, "following a futile altercation."[17] A new incident was recorded on 26 November when a soldier wanted to arrest a woman who had just stolen a bag of rye. He was assaulted by a crowd of twenty people; some fired at him six times but missed, and he had to wait for a patrol to arrive to be released.[18] The circumstances had led many people to carry a gun;[19] the minutes of evidence of the court of first instance show that a fair majority of people arrested for insulting behavior were carrying a weapon without a license.

Economic delinquency was also on the increase, in percentages if not in actual numbers. Burglary, robbery, theft, and all kinds of fraud amounted to less than one-fourth of all cases tried in July 1914 (23.9 percent). These offenses increased regularly and peaked at 45 percent six months later. The most frequent offense was theft. There were fewer burglaries, which can easily be explained by the recruitment into the army of the habitual criminals. Frauds are a much more interesting topic, as this particular kind of offense relates to shopkeepers trying to dupe their customers. Before the war broke out, the suspects were accused in most cases of using fake weights. It was a common practice in nearly every marketplace in the early

twentieth century. In October 1914, twenty-seven such cases were tried by
the court of first instance, eight on the following month, and seven in December. But the offense was then of a totally different nature, as shopkeepers were charged with watering down either their milk or their wine.
In May 1915, the superintendent made this comment: "The court is really
harsh on defrauders, who are punished with prison sentences going from
eight days to a fortnight, with reprieve, but with fines from twenty-five
francs to one hundred (no reprieve), publication of the judgment in the
papers, and advertising for seven days at the town hall and the merchant's
door. The court of appeal always follows the court in this way."[20] In the
first week of January 1916, twelve milkmen were given sentences ranging
from eight days to one month imprisonment, and from fifty to two hundred
francs in fines for the same offense.[21]

It is easy to realize that beyond a simple decrease in the total amount of
offenses committed, the state of war caused a real change in patterns of
delinquency. Violent behaviors were more common, and for some people
it was tempting to try and make a profit—however illegal—out of this new
situation. The departure to the warfront of the most troublesome characters
certainly helped to reduce the global amount of law-breaking, but it was
not long before their places were taken over. The superintendent noticed
no later than 11 May 1915: "The amount of misdemeanors is low for
adults, but it is rising as far as minors are concerned; we are talking about
theft, assault, insulting behavior, pilfering. Many of them are not convicted,
eight out of ten are handed back to their family, some others are on parole,
a few of them are placed in a house of correction."[22]

With the war extending longer than expected, things were getting worse
as soon as the second half of 1915. On 6 October, the chief superintendent
noticed that "some bad characters are back as they are unfit for the service,
injured, etc."[23] A new alert occurred in July 1916: "Public security is really
bad in Bordeaux; there have been many assaults at night on drunkards;
many thefts did happen as well as attempted burglaries."[24] A weekly survey, dated 29 June 1917, mentioned again the "always increasing" burglaries in the small, peripheral towns.[25] 1918 was remarkable for yet another
outburst of delinquency (reports for the previous year are missing). Gone
were the days when the people of Bordeaux were safe: "In Bordeaux, which
was a rather quiet and peaceful city, insecurity has grown and become
blatant and could turn out to be very dangerous."[26]

No relief was brought by the end of World War I. The surveys of the
Préfet for the first four months of 1919 kept mentioning this problem: "It
is urgent to reorganize the police forces, if only to fight the ever-increasing
crime and delinquency";[27] "criminality is on a daily increase. Robberies,
burglaries, assaults at night, murders are growing in an alarmingly way";[28]
"the town is really insecure at night, and robberies and burglaries are on
the increase."[29]

Table 2

Crimes and Misdemeanors Known to the Police in the Bordeaux Conurbation
1918–1919

| | 1918 | | | | 1919 | | | |
| | RECORDED | | UNSOLVED | | RECORDED | | UNSOLVED | |
	C	M	C	M	C	M	C	M
BORDEAUX	4462		2237		4677		2284	
LE BOUSCAT	42		20		44		23	
CAUDERAN	85		32		80		38	
TALENCE	18		14		82		37	
BEGLES	96		43		96		41	
PESSAC	-	41	-	14	-	40	-	10
MERIGNAC	24	60	18	26	23	56	13	21
BRUGES	-	25	-	14	5	11	-	5
BASSENS	1	36	-	11	2	87	-	9
LORMONT	1	27	-	8	2	54	-	18
CENON	-	6	-	2	1	7	1	-
FLOIRAC	12	82	1	18	3	62	-	22

C: CRIMES

M: MISDEMEANORS

Source: A.D.G., 4 M 174.

It is possible to check those assertions with the help of a totally different document. The Head of the French Criminal Investigation Department sent a letter to the local *Préfet* in 1920, asking for a return of all the misdemeanors committed in Bordeaux and the nearby towns for the two previous years. The government was working on the creation of a national police force to reinforce the existing municipal ones, and this return was to provide food for thought. The *Préfet* in turn asked the respective superintendents to send him the required figures. The Gironde Archives has kept a copy of each return (see Table 2).[30] They may seem disappointing at first sight, as nothing is said about the level of criminality for the previous years. Moreover, all of the local superintendents, except for the one of Bègles, contented themselves with indicating global figures without differentiating between crimes and misdemeanors, and without indicating the proportion of each offense in the total amount. Nevertheless, this is a unique document in the *Préfecture* archives. It offers a rather detailed picture of law-breaking and law-enforcement, including the proportion of unsolved cases, for those two years.

Taken as a whole, delinquency did not increase in a particularly striking way from 1918 to 1919: 5,336 offenses were recorded in 1919, which is only a 6 percent increase over the previous year. Yet the figures differ widely from one place to another. In Talence, the number of offenses jumped from eighteen to eighty-two, a 355 percent increase. A 140 percent increase happened in Bassens, and the figures doubled exactly (twenty-eight to fifty-six) in Lormont. We can reasonably assume that such reports were responsible for most of the alarm raised by the police services. However, taking a look at the figures for Bordeaux—the main town of the conurbation, and consequently the hotbed of delinquency—one will notice a lesser increase in the figures (4.8 percent compared to 6.3 percent), while there was an actual decrease in many other places such as Pessac (−2.4 percent), Caudéran (−5.8 percent), Mérignac (−5.9 percent), Floirac (−30.8 percent), or Bruges (−36.1 percent).

An argument that this alleged crime wave was feeding on the police's lack of efficiency would be untrue. Out of the twelve towns—Bordeaux being excluded—the proportion of unsolved cases was accruing only in Lormont (four percentage points), Le Bouscat (five), Caudéran (ten), and Floirac (fourteen); it was receding in all the other towns, and particularly where there were many offenses—such as in Talence or Bassens. A thorough study of the 1920 police survey is thus somewhat contradictory with the alarming reports sent to the Home Minister. Yet the chief superintendent and the *préfet,* who were in charge of law enforcement, were deeply worried about yet another kind of delinquency, which had more to do with moral than with public order. It was the alleged crime of prostitution.

Prostitution was not an offense in itself; only soliciting was targeted as reprehensible. As early as August 1914, about ten prostitutes a night were arrested. It turned out to be a recurring topic in all the wartime police reports, with special emphasis on the spread of venereal diseases. A circular from the war minister to the Military Health Service raised the matter again in January 1916, underlining the spread of such diseases at the national level, and especially the dreaded syphilis, which was branded "a national danger."[31] In a similar vein, the superintendent was pointing out to the *Préfet* that "syphilis cases are increasingly common, due to Senegaleses, Negroes, Arabs; many a servicewoman, honorable up to here, has contracted the illness . . . society women, Red Cross nurses would have been seeking those Negroes."[32] The *Préfet* repeated it to the minister in his monthly report for February 1918: "Prostitution is still spreading fast, which is worrying for hygiene as much as for morals. It is parading with no shame at all and, as we get accustomed to it, we are no longer shocked by the scandalous scenes which happen in broad daylight, caused by women and above all young girls looking for American soldiers or any other kind of client."[33] He reported again, on 13 May 1918: "Night raids are always fruitful. We are picking up many unfortunate women, registered or not as prostitutes."[34]

The ever-present fear of syphilis and of all venereal diseases can be found in many reports. It is noteworthy that this fear was always intricately linked to the presence of the colonial troops, on the one hand, and of female factory workers on the other. These were two groups that were located, in the reporters' point of view, at the margins of society. For example, there was a gunpowder factory with an all-women staff in the nearby township of Saint-Médard, while colonial troops were quartered in the military camp of Souge, only a few miles from the factory. Two reports were sent by the police superintendent to the *Préfet* in March and June 1916, dealing with this particular aspect of the situation. While the first one dismissed any suspicious claim that reproachable things were going on, the second one was written in a totally different way. Since the number of soldiers barracked there had more than doubled, venereal diseases were increasing in a similar proportion. Things were made worse as those troops consisted of "colonial soldiers all more or less suspect on a sanitary point of view. . . . a great many of them are suffering from very obstinate cankers. . . . syphilis is endemic among the Annamites."[35] Yet it is interesting to read in the same report that "prostitutes would not be found among the women living in Saint-Médard, but much more among the 2,000 ones who live in Bordeaux, where they can exercise their trade of pleasure-seller very easily."[36]

This last remark refers once again, and rather pointlessly, to the conception that a prostitute cannot be anything but an element foreign to local society. In this case, Bordeaux, the big city, is seen as contributing to the spread of vice in the wholesome township population. The 9 March 1916 report indicated that because of working together, male and female factory workers were quite promiscuous. But it insisted that there was no soliciting, nor were women "openly living off the profits of debauchery."[37]

It is rather difficult to say to what extent this alleged spread of venereal diseases was true, as there are no reports available for the entire war period. A survey dated 21 April 1916 simply indicates that for the first two months of the year, eighty-three new cases of syphilis were recorded among the armed forces of the eighteenth military division (that is, the one of Bordeaux), ranking at eighth in the twenty-two divisions for this particular disease.[38] Bordeaux, being far from the front, had of course a smaller concentration of troops. While such a high position does indicate that there was some cause for alarm, we are lacking any factors for further comparison.

We have seen that police or prefectoral reports were more often than not alarming in tone. Nevertheless, it is true that the fight against delinquency was devoted to another far-reaching task that was at the center of the police and civilian authorities: the enforcement of law and order.

LAW ENFORCEMENT IN WARTIME BORDEAUX

The breakout of the war did not affect only delinquency. There were, during the following weeks, some incidents easily explained by the exacerbation of bellicism and patriotism. People became excited as the news broke that Austria was waging war on Serbia. Police reports were perfectly clear: on 28 July, twenty or so monarchist activists, the *Camelots du Roy,* were demonstrating in the main streets, followed by "about thirty people of dubious character;"[39] 200 young men were in the streets on the day after, demonstrating in favor of war, causing some trouble to the police forces.[40] All this agitation, however, was only a flash in the pan. There were still some minor incidents at the beginning of August when a number of people were accused of making common cause with Germany, if not of being German spies. Two grocers' shops advertising for Maggi products (an Alsatian firm) were ransacked on 4 August, as they were in many other French towns. Police intervention prevented the situation from getting worse, as the grocers themselves were close to being lynched, but it does not seem that the rioters were tried. Yet no similar event was reported by the police after the middle of August.

The supervision of the political activists was a more important task. There existed in the 1910s what was called the *Carnet B:* A file with the names of all the spies, or suspected ones, and antimilitarist activists who would try to hamper the war effort. All of them were to be arrested if necessary. Jean-Jacques Becker has shown how this plan had been made obsolete, given the patriotic enthusiasm of the *Union Sacrée.*[41] Indeed, there was in Bordeaux only one person arrested because of the said *carnet,* on 28 July; still, this person, described as an antimilitarist activist by the police report, had been arrested for having shouted "Long live Germany."[42] A like incident happened three days later, but it was a Spanish man who was arrested (there was a rather large Spanish community in Bordeaux). As a matter of fact, the police had been needed to protect the Spaniard from the anger of the crowd.[43] A report dated 1 August still mentioned a few seditious cries ("Long live Germany," "Down with the police," etc.), but there were no more than six such cases.[44]

The fight against any kind of pacifist propaganda remained a major activity of the second department of the *Préfecture* throughout the war. Yet its task was by no means an overwhelming one: The city, as it was far from the front, was not a den of activists. There were few incidents and they were by no means outstanding ones, even though official reports kept referring to them as such. On 9 May 1915, a lecture was held by a Norwegian at the Alhambra theatre. An informer, who was sent by the superintendent, reported that the speaker had shown pictures of emaciated German prisoners sick with typhus and full of vermin, compared with snapshots of well-fed French prisoners in Germany. There was an unmistakable message: The real barbarians were not those who were supposed to be. This lecturer was forbidden to come back to Bordeaux ever again, even though his lecture had been a rather unsuccessful event (only a hundred people had come to listen).[45]

The local anarchists were also under police supervision and informers were standing at every meeting to report the usual verbal excesses. On 3 July 1915, some Spanish activists who were meeting in a squalid pub said that it was necessary "to chop their heads off" to all the leaders of the countries at war, after which they plainly disbanded.[46] Although pacifist propaganda was quite active at a national level in 1917, it was rather discreet in Bordeaux. When a ministerial circular was issued, reminding of the need to fight subversive activities, and that "the line to hold on such a case (was) to arrest and to take to court,"[47] a prefectoral report answered that there was little to worry about. In January, a man pretending to be a military almoner was preaching in favor of immediate peace as he was travelling through the south of France. He went through Bordeaux, but did not stay long enough for the police to get their hands on him. That same month, various pacifist tracts were found in letter boxes and duly reported to the military authorities; the people responsible for these could not be arrested, and the whole affair petered out.[48]

Nevertheless, prefectoral reports were changing in tone throughout the war. During the first two years, local authorities feared, or pretended to fear, a handful of activists supporting a generous, yet utopian cause. The year 1917, however, was marked by the outbreak of a much more subversive type of propaganda that refered to the Marxist-Leninist concept of revolution; it was a new source of concern for the people in charge of law and order.

The shadow of revolution spread over most of the reports about the population's state of mind from the beginning of 1917 onward. It is rather amusing to find as early as March 1916 a letter from an inhabitant of Bazas, a township fifteen miles from Bordeaux, who was trying to persuade a local member of Parlement of the imminence of revolution: "[There are] rumours in the area: the bourgeois and priests are the ones responsible for the war. . . . Nowadays, the talk of 'revolution to be done' follows those words almost invariably."[49] But it was only a foretaste of what was to come, words written at random by a somewhat excited person. A more serious matter was to arise about one year later, as is shown in a report from the chief superintendent dated 12 June 1917: "Some kind of popular uprising is to be expected at a date yet to be determined, which could be brought closer by the evolution of the war. The word 'revolution' is on nearly every person's lips."[50]

The ending of the war did little to cool the spirits of the weary inhabitants. As the superintendent warned again in November 1918: "Hunger will be tomorrow's enemy and if decisions are not quickly taken and put into practice, it will be necessary to think of police reinforcement so that the public community will be protected against any kind of excess."[51] The return of the demobilized soldiers was seen as another potential danger, as they could spread subversive ideas: "[Those soldiers] are prone to indiscipline and brutality, which leads to fear it will be even worse when the younger elements are demobilized."[52]

Protecting law and order against any possible kind of revolutionary agitation and fighting an ever-increasing delinquency seem to have been the two imperious tasks delegated to civilian authorities in the years 1917–1919. A reorganization of the police forces was urgently required, if we are to believe what was written in many reports.

The chief superintendent, eager to persuade the *Préfet,* repeatedly insisted on the critical situation his police forces were placed in: "It seems urgent to remedy the police force situation: in all center towns, it should be brought back to its prewar level."[53] "It will not be long before the police services are physically unable to fulfill their duty, at a time when they will be most wanted."[54] The *Préfet* in turn tried to convince the home minister by sending him a rough numerical account of available forces: 5,000 soldiers quartered in the nearby Souges military camp, 100 *Gendarmes,* plus the 300 men from the local police forces. But he added that "it is impossible to rely on the soldiers; should any riot occur in the streets, they would not obey orders."[55] There was only one solution, which was to set up a nationwide police force to alleviate the shortcomings of the local forces. In a report dated 17 June 1917, the *Préfet* was more precise and unveiled a real scheme for remodelling the country's police forces. All the local forces would be incorporated into a 500-strong state police corps whose authority would reach the whole of the conurbation. The forces would be recruited from among the demobilized senior policemen, as well as hired on a voluntarily basis. They would not be paid less than six francs a day in order to achieve maximum motivation and efficiency.[56]

There were many other prefectoral reports devoted to this topic during the last months of the war as well as during the first half of 1919, when social unrest was running high throughout the country.[57] In 1920 a reform of the police was carried out by the Parlement, setting up the *police nationale.* Yet it did not totally supersede the local police forces, which kept on doing their business and still exist to this day. Nevertheless, it seems rather hazardous to proclaim the chief superintendent or the *Préfet* of Bordeaux as the instigators of this reform.

LOCAL SOCIETY AND THE INFLUX OF FOREIGNERS

There were three different kinds of foreign persons in Bordeaux during World War I: refugees from the German occupied territories, prisoners of war, and American soldiers. The first trains of refugees arrived in August

1914, as the German armies were invading Belgium and the North of France. They were carefully scattered among the nearby towns and villages, as the civilian authorities were eager to avoid Bordeaux becoming over-crowded with them. Consequently, it had not been a source of disorder, apart from a few anecdotal cases. It was different when prisoners of war were given cantonments in the town itself. The reasons for such a decision were obvious. As Bordeaux was far from the war front, there was no real danger of the prisoners trying to help a German attack by breaking into a sudden revolt and opening up a second front behind the Allied positions. At the same time, it was necessary to place them in Bordeaux itself, as a larger number of soldiers and policemen were available to watch over them than in the rest of the area. Most of these prisoners were German and there were a few Austrians. They were used for loading and unloading ships on the right-bank wharves. Yet a series of reports indicate that things did not go as expected.

On 21 February 1916, the superintendent in charge of supervising all means of transport sent a letter to the general in charge of the Eighteenth Military Division. He was worried that the watch of the prisoners on one of the quays was defective (militarymen were in service instead of police-men).[58] It turned out that some women factory workers had come and talked to them. Such a scene was really out of place, yet it was occurring repeatedly. On 21 February 1918, two women picking up chips of wood (the prisoners were used for wood planing) started talking with two German men. One of the women had been seen before at the same place and time, and "had taken no account of what had been said to her"; to make things worse, their husbands were in the army and could be killed anyday.[59] It was a less shocking incident when this foreman was arrested in a café in October 1918: He was providing a drink to his two German workers as "they had been doing a good job and were under his respon-sibility; he did not think he was doing wrong."[60]

A summary note from the superintendent explained to the *Préfet* that all the trouble was coming from "too much freedom being given to the pris-oners of war by non-commissioned officers who do not care and inspire no fear to the prisoners."[61] Beyond these reports, which sounded somewhat shocked or aggrieved in tone, is the impression that the prisoners of war were quite well accepted by the local population. Moreover, those who had been sent to work on farms were praised for the quality of their work. Finally, the reports never suggest that those foreigners may have been trou-blemakers or criminals. It sounded quite different as far as the American soldiers were concerned.

In all official circumstances, the local authorities praised highly the age-old French-American friendship. But the prefectoral services were literally flooded by reports that show how uneasy the cohabitation was. Basically, the soldiers from the United States were being reproached with behaving, if not like being in conquered territory, at least like working in a banana republic. As a matter of fact, there were two different sets of problems. The first consisted of all the offenses committed that were related simply to their presence. The second comprised the incidents caused by what might be called the incompatibility of temperament between the French and the Americans.

The existence of a 500,000-plus strong expeditionary corps was likely to have bad consequences on local delinquency, no matter what precautions were taken. These newcomers were all young and strong, and waiting for their imminent departure for the front. They were in the first place an easy target for the local thieves. The thieves were not really interested in the soldiers' personal belongings, but in all the military gear the U.S. army was carrying along. Any stolen item was likely to be sold at a high price. Weapons were reported to have been stolen,[62] as well as foodstuffs from the American trucks, which were eventually sold on the black market.[63]

Only a few American soldiers appeared as victims in the reports submitted to the *Préfet*. The first months of 1918 were crammed with the incidents they caused. In February, a police report mentioned that two "Black" soldiers had robbed a worker from the Saint-Médard gunpowder factory, and then some other passers-by downtown.[64] Another one insisted on the growing number of thefts made by those rather embarrassing allies.[65] The following month two militarymen were courtmartialed for having stolen a horse.[66]

The expeditionary corps men were also quick tempered, as there were a number of brawls recorded by the French civilian authorities: some twenty or so for the last twelve months of the war (November 1917–November 1918). There was hardly a month that passed by without such an incident. They involved intoxicated groups of American soldiers and passers-by who replied to them. The incidents demonstrate that relations were not quite amicable between the American troops and the local population, even when no indictable offense was committed.

First of all, the local people continually reproached their "allies" for their offhandedness. This was commonplace in the letters and petitions sent to the *Préfet*. For example, there was a letter that eight inhabitants of Saint-Sulpice-de-Cameyrac signed. It was a small village nearing the Souges military camp, where some troops were quartered before leaving for the front. Those eight persons complained about the damages made by "the American soldiers and their *dollies* (their emphasis) in our fields sown with wheat, rye and oats."[67]

Second, there was also matter for complaint about the way the "Yankees" were driving—it must be remembered that cars were quite a curiosity in France outside Paris. Indeed, driving accidents increased as soon as the Americans arrived, and occasionally such accidents could cause death.[68] The *Préfet* was so depressed that he wrote to the superintendent: "those incidents are a real nuisance which is due to end; it has a bad effect on the population, who are worried and asking for protection."[69]

The atmosphere reached the point where a real scare prevailed among the local population, as can be seen from this letter dated 19 February 1918: "People are afraid of going out at night; this is so because of the risks of being assaulted or robbed, but also because many American soldiers are drunk and wandering around until late. Others are in the company of women and are behaving in a scandalous way. Moreover some people are afraid, and rightly so, of the often unjustified use of their gun by military policemen."[70]

This letter brings forward another interesting topic found in many reports. The German prisoners of war were not the only ones to be the darlings of the ladies. Moreover, the charm of the exotic favored the American soldiers. A large number of complaints were recorded, coming from dwellers horrified at the comings and goings of those very peculiar admirers: A shed was being used for nightly meetings, and scandalous scenes could be seen by everyone. Of course, there was the ever-present fear of the spread of venereal diseases. "The American soldiers are seeking the female workers of the gunpowder factory, who are living in barracks and are really easy. Cases of venereal diseases have been recorded among them."[71]

The French and American authorities reacted differently, and there was a clear lack of coordination, which eventually led to further tensions. The French were at first prone to deny the evidence. For example, the chief superintendent replied to one of his subordinates that "no violent behavior [was] known, and [that] the cooperation of [the American] police [was] most useful."[72] There was also the possibility of discarding the plaintiff's claim as an exaggeration. But as it was most important to calm the people down, law-enforcing measures were secretly taken. In February 1918, the headquarters of the French military police of Bassens (on one of the right-bank wharves, placed under strict supervision) decided to forbid all American soldiers to enter a café; all infringers would be imprisoned. Similarly, any soldier found with a woman of "disreputable character" would be treated the same.[73] Three months later the access to the female workers barracks in Saint-Médard was forbidden as well.[74]

The American police, who were in charge of the physical and moral safety of the expeditionary corps, decided to take similar action and to confine their soldiers. According to a report of the superintendent to the *Préfet,* this was the wrong decision, as it would hamper the French police efforts against prostitution. "It can not be totally eradicated in such a large city as Bordeaux, but we were about to contain it outside [*sic*] the perimeter fixed by the Mayor's decree. How could we do it if the U.S. troops are banned from the streets where women of bad character are relegated? It is obvious that they will try to violate the said decree, and non-registered prostitutes, who, to my opinion, are the worst of all, will try to escape our supervision."[75] The superintendent was not far from being right. In September 1918, some American soldiers were reported as regular customers in a non-registered brothel run by a Parisian madam and her lover.[76] Yet, despite the obvious breach of the regulations and the petitions of the neighbors complaining about the noise, no measures seem to have been taken against it.

The American soldiers and the local population did not get along well in Bordeaux, which was the cause of more problems than the presence of German prisoners of war. Perhaps it was the consequence of the clash of two different worlds, giving way to reflexes that may have blurred the expected allies/enemies distinction. Nevertheless, those problems could occasionally be put aside, as on 4 July 1918, when 100,000 people showed that soldiers of the United States could sometimes be popular.

World War I had a more disruptive effect on the local society than what might have been expected at first glance. In particular, we have tried to question the usual assumption of war bringing about a decrease in delinquency. The evidence suggests that there was some decrease in crime, but beyond that fact, we saw how a "war delinquency" had relieved a "peacetime" one. Similarly, a new criminal population emerged. The landing of the American troops, though leading to a quicker victory, opened the way to many troubles, which were not always free from xenophobic connotation, while there was no such behavior in the relations with the German and Austrian prisoners of war. Through its exceptional length and scope, World War I was a turning point in the field of delinquency as in so many others in the early twentieth century.

NOTES

1. Daily reports from the chief superintendent of Bordeaux to the *Préfet* of the Gironde, Archives départementales de la Gironde (hereafter A.D.G.), series 4 M 151–153.

2. Weekly reports on the state of mind of the population, A.D.G., series 1 M 413–415.

3. Supervision of suspect persons during World War I, A.D.G., series 4 M 970–973; press censorship, supervision of the mail, series 1 M 452–461.

4. Supervision of refugees, A.D.G., series 4 M 489–490.

5. Supervision of Austrian and German persons living in the area, A.D.G., series 4 M 970–973; supervision of the prisoners of war, series 9 R 3.

6. American troops in France: incidents, varia, 1917–21, A.D.G., series 10 R 54.

7. Minutes of evidence of the court of first instance of Bordeaux, 1914–18, A.D.G., series U 3486–3548.

8. Especially the daily newspaper *La Petite Gironde,* the last five months of 1914, Bordeaux town library.

9. "L'ordre public n'est pas troublé; les esprits sont indifférents à la guerre," 29 July 1914, A.D.G., 1 M 413.

10. "Sécurité publique: tout est tranquille à Bordeaux," 15 Dec. 1914, A.D.G.; ibid.

11. "La sécurité publique est toujours satisfaisante à Bordeaux," 15 July 1915, A.D.G., 4 M 153.

12. "Le tribunal correctionnel a moitié moins d'affaires à juger qu'en temps de paix. cela tient au départ pour l'armée de nombreux récidivistes, mais aussi à la sévérité toute spéciale, et à ce jour inconnue, du Tribunal et de la Cour," 22 July 1915, A.D.G., d°.

13. Superintendent's daily reports, Aug.–Oct. 1914, A.D.G., 4 M 151.

14. Minutes of evidence of the court of first instance, A.D.G., U 3486–3548.

15. Ibid.

16. Ibid., "Un énervement de la population est perceptible, la cause en étant les nouvelles contradictoires dont elle est assaillie," 25 Aug. 1914, A.D.G., ibid.

17. "A la suite d'une discussion pour un motif futile."

18. Ibid.

19. People arrested for unlawfully carrying a weapon, Aug.–Sept. 1914, A.D.G., 4 M 151. There were still many similar cases in 1918, according to a report to the *Préfet* dated 8 April 1918, A.D.G., 4 M 153.

20. Ibid., 11 May 1915, A.D.G., "Le tribunal se montre très sévère pour les fraudeurs, qu'il punit de peines de prison allant de huit à quinze jours, avec le bénéfice du sursis, mais avec des amendes de vingt-cinq à cent francs (sans sursis), insertion dans les journaux et affichage pendant sept jours à la porte de la Mairie et au domicile du délinquant. La Cour d'Appel suit le Tribunal dans cette voix."

21. 7 Jan. 1916. A.D.G., ibid.

22. Ibid., 11 May 1915, A.D.G., "Le nombre des délits est peu élevé pour les adultes, mais il s'élève en ce qui concerne les mineurs; il s'agit pour ceux-ci de vols, de violences, outrages à agents, maraudage. Beaucoup sont acquittés, huit sur dix rendus à leur famille, d'autres sont placés en liberté surveillée, quelques uns en maison de correction." Ibid.

23. Ibid., "Quelques mauvais éléments ont fait leur rentrée comme réformés, blessés etc.," A.D.G.

24. Ibid., 12 July 1916, "La sécurité à Bordeaux est très médiocre; il y a eu plusieurs agressions nocturnes sur des individus pris de boisson; de nombreux petits vols ont eu lieu et des tentatives de cambriolage."

25. "Les cambriolages se font toujours plus nombreux dans les communes de la périphérie," 29 June 1917, A.D.G., 1 M 413.

26. "Déjà à Bordeaux, ville plutôt calme et suffisamment policée, l'insécurité s'y manifeste assez sérieusement et pourrait devenir dangereuse." Prefectoral report on the state of mind of the population, Dec. 1918, A.D.G., 4 M 415.

27. Ibid., Feb. 1919, "Il est urgent de réorganiser les forces de police, ne serait-ce que pour combattre les crimes et les délits ordinaires qui tendent à se multiplier."

28. Ibid., March 1919, "La criminalité augmente chaque jour; les vols, les cambriolages, les attaques nocturnes, l'assassinat se multiplient de façon particulièrement inquiétante."

29. Ibid., April 1919, "L'insécurité est grande la nuit dans la ville, où les attaques et les cambriolages se multiplient."

30. Return of crimes and misdemeanors committed 1918–1919, A.D.G., 4 M 174.

31. "Un fléau national," prostitution and venereal diseases, A.D.G., 4 M 337.

32. "Les cas de syphilis sont de plus en plus nombreux, due aux Sénégalais, Noirs, Arabes; de nombreuses femmes mobilisées, honnêtes jusque là, ont contracté la maladie . . . les femmes du monde, les infirmières de la Croix Rouge, auraient recherché le contact de ces Nègres," Superintendent's daily reports, A.D.G., 4 M 153.

33. "La prostitution continue de se développer dans des proportions iquiétantes pour l'hygiène et pour la morale. Elle s'étale sans la moindre pudeur et, l'habitude aidant, on finit par ne plus guère s'offusquer des scènes scandaleuses qui se produisent en plein jour de la part de jeunes femmes et surtout de gamines à la chasse de soldats américains ou de tout autre client," prefectoral report on the state of mind of the population, Dec. 1918, A.D.G., 4 M 415.

34. "Les rafles, la nuit, sont toujours fructueuses. On ramasse souvent de nombreuses femmes de mauvaise vie, inscrites ou non sur les contrôles de la prostitution," 13 May 1918, A.D.G., 4 M 153.

35. "Des soldats coloniaux qui sont tous plus ou moins suspects au point de vue sanitaire. . . . Beaucoup souffrent de chancres très tenaces. . . . La syphilis est endémique chez les Annamites," prostitution and venereal diseases, 5 June 1916, A.D.G., 4 M 337.

36. Ibid., "On ne trouvera pas de prostituées parmi les femmes habitant à Saint-Médard, mais plutôt parmi les 2000 d'entre elles qui vivent à Bordeaux, où elles peuvent exercer leur activité de marchande de plaisir."

37. Ibid., "Il n'y a pas de racolage, ni de femmes vivant ouvertement du profit de la débauche."

38. Ibid.

39. "Une trentaine de jeunes gens douteux," superintendent's daily report, 28 July 1914, A.D.G., 1 M 413.

40. Ibid.

41. Jean-Jacques Becker, Le Carnet B. Les pouvoirs publics et l'antimilitarisme avant la guerre de 1914 (Paris, 1973).

42. "Un antimilitariste a été arrêté, qui avait crié 'Vive l'Allemagne,' " A.D.G., 4 M 151.

43. 31 July 1914; A.D.G., 4 M 151.

44. Supervision of public meetings and pacifist propaganda, A.D.G., 4 M 435.

45. Ibid.

46. Ibid., "Il faut couper le cou à tous les chefs des nations belligérantes."

47. Ibid., 13 Jan. 1917, "La ligne à tenir en pareil cas est la suivante: arrêter et traduire en justice."

48. Letter annexed to a prefectoral report, A.D.G., 1 M 414.

49. Ibid., "Des bruits courent dans les campagnes: les bourgeois et les curés sont les auteurs de la guerre. . . . Aujourd'hui, le mot de révolution à faire accompagne presque toujours ces paroles."

50. "Un mouvement populaire est à prévoir, à une époque encore indéterminée-

mais que les événements de la guerre peuvent rendre assez prochaine; le mot de révolution est devenu à peu près familier à tous," A.D.G., 4 M 415.

51. Ibid., Dec. 1918, "La faim sera l'ennemi de demain, et si des mesures pratiques n'ont pu être prises en temps voulu, il sera nécessaire de prendre des mesures de police susceptibles de garantir la communauté contre les excès de certains."

52. "(Ces soldats) manifestent un état d'esprit qui révèle une indiscipline plutôt brutale, qui conduit à craindre une brutalité encore plus accentuée de la part des éléments d'âge moins rassis des classes à libérer," Superintendent's report to the *Préfet*, 12 June 1917, 1 M 414.

53. "Il semble qu'il y ait urgence à rémédier à l'insuffisance des forces de police qui devraient être rétablies, dans les centres, aux contingents d'avant-guerre, pour le moins," Aug. 1918, A.D.G., 4 M 415.

54. "Les services de police, de plus en plus réduits, seront sous peu de temps dans l'impossibilité matérielle d'assurer leur mission et cela au moment même où leur concours serait des plus nécessaires," 17 June 1917, A.D.G., 1 M 414.

55. Ibid., "On ne peut compter sur les hommes de troupe si un mouvement important se produisait dans la rue, ils n'exécuteraient pas les ordres."

56. 17 June 1917, A.D.G., 1 M 414.

57. Ibid.

58. A.D.G., 9 R 3.

59. Ibid., "L'une de ces femmes a déja été vue au même endroit et n'a tenu aucun compte de ce qui lui a été dit."

60. Ibid., 2 Oct. 1918, "Ils avaient bien travaillé et étaient sous sa surveillance; il ne pensait pas mal faire."

61. Ibid., 12 Sept. 1918, "Tout le problème vient de la trop grande liberté laissée aux prisonniers de guerre par une surveillance de sous-officiers indifférents et n'inspirant aucune crainte aux prisonniers."

62. 28 Aug. 1918 and 6 July 1919, A.D.G., 10 R 54.

63. Ibid., Reports dated June and September 1918.

64. Ibid.

65. Ibid., 19 Feb. 1918.

66. Ibid., 6 March 1918.

67. Ibid., 12 May 1918, "Les soldats américains et leurs *poupées* dans nos terrains ensemencés en blé, seigle, et avoine."

68. Ibid., 14 and 20 March, 14 May 1918, and 16 April 1919.

69. Ibid., 14 May 1918, "Ces incidents constituent de véritables violations auxquelles il est urgent de mettre fin, produisent une fâcheuse impression dans le public qui s'émeut et demande protection."

70. Ibid., 19 Feb. 1918, "Les gens n'osent plus sortir de chez eux dès la nuit tombée; cet état d'esprit s'explique non seulement par les actes d'agression et de rapine précités, mais par la raison que de nombreux soldats américains, en état d'ivresse manifeste, parcourent et jusqu'à une heure trop tardive les rues et les chemins. D'autres, que ces militaires sont en compagnies de filles et se livrent à des scènes scandaleuses. Il faut joindre à cela la crainte bien justifiée de l'emploi, parfois bien abusif, du revolver par les policemen militaires."

71. Ibid., 16 Feb. 1918, "Les soldats américains recherchent les ouvrières de la poudrerie qui sont cantonnées dans des baraquements, et en général de moeurs faciles. Des cas de maladies vénériennes sont constatés parmi le personnel fémin."

72. Ibid., 21 Feb. 1918, "Aucun fait de brutalité n'est connu, et la coopération de cette police est fort précieuse."

73. Ibid.

74. Ibid.

75. Ibid., Police report dated 26 Oct. 1918, "(La prostitution) ne peut être totalement éradiquée dans une ville aussi grande que Bordeaux, mais nous étions parvenus à la contenir en dehors du périmètre que le Maire avait déterminé par décret. Comment pourrons-nous y parvenir si les soldats américains se voient interdire les rues où les femmes de mauvaise vie sont reléguées? Il est évident qu'elles tenteront d'enfreindre ledit décret, et les prostituées qui ne sont pas en carte, qui sont, à mon avis, les pires, tenteront d'échapper à notre surveillance," prostitution and venereal diseases, superintendent's report, 13 March 1918, A.D.G., 4 M 337.

Authority, Control, and Class Justice: The Role of the *Sondergerichte* in the Transition from Weimar Germany to the Third Reich

Anthony McElligott
University of St. Andrews

INTRODUCTION

The subject of "political" or "class" justice and the German judiciary has been discussed for the early years of the Weimar Republic,[1] and it has received some treatment for the middle years, concentrating mostly on the trials of major figures on the left.[2] But the subject has been scarcely dealt with for the critical period of transition from the late Weimar years to the Third Reich. The purpose of this chapter is to offer a preliminary discussion of this virtually unexplored subject.

The period of transition from a liberal democratic state-form to an authoritarian state-form commenced in 1930 and climaxed in 1933–1934 with the consolidation of Adolf Hitler's personal dictatorship. An insight into both the means and character of this return to the authoritarian state can be found in the courtroom practice of German judges and state prosecutors. The judiciary, I shall argue, was guided by its own set of political values, professional mores, and social prejudices, which were independent of, though not necessarily fully different from, those of the Nazis.

The first part of this chapter presents a general but necessary introduction to the political situation and the position of the judiciary in the transitional period from the Weimar Republic to the Third Reich. The second part discusses in broad terms the historical context, politics, and role of the *Sondergerichte*—summary courts—after their introduction in August 1932 until the end of that year, and from their reintroduction in March 1933.

In order to illustrate my overall thesis, the third part draws on a particular case that occurred in the north German city of Altona. Altona was part of the manufacturing conurbation and port complex centering on Hamburg, and as such it was considered a stronghold of the political left. The city administration was led by the Social Democrats, and the two main parts of the city, Ottensen and Altstadt, were identified as being either socialist or communist in political configuration. During the late Weimar period the city became increasingly contested by both the far-left led by the KPD (*Kommunistische Partei Deutschlands*), and the far-right united around the NSDAP (*Nationalsozialistische Deutsche Arbeiterpartei*), with the Altstadt in particular becoming the location for some of the worst scenes of violence to mark the demise of the Weimar Republic.

A judicial process under the auspices of the *Sondergerichte* followed a particularly violent clash on 17 July 1932 and culminated in the so-called "Altona Bloody Sunday Trial," which lasted from 8 May to 2 June 1933. The court passed death sentences against four of the fifteen defendants, which were carried out on 1 August. These were the first judicial killings to take place in the Third Reich and anticipated the flood of miscarriages of justice, invariably ending in capital verdicts, that followed on the heels of the *lex van der Lubbe*.[3]

THE POSITION OF THE JUDICIARY IN THE TRANSITION FROM THE WEIMAR REPUBLIC TO THE THIRD REICH

The degree to which the German judiciary had been "nazified" by the early 1930s,[4] or how pervasive its "co-ordination" under Hitler's regime was, is still the subject of some debate among historians. On the one hand, a number of historians see the German judiciary as being either pressed into service by nazism or remaining by and large at a distance from it, or as openly cooperating only in order to prevent far worse from happening. Thus the average German judge either "stood at a distance to National Socialism" or turned out to be a "courageous resister."[5]

On the other hand, there is a contrary view that is less sympathetic toward Germany's judiciary, and is summed up in an observation by the exiled leadership of the Social Democrats in early 1935. Since 1933, "Justice," it was said, "has lowered itself to become the prostitute of politics."[6] While this position castigates the judiciary for its willingness to abandon principles of justice and democracy, it ultimately exonerates the judiciary from full culpability for the crimes of the Third Reich on the assumption that the legal system and its personnel became increasingly subject to Nazi manipulation (*Lenkung*). The logic of this position would be to deny the judiciary its historical role and any responsibility for miscarriages of justice. This view has recently been echoed in a number of meticulous studies, not least the pioneering work of Werner Johe on Hamburg and the *magnum opus* of Lothar Gruchmann.[7]

However, Emil Gumbel and Franz Neumann, among others, pointed out half a century ago that the German judiciary, and judges in particular, were happy to twist justice to suit their view of the world. Nor had they ever flocked to the banner of democracy and republicanism; indeed, they bore a heavy responsibility for Weimar's eventual downfall.[8] Klaus Marxen has gone even further in suggesting that the courtroom activities of the judiciary during the Third Reich were not subordinated to the political imperatives of the regime, but vice versa; politics underwent a process of judicialization.[9] This is to argue that the judiciary, rather than being the tool of the Nazis, actively participated in the shaping of politics wherever their interests dovetailed with those of the Nazis, at least until the later 1930s.[10]

It is well known that before March 1933 the majority of German judges and state prosecutors stood apart from the NSDAP, tending instead more toward the politics and views common to the ultra-conservative and nationalist camp. Even after many of their profession joined the party in the first few years of the Third Reich and their organizations were coordinated, they still managed to retain a degree of autonomy in spite of political pressure from the Nazis. The various sections of the German legal profession were neither comprehensively nor equally affected by the process of coordination (*Gleichschaltung*) and the purges that accompanied this process. It is an almost impossible task to construct a comprehensive national picture, because the necessary sources are both sparse and inconsistent. Therefore, one can only provide a general and impressionistic picture by extrapolating from particular case studies.

Lothar Gruchmann, in what must be the most authoritative work to date on the judiciary during the Third Reich, shows that there was a widely differing practice between the *Länder* in implementing the Law for the Restoration of the Professional Civil Service and the Law for the Admission to the Practice of Law, both passed in April 1933.[11] Prussia proved to be the most draconian in executing these laws.

Gruchmann shows how the impact on overall membership was a lot less dramatic than hitherto portrayed. Those most affected by the new laws in Prussia—as indeed elsewhere in the country—were the Jewish lawyers and notaries registered at the thirteen provincial high courts (*Oberlandesgerichte*). They formed the great majority of the 11 percent and 16 percent respectively of lawyers and notaries purged.[12] Both he and Shorn show that judges and state prosecutors, enjoying higher civil servant status (*höhere Beamte*), were less affected by the laws: barely 2 percent were purged, and again, these were mostly Jewish personnel.[13]

The judicial administration of the province of Schleswig-Holstein was hardly affected by the changes of 1933.[14] To be sure, the province's long-serving chief state prosecutor in Kiel, Dr. Peter Hansen (1921–1933), was replaced by Dr. Viktor Sauer, a nationalist and jurist of the "old school," as was the province's chief judge, Dr. Gottfried Kuhnt (1928–1933) by Dr. Karl Marten.[15] But the personnel at the county court in Altona, which came under the chief prosecutor's jurisdiction, appear to have remained undisturbed by the political change in 1933.[16] It is also important to note that the replacements of purged personnel were not necessarily fanatical Nazis.

Very often experience took precedence over party membership, which explains why less than half of the fourteen new provincial state prosecutors (*Generalstaatsanwälte*) after 1933 were Nazis.[17]

In general, there was little discontinuity in personnel from one regime to the other. Of course, continuity in personnel does not necessarily mean continuity in the dispensation of justice (*Rechtsprechung*), but this, too, was largely unchanged. Contrary to the older but still widely held view that some rupture in the role and practice of the courts occurred between Weimar and the Third Reich,[18] the evidence can be interpreted to suggest less disturbance in the verdicts of the courts, especially in the crisis years of 1932 and 1933 when the *Sondergerichte* came into operation. This court gave Germany's politicized judiciary the necessary tool with which to refashion the criminal justice code, which, in their view, had grown flabby in the liberal climate of Weimar. They were thus able to deploy legal terror against the working class per se, in whom they identified the causes for national decline and an obstacle to the reassertion of authority.[19]

AUTHORITY BETWEEN CRISIS AND CONTROL AND THE ROLE OF THE *SONDERGERICHTE*

Germany's leaders experienced the last months of the Weimar Republic with a sense of deepening crisis of their authority as the country plunged further into social and economic distress, accompanied and exacerbated by a rising tide of political violence fought out mostly between Communists and Nazis.[20] The election month of July in particular saw maimings and deaths perpetrated on both sides, which shocked a German public that by now had become all too familiarized with violence[21] though not necessarily accepting it. In Prussia alone during June and July, there were an estimated 461 incidents of violent clashes resulting in eighty-two deaths.[22] While some of this violence was not always under the control of either party's leadership, many of these deaths resulted from the murderous street battles provoked by the Nazis and their paramilitary organizations as they staged so-called *Werbemärsche* (propaganda marches) through mainly working-class districts of towns and cities. For some residents of such areas, these invasions of "red territory" recalled the sieges laid by *Freikorps* detachments during the counterrevolution of the early days of the Weimar Republic.[23]

The list of casualties grew longer as the election of 31 July drew closer. On Sunday, 10 July, street battles occurred in a number of cities throughout the Reich, claiming a total of at least eleven lives. The following Sunday, 17 July, the worst battle of all during this crisis period took place in Altona, when some 7,000 Nazi storm troopers attempted to march through some of the so-called "purely Communist" and "meanest streets" of the poorer districts of the city.[24]

The political consequences of the "Altona Bloody Sunday" shook the republic to its foundations. The death toll eventually rose to eighteen, with over a hundred more persons injured.[25] Blame for the deaths was attributed to communist gunmen. The police authorities claimed that their officers had come under a barrage of sniper fire from the rooftops and windows of the houses lining the narrow streets through which the Nazis marched.[26] They, the police, had been as much the targets for communist fire as the Nazis, and had fought a serious engagement with an enemy hidden from view by a largely sympathetic local population.[27] A picture of the forces of law and order under siege soon emerged from official reports.[28]

In the public domain, politicians and the media frequently spoke of a "civil war situation," and portrayed the state as endangered from the combined forces of communism and social anarchy.[29] This idea of an insurgent working class, which was both insubordinate and contemptuous of authority, seeking to wage war openly on state and society, was firmly planted in the mind of the conservative Dr. Diefenbach, who functioned as commissarial chief of police in Altona for eight critical months from 24 July 1932 to 28 March 1933.[30] In his assessment of "Altona Bloody Sunday," the communists and local population had not acted from self-defense, but instead had set out deliberately to "strike a blow at authority in order to cause the state to totter."[31] In his view, "only stern and consequential measures can restore respect and obedience" and thus bring the rebellious working class to heel.[32]

Meanwhile, the Nazis, who had been the original cause of the trouble, metamorphosed into victims of working-class and Communist rowdyism and violence. For instance, four days before the massacre, Joseph Goebbels, ignoring entirely the fact that much of the violence of that summer was being generated by his own movement, wrote in his diary of the "red murder raging through the country."[33] And on hearing the news from Altona and of the deaths of two local storm troopers, Heinrich Koch and Peter Büttig, he expressed his horror, exclaiming, "The KPD attack in an organized assault upon our marching S.A. . . . Civil war is declared. When will the state act?"[34]

The answer to his question came three days later. Authoritarian conservatives led by the Reich Chancellor, Franz von Papen, the Reich interior minister, Wilhelm von Gayl of the German Nationalist Party, and the army minister, General Kurt von Schleicher, took events in Altona as the excuse to dismiss the Prussian coalition government led by Social Democrat Otto Braun on 20 July.[35] Papen's coup d'etat stepped up the counter offensive against the left and its allies and, indeed, against the remnants of the republic's parliamentary democracy.[36]

However, the purging of the "red system" in Prussia and its replacement by a commissarial administration with special powers to "restore law and order," while accepted by Goebbels as a step in the right direction,[37] was still not enough to satisfy everyone. An editorial in the Nazi provincial newspaper, the *Schleswig-Holsteinische Tageszeitung,* lamented the weakness of Weimar justice, while at the same time it promised retribution for the deaths of the two S.A. men. "It cannot be vengeance if this or that person gets three months prison for the illegal carrying of weapons. Vengeance must be radical. The whole murderous communist plague must be cleared out!" The newspaper concluded that "there would be no pardon and no half-measures."[38] How the deaths of Koch and Büttig were to be avenged was not exactly clear. Certainly, at this point few Nazis placed any faith in Weimar's code of criminal justice, disparaged by many conservatives as a "Magna Carta for the criminal."[39]

During this critical phase of reasserting authority and control—from the summer of 1932 to the early months of 1933—a string of legal measures were taken to neutralize opponents. These began with the emasculation of parliamentary government, starting with the Emergency Decree that dissolved the Prussian government on 20 July 1932 and concluding with the Enabling Act of 23 March 1933.[40] These measures against parliamentary rule must be seen in the context of the attack upon the extra-parliamentary political life that found its climax with the abolition of political parties in the summer of 1933 and the use of terror.

Together, these measures formed a cycle of legally ordained changes to the lawful and constitutional life of Germany which, to paraphrase Ernst Rudolf Huber, were the means to defeat the "old enemy."[41] As Franz Neumann in his celebrated book on the nature and practice of the Third Reich, *Behemoth,* pointed out, "Law is the most pernicious of all weapons in political struggles, precisely because of the halo that surrounds the concepts of right and justice."[42] The introduction of the *Sondergerichte* in early August must be seen as part of this process of instrumentalization of law, one central to the reassertion of the right's political authority, which had suffered in 1918 after the collapse of the "inner front."[43]

Therefore, the purpose of the *Sondergerichte* was solely to strike legal terror into the ranks of the participants of extra-parliamentary politics. Conservative nationalists in and out of government believed they faced a revolutionary situation in the summer of 1932, with a possible united front composed of the two left parties emerging.[44] Government officials agreed that unless tough action was taken, they would lose their political grip. As von Papen was to explain to the international military tribunal in the summer of 1946, "punishable political acts had to be brought to expeditious trial under the law," and the *Sondergerichte* were the best means to achieve this.[45] However, it was a wave of Nazi-inspired violence in the days following the July election that provided the immediate context leading to their introduction.[46] Not surprisingly, Goebbels envisaged the courts operating more against Nazi activists than communists.[47] But, as we shall see, this was not the case.

Similarly, when twenty-six special courts were reintroduced on 21 March 1933,[48] the fragility of the political situation throughout Germany made them necessary. During the cabinet meeting immediately prior to their reintroduction on 21 March, Franz Schlegelberger, the secretary of state at the Reich Justice Ministry, pledged judicial support for the "present government of national renewal" in its fight against "treasonable" acts.[49] A leading jurist in the Justice Ministry who had joined the NSDAP in the autumn of 1932, Dr. Crohne, wrote in *Deutsche Justiz:*

The *Sondergerichte* are called upon in peacetime during periods of political tension through a speedy and emphatic delivery of penal authority to ensure that restless spirits will be warned or removed and that the smooth running of the state machinery will not be disturbed. . . . The sentences will be tightened up and immediately and ruthlessly carried out in order to frighten the like-minded.[50]

Reliable information on the precise number of indictments, trials, and defendants of the *Sondergerichte* before 1933 is difficult to obtain and can be conflicting. Nonetheless, the examples provided here give some idea of their widespread use from the summer of 1932. According to a report published in late November by the Social Democrat weekly, *Vorwärts,* since 12 August (when the courts came into operation) there had been 306 trials before forty-five *Sondergerichte* throughout the Reich, involving no fewer than 1,439 defendants.[51] This may be an underestimate, for an unpublished source in the archives of the Prussian administration shows that until 20 December, when the decree that had introduced the *Sondergerichte* was rescinded, there had been 16,328 cases brought before the thirty-nine *Sondergerichte* operating in Prussia, the majority of which were then transferred to the ordinary courts. The remaining indictments concerned at least 3,278 defendants.[52] In the first weeks and months after Hitler came to power thousands of opponents were rounded up and later brought before the special courts. Official data published in the Reich Statistical Yearbooks suggests a rise for 1933 (March to December), when 5,365 indictments were brought before the special courts, and of which nearly half were in Prussia.[53]

Defendants in many cases had to face the arbitrary and unequal force of the *Sondergerichte.* The position of the prosecution was greatly strengthened at the expense of the defense as a result of a number of innovations "eliminating formalism" and intending to speed up the process of legal retribution "with the greatest possible thoroughness and speed, and at the lowest cost."[54] Inevitably, such innovations led to a reduction in the safeguards guaranteeing the protection of the defendant.

For instance, the pretrial judicial investigation determining whether or not the charges were justified was dispensed with, as were the opening statements of counsel. The defense was denied access to the charges and lost the power to negotiate the setting of a trial date. A shift toward authoritarian justice was indicated in the removal of the right to be tried by one's peers, leaving judgment in the hands of three professional judges whose chairman had wide powers, including the right to deny defense counsel's submission of evidence to the court. Moreover, after sentence had been passed there was to be no legal means of appeal, and a retrial could only take place if new facts or evidence were unearthed that convinced the prosecutor (!) of the necessity for a new investigation in the ordinary courts.[55] In short, the role of the trial was to legally *affirm* the guilt of the defendant and to punish him or her without consideration of mitigating circumstances.[56]

In spite of public claims in 1932 that the *Sondergerichte* were a necessary means to combat political violence of *all* persuasions, in fact they transpired to be vehicles mainly for the repression of the left.[57] The author of the *Vorwärts* article cited above marshalled evidence to show how the courts were being used to suppress communists and socialists alike (Table 1). He showed that of the 1,439 defendants, a total of 914 (or 63.5 percent) from all parties were found guilty and convicted. But of this number well over half were members of the Socialist and Communist parties, who also stood a greater chance of conviction (Stahlhelm excepting). They also received sentences that far outstripped those passed against the right.

These figures hide a complex social history of attrition. While it is true that very little political discrimination seems to have operated in bringing miscreants before the courts, clearly the decisions of the judges displayed the hallmarks of a politicized class justice. This is a pattern that conforms with Emil Gumbel's findings for the early years of the Weimar Republic.[58]

The practice of the Weimar *Sondergerichte* led to widespread concern over the issue of infringements of civil liberties. Nonetheless, this concern was by no means universal. In the Prussian State Chamber, the *Staatsrat,* a heated debate erupted over the courts.[59] The moderate parties protested against the denial of basic rights and the tendency to bring nonpolitical misdemeanors before the courts, as well as the retrospective application of the *Sondergerichte*'s jurisdiction for political acts before 10 August. The latter feature of the courts threatened the principle of *nulla poena sine lege,* and led most political parties in the Prussian State Chamber (*Staatsrat*) to support the Catholic Center Party in its motion calling upon the government to abolish this part of the decree.[60]

On the one hand, the chamber's working committee on constitutional law, dominated by the center right and liberals, acknowledged that the practice of the *Sondergerichte* infringed the basic rights of the individual. Some members stressed, however, that the interests of the state came first.[61] They were prepared to see some regulation of practice but not the removal of the courts. Social Democrats and communists, on the other hand, wished to see the courts revoked entirely and made motions to that effect.[62] The

Table 1
Sondergericht Convictions, August–November 1932

Pol. affil.	Nos. tried	conv.	% total conv.	total sentences[a] 1	2	3	4	5
SPD	302	192	63.5	21.0	–	31.4	90.11	–	3550
KPD	473	325	68.7	35.6	–	244.2	155.7	53	200
NSDAP	539	300	55.6	32.8	5[b]	91.5	139.7	13[c]	1130
Stahlhelm	3	3	100.0	0.3	–	–	9.6	–	–
No Aff.	122	94	77.0	10.3	3	49.1	34.4	15	180

Notes: a (years and months) 1: death penalty; 2: penal

servitude; 3: prison; 4: loss of citizenship; 5: fines

in Marks.

b: convicted for the Potempa murder, but commuted to

life sentence;

c: plus one life term.

Source: "Opfer der Sondergerichte. Eine furchtbare Statistik," *Vorwärts* 562, 29 November 1932.

left was keenly aware of the political bias in the verdicts and called for a reduction in the severity of sentencing.[63] Even the deputies of the NSDAP in the Prussian diet—possibly with the Potempa murderers in mind—complained bitterly about the practice of the courts.[64]

The *Sondergerichte* were eventually withdrawn at midnight on 21 December, under a new Emergency Decree issued by von Schleicher and Gürtner.[65] Unfinished investigations were to be transferred to the ordinary courts.[66] However, this transfer did not necessarily entail a change in the court personnel dealing with individual cases. Moreover, when the courts were reintroduced in March, a simple transfer of cases and personnel back to the *Sondergericht* was effected. The reintroduction of the *Sondergerichte* was welcomed by judges and prosecutors, many of whom could now be assured that the most effective legal means were once more at their disposal in the purging of the "restless spirits" and their "like-minded comrades," as Crohne called them, from the regenerated national community.

PREJUDICE AND POLITICS: THE *SONDERGERICHT* AND CLASS JUSTICE IN ALTONA

There were three *Sondergerichte* in operation in Schleswig-Holstein from the late summer of 1932: Kiel, Flensburg, and Altona, of which the latter was by far the busiest.[67] Unlike the violent clash that led to it, the Altona Bloody Sunday trial has hardly received any attention from academic historians.[68] This is partly because it was only until very recently that the *Sondergericht* files pertaining to the case were made available for scrutiny. And yet the trial provides a concrete example of the deployment of class justice through the courts during the transitional period from Weimar to the Third Reich.

The original list of accused on the indictment sheet of December numbered twenty-one, but by April the list had been shortened to fifteen. Most of the men had been detained since 17 July. Some had been detained then released, and then, on the basis of witness accounts, rearrested at a later date. Other individuals were picked up as the investigation progressed, sometimes as the result of denunciation. Such features in the construction of a *Sondergericht* case were not unlike those that led Rudolf Olden, a prominent Jewish lawyer, to comment in the left-wing literary journal, *Die Weltbühne*: "It is also important how the conflicting parties are brought before the court. Who sits in the dock and who is allowed to raise their hand as a witness? Often the trial is decided before the charge is even made known, and the verdict is not always just."[69]

The fifteen defendants who eventually came to trial in early May were divided into three categories: (1) the Communist leadership with overall responsibility, (2) the snipers, and (3) leaders of the house protection formations and barricade builders. This division roughly corresponded to the three platforms upon which the case against the men had been built: that there was evidence of a Communist conspiracy to attack the S.A. and police with the intention to kill; that there were witnesses who could identify four of the alleged snipers and leaders of the popular house and street resistance; and that there was forensic evidence to substantiate the charges of conspiracy and murder.

Thirty-five-year-old August Lütgens and thirty-seven-year-old Stanislas Switalla (who was being tried in absentia) were cast into the first group; twenty-seven-year-old Walter Möller and twenty-year-old Karl Wolff, both from Hamburg, were put into the second group accused of being communist gunmen, joined by twenty-five-year-old Peter Wolter and nineteen year old Bruno Tesch from Altona. The remaining defendants were banded into the last group. Among the charges the men in the first two groups faced were conspiracy to murder, murder, serious tumult, and attacks against the state. The others faced charges ranging from accessary to murder and serious tumult to disturbance of the peace. The trial lasted four weeks and concluded on 2 June with the death sentence and loss of civil rights in perpetuity given to Lütgens, Möller, Tesch and Wolff; six others faced sentences of penal servitude or prison totaling forty years and six months, and the loss of civil rights for thirty-four years for their alleged part in Bloody Sunday. Three of the defendants were acquitted, while a fourth had charges dropped under the presidential amnesty of 20 December.[70] These four men were taken into "protective custody" immediately after the trial.[71]

The trial had opened in Altona amidst wide public interest on 8 May, after an initial investigation led by a county court judge, Dr. Hildebrand, and a more detailed judicial inquiry by an eleven-man team headed by the state prosecutor in Altona, Dr. Behrens. Behrens and his men were appointed to the *Sondergericht* on 12 August. Hildebrand was also assigned to the *Sondergericht* and continued with his pretrial investigations until April. It was on the basis of their inquiries between July 1932 and April 1933 that the fifteen defendants were to face trial. The judge presiding at the *Sondergericht* was Dr. Block (originally appointed November 17th), with two deputies, one of whom had been appointed on 14 September.[72]

Hildebrand's task originally had been to ascertain for the ordinary courts the involvement in Bloody Sunday of the ninety or so persons taken into custody on 17 July and in the days following. Initially he worked quickly, for by 25 July he had issued warrants for seventy-one detainees, and within ten days could signal the go-ahead for court proceedings for minor charges.[73] This part of the investigation, even before the introduction of the *Sondergericht*, lacked impartiality, for the judge and police acted on the assumption that the men they interrogated were guilty. After the introduction of the *Sondergerichte* and the arrival of Dr. Behrens on the scene, any semblance of legality also appears to have vanished.

As we noted above, the procedural construction of the *Sondergerichte* was not designed to uphold the civil liberties of the defendant. To sift through the many eyewitness accounts and reports upon which the evidence collected by the police and the *Sondergericht* would require much more space than is possible here. What is absolutely clear and is borne out by a detailed analysis of the existing source material is that, in spite of reservations in some quarters of the investigation as to the quality of the testimonies,[74] Behrens was happy to find support for his case from questionable witnesses, many of who were political opponents or who had a pecuniary interest.[75] Moreover, as we shall see, he was also prepared to distort evidence in his quest to substantiate the alleged Communist conspiracy against the NSDAP, police, and state. The court was happy to connive in this.

In court, the prosecution alleged that Lütgens, as a high-ranking member of the Red Front Fighters League, had had overall command of the attack, delegating to his subalterns the placing of snipers organized in ten, five-man fire-groups (*Feuer-Gruppen*) in various parts of the Altstadt. In the case of Wolff and Möller, chief prosecutor Behrens claimed that "without any doubt" they belonged to the squad of gunmen at the corner of Christianstraße and Große Johannisstraße, from where the fatal shots killing Koch and Büttig were said to have been fired. Tesch was said to have been active outside a well-known communist tavern, *Korkenzieher*, on the corner of Große Marienstraße and Große Johannisstraße. Other unidentified snipers were said to have fired from the upper windows of numbers 55 and 62 Große Marienstraße.[76]

The *Sondergericht* was unable to directly prove the involvement of Lütgens, nor could it show beyond doubt that Tesch had either held or fired a gun, nor with certainty that Wolff and Möller were members of the apparent Christianstraße group.[77] The witness accounts seriously contradicted one another on particular points, especially as to the positions, clothing, and physical characteristics of the alleged snipers.

For instance, some of the prosecution witnesses who identified Möller as being among the crowd of men in the Christianstraße stated that Möller had not fired a weapon, and he was dressed differently from the supposed gunman. Also, the general demeanor of the alleged snipers was described as calm and collected, even insolent (*frech*), continuing to shoot at the police as they retreated into the courtyard of Christianstraße 29. Möller, in particular, was imputed by one witness to have fired with "careful consideration" (*Wohlüberlegung*). The S.A. man who claimed this stated how he "had been amazed by Möller's audacity at this moment."[78] Yet at the time of his arrest he was shaking all over, convulsed by extreme nervous agitation brought on by the noise and confusion of gunfire and panicking crowds. The court knew that Möller cut an unlikely figure for a Communist gunman; he was said to have a low mental age and probably suffered some physical disability arising from a series of accidents between 1918 and 1931.[79]

However, such details and anomalies appear to have been ignored by the court. So too were the witnesses for the defense who were able to offer alternative accounts of where individuals had been or what they had been doing at the time of the clash. Nor were they put under oath, and consequently their evidence was spurned by the judges.[80] Furthermore, evidence that had been given during the judicial investigation the previous autumn by key witnesses that was later retracted, thus rendering it unreliable, reappeared as central to the prosecution and was accepted by the tribunal.[81]

The prosecution made a great deal of its employment of scientific techniques to corroborate evidence. The case against Lütgens rested on the existence of a map, said to be in Lütgens's hand, showing the proposed route of the Nazis and the points for attack. This map had been delivered to the police by a man who claimed he had found it in the apartment of Lütgens's lover in the Schauenbürgerstraße.[82] The prosecution relied on the findings of a graphologist as proof that Lütgens was the author of the map. This expert, a retired court official who lived in Paulsenplatz, a relatively middle-class area with a strong nationalist and Nazi affiliation before 1933,[83] found at least twenty-two similarities of style between the map and what he believed to be a sample of Lütgens's handwriting. Yet even to the uninitiated observer, a comparison between the map and the letters Lütgens sent from prison shows absolutely no resemblance between the two.[84] A recent reexamination of this map has also cast into doubt the authenticity of the markings for the positioning of sniper groups, leading the author to conclude that these must have been added retrospectively.[85]

The alleged murder weapon discovered by the police in a cupboard in one of the court houses of Christianstraße 29, where Möller and Wolff had fled along with others to escape the gunfire and the police, was a rusty old Ortgies 7.65mm.[86] Tests carried out in September at the municipal Chemical Investigations Office in Stuttgart on two bullets said to have come from the bodies of Koch and Büttig confirmed that they had been fired from this weapon.[87] According to the prosecution, it was thus beyond doubt that "Koch and Büttig were killed by bullets which were fired by the sniper group on the corner of Christianstraße. This conclusion corresponds with the evidence of the direction of the trajectory of the fatal wounds of the dead."[88]

But it did not. The bullet that killed Koch penetrated the left side of his chest, 3mm from the center and 8mm above the nipple. It created a 5mm opening, damaged his left lung and heart, penetrated the right lung, traversed the 5/6 rib about 6mm from the spine, finally coming to rest approximately 9mm from the spine in the height of the lower part of his shoulder blade. The bullet's trajectory showed a slight decline from left to right, but not enough to suggest he was shot from a window. The impact of the bullet indicated he was shot at close range.[89] Contrary to the assertion made by the prosecution, Koch could not have been shot by anyone standing at the corner of Christianstraße, for were this the case, the bullet would have entered from the right or from the front, given his position at the time.[90]

A similar discrepancy arises in Büttig's case, too. The pathologist's report shows that the bullet entered the right side of his chest at armpit height, leaving a kidney-shaped wound. It made a downward course to the stomach and finally lodged in the lower spine, causing extensive damage to the vertebra. Its trajectory had a sharp incline, having entered the body from above and from a distance.[91] The line of fire suggests, perhaps, a shot fired from horseback, and the direction possibly from the Schauenbürgerstraße into which the S.A. were turning. Nowhere in the records is there any mention of "communist snipers" active there; rather, accounts place only mounted police and the retreating S.A. men there.[92]

The court could not discount out of hand the evidence of the pathologist that stood in contradiction to the allegations of the prosecutor. Dr. Block, as chairman of the tribunal, had to do an acrobatic act in order to get around this problem. In this summing up at the end of the trial, he asserted: "There can be no doubt as to the perpetrators: Möller, Wolff, and Tesch acted as snipers at the corners of Christianstraße and Große Marienstraße. Möller fired from the Ortgies pistol." He then conceded that in Möller's case, "It is not possible to ascertain that he is the one from whose hand the two S.A. men were shot, for the trajectory of the wounds in the corpses could not have stemmed from a kneeling sniper. Also, in the opinion of the court, the fatal shots cannot have been fired from a window."[93] It is not clear if Block was fully aware that he had virtually admitted the spurious nature of the charges.

There was one further and vital piece of evidence that challenged the case against Möller. According to the prosecution, the ballistics evidence from Stuttgart revealed conclusively that the murder weapon was the Ortgies and therefore this "fact" was beyond contention (*unwiderlegbar*). Because the defendants' lawyers had no access to the evidence gathered by the judicial inquiry, and because under the rules governing the *Sondergerichte* the prosecution and chairman of the court decided which evidence could be submitted, counsel for the defense was unable to challenge Behrens's presentation of the forensic material. Had they been allowed access, as permitted under normal court procedure, they would have found that the pathologist's reports contradicted in a disturbing manner the forensic findings. Koch's autopsy showed that the weapon that killed him was a 6.35mm, while Büttig's autopsy revealed that he was killed by an 8mm Browning,[94] two very different weapons altogether from the 7.65mm caliber Ortgies pistol alleged to have been used by Möller. The disturbing fact is that neither bullet obtained from the bodies bore any resemblance to the ones sent to Stuttgart by Behrens and the police during the judicial inquiry the previous autumn.

Would the court's admission of witnesses who offered an alternative version of events, its disregarding of contradictory accounts by dubious witnesses, and the exclusion of manipulated and, indeed, fabricated evidence, have made any difference to its decision to condemn these men to a horrible fate? It is doubtful. The changed political circumstances after 1933 meant that the courts could act freely in dispensing a class justice through the medium of the *Sondergericht*. Already, in 1932, the judiciary was becoming increasingly detached from the political constraints imposed by Weimar's constitutional system, which until now had been able more or less to rein in a too excessive dispensation of justice. With the Nazis in power, the judiciary could rely on even more favorable political sanctions in its efforts to overcome the storm of a perceived "epochal cultural crisis" by dismantling Weimar's "magna carta of the criminal" and its substitution by a more authoritarian justice.[95]

As we saw above, the general practice of the *Sondergerichte* in 1932 was draconian, especially where the politically organized working class was concerned. Under Block's chairmanship, and powered by Behrens's zeal, the special court in Altona before 1933 was more likely than not to find a defendant guilty, was inclined to hand down a sentence of penal servitude than prison, and was willing to mete out sentences that were quite severe when compared to elsewhere.[96] The travesty of justice manifested in the proceedings of the Bloody Sunday Trial and the vicious sentences of death passed on 2 June 1933, were, therefore, not anomalous nor products of "Nazified justice."

The language employed by the court, the prosecutor's office, and by other state officials from the prison director to the prison social worker, who were subsequently consulted during the appeals for clemency from June to the eve of execution, reveals the contours of class prejudice as practiced by a politicized state bureaucracy. All the agencies concerned couched their assessments of the condemned men in terms of the "slum" paradigm and a pseudo-sociological discourse of "criminal types."[97] Indeed, of the fifteen men in the dock, nine had previous convictions, including two of the condemned men.[98] A careful reading of this language and an understanding of the discourse from which it derived, together with a knowledge of the political landscape of Germany during the period, intimates that it was not only the fifteen men who stood in the dock but also the Altstadt's working-class community per se, the proletarian inhabitants of one of Germany's many "little Moscows." By making an example of these men, the government believed, the community itself would heed the lesson.

The city's erstwhile liberal newspaper, *Altonaer Nachrichten*, in a thinly veiled reference to the Paris Communards, reported at the end of the trial as follows:

The intelligentsia of the Altona Commune sit in the dock: There is Lütgens, a man of maturity who one should think capable of sense. He is considered to be the leader of this armed uprising, who behind the scenes held all the threads in his hand. There as well are Tesch and Wolff. One cannot tell from their appearance that they are two assassins of Bloody Sunday. They must have been active in this way a long time because for this "work" only selected experienced fellows from so-called armed formations (*scharf Staffeln*) are chosen. Möller, the third sniper, looks "genuine." One sees the cast of mind of the leaders of the (house) formations (*Häuserstaffeln*) more easily, yet they appear more honest than the others. Only Wendt, the technical leader, makes an exception here. (He) is a *poseur* and a blusterer and seeks, to his comrades cost, to escape his reponsibility for the affair, a typical case of repulsive cowardice.[99]

The observations could also border on the ludicrous. According to Behrens,[100] Lütgens as an illegitimate child from a large family who had little education was, in view of his age, beyond redemption. Behrens reported how Lütgens's "moral inferiority is also revealed by the fact that for years he has left his mother without any news of himself." Moreover, he had a relationship with a local woman, in spite of having a wife and two children in Russia. He would remain a "fanatical bolshevik" who would continue to attack the state. The prosecutor, therefore, energetically opposed clemency.

In the cases of Tesch, Möller, and Wolff, they had grown up in morally degenerate areas, dominated politically by the left. Their lawyer, Harry Soll, wrote to Goering in June pleading clemency on the grounds that "because of their youth they were unable to escape the influence of their environment. They were drawn into communist circles by their work colleagues and friends, and there, because of their political immaturity, fell under the spell of communist ideas."[101]

Such arguments, however, cut little ice with the authorities. The police and the prison director saw in Tesch "a spirited communist" (*ein rühriger Kommunist*) who could not escape his milieu. His biological father was an unknown Italian, and his mother stemmed from a Croat family, considered by the authorities as a volatile and violent mix indeed. Wolff and Möller, who had received more positive social and police reports, were nonetheless described respectively as "troublesome" and of "little intelligence" and "too fond of alcohol," with no corroboration for such allegations. All four were considered to be "fixed in their views" (*unbelehrbar*) and "unrepentant."[102]

Even though Hermann Goering as minister president of Prussia was the ultimate authority who decided whether or not clemency could be granted, the actual decision lay with the chief provincial prosecutor in Kiel, Dr. Viktor Sauer. Sauer was no friend of the working class, and had had occasion in the past to demonstrate this.[103] Although he had been a Nazi choice for chief prosecutor in 1933, he was not a Nazi. Nonetheless, his position was unmistakably close to that of the young Nazi jurist Roland Freisler, who, in 1933, also called for a more authoritarian justice that would not shirk from the extirpation of "asocial elements."[104] In Sauer's view:

The survival of the German *Volk* and the state absolutely demands that this enemy be annihilated with all means. . . . The hitherto inadequate and thus unsuccessful struggle against communism . . . forces the severest measures, of which only the obliteration of this most bitter and dangerous enemy of the nation can be expected. . . . Also, leniency would not be respected by the great majority of the supporters of bolshevism. Instead, it would be inferred as a weakness. . . . The carrying out of the punishments would demonstrate indelibly to communist inclined circles the entire gravity of the situation; it would be a lasting warning to them and work as a deterrent.[105]

The need to strike terror effectively was all the more necessary because, in mid-1933, the process begun the previous summer of reasserting conservative authority was still incomplete. The state was still not sure of itself in the face of continuing popular and organized resistance. Its apparent insecurity was flaunted in its face by Lütgens himself, who turned Sauer's analysis on its head. He is said to have told his captors, "The government would reprieve him if it felt strong enough, but if it felt weak, it would confirm the verdict and carry it out."[106]

CONCLUSION

In *Mein Kampf,* Adolf Hitler expressed in crude but vivid terms the task of the political right in Germany in its fight to reestablish authority over the organized working class. He wrote, "The first requirement [is] always the elimination of the Marxist poison from our national body. And in my opinion, it [is] therefore, the very first task of a truly national government to seek and find the forces which [are] resolved to declare a war of annihilation on Marxism."[107] The judiciary provided Hitler with the allied and necessary force to fight his "war of annihilation." But this is not to argue that it was merely a tool pressed into the service of Nazism.[108] It has been the contention of this chapter that German judges and prosecutors shared a tradition of conflict with the working class in both its social and political entities; It was their "war of annihilation" too, and in 1932–1933 the *Sondergericht* was their preferred weapon.

NOTES

1. E. J. Gumbel, *Vier Jahre politischer Mord* (1922, reprint Heidelberg, 1980).

2. Heinrich and Elizabeth Hannover, *Politische Justiz 1918–1933* (Frankfurt am Main, 1966); Gotthard Jasper, *Der Schutz der Republik: Studien zur staatlichen Sicherung der Demokratie in der Weimar Republik 1922–1930* (Tübingen, 1963).

3. I will not be reconstructing the events of "Bloody Sunday," nor presenting the minutiae of the the trial itself; that would breach the parameters of the present chapter. For the Reichstag Fire trial and the *lex van der Lubbe,* see Martin Broszat, "Zum Streit um den Reichstagsbrand," in *Vierteljahreshefte für Zeitgeschichte* 8 (1960); idem., *Der Staat Hitlers: Grundlegung und Entwicklung seiner inneren Verfassung* (Munich, 1969), 405; and Lothar Gruchmann, *Justiz im Dritten Reich* (Munich, 1990), 826f.

4. "Frühling am Reichsgericht," *Leipziger Volkszeitung,* 14 April 1931, cited in Bundesminister der Justiz, ed., *Im Namen des Deutschen Volkes: Justiz und Nationalsozialismus* (1989), 57–58. Hermann Weinkauff estimates that before 1933 only about thirty of the 7,000 judges in Prussia belonged to the NSDAP and

that these were most likely to be younger members of the profession. Hermann Weinkauff, *Die Deutsche Justiz und der Nationalsozialismus: Ein Überblick. Die deutsche Justiz und der Nationalsozialismus* Part. 1 (Stuttgart, 1968), 108. For an introduction to the subject, see Dieter Simon, "Waren die NS-Richter 'unabhängige Richter' im Sinne des Š 1 GVG?," Bernhard Diestelkamp and Michael Stolleis, eds., *Justiz im Dritten Reich* (Frankfurt am Main, 1988). A concise overview of the literature can be found in Klaus Bästlein, "Als Recht zu Unrecht wurde: Zur Entwicklung der Strafjustiz im Nationalsozialismus," *Aus Politik und Zeitgeschichte: Beilage zur Wochenzeitung Das Parlament* B13–14/89 (24 March 1989).

5. Weinkauff, *Die Deutsche Justiz,* and Gerhard Kramer, "The Courts of the Third Reich," *The Third Reich* (London, 1955), 626, for the quotes. Eberhard Kolb, "Die Machinerie des Terrors. Zum Funktionieren des Unterdrückungs-und Verfolgungsapparates im NS-System," in Karl Dietrich Bracher, Manfred Funke and Hans-Adolf Jacobsen, eds., *Nationalsozialistische Diktatur 1933–1945. Eine Bilanz* (Bonn and Düsseldorf, 1983): 270–84, art 280; and Hinrich Rüping, "Strafrechtspflege und politische Justiz im Umbruch vom Liberalen Rechtsstaat zum NS-Regime", in Josef Becker, ed., *1933: Fünfzig Jahre danach: Die national sozialistische Machtergreifung in historischer Perspektive* (Munich, 1983), 159, 163.

6. SOPADE 1935 (Salzhausen and Frankfurt am Main, 1980), 251.

7. Werner Johe, *Die gleichgeschaltete Justiz: Organisation des Rechtswesens und Politisierung der Rechtsprechung 1933–1945, dargestellt am Beispiel des Oberlandesgerichtsbezirks Hamburg* (Frankfurt am Main 1967), 93; and Gruchmann, *Justiz,* 1143–44.

8. Franz Neumann, *Behemoth: The Structure and Practice of National Socialism 1933–1944* (New York, 1942, 1944, reprint 1963 and 1983), 20–23; Ralph Angermund, " 'Recht ist, was dem Volke nutzt.' Zum Niedergang von Recht und Justiz im Dritten Reich," in Karl Dietrich Bracher, Manfred Funke and Hans-Adolf Jacobsen, eds., *Deutschland 1933–1945: Neue Studien zur nationalsozialistischen Herrschaft* (Bonn and Düsseldorf, 1993), 75; and Gotthard Jasper, "Justiz und Politik in der Weimarer Republik," in *Vierteljahreshefte für Zeitgeschichte* 30 (1982): 169–70.

9. Klaus Marxen, "Strafjustiz im Nationalsozialismus Vorschläge für eine Erweiterung der historischen Perspektive," in Diestelkamp and Stolleis, *Justiz im Dritten Reich,* 102.

10. Martin Broszat, "Zur Perversion der Strafjustiz im Dritten Reich," *Vierteljahreshefte für Zeitgeschichte* 6 (1958): 390, 397, 403; and Dietmut Majer, "Justiz und NS-Staat. Zum Einfluß der NSDAP auf die Organisation und Personalpolitik der Justiz 1933–1945," in *Deutsche Richterzeitung*.

11. RGBl (1933) I, "Gesetz zur Wiederherstellung des Berufsbeamtentums, Vol. 7, April 1933," 175–77.

12. Gruchmann, *Justiz,* 151f1., 1117. Ingo Müller, *Hitler's Justice: The Courts of the Third Reich* (Cambridge, MA, 1991), 61, gives 1,500 as the number affected by the measures. The authors mentioned here make the distinction between lawyers admitted to the bar and legal personnel (prosecutors, judges, etc.) employed by the state. For the older view, see Weinkauff, *Die deutsche Justiz,* 151, 160; Kramer, "The Courts of the Third Reich", 626; and K.-D. Bracher, *The German Dictator-*

ship: *The Origins, Structure and Consequences of National Socialism* (Harmondsworth, 1970), 269–71.

13. Gruchmann, *Justiz,* 150, 221–40; and H. Schorn, *Der Richter im Dritten Reich: Geschichte und Dokumente* (Frankfurt am Main, 1959), 730.

14. Based on the Statistik des Preußischen Justizministeriums cited by Schorn, *Der Richter.*

15. Gruchmann, *Justiz,* 228.

16. See, for instance, STAH 421-5, Regierung Schleswig, Akten der Dienststrafkammer (Reichsdisziplinärkammer Schleswig), DK1-46.

17. Gruchmann, *Justiz,* 226.

18. Rüping, "Strafrechtspflege", 161, 168. Weinkauff, *Die deutsche Justiz,* portrays a beleaguered, angry, but impotent judiciary during the "two years of Nazi lawlessness" (i.e., 1933 and 1934), 113; and Johe, *Die gleichschaltete Justiz,* 107.

19. Müller, *Hitler's Justice,* 45, 52–53.

20. "Niederschrift des Staatssekretärs Planck über eine Unterredung mit den deutschnationalen Abgeordneten des preußischen Landtages v. Winterfeld und Borck am 8. Juli 1932," *Akten der Reichskanzlei Weimarer Republik: Das Kabinett von Papen 1. Juni bis 3. Dezember 1932,* Band 1: Juni bis September 1932, bearb. von Karl-Heinz Minuth (Boppard am Rhein, 1989) [hereafter, *Akten der Reichskanzlei:* Kabinett von Papen], Doc. 53, 190–191; and Gotthard Jasper, "Zur Innerpolitischen Lage in Deutschland im Herbst 1929," *Vierteljahreshefte für Zeitgeschichte* 8 (1960):281.

21. Richard Bessel, *Political Violence and the Rise of Nazism: The Storm Troopers in Eastern Germany 1925–1934* (New Haven and London, 1984); and Eve Rosenhaft, *Beating the Fascists? The German Communists and Political Violence 1929–1933* (Cambridge, 1983).

22. See *Akten der Reichskanzlei:* Kabinett von Papen, 249 n.1; and *Preussen contra Reich vor dem Staatsgerichtshof: Stenogrammbericht der Verhandlungen vor dem Staatsgerichtshof in Leipzig vom 10. bis 14. und vom 17. Oktober 1932* (Berlin, 1933), 14–17.

23. Helmut Heins, "Der 'Altonaer Blutsonntag' Hintergründe, Erlebnisse, Zusammenhänge, Entwicklungen," idem. et al., *Bruno Tesch und Gefährten: Erinnerungen an den 'Altonaer Blutsonntag'* (Hamburg, 1983), 15–16.

24. *London Times,* 2 Aug. 1933; Institut für Marxismus-Leninismus beim ZK der SED, Zentrales Parteiarchiv, IV 3/2/1078 (hereafter, IML, ZPA, IV 3/2/1078, followed by serial number), St. 18/217 Preussisches Ministerium des Innerns, Bl. 53 ff: Copy of nine-page report—Der Minister des Innerns, II 1272 OP Schleho/ 65, Berlin 17 Aug. 1932, "Entwurf," 4. This provisional report was actually formulated by *Oberregierungsrat* Rudolf Diels together with a colleague, R. A. Dr. zur Nedden. Diels later forged a successful career under the Nazi Regime. Rudolf Diels, *Lucifer ante portas* (Stuttgart, 1950).

25. Landesarchiv Schleswig Rep. 352 *Sondergerichtsakten* (hereafter LAS followed by serial number), 352/1241, Der Oberstaatsanwalt als Leiter der Anklagebehörde. Altona, 11 Son. J. 3/32. Namenverzeichnis zur Strafsache gegen Meyer u. Gen. wegen Aufruhrs: Getötete und verletzte Personen.

26. LAS 352/1244 Sub-files 249 and 252: Reports of Pol. Maj. Wendt and 352/ 1242 Sub-file 102: Report of Pol. Lt. Schieritz, responsible for clearing Gr. Marienstrasse 62 and the surrounding area. For copies of the official report from the

office of *Regierungspräsident* Abegg, see LAS 301 (Akten der Preußische Provinzialregierung, Akten des Oberpräsidenten), 301/4709, Der Regierungspräsident Schleswig An den Herrn Preuss; Minister des Innern—Betrifft: Blutige (*sic*) Ausschreitungen der Kommunisten in Altona am 17. d. Mts. (Berichterstatter: Regierungsassessor Dr. Krüger, Polizeimajor Röh, 19 July 1932); and "Bericht des Regierungspräsidenten in Schleswig Abegg an den Preußischen Innenminister Severing," *Akten der Reichskanzlei: Kabinett von Papen*, Doc. 67, pp. 248–56.

27. IML, ZPA, IV 3/2/1078, St. 18/217 Bl. 63f1.: Der Pol. präs. A/W IA 3557/32, 17 Sept. 1932—Betr. Politische Ausschreitungen und Strassenunruhen v. 17.7.32.

28. Ibid., Bl. 87–100: Der Pr. Min. des Inn. II 1272 O. P. Schleho, Berlin 18 Nov. 1932 (final report). In this final report from the Prussian Interior Ministry, the authorities claimed that at least ten armed, five-man groups had fired on the police. This version of events has carried over into the literature: E. R. Huber, *Deutsche Verfassungsgeschichte seit 1789* (2nd ed., Stuttgart, Berlin, Cologne, and Main, 1991), vol. 7.: Ausbau, Schutz und Untergang der Weimarer Republik, 1052–53; Ursula Büttner and Werner Jochmann, *Hamburg auf dem Weg ins Dritte Reich: Entwicklungsjahre 1931–1933* (Hamburg, 1983), 30–31; Wolfgang Kopitzsch, "Der 'Altonaer Blutsonntag,'" in Arno Herzig, Dieter Langewiesche and Arnold Sywottek, eds., *Arbeiter in Hamburg: Unterschichten, Arbeiter und Arbeiterbewegung seit dem ausgehenden 18. Jahrhundert* (Hamburg, 1983), 509–16.

29. "Minister Besprechung vom 11. Juli 1932, 16.30 Uhr," *Akten der Reichskanzlei: Kabinett von Papen*, Doc. 57, pp. 204–8.

30. "Ministerbesprechung vom 20. Juli 1932, 18 Uhr," ibid., Doc. 72, 265–66; "Sitzung des Preußischen Staatsministeriums vom 21. Juli 1932," ibid., Doc. 76, pp. 281–82. Diefenbach was transferred to Altona from his post as an *Oberregierungsrat* in Hannover. He had served once before as commissarial police president in Altona, from Nov. 1922 to March 1923. Gerd Stolz, "Die Schutzpolizei in Altona und Wandsbek 1869–1937," *Zeitschrift des Vereins für Hamburgische Geschichte* 63 (1977): 46–47, and soon found himself in conflict with the Social Democrat Lord Mayor, Max Brauer—LAS Rep. 309 (Akten des Regierungspräsidenten Schleswig-Holstein), 309/22721, Der Polizeipräsident Altona-Wandsbek in Altona an den Herrn Regierungspräsident Schleswig, 22 Dec. 1932.

31. "Politische Ausschreitungen und Straßenunruhen v. 17.7.1932."

32. Some idea of the sort of "stern and consequential measures" Diefenbach and his ilk preferred can be gauged from the order of the Reich minister of the interior, von Gayl, to the police to make ample use of their firearms, with impunity. LAS 309/22804, Polizeifunkdienst, Berlin 25.7.32.

33. Elke Fröhlich, ed., *Die Tagebücher von Joseph Goebbels: Sämtliche Fragmente: Teil I Aufzeichnungen 1924–1941*, Bd. 2 1.1.31–31.12.36 (Munich, New York, London, Paris, 1987), diary entry 13 July 1932, p. 204.

34. Ibid., diary entry 17 July 1932, p. 206.

35. *Preußen contra Reich*, 18–86; Thomas Trumpp, "Franz von Papen, der preußisch-deutsche Dualismus und die NSDAP in Preußen. Ein Beitrag zur Vorgeschichte des 20. Juli 1932" (Ph.D. Dissertation, University of Tübingen, 1963); and Hagen Schulze, *Otto Braun oder Preußens demokratische Sendung: Eine Biographie.* (Frankfurt/Main, Berlin, and Vienna, 1981).

36. And much to the consternation of the *Land* administrations who feared for

their own positions: Staatsarchiv Hamburg (Hereafter StAH), Senatskanzlei Präsidialabteilung A69, Bl.1 f. (political situation); "Besprechung mit den Staats—und Ministerpräsidenten der Länder in Stuttgart am 23. Juli 1932, 10.45 Uhr," *Akten der Reichskanzlei: Kabinett von Papen*, Doc. 83, 295–313; and Wilhelm Hoegner, *Flucht vor Hitler: Erinnerungen an die Kapitulation der ersten deutschen Republik 1933* (Frankfurt am Main, 1979), 24–28.

37. Fröhlich, *Die Tagebücher von Joseph Goebbels*, diary entry 19 July 1932, p. 207.

38. *Schleswig-holsteinische Tageszeitung*, 20 July 1932.

39. E. R. Huber, *Verfassungsrecht des Grossdeutschen Reiches* (Hamburg, 1937), 280.

40. RGBl. I (1932), "Verordnung des Reichspräsidenten, betreffend die Wiederherstellung der öffentlichen Sicherheit und Ordnung im Gebiet des Landes Preußen. Vom 20. Juli 1932," 377–78; and RGBl. 1 (1933), "Gesetz zur Erhebung der Not von Volk und Reich. Vom 24. März 1933," 141.

41. Huber, *Verfassungsrecht*, 40.

42. Neumann, *Behemoth*, 20.

43. Müller, *Hitler's Justice*, chap. 18, who argues persuasively how the purpose of the *Sondergerichte* changed to become that of strengthening the "inner front" during World War II.

44. "Vermerk des Ministerialrats Wienstein über eine Besprechung in der Wohnung des Regierungsrats Diels am 19 Juli 1932," *Akten der Reichskanzlei: Kabinett von Papen*, Doc. 66, 246–47. See Diefenbach's report to the *Regierungspräsident* (22 Dec. 1932) in LAS 309/22721, the context of which was a united stand between communists and socialists in the city parliament to force Diefenbach to close down a Nazi base in the Altstadt (*Sturmlokal*).

45. International Military Tribunal, Nuremberg Trials Major War Criminals (London, 1947), 16: 281. See also the evidence of Schlegelberger, ibid., vol. 20, 233; Huber, *Verfassungsgeschichte*, vol. 7, p. 1054; and *Reichsgesetzblatt* (Hereafter RGBl), Teil I (1932), "Verordnung der Reichsregierung über die Bildung von Sondergerichten. Vom 9 August 1932," 404–7.

46. See for instance, Paul Kluke, "Der Fall Potempa," in *Vierteljahreshefte für Zeitgeschichte 5* (1957); and Richard Bessel, "The Potempa Murder," *Central European History* 10 (1977), and *Political Violence*, chap. 6 passim.

47. Fröhlich, ed., Die *Tagebücher von Joseph Goebbels*, diary entry 9 Aug. 1932, p. 221.

48. RGBl I (1933), "Verordnung der Reichsregierung über die Bildung von Sondergerichten. Vom 21 März 1933," 136–38.

49. "Ministerialbesprechung vom 21 März 1933, 16 Uhr," *Akten der Reichskanzlei Weimarer Republik: Die Regierung Hitler Teil 1: 1933/34*, bearb. von Karl-Heinz Minuth, 2 vols. (Boppard am Rhein 1983), Doc. 70, p. 244.

50. Dr. Crohne, "Bedeutung und Aufgabe der Sondergerichte," *Deutsche Justiz* (1933): 384–85.

51. *Vorwärts* 562, 29 Nov. 1932, "Opfer der Sondergerichte. Eine furchtbare Statistik."

52. Geheime Staatsarchiv Preußischer Kulturbesitz (hereafter GStA), Rep. 84a 797, Bl.398–399: Übersicht über die Tätigkeit der Sondergerichte (Preußen) o.D. (Dez. 1932).

53. *Statistisches Jahrbuch für das Deutsche Reich 1935* (Berlin, 1935), 529. Cf. Broszat, *Der Staat Hitlers*, 407–9.

54. Supreme Court Judge Otto Schwarz, cited in Müller, *Hitler's Justice*, 153–54.

55. "Bildung von Sondergerichten. AB. d. IM. v. 9. 8. 1932 (I 4197)," *Justiz-Ministerial-Blatt für die preußische Gesetzgebung und Rechtspflege* Jg. 94, Nr. 31, 10 Aug. 1932, Sondernummer Ausgabe A, 195–96. For further details on the operational procedures of the *Sondergerichte*, see Gruchamann, *Justiz*, 949–50, and Johe, *Die gleigeschaltete Justiz*, 81–116.

56. Huber, *Verfassungeschichte*, 7: 1054.

57. Gruchmann, *Justiz*, 947.

58. Between 1919 and 1922, 354 political murders were committed by the right, for which the perpetrators received a total of ninety years imprisonment. The left carried out twenty-two political killings in the same period, for which ten of its adherents faced execution, and 248 years of prison was meted out. Gümbel, *Vier Jahre*, 73–81.

59. Preußischer Staatsrat 24. Sitzung am 9 Sept. 1932, "Allgemeine Verfügung vom 9 August 1932, betr. Bildung von Sondergerichten," col. 540–41.

60. The motion was carried with a sizable majority, but the result had no immediate effect. Ibid., col. 550.

61. Ibid., col. 544.

62. Ibid., cols. 540–42 (Drucksache 266, SPD), and cols. 543–44 (Drucksache 249, KPD).

63. Preußischer Landtag, 4. Wahlperiode, I. Tagung 1932, Nr. 854 Urantrag (Winzer, Gehrmann, Kuttner, SPD).

64. Preußischer Landtag, 4. Wahlperiode, I. Tagung 1932, Nr. 1157 Urantrag (21 Oct. 1932), (Kube, Lohse, Haake, Hinkler, Dr. Freisler, NSDAP). For the Potempa murder, see Preußischer Staatsrat, col. 541; and Kluke, "Der Fall Potempa."

65. RGBl (1932) I, "Verordnung der Reichsregierung über die Aufhebung der Sondergerichte. Vom 19 Dezember 1932."

66. GSTA Rep. 84a/797, Der Pr. JM. Funkspruch, Aufhebung v. Sondergerichte, 21.12.32.

67. "Übersicht über der Tätigkeit der Sondergerichte." To date, there has been little systematic work on any of these three special courts, the composition of their personnel, activities, judgments, etc. Nor has there been any attempt to draw a comparison between them, even though the archives of the *Sondergerichte* offer a rich vein of historical material for the historian. See Klaus Bästlein, "Die Akten des ehemaligen Sondergerichts Kiel als zeitgeschichtliche Quelle," *Zeitschrift der Gesellschaft für Schleswig-Holsteinische Geschichte* 113 (1988): 157–211; and Peter Hüttenberger, "Heimtückefälle vor dem Sondergericht München", in Martin Broszat, Elke Fröhlich, and Anton Grossmann, eds., *Bayern in der NS-Zeit* IV (Munich and Vienna, 1981), 435–526.

68. Wolfgang Kopitszch, "Der Altonaer Blutsonntag" (Staatsexamsarbeit für das Lehreramt, University of Hamburg, 1974), 2 vols, and Leon Schirmann, "Der Altonaer Blutsonntag und die Altonaer-Hamburger Justiz 1932–1991," *Demokratie und Recht* 19 (3/1991), 329–40.

69. R. Olden, "Sondergerichte," *Die Weltbuhne* XXVIII Jg., Nr. 33 (16 Aug. 1932), 224. See the "letter from a lawyer, April 1939," published in *Uncensored*

Germany (London, 1940), 12: "When a German judge of today receives the dossier of a case for study he does not examine the various incidents or the motives of the defendant, or the circumstances of a particular action. He does not consider the case independently of the position of the parties. . . . Men are condemmed to death when there is not a single witness available, and [when] even the circumstantial evidence is not enough to warrant a verdict of guilty. It is sufficient for someone to say that he has 'heard.' "

70. The fifteenth defendant, Stanislaus Switalla, was believed to have escaped to the Soviet Union after Bloody Sunday. LAS 352/1240, Staatsanwaltschaft bei dem Landgericht Hamburg-Altona, Not-Akte Switalla u. And., 11 Son. J. 3/33 Sdg. 7/33, "Im Namen des Volkes!"

71. *Altonaer Nachrichten* 127, 1. Beilage (2 June 1933).

72. GSTA Rep. 84a/24143 Landgericht Altona, Bd. IX (1931–1934), Bl. 108: Der Landgerichtspräs. III A 6/10292, to O/G. präs. Kiel, 8 Aug. 1932; Bl. 119: Der OP VA 117/4795I, 14 Sept. 1932; Bl. 140: Der OP VA 117/6643, 14 Nov. 1932; ibid., 84a/797 Bl. 79: Abschrift: Der Oberstaatsanwalt und Leiter der Anklagebehörde VII 96, Altona 12 Aug. 1932 (Bildung von Sondergerichten A.V. 9/8.32).

73. IML ZPA St 18/217, Bl. 31, 34, 39. STAH Dienststelle Altona, 424-10 (Gefängnis Altona), lists of arrested; and Hamburger Echo Nr. 173, 20 July 1932, 2. Beilage.

74. LAS 352/1246, Sb.E Strafsache Reese u. Gen. (Meyer u. Gen), Wegen Beihilfe zum versuchten Mord, Bl. 13, Vermerk (Gerichtsassessor de la Motte).

75. It is not possible to provide here a detailed account of the witnesses or their evidence. Some witnesses were attracted by the possibility of earning a money reward. Others, such as most of the young S.A. men and their *Sturm* leaders, were in pursuit of personal and political vengeance. Much of the evidence they gave was either contradictory or vague; some of it was eventually discounted by the police or manipulated by the prosecutor. There is also a suggestion that the state prosecutor had 'turned' some of the defendants who had been physically and mentally weakened by up to six months of solitary confinement with either threats or promises regarding their punishments. See, for instance, LAS 352/1242, files 90, 102, 122, 147, 148; 352/1244, files 278, 280, 281; 352/1245, file 304; and the series of files in 352/1246. IML ZPA St. 3/129, Bl.16-30f1, for the reward money of 5,000 marks approved by the authorities in July 1932 for information leading to arrest and conviction of (Communist) participants in Bloody Sunday. Thus, the worker Wilhelm M. from Lübeck received 100 marks for his part in getting Möller convicted of murder.

76. As well as 352/1240: "Not-Akte Switalla": "Im Namen des Volkes!" (Gründe), 67–98. See also the reports in *Altonaer Nachrichten*, Nrs. 107 (8 May 1933), 108 (9 May 1933).

77. Evidence of defense counsel recapitulated in *Hamburger Anzeiger*, 30 May 1933; *Schleswig-holsteinische Tageszeitung*, 1 June 1933; and ibid., 2 June 1933.

78. "Not-Akte Switalla," 132.

79. LAS 352/1251 (1252), Gnadensachen: Wolff, Tesch, Lütgens, and Möller, Beglaubigte Abschrift. Staatspolizei 16965/33[4a], 19.6.1933 Bl. 36–38: Police report on Möller.

80. Verein der Verfolgten des Nationalsozialismus, Hamburg: Nachlaß Emil Wendt, "Altonaer Blutsonntag Mitschrift des 1. Prozesses" (Hamburg n.d.). This

is a seventy-page, hand-written protocol of the trial hearing. Its exact provenance is unclear, but there is some speculation that it was possibly written by Emil Wendt. I would like to thank Herr Herbert Diercks for kindly making available to me a copy of this unusual document.

81. LAS 352/1240, Antrag auf Wiederaufnahme des Verfahrens, 31 July 1933, S.A. men Kurt Evers and Walter Andersson concerning the role of Tesch.

82. 352/1242, Sub-file 148: Handakten Lütgens, evidence to the police of the butcher Bertel Sternkopf, 26 Aug. 1932.

83. W. had been a *Justizoberinspektor;* the area he lived in was in the electoral district 29, which had presented a higher than average support for the NSDAP in the elections of July 1932. For the social composition of Paulsenplatz, see Altona Adreßbuch 1929 and 1932. The voting behavior of the area is computed from the data published in the relevant issues of the municipal gazette, *Altona Amtsblatt.*

84. The map and letters can be found in "Handakten Lütgens."

85. Schirmann, "Altonaer Blutsonntag," 331–32.

86. LAS 352/1242, Sub-file 98 (Cieskowski).

87. Ibid., Letters from Chemisches Untersuchungsamt Stuttgart, to Oberstaatsanwalt als Leiter der Anklagebehörde beim Sondergericht, Altona, 19 Sept. and 15 Oct. 1932.

88. "Not-Akte Switalla," 91–92.

89. LAS 352/1243, Sub-file 230: Autopsy report by Koch.

90. Based on eyewitness accounts to the investigation, ibid.

91. Ibid., Sub-file 223: Autopsy report by Büttig.

92. Even a close reconstruction from witness and judicial inquiry reports still leaves open the question of where exactly the shots were fired from.

93. Altonaer Nachrichten Nr. 127, 2 June 1933, "Die Urteilsbegründung."

94. Autopsy reports, op. cit., Sub-file 230, p. 6 and Sub-file 233, p. 9.

95. G. Dahm and F. Schaffstein, *Liberales oder autoritäres Strafrecht?* (Hamburg, 1933), 3f1., cited in Martin Hirsch, Diemut Majer, and Jürgen Meinck, eds., *Recht, Verwaltung und Justiz im Nationalsozialismus: Ausgewählte Schriften, Gesetze und Gerichtsentscheidungen von 1933 bis 1945* (Cologne, 1984), 447.

96. For instance, the *Sondergericht* in Altona passed a total of 209 years and four months in 167 cases, whereas the *Sondergericht* in Königsberg, another black-spot, gave sentences totaling 190 years in 271 cases, while the Bochum *Sondergericht* handed down a total of 77 years and seven months in 158 cases. "Übersicht über der Tätigkeit der Sondergerichte."

97. O. Rietzsch, "Die Abwehr des Gewohnheitsverbrechertums: Deutsche Gesetze und Gesetzentwürfe bis zur Machtübernahme," *Deutsche Justiz* (1938), 134f1; Gruchmann, *Justiz,* 719–45; and Reinhard Mann, *Protest und Kontrolle im Dritten Reich: Nationalsozialistische Herrschaft im Alltag einer rheinischen Großstadt* (Frankfurt and New York, 1987), 157–58.

98. See the "Anklageschrift" in 352/1240: "Not-Akte Switalla."

99. "Der Blutsonntag und seine Sühne."

100. LAS 352/1252, "Gnadensachen Wolff, Tesch, Lütgens, Möller": Der Oberstaatsanwalt als Leiter der Anklagebehörde bei dem Sondergericht, 6 July 1933: Strafsache geggen Switalla und Genossen wegen Landfriedensbruch pp. Betrifft Gnadenverfahren hinsichtlich der zum Tode verurteilten Lütgens, Möller, Wolff und Tesch, 1–4.

101. Ibid., Rechtsanwalt Harry Soll, 24 June 1933, In der Strafsache gegen Switalla und Genossen an den Herrn Ministerpräsidenten, in Berlin: *Gnadengesuch*, 3.

102. Ibid. This section and its quotes are culled from the different reports held in the file.

103. It was he, after all, who had been at the center of the notorious Marburg student case in 1922, when as the prosecuting counsel he pleaded with the judge to acquit the student members of a Free Corps detachment on trial for cold-bloodedly gunning down fifteen unarmed and innocent workmen from Bad Thal, Thuringia. Gümbel, *Vier Jahre*, 57–58; and Gruchmann, *Justiz*, 128.

104. Freisler, in Hirsch et. al., *Recht*, 432–34.

105. "Gnadensachen," Der Generalstaatsanwalt, E. R. 403/32, 13 July 1933, Äusserung in der Strafsache geen Switalla und Genossen, 3–4.

106. "Gnadensuchen," Der Oberstaatsanwalt, Gnadenverfahren, 3.

107. Adolf Hitler, *Mein Kampf* (transl. Karl Mannheim, introduction by D. C. Watt, London 1969), 621.

108. Gruchmann, *Justiz*, 1112, 1142.

The Decline of Women in the Criminal Process: A Comparative History

Malcolm Feeley

Hebrew University, Jerusalem

INTRODUCTION

In a recent book the distinguished criminologists Michael R. Gottfredson and Travis Hirschi observed, "[G]ender differences appear to be invariant over time and space."[1] This is not a new or novel view, but represents the consensus within the field.[2] Indeed, it is more than a consensus; it is a "fact" so taken for granted that like the air we breathe it usually goes unnoticed. To the extent that the relationship between gender and crime has been the object of focus, it has been to underscore the fact that crime is overwhelmingly a male pursuit. Indeed, until very recently even those few scholars who have dealt with female criminality have either focused on distinctively female offenses, or considered female deviancy a physiological, sexual, or psychological idiosyncrasy.[3] Even now most feminist criminologists accept the notion that overwhelmingly crime is a male pursuit. Only recently, with the work of Freda Adler, Rita Simon, Carolyn Smart, and a handful of other scholars, has variation in the level of female criminality become a central concern of sociological scholarship. But this work lacks deep historical perspective. The conventional view of women as marginal to crime persists, as the recent observation of Gottfredson and Hirschi attests.[4]

This article challenges this conventional wisdom. It argues that women were once heavily involved in the criminal process, and that a central problem for social scientists and historians is to explain the extent, nature, and reasons for the marked decline. In particular, it argues that at periods in the seventeenth and eighteenth centuries, women constituted 30–50 percent of the cases in the criminal process, and that by the late nineteenth century and throughout the twentieth this figure dropped to 5–15 percent. The question is, what accounts for this two and one-half to fourfold decrease in women's involvement? What does it say about the changing nature of crime, changes in the criminal process, and the shifting role of women? There is also a prior question: Why has this dramatic drop been virtually ignored by scholars until quite recently?

The answer to this latter question lies, I believe, in the division of labor of the academic disciplines. One of the common observations made about historians (usually made by social scientists) is that they are data rich but theory poor. And one of the common observations made about sociologists (usually by historians) is that they are theory rich but data poor. Whatever the general truth of these observations, they certainly ring true for the study of crime and the criminal process. Most sociological theories of crime and criminality—which for the most part purport to be universal or general— have been formulated by Anglo-American criminologists writing since the turn of the century and generalizing broadly from this limited experience.[5] As a consequence, these theories have been anchored in a relatively narrow range of human experience, and as such their generalizability and univer- sality ought to be an open question. But if social scientists have been care- less in generalizing from limited experience, historians of crime have eschewed theorizing and failed to explore the broader implications of their particular findings. By examining a social phenomenon only within its own context, there is the danger of missing what might be an important pattern, which in the case of women's involvement in the criminal process is a significant decline in their proportions in the seventeenth and eighteenth centuries.

There are, of course, exceptions to this lack of inquiry, and the concern expressed here is by no means unique.[6] Indeed, in recent years the study of gender and crime has become a minor growth field among both social scientists and historians. For instance, sociologists Freda Adler and Rita Simon have examined reported shifts in arrest rates for women in the United States in the 1960s and 1970s, claiming to detect a general trend of increasing criminal involvement, and each has offered a different theo- retical explanation relating to shifting gender roles to account for it. This work has been seriously challenged at two levels. Some have rejected the interpretations of the data, and have convincingly argued that there has been no distinct trend toward increased criminality among women during the period under consideration.[7] Others have offered a theoretical critique that has questioned the viability of sex role theory, as applied by Adler, Simon, and others, for providing a basis for explaining gender differences and crime. Carolyn Smart, for instance, argues that before it can become a viable explanatory base, the concept of role must itself be located within a theory that first can account for the existence of specifically differentiated roles as well as other features of human activity (like criminality), and then can treat both as the outcome of socioeconomic, political, and historical factors, rather than treating one (crime) as the outcome of the other (sex roles).[8]

Despite its flaws, the work of Simon and Adler is pioneering. It asked an important question. It problematized women and crime in a way that had not heretofore been done (at least by contemporary Anglo-American academic criminologists). And it sought to account for *variation* in the level of women's criminality.

Since the issue was first put in this form, interest in women and crime has continued to grow. But ironically the questions Adler and Simon posed have only occasionally been pursued. With but a handful of exceptions,[9] women continue to be relegated to the margins of research on criminality, and what limited interest in women and crime there is, continues to be dominated by a concern for distinctively "female" issues. In my view the most interesting work now being done is by historians rather than criminologists; the former have begun to note the presence of women in the criminal process and have found that women were once much more likely to be involved in the criminal process than they are today. But even they have been neither especially interested in theorizing nor perhaps even aware of the conventional wisdom of sociological theory, which holds that crime is overwhelmingly a male activity. Their work is important because it reveals important patterns that should frame the central concerns with respect to women and crime: It points to a far higher level of women's involvement in the criminal process in the past than there is today. The preponderance of the evidence points in the same direction and to the same conclusion: Women were once two and one-half to four times more likely to be involved in serious crime than they were at the end of the nineteenth century and have been throughout the twentieth. This pattern is significant; it should form the foundation for sustained inquiry into the extent and nature of general transformation of the role of women in the criminal process, and perhaps even the changing role of women in society.

This is both a sweeping and an ambiguous assertion, one that must be qualified and unpacked in any number of ways. One obvious question is whether the evidence is sufficient to draw such a sweeping conclusion. I believe it is, at least tentatively, and the evidence considered here is only a first effort in an ongoing investigation. Another question is whether the evidence suggests that this pattern holds for both violent and nonviolent offenses. Here, too, I believe that it does, although the evidence reveals that women have consistently been much less likely to be charged with violent offenses than men, and that their declining level of involvement in such cases is not as great as with other types of offenses. Still another question arises, over what period of time? And, of course, the theorist wants to know, "Why"—what does this shift say about the changing nature of crime, and the changing role of women in society? Some possible explanations are explored here.

GENERAL PATTERNS OF THE VANISHING FEMALE

In this section I review a number of studies that have dealt with women's criminality, extracting data (almost always presented for purposes quite different from my own), and contrasting them with estimates for the late nineteenth and twentieth centuries. It should be acknowledged that in undertaking this task, I am at times wrenching these data out of context, generalizing beyond the intentions of the authors, and ignoring many qualifications that should be introduced. But I do not think that the meaning of these data is distorted beyond recognition. They are, I believe, satisfactory for providing a rough but convincing picture of broad trends, although they become problematic if one wishes to present a more nuanced portrait, particularly in charting the nature and rate of the decline of women's involvement in the criminal process over time. For a more nuanced picture, offense categories must be more refined, and more data points used. But what is remarkable about these studies is that almost all of them point in the same direction and to the same conclusion, namely, that women were once two and a half to four times as involved in the criminal process as they are today.

Although these data reveal a marked decrease in the level of women's *involvement* in the criminal process, the nature of this involvement is not clear. Does it represent shifts in criminality or shifts in the form and nature of social control? This issue is well known to anyone who has worked with official statistics, but the message bears repeating here.[10] Indeed it is for this reason that I have used the phrase, *"involvement* in the criminal process." But as will become more evident in the concluding section, the interpretation advanced here tends to emphasize shifts in the *modes of social control* applied to women. Modes of social control, however, can in fact have some effect and affect levels of criminal activity as well.

In the section below, the central findings of these several studies are tabulated as they pertain to the concerns of this chapter. To facilitate comparisons across time and jurisdictions, as well as to emphasize a concern with the contrast to contemporary levels of involvement, the figures and estimates provided in each of these studies have been expressed in graph form. These graphs are reproduced in the Appendix.

THE ENGLISH DATA

There are now several studies drawing on court records from greater London that consider the proportion of women involved in the criminal process over time. They all reveal the same trend: a substantial decline in the pro-

Figure 1
Old Bailey: Percent Women (All Offenses: 1687–1950)

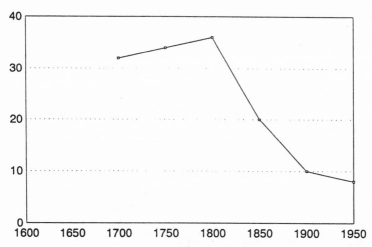

Source: Estimates from Feeley and Little (1991) and Home Office.

portion of women over the eighteenth and nineteenth centuries. In our study of the Old Bailey Sessions Papers from 1687 to 1912, Deborah Little and I found that women constituted well over one-third of the caseload at the Old Bailey in the early eighteenth century, after which they steadily declined (see Figure 1). We account for much of the continuing decline in the nineteenth century to shifts in jurisdiction between the Old Bailey (and crown court generally) and magistrates court,[11] and conclude that a substantial portion of this decline must be attributed to "real" decline in the level of involvement of women in the criminal process. In a replication of our study, David Greenberg reexamined records for the Old Bailey, drew a different sample, and found the same pattern.[12]

In his pioneering study of courts and crime from 1660 to 1800, John Beattie focused at some length on women in the criminal process. He showed how women in rural Sussex were much less likely to be involved in the criminal process than were women in more urban Surrey. Little and I reanalyzed his data, focusing on variation over time, and found for Surrey much the same pattern we had found for the Old Bailey (see Figure 2). And in more recent, ongoing research that has more carefully combined various levels of courts (to control for shifting jurisdiction), Beattie has found that at times in the eighteenth century women constituted 50 percent or more of all criminal defendants.[13]

Similarly, Professor Norma Landau is in the midst of a major study of

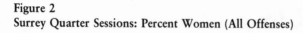

Figure 2
Surrey Quarter Sessions: Percent Women (All Offenses)

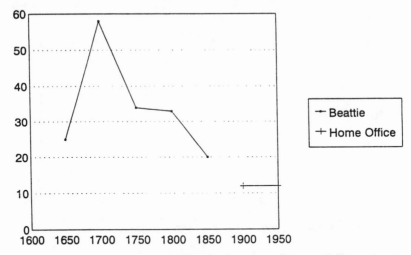

Source: Estimates from Beattie (in Feeley and Little, 1991) and Home Office.

the Middlesex Court of Quarter Sessions, and graciously allowed me access to some of her unpublished materials. Figures she has collected for all indictments brought, as well as selected cases involving fraudulent takings and receiving, reveal that throughout the eighteenth century women constituted 35 percent or more of the cases in these categories, and that the level of women's involvement was slightly higher during the early part of the century.[14]

Lucia Zedner has recently made the issue of changes in the level of women's involvement in the criminal process in the latter half of the nineteenth and early twentieth century the central focus of a major book (see Figure 3).[15] It is the first full-length study of shifts in the levels of women's involvement in the criminal process over time, and as such will do much to establish this field of inquiry. For this reason it is worth considering her findings at some length. The opening sentences of her book set forth her concern, one that is wholly consistent with the central concern of this chapter:

In Victorian England women made up a far larger proportion of those known to be involved in crime than they do today. During the second half of the nineteenth century over a fifth of those convicted of crime were women—today they make up only an eighth. And whilst a hundred years ago women made up 17 per cent of the daily average local and convict prison population, today the figure is less than 4 per cent.[16]

Figure 3
England: Percent Women (Larceny Offenses)

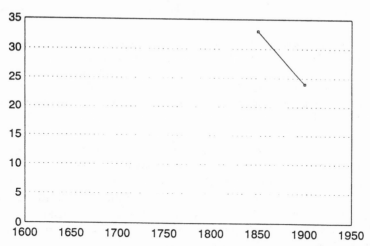

Source: Estimates from Zedner (1991).

At several places in her book, Zedner marshals impressive evidence to show that mid-nineteenth century women constituted a much higher proportion of arrestees and convicts than did women at the end of this century, and that there was a more or less steady decline in most (but not all) types of criminal offenses during the period 1857–1912.[17] Some illustrative findings: With respect to summary offenses, in 1879 "women made up roughly one third of convictions for larceny under 5 shillings," and "women consistently outnumbered men . . . [for] 'offenses against the Pawnbroker's Act.'" (Thirty or forty years later the figures were considerably less.)[18] With respect to indictable offenses, she reports that women made up a third of all those tried for "receiving stolen property" in midcentury, a figure that fell to 24 percent by 1890.[19] Women also constituted substantial portions of those charged with "forgery and offences against the currency." In the early nineteenth century, women constituted nearly one-third of those tried for "uttering" counterfeit coins, a proportion that dropped to a quarter in 1890.[20] And women at midcentury constituted 33–40 percent of those charged with "forgery" and "coining and having in possession implements for coining," a percentage that fell over time. She also found that during the early years of the Victorian era, women constituted a strikingly large portion of all those charged with violence against the person—one year they constituted 40 percent of those charged with murder.

Women's relatively high involvement in crimes of violence and property crimes is of particular interest to Zedner. She writes: "Women's relatively high level of involvement in these activities where the usual hindrances did not apply seems rather to belie contemporary assertions about women's innate non-criminality." She then concludes:

In the main, then, women tried on indictment were charged with financially motivated crimes. They were often planned, organized, and in the case of currency offenses at least, highly sophisticated ventures. Even taking into account their dubious reliability, such figures do seem to belie the widely held notion of female criminals as sexually motivated or driven by impulses to commit irrational, behavioral offenses. (40)

Patterns found by Zedner in the Judicial Statistics[21] for the nineteenth century are also seen in other data sources, namely, Home Office Reports of criminal offenses and other parliamentary reports.[22] Indeed, all the evidence on England points to a distinct and dramatic downward trend throughout the eighteenth and nineteenth centuries.[23] For instance, figures for the period 1805–1818 report a steady decline in the proportion of cases in which women were criminal defendants.[24]

Other historians who have examined still other sets of court records have noted the high proportion of women—relative to twentieth-century levels—involved in the criminal process. For instance, David Phillips examined figures from records in the Black Country from 1835 to 1850, and observed, "This general male-female ratio of 3:1 is of interest, differing markedly from the situation today, where the sex ratio in indictable offenses is about 7:1."[25] In his survey of crime in early modern England, James Sharpe also noted this phenomenon.[26] John Langbein, examining other sources, noted in passing that women in the eighteenth century appeared to constitute a far higher proportion of the caseload than they do today.[27] But with the exception of a handful of scholars, and particularly Lucia Zedner, researchers who have observed this phenomenon have not paused to puzzle over it.

CONTINENTAL EUROPEAN SOURCES

There are a number of historical studies of court and prison records on the Continent that address the issue of women and crime. Like most of the English studies, many authors have not been primarily interested in women's involvement in crime. Nor have they been interested in ascertaining if there were sweeping shifts between the eighteenth and twentieth centuries. When they have shown interest in the subject, their study has been limited to a particular period, or a particular type of offense, rather than an exploration of sweeping transformations of the role of women in the criminal process. Nevertheless, these studies contain valuable information that illuminates the thesis developed here. Overall, they suggest a dramatic decrease

Figure 4
Amsterdam: Percent Women (Selected Offenses)

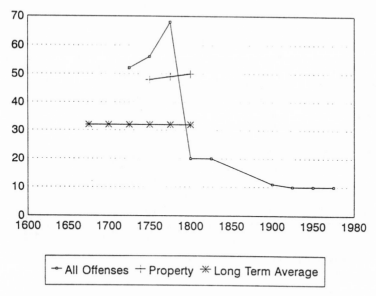

Source: Estimates derived from Faber (1983), Diederiks (1990), Interpol.

in the level of women's involvement in the criminal process. Figures 4–11 translate figures reported in these various studies into graph form in order to summarize conveniently levels of women's involvement in the criminal process in several communities in the eighteenth and nineteenth centuries, and to compare them to late nineteenth- and twentieth-century estimates. Again, the reader is warned that these figures are crude, because at times they represent averages over long periods (several decades), collapse different types of offenses into a single category, and represent irregular and incomplete data sets. Still, the overall trend is evident, compelling, and consistent with the English data.

Sjoerd Faber and Herman Diederiks have both examined Amsterdam court registers for selective years during the period 1737–1768, and still other records for 1680–1811.[28] Although they do not offer a sustained discussion of the nature of women's involvement in the criminal process or elaborate on the data they have gathered, their work offers some intriguing findings. The overall proportions of women offenders, as indicated by official records recording *all* offenses, range from 53 percent in 1737 to 67 percent in 1768 (see Figure 4). Diederiks reports that throughout most of the eighteenth century in Amsterdam, women constituted on average over

Figure 5
Amsterdam: Percent Women (Serious Offenses [*confessieboeken*])

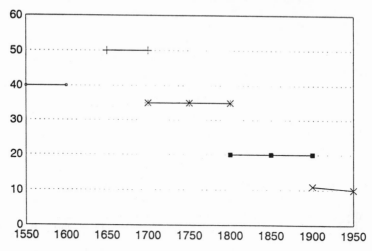

Source: Estimates from van de Pol (1987).

32 percent of all criminal cases.[29] Looking only at property offenses for the middle part of the eighteenth century, women constituted over 30 percent of all those compelled to appear in court, and in some years—1745, 1760, and 1766—they constituted over 50 percent of those charged with property offenses.

Lotte C. van de Pol has also examined the proportion of women in the criminal process in Amsterdam during the eighteenth century,[30] and her findings reinforce Faber's and Diederiks's. Hers is one of the few studies that self-consciously contrasts women's involvement in the criminal process in the seventeenth and eighteenth centuries with much lower levels in the nineteenth and twentieth. Despite this, she too looks at averages over long periods of time so that it is impossible to chart the rate of change over time. Her findings, however, are striking. For instance, women constituted 40 percent of the entries in the confession books during the latter half of the sixteenth century, 50 percent during the latter half of the seventeenth century, 35 percent during the eighteenth century, but only 20 percent during the nineteenth century (see Figure 5). Her summary interpretation of these findings is as follows:

Female criminality was much higher than is common nowadays. In Amsterdam in the second half of the seventeenth century half the trials before the criminal court were against women. A third of these women were prostitutes and procuresses, another third were thieves, receivers and swindlers. Offenses against property were committed by women as often as by men. (p. 148)

Pieter Spierenburg's study of prison records in Amsterdam during the eighteenth century reveals a similar pattern of higher levels of involvement by women in serious crime in the eighteenth century. He found that women constituted 25 percent or more of those sentenced to periods of confinement, a figure several times higher than contemporary figures.[31]

In her ongoing research on women and crime in Rotterdam, Christine Boerdam has examined magistrates' record books for the period 1750–1787.[32] During this period she has found, on average, that women constituted nearly 37 percent of the criminal case load. She also broke the cases down into minor (reported in the Quade Klap) and serious (reported in the Examenboeken) offenses and found a curious pattern. Women constituted an average of 29 percent of all those charged with minor offenses but nearly 47 percent of those charged with serious offenses! (see Figure 6).

Els Kloek has examined the criminal caseload in Leiden during the period 1678–1794, and has also considered the proportions of men and women separately.[33] Although she, too, examines average proportions over long periods of time (i.e., one hundred years), rather than tracing variation over time, her findings are illuminating nevertheless (see Figure 7). She found that on average women constituted 41.2 percent of all those listed in the criminal court registers. When broken down into minor and serious of-

Figure 6
Rotterdam: Percent Women (Selected Offenses)

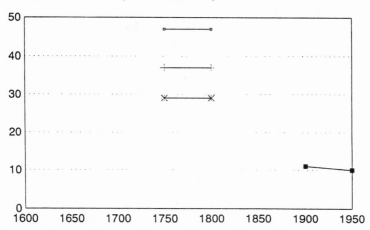

Source: Estimates from Boerdam (1993) and Interpol.

Figure 7
Leiden: Percent Women (Selected Offenses)

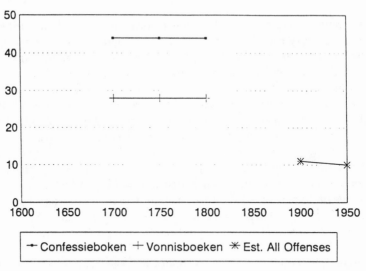

Source: Estimates from Kloek (1987) and Interpol.

fenses, women constituted 44.3 percent of those listed in the Confession-boeken (minor offenses), and 28.4 percent of those listed in the Vonnisboeken (more serious offenses).

Herman Diederiks has also examined the criminal court records of Leiden.[34] Although he focused on differences between textile workers and non-textile workers, he does report on the proportion of women charged with various types of criminal offenses between the years 1601 and 1811. In this regard the pattern he finds is consistent with the patterns reported above: Women constituted a small percentage of all defendants in the early 1600s, but their proportions rose steadily over the next seventy-five to 150 years, at which time they began to decline (see Figure 8). Diederiks also singles out property offenses for special consideration, again distinguishing between men and women. Here, too, he finds that patterns for textile and nontextile workers closely track each other. But for our purposes what is most important is that overall the level of involvement of women is relatively high as compared to late nineteenth- and twentieth-century levels. In the early 1600s, women constituted 35–40 percent of all those charged with property offenses, a figure that jumped to 65–74 percent fifty years later. After that it plummeted to a low of 18–20 percent in 1725, only to increase again over the next hundred years. As Diederiks himself notes, the levels of women's involvement were considerably higher throughout the seventeenth and early eighteenth century than they have been since the late nineteenth century.

Figure 8
Leiden: Percent Women (Delinquents: All Offenses and Property Crimes)

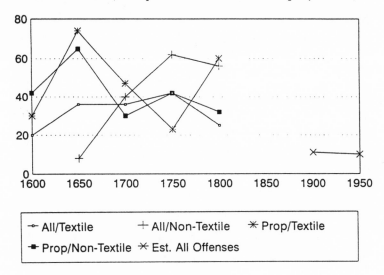

Source: Estimates from Diederiks (1990) and Interpol.

Diederiks also briefly comments on findings for other communities. In a brief discussion of criminal court records in Delft between 1591–1811, he reports that the average level of female offenders appearing in court for all charges during this period was 36.3 percent. When disaggregated and reported in averages for intervals of twenty-five years, the levels vary from a low of 28 percent in 1600–1625 to a high of 47 percent in 1751–1775. Diederiks contrasts these figures with comparable figures from the years 1896–1940, during which women constituted between only 8.4 and 11.2 percent of the criminal court caseload (see Figure 9).[35] Thus, on average there was a three- to fourfold decrease in the level of involvement of women in the criminal processes, a figure that is suggested by much of the data for other courts that is reviewed in this paper.[36]

A. M. Roets examined court records in Ghent during the period 1700–1789, and reports averages of men's and women's criminal cases for three groupings within this period, 1700–1749, 1750–1769, and 1770–1789.[37] With respect to violent offenses during the three subperiods, the proportions of women are 11, 14, and 4 percent respectively. With respect to offenses against property and offenses against public order (excluding sexual offenses), women constituted a slightly declining portion of those involved: 26, 19, and 18 percent of those charged with property offenses and 21, 19, and 3 percent of those charged with public order offenses (see

Figure 9
Delft: Percent Women Convicted (All Offenses 1591–1811 and 1896–1940)

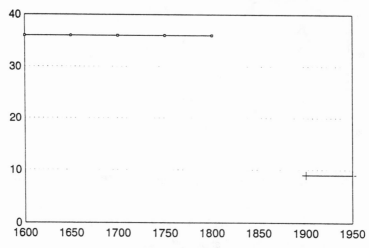

Source: Estimates from Diederiks (1990) and Interpol.

Figure 10). In contrast, the proportion of women charged with vagrancy nearly doubled over the period, jumping from 24 and 26 percent during the periods 1700–1749 and 1750–1769, to 46 percent from 1770–1789.

Overall, these figures reveal that women in Gent constituted a significantly larger portion of the criminal caseload in the latter part of the eighteenth century than they do today. But the figures here are somewhat lower than they are for London and Amsterdam during roughly the same period. This may be a consequence of different categorizations (Roets carefully separates out sexual offenses in a way some other scholars do not, and this might account for the somewhat lower proportions of women), or it may simply reflect differences in the composition of defendants in the different jurisdictions.

Finally, Nanon Borgerhoff has examined court records for the period 1700–1789 for the very small community of Tongeren, Belgium, and found that women constituted on average about 10 percent of the criminal caseload.[38] This is a "modern" level, and thus runs contrary to my thesis. It is, however, consistent with John Beattie's findings, which reveal markedly lower levels of women's involvement in the criminal process in rural as opposed to urban areas (see Figure 11).

NORTH AMERICAN DATA

North American data present more problems in dealing with the central concerns of this chapter, because the population was so sparse in the early

Figure 10
Gent: Percent Women (Selected Offenses)

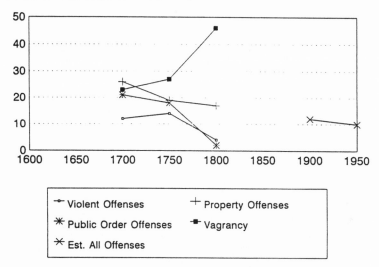

Source: Estimates from Roets (1982) and Interpol.

part of the eighteenth century. Still, there is some readily available if scattered evidence. N.E.H. Hull, for instance, notes that women constituted a substantially larger portion of those charged with serious criminal offenses in colonial New England than they do today.[39] However, she focuses on infanticide and does not carefully distinguish distinctively "female" offenses from other types of offenses. Thus, for purposes of this article, her findings must be read with extreme caution.

However, in a study of Toronto, Helen Boritch and John Hagan have addressed the problem in a way that is compatible with the aims of the present study. They compared rates of men's and women's arrests in Toronto between 1859–1955, and found a generally declining level of women's involvement.[40] Their data are especially valuable because they are carefully presented in three-year intervals, broken down by various types of offenses—violent, property, public order, theft, and fraud—and are presented as rates per 100,000 males and females rather than proportions of all offenses (as are most of the other data sets examined in this paper). This latter point is especially important because it underscores the fact that the decline they find represents a decline in the level of women's involvement rather than an increase in men's involvement. Their data reveal a general decline in the rates of women's involvement over a hundred-year period, a pattern that holds for the three major types of offenses—violent, property, and public order, although it is most pronounced for property offenses and much less so for violent crimes.

Figure 11
Tongeren, Belgium: Percent Women (Selected Offenses)

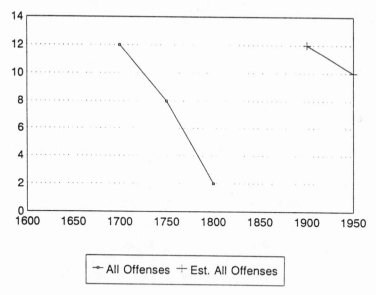

Source: Estimates from Borgerhoff (1993) and Interpol.

SUMMARY AND DISCUSSION

The material discussed above hardly constitutes a systematic sample of criminal court records, let alone a detailed comparison of the level of women's and men's criminality in the seventeenth and eighteenth centuries in contrast to contemporary levels. Taken together, these data do provide an important sketch that outlines a fairly convincing pattern: Women once constituted a much larger portion of the criminal caseload than they do today. And although individually the data are problematic in many ways—most particularly some of them combined sex offenses with other types of offenses so as to confound figures for women's involvement in "ordinary" crime—what is striking is that almost all of the studies report similar trends. From all this, several tentative conclusions can be drawn.

1. Levels of female involvement in crime in the seventeenth to nineteenth centuries are from two and a half to four times as high as in the late nineteenth and twentieth centuries. Because the available data are fragmentary and because some studies aggregate data across broad time spans, it is not now possible to trace the precise path of this decline, if indeed there is even a single pattern. Some studies suggest that it took place in the latter

part of the eighteenth century, others the latter part of the nineteenth century, and still others suggest that it was a steady trend across both centuries.

2. Some of the data suggest that the level of women's involvement may follow a curveliniar path, with an increase in women's involvement in the late seventeenth and early eighteenth centuries, followed by a distinct decline over the latter part of the eighteenth and much of the nineteenth century. This observation is speculative, and requires more data and more careful evaluation of the seventeenth-century records before it can be confirmed. But if it is a general pattern, it may reflect the importance of a particular set of social factors for a brief period.

3. The pattern of declining involvement appears to hold true for both minor and more serious offenses. Although most of the studies do not clearly indicate the levels of seriousness of the offenses involved (i.e., group them by levels of possible punishments), nevertheless the higher level of involvement during an earlier era does not appear to be restricted to either a handful of types of "female" offenses or selected types of minor offenses. Although most pronounced for property offenses, and least pronounced for violent crimes, the pattern appears to hold in general.

4. With some exceptions, the variation in the level of women's involvement in crimes of violence is not as great as it is for other sorts of offenses.[41]

5. The highest levels of women's involvement in crime throughout the entire period considered here were greater in urban settings—London, and urban parishes in Surrey, Amsterdam, and Leiden—than smaller and more rural communities (e.g., Tongeren, Belgium, and rural Sussex).

EXPLAINING THE PATTERN: IS IT MORE APPARENT THAN REAL?

In "The Vanishing Female," which examines the proportion of women in the caseload of London's Old Bailey, Deborah Little and I found that at times in the early eighteenth century women constituted over 40 percent of the caseload. As social scientists familiar with the criminological literature that holds that crime is a male pursuit, our first impulse was to search for factors that would "explain away" this apparently "inconsistent" finding, to show that it was more apparent than real. We considered five distinct possibilities, three of which are worth raising again in light of these additional data. The first was that the "decline" in women's involvement was in fact only a *shift* due to changes (both formal and informal) in the court's jurisdiction, one that transferred selected types of offenses (disproportionately involving women) from an upper level trial court to a lower level one (e.g., from the Old Bailey to magistrates court and the court of quarter sessions). If this were the case, a decline in the proportion of women in one court should be accounted for by an offsetting increase in another, and if so, the social significance of the shift would be minimal. However, when we considered available data from the combined caseloads of crown and magistrates courts, this possibility did not receive much support, at least for the mid-seventeenth century.

Data and additional analysis supplied by John Beattie and Norma Landau reinforced this conclusion. In particular, when Beattie combined the caseloads of two courts he found that the decline was "real," and not merely a result of informal shifts in jurisdiction.[42] There is, however, some evidence to suggest that some of the marked decline of women charged with selected property offenses in the nineteenth century was due to shifts in jurisdiction that transferred jurisdiction for many types of lesser property offenses to magistrates courts.[43] However, the data from several additional studies from other quite different jurisdictions suggests that the "shifting jurisdiction" explanation cannot provide a general explanation for the observed changes.[44] Indeed, a number of these studies combined findings from two levels of courts, and thus in effect controlled for the possibility of shifting jurisdiction. Thus, this possible explanation should be rejected.

A second possibility is that the shift could be accounted for in terms of demographic changes in the population. In our Old Bailey study, we focused on the *proportion* of women among those caught up in the criminal process, as do most studies. We did, however, also examine the *rate* of women's involvement, and the same pattern held. The more general findings presented in this paper, some of which examine rates as well as proportions, cast further doubt on this plausible explanation. Nonetheless, demographic factors should be considered at greater length so that the rates—as opposed to the proportions considered here—of women's involvement can be considered.

A third possibility was that for a period of time the courts were vigorous in enforcing "women's offenses," or that there were moral panics involving women that accounted for the relatively high proportion of women in the criminal process during selected years. But here, too, we rejected the possibility. Witchcraft, infanticide, and charges related to food riots, which disproportionately involved women, did not constitute even a trace of the offenses studied during the period under consideration. As prostitution was not a capital offense, it was not represented in cases at the Old Bailey or in other courts that dealt with "serious" offenses. We did find that women were overrepresented in property offenses, and underrepresented in violent crimes throughout the two hundred-year period, but property offenses constituted the overwhelming majority of offenses of both men and women. The additional materials presented in the studies reviewed above lend support for the rejection of this possible explanation. Rather, there is a general trend of declining levels of women's involvement in the criminal process.

A fourth and related possibility was that the high percentage of women defendants in the eighteenth century was due to women following men into crime, and that at one time—or perhaps intermittently—women accomplices were vigorously prosecuted. Controls established for the Old Bailey data lead to a rejection of this hypothesis. Although additional studies examined here do not control for this possibility, the widespread pattern of women's involvement renders it an implausible explanation. The additional materials reviewed above can only reinforce the decision to reject this possibility as a significant explanation.

A fifth possible explanation for the high levels of women's involvement is that women were overrepresented in the criminal process during periods of military mobilization, when men were removed from civil society and the ordinary criminal process, and thus were subject to an alternative form of social control. The central argument is this: During periods of war, men are subject to alternative forms of control and absorbed in military affairs, and removed from civil society, thereby decreasing the likelihood of their involvement in the criminal process. Immediately following wars, large numbers of men are released from military service and are dislocated, thereby increasing the likelihood of their criminal activity and involvement in the criminal process. Some writers have suggested that this might account for fluctuations in the proportion of women involved in the criminal process. At least since John Howard considered the possibility, a number of scholars have explored this hypothesis and have used it to account for fluctuations in the proportion of women involved in the criminal process.[45] Figures on criminal involvement in the studies reviewed here could be correlated profitably with periods of military mobilization and demobilization. In our study of the Old Bailey, for example, we concluded that war and peace account for some of the fluctuation, but that this alone did not account for the distinct decline over time. Similarly, the general pattern of decline suggests a general pattern of decline independent of such factors.

Some of the possible explanations discussed above have been firmly rejected, but others no doubt account for at least some of the variation that has been found. However, none of them—alone or in combination—can account for all the changes in each of the communities. The pattern is simply too sweeping, and it calls for a general explanation. But before pursuing this, several additional plausible explanations that have been advanced merit consideration, and are discussed below.

THE LIMITS OF "LOCAL EXPLANATIONS"

Several scholars whose findings were outlined above have attempted to account for the declining level of women's involvement in the criminal process in terms of factors particular to the setting on which they focused. But such explanations are, in my view, too constrained; they are limited in time and place, and offer local rather than general explanations. Even those encompassing a sweeping time period are limited to one or two communities, and usually seek explanations that are tied to local conditions. As a result, one of the most important "facts" highlighted in the discussion above has been ignored, namely that the decline of the level of women's involvement in the criminal process is a general and long-term trend found in a number of societies. As such, an explanation linked to particular local conditions is not likely to provide a sufficiently general explanation to account for what appears to be a very broad trend. Some of these plausible explanations, and their limitations, are examined below.

Herman Diederiks and others[46] have related shifts in the proportion of women in the criminal process to changing economic conditions, arguing that as times got tougher (as measured by the price of grain, etc.) the proportion of women caught up in the criminal justice system increased. Diederiks has termed this pattern a "survivalist strategy," and claimed to have found some support for it. Still others have asserted economic hardship as an explanation without careful examination. Such an inference has a number of problems. Foremost is the problem of drawing individual-level inferences from aggregate data. It is risky business. Indeed, this type of inference is widely known among applied statisticians as the "ecological fallacy," since there is no direct evidence that those whose changed behavior is to be explained are those included within the shifting aggregates. Apart from this, it is not clear why economic hardship that leads to crime should fall disproportionately upon women. One might expect fluctuations in crime for both men and women in response to changing economic conditions.[47] When the decline in the proportion of women in the criminal process is seen as a *general* pattern, across many communities and countries, each with a different economy, different employment cycles, and the like, a simple economic explanation cannot rise to the occasion. For example, there were significant fluctuations in the economy within the seventeenth, eighteenth, and nineteenth centuries, yet during the first three centuries there appears to have been a steady decline of the level of women's involvement in the criminal process. Thus, even though economic cycles may to some degree account for fluctuations in the levels of women's involvement in the criminal process, such cycles cannot easily be used to account for the long-term decline in their involvement.

In contrast to such economic arguments, Lucia Zedner has offered an explanation anchored in changing social values and popular explanations of crime.[48] She argues that the decline in the proportion of women involved in the criminal process is a result of shifting conceptions of women's deviance. She not only detects a trend—the decline of women's involvement in the criminal process—her book is essentially a sustained explication of a theory of this decline. Her argument is that it is a consequence of the "gradual . . . transition in explanations of and response to crime" [during the latter half of the nineteenth century]. The Victorian era opened "with moralistic understandings of crime and quasi-religious attempts to reclaim the offender, [and] concludes with the rise of secular, 'scientific' explanations of deviance, which in their turn led to medically oriented attempts to replace punishment with treatment and containment."[49] She then uses this phenomenon to account for the decline in the proportion of women in the criminal process. She puts it succinctly: Women were redefined from "bad to mad," and as a consequence were transferred out of the criminal justice system into an emerging new mental health system. She writes:

Removed from the penal sphere, diagnosed as sick rather than sinful, even these most dangerous of feeble-minded women were effectively decriminalized. The impact of this changing diagnosis of serious female offenders as mad rather than bad had a significant impact on the rates of those entering the criminal justice system. The proportion of women making up the daily population of convict prisons more than halved over the second half of the nineteenth century. Putting aside the possibility that women were actually becoming less criminally inclined and more prone to mental illness, we must turn yet again to the social construction of images of deviant women for explanation of these trends."[50]

This is an elegant and powerfully argued explanation, and appears to be supported by data that show that shifting conceptions of women's criminality track closely with shifting levels of involvement in the criminal process. Despite this, it, too, is a "local" explanation that cannot easily account for a general pattern across several societies and at different times. Indeed, there are a number of problems with its applicability even to the English setting for which it was developed. Before it can be convincing, Zedner must address additional issues. First, it hinges on shifts in conceptions of women's criminality *within* the Victorian era, from the middle to the end of the nineteenth century. But as was suggested in the discussion earlier, the decline in the proportion of women in the criminal process occurred over a long period, was probably greatest long before the period considered by Zedner, and at any rate occurred in a number of different countries that did not experience the peculiarities of the Victorian era. By focusing on change within a relatively brief period, and attempting to base an explanation for this change on factors limited to this period, one runs the risk of misunderstanding the nature of the change and ignoring other more general and perhaps more important and longer-term factors. In England, it appears that there was a steady decline over possibly a 200-year period, and by focusing on factors distinctive to a fifty-year period within the longer time span there is the risk of misunderstanding the phenomenon.[51] In short, a convincing explanation must be located outside the peculiarities of the Victorian era because the greatest decline in England—as well as in a number of other countries—took place before the onset of the changes wrought by the era.

Additionally, Zedner's explanation for the decline of women in the criminal process is that some of them were redirected into another social control institution, namely the mental health system. But in order for this explanation to be convincing, one must present convincing evidence that there was in fact an increase in the rate of civil commitments of women at a rate faster than men's (who presumably continued to be processed by traditional methods, through the criminal process). And this displacement hypothesis would also have to confront an alternative explanation that has occasionally been put forward, namely the rise and widespread use of "treatment" regimes and institutions represented not a displacement of traditional penal strategies, but a supplement—a widening of the net of social control.[52]

We are left where we began, with the finding of a precipitous decline in women's involvement in the criminal process sometime in the eighteenth or early nineteenth centuries. This decline was real and is significant. It represents a transformation in the role of women in the criminal process. Thus our question remains: Why did women once constitute such a large proportion of those charged with crimes, and why do they now account for a much smaller portion? It is beyond the scope of this chapter to develop the sort of general theory that is called for by these data. But one cannot help but speculate about some directions for fruitful theoretical development.

THEORIES OF WOMEN'S INVOLVEMENT IN THE CRIMINAL PROCESS[53]

Until recently, criminological theory has not addressed itself to women's criminality. However, in recent years, a number of feminist theorists have begun to approach the issue, although for the most part they have formulated it in terms of why women commit such few crimes, and not why has the proportion of women involved in crime declined precipitously. Most of these theories emphasize patriarchy—a system of male domination of women. Patriarchy, of course, has different forms, and it looks different in different historical contexts.

One such theory, sex role theory, explains the lack of female deviance by arguing that women are "socialized" to be more conforming than men. For instance, Freda Adler argues that the increased emancipation of women and a change in their gender roles (less sex-role differentiation) in the 1960s and 1970s were responsible for rising female crime rates.[54] However, as Smart has observed:

To improve the status of the role theory approach the concept of role must itself be located within a theory which first can account for the existence of specifically differentiated roles as well as other features of human activity (like criminality) and second treats both as the outcome of socioeconomic, political, and historical factors, rather than treating one (crime) as the outcome of the other (sex roles).[55]

Thus, effective use of sex role theory would require an analysis of the structures in which roles are reproduced and maintained, and an understanding of the social, economic, and historical bases of these structures. More problematic than the lack of clarity in explaining the causes of roles, however, is the failure to explain why greater female independence and autonomy would cause women to be more criminal. What greater equality does is make women equally subject to the forces that promote male criminality, whatever these forces may be. The removal of patriarchal controls does not cause crime; at best it can only remove an intervening variable.[56]

Differential opportunity theory, as developed by Simon, can be seen as an effort to overcome some of these problems.[57] Simon argues that as women enter the labor force, they are exposed to both legal and illegal opportunities, and that the increased opportunity to engage in illegal acts explains increases in female property crime. Many have successfully challenged these claims as well.[58]

More generally, however, this research points to the complexity of theorizing about women and crime, and shows the inadequacy of understanding female criminality solely in terms of women's exclusion from or participation in productive work.[59] Both sex role and differential opportunity theory lack an adequate understanding of patriarchy. What follows is an effort to link more tightly general theories of patriarchy with criminological theory that focuses on gender. I do this by integrating the work of Mitchell[60] and several other gender theorists with the work of criminologists who have grappled with female crime in the context of patriarchal structures. When developed more fully, this should provide a theoretical basis for confronting the patterns of women's criminality posed by the pattern reported above.

Patriarchy in the broadest sense is a system in which men (individually or as a group) control women (individually or as a group). These social controls occur in different structures. Women's subordination should be understood by examining four structures of male control—production, reproduction, sexuality, and socialization (childrearing as opposed to childbearing). Male domination is not constant in all four, so all arenas must be examined at any given historical moment. As Walby notes,[61] patriarchy differs historically in form (the overall type of patriarchy as determined by specific relations between patriarchal structures) and intensity (the intensity of oppression in a specific arena), and both must be evaluated. Much feminist theory looks at domination in production or in the family (the structure in which much of sexuality, reproduction, and socialization take place).[62] Control theories of female crime have also looked at these spheres.

Hagan, Simpson, and Gillis focus on the family, specifically the process of socialization, to explain gender differences in crime.[63] They assert that there is a "family based sexual stratification of the social control of children in industrial societies."[64] The source of the controls is the "gender based

power structures of patriarchal families that characterize industrial societies."[65] The controls make women less inclined to take the risks associated
with deviance. These theorists begin to combine questions of patriarchal
control of women with more conventional theories of crime. However, they
tend to limit control to the family.[66] A more comprehensive theory would
look not only at the family, but also at patriarchal controls in other arenas.

Other theorists[67] have drawn from control theory to analyze patriarchal
controls in both production and the family or reproduction. Control theory
asserts that control, either personal/psychological or social/institutional, is
necessary to repress deviant tendencies in all of us.[68] Theorists argue that
women's social location contains more factors constraining criminal activity than does the location of men.[69]

Heidensohn details the myriad ways in which women are subject to
greater social controls than men, in both the public and private spheres of
Western capitalism.[70] She argues that women themselves participate in and
accept these controls. In terms of traditional control theory, women are
more attached to the institutions of law-abiding society. However, feminists
point out that women are also controlled by patriarchal relations within
these institutions, and thus are "overcontrolled," to use Hagan, Simpson,
and Gillis's term.[71]

Although control theory offers a more plausible framework for explaining female criminality and conformity, shifts in patriarchal controls must
be examined historically. Patriarchy has changed form with the development of modern societies, a strong and centralized polity, and extensive
division of labor in production. In particular, there was an intensification
of "private" patriarchy followed by a shift from private to "public" patriarchy. The shift reflects a change from the control of women by men as a
group, acting primarily in the state,[72] or in the state and the economy.[73]

Fully developed private patriarchy in the nineteenth century encompassed
the exclusion of women from the productive and political spheres and their
relegation to housework and childcare in a private home. Individual male
control as head-of-household was gradually reduced in the twentieth century as state intervention into the family gave women and children rights
vis-à-vis individual men, as women began to enter the industrial workplace.
However, the decline of the patriarchal power of male household heads
was offset by the rise of the power of the state and the market over women.
Thus, it may be that the entry of women into the workforce in the mid-
twentieth century did not lead to higher female property crime because
there was no real lessening of patriarchal controls. While increased participation in production did mean greater female autonomy and independence
vis-à-vis individual men, women entered the workforce in the context of
public patriarchy (in which women are controlled as a group through
things like segmented labor markets, the job segregation of women in primarily low-wage and low-power work, the continued treatment of women's

work as "supplemental" to the male wage, and the like). It appears that increased female labor force participation in the twentieth century did not produce increased female criminality because this participation occurred in the context of continuing patriarchal control.

The data considered in this paper, however, covers the period of the intensification of private patriarchy. What I propose is an analysis that focuses on social controls, especially patriarchal controls, to account for female conformity and criminality. The "patriarchal control theory" suggested here draws from traditional control theorists, but expands their notion by looking at patriarchy as a concrete and historically variable phenomenon. It looks both at female participation in various structures (reproduction, sexuality, economy), and at the type and intensity of male controls within these structures at different historical moments. Therefore, it asks, how does this theory help us account for the decline in female participation in crime, particularly property crime, during the eighteenth and nineteenth centuries?

PATRIARCHAL CONTROL THEORY AND CRIME: AN EXPLORATORY ANALYSIS

The eighteenth century is generally known as the time of the "Bloody Codes," a period when over 200 crimes were legally punishable by death. Rising commercial classes called for deterrents against property crime.[74] Criminal control mechanisms were informal—there was no organized system of police, and prosecution depended upon private initiative. This initiative was promoted through a system of rewards for successful prosecution and pardons for defendants who became informants.[75] Some have argued that the severity of punishment coupled with private and/or official lenience after indictment or conviction reinforced the dependence and deference of the lower classes, who were the primary objects of criminal prosecution.

The pressures toward criminality were similar to those in the twentieth century—unemployment, underemployment, destitution. In London, Beattie tells us, "a considerable proportion of the work force depended on casual labor that was irregular in supply, to some extent seasonal, always capricious."[76] Events like war, a rise in food prices, interruptions in export trade, seasonal layoffs, and the movement of upper-class families in and out of the city, could change the lives and fortunes of those in a city overstocked with workers.[77] This is significant because, as Dorothy George reports, the majority of work in London in the eighteenth century was seasonal.[78] I am not as familiar with social histories of the Netherlands for this period, but presumably the economy and social conditions of its port cities were similar. (Obviously, a careful comparative history must be undertaken.) These, then, were the general pressures toward criminal involvement in the late seventeenth and eighteenth century. Why did women become equally subject to them during this period? And why did their involvement decline over the next 100 or 150 years?[79]

From 1650 to approximately 1900, Europe changed from feudal, rural, agricultural societies to countries with capitalist, urban, industrialized communities. This was especially true for England and the Low Countries, for which the bulk of the crime data presented earlier came from. Over this same period, there were major changes in social relations between men and women and in the form and intensity of patriarchal controls. In the broadest terms, there was an intensification of "private" patriarchy. Women's participation as more or less equal participants in household production and the provisions of subsistence diminished; men became primarily economically responsible for wives and children. Women were excluded from much of developing industry or segregated into fewer and fewer low-wage occupations. Their time was increasingly devoted to childcare, as children, too, were removed from productive work. These changes are generally regarded as having been harmful to women's status. The loss of their economic functions led to a loss of power and autonomy within the family; male head-of-household authority was solidified. By the end of the nineteenth century, there was a clear separation of home and work, a firmer sexual division of labor, the exclusion of women from the public sphere and from productive work, and the confinement of women to reproductive and domestic work in the home. This was not a uniform or unilinear process. In fact, modern historians stress the unevenness of these developments throughout England.

Women and Economic Participation

Alice Clark, in her pioneering 1919 book examining the impact of the economy of women's roles in England, traced the impact of changes in the modes of production on the position of women in the seventeenth and eighteenth centuries.[80] She posited a three-stage process of economic development. The first stage of preindustrial economy was a "domestic economy," a form of production in which "goods were produced largely for the use of the family and were not therefore subject to an exchange or money value." This was followed in the seventeenth and eighteenth centuries by the "family economy," the "form [of economic production] in which the family becomes the unit for the production of goods to be sold or exchanged."[81] The final, advanced stage was "capitalistic industry or industrialism," in which "production is controlled by owners of capital and the labors or producers . . . receive individual wages."

Examining the changes in the mode of production in agriculture, textiles, the crafts, trades, and the professions, Clark traces the shift from family industry to modern wage-labor industrialism. She argues that the middle stage—the period of family economy—was a period of significant economic participation by women. During this period, "the part which women played in industrial and professional life was in addition to a much greater productive activity in the domestic sphere than is required of them under modern conditions."[82]

Furthermore, "if women were upon the whole more actively engaged in industrial work during the seventeenth century than they were in the first decade of the twentieth century, men were much more occupied with domestic affairs then than they are [in the twentieth century]."[83] All this changed with industrial capitalism, "which broke away from the family system, and dealt directly with individuals, the first fruit of individualism being shown by the exclusion of women from the journeyman's associations."[84]

Hans Medick, examining German and other continental sources for this same period, draws the same conclusions. Indeed, he states the proposition even more strongly.[85] Not only did both men and women engage equally in agricultural work, but both were engaged in household work to the point of "sex role reversal." Although Medick's and others' views, and those of various proponents of "proto-industrialization," are controversial, there does appear to be widespread agreement that the period just prior to large-scale industrialization (embraced at different times in different places and for different industries) was a period in which women were much more involved in a wide variety of tasks in the labor force than they were once the factory system was widely adopted.

While historians no longer characterize the shift to industrialization in such a schematic three-stage movement, Clark's argument that women played a central role in production for the family has been generally accepted. Louise Tilly and Joan Scott argue that marriage, in the eighteenth century, was an economic partnership.[86] Everyone worked, including women and children. In rural areas women farmed, engaged in dairy work, and sold home-manufactured products in local markets. In urban areas, where much of the production of food and clothing had moved outside the home, women spent more time in consumption activities (shopping) to meet the subsistence needs of their families. Women in families of craftsmen or shopkeepers assisted in the craft or shop. While occupational designations were male, when husbands died guild memberships passed to their wives. Some women practiced independent trades, such as bakers, grocers, innkeepers, milliners, butchers, and the like. When their husbands were unskilled laborers, women worked in the informal economy as petty traders and hawkers, or sold their labor, carting goods or water, sewing, or doing laundry. In London, where the widest range of occupations was practiced, women were expected to work, and they engaged in the full range of productive activities:

The wife was expected to contribute to the family income. The wife of a day-labourer usually hawked fruit or fish or carried loads through the streets from the markets. . . . The journeyman's wife in trades where women were not employed often had a small shop or took in washing or needlework. A shopkeeper's wife generally served in the shop or superintended it unless she had a separate business of her own; if she had been a widow she frequently continued in nominal or actual charge of her first husband's business. Marriage was a business partnership—the wife's portion was often the means of setting her husband up as a master.[87]

In London, widows who did not inherit a guild membership had a difficult time, and many had to send children to charities, unable to support them with low-wage work. However, many widowers had similar problems, suggesting that two adults were necessary for the economic well-being of a family.[88]

This is not to argue that women were equal to men in the eighteenth century. Sonya Rose reminds us that women were low-waged labor, paid much less than men even before industrialization.[89] Women were denied membership in many guilds as long as their husbands were alive. Additionally, husbands were the legal heads of the household, with rights to physically chastise women and children. As Lawrence Stone has pointed out,

All that productive work entailed for most married women in the sixteenth, seventeenth and eighteenth centuries was, therefore, a crushing burden of labour added onto their normal household chores of marketing, cleaning, cooking, and child care. The work did not bring any compensation in an independent income to spend on personal luxuries, nor greater status, nor greater participation in male leisure activities.[90]

However, Stone acknowledges that economic changes that led to the wife having greater participation in the household economy and control over certain aspects of production did give some eighteenth-century women a measure of autonomy and power. Regardless of the legal status of dependency, a wife was an economic asset to the family, and this undoubtedly lessened patriarchal controls over her.

Moreover, food was the major component of a family's costs, and women controlled this part of the budget. A wife's ability to provide through work and careful budgeting might mean the difference between eating adequately and not eating at all.[91] This control gave her real power in the family.

In England, and presumably in the Low Countries, during the eighteenth and nineteenth centuries, work moved out of the control of the family, and workers were employed first in the putting-out system and then in factories. Ivy Pinchbeck marshals an impressive—and unequalled—array of data in her 1930 study to support the contention that in industry after industry—

textiles, the domestic industries, the mines, crafts, and business—employment for women shrank dramatically throughout this period.[92] Focusing in depth on the textile industry, she argues that in the late eighteenth century "a total revolution occurred."[93] Just preceding the rise of the factory, she argues, "many women were accustomed to assisting their husbands and fathers at the broad loom which required two workers before the use of the flying shuttle."[94] Thus, up until the mid-eighteenth century, women and children pursued work alongside their husbands and fathers, combining spinning and the like with housework. Unlike men, however, women did not specialize. With the rise of wage labor, these jobs were transferred out of the house and into the factory, and "the industry fell naturally into the control of men."[95] Thus, by 1830 this industry had been entirely removed from the cottage into the factory, "and was now performed by a class of skilled workmen on complicated machinery."[96] In the case of London, the movement from the putting-out system to the factory meant that silkwinding and silk-throwing, occupations that employed large numbers of women, disappeared as production moved to textile factories outside of London.

Clark concludes that as industry shifted from the family-based household to the individual-oriented factory, two things occurred. First, the new form of organization required specialized knowledge and training, which men had already begun to monopolize.[97] Second, there was the development of the "doctrine of the subjugation of women to their husbands."[98] Industrial capitalism "freed men to some extent from economic dependence on their wives, and from henceforth the ideal of the subjugation of women to their husbands could be pursued, unhampered by fear of the dangers resulting to the said husbands by a lessening of the wife's economic efficiency."[99] These factors, Clark continues, led to a theory of "inferiority" that was reinforced by the emerging political theory of the times (which had little to say about women). The result, in her view, was that industrial capitalism exerted a "momentous influence" on the economic position of women that contributed to a substantial decline in their economic well-being and opportunities, from which they have still not recovered.

Pinchbeck generally agrees with Clark, although she locates formative changes some time later. Like Clark, Pinchbeck argues that as production shifted from the family as a joint economic unit to a wage-labor economy, women were squeezed out of economic participation as a "whole host of factors" restricted the best-paying jobs to men. In her 1989 update of Pinchbeck's work, Bridget Hill reviews a mountain of material published since 1930, and concludes that Pinchbeck's thesis has withstood the test of time.[100] Thus, there continues to be substantial support for the argument that women participated to a large degree in a wide range of economic activities prior to and during the early period of industrialization, and that it was only later that most of this productive work became the exclusive domain of men. With the rise of capitalist forms of production, the rage of occupations open to women narrowed. Hill concludes, "Side by side with the 'masculinization' of some tasks and trades went the feminization of others. By the end of the century, female blacksmiths, carpenters, bricklayers, and coopers had become rarities. On the other hand, domestic service was in the process of becoming feminized.[101]

Along with changes in the mode of production came a growing view about gender and work. Exclusionary provisions were justified on the grounds that certain work was "unsuitable, unfeminine, and inclining to immoral habits because it required being in close proximity to men."[102] When women worked, only occupations that coincided with their "natural sphere" were encouraged. As Hill observes, "Far from industrialization meaning the emancipation of women, for many the first phase must have meant a greater servitude and conditions where they had no defence against the arbitrary yielding of patriarchal power."[103]

Hill, like Clark, and Pinchbeck, attribute these changes to shifts in the mode of production—away from family-based industry which minimized role differentiations between husbands, wives, and children, and often allowed widows to maintain themselves in the absence of husbands—to the wage-labor system and an increased division of labor that quickly came to discriminate against women and greatly restricted their participation in work. Even without discrimination against women, the transition to a family wage economy in which households needed cash and not labor meant that women's capacity to make a productive contribution was now limited by their domestic childbearing and childrearing duties. All this was reinforced by accompanying theories of femininity, which further restricted the range of socially acceptable behavior permitted to women.

The restriction of women's participation in industry continued throughout the nineteenth century. Trade unions used exclusionary practices to keep women out of some areas of employment.[104] The development of the "family wage" and protective legislation further restricted female employment. Accompanying these restrictions was the rise of the "cult of domesticity" in the middle classes, an ideology which portrayed women's proper role as a subservient, virtuous, and pious wife and mother.

In London, and presumably other urban areas in Europe, this process was both less dramatic and more gradual. In an urban area in which trades, crafts, and casual employment predominated, women did not experience the rapid transition from putting-out to factory work so carefully detailed by Pinchbeck for agricultural workers. Some women continued to work in their husbands' trades well into the nineteenth century. However, probably less than 10 percent of the women in London were married to tradesmen.[105] Moreover, as work moved from the home to the workshop and male tradesmen acquired capital, they began to hire larger numbers of male journeymen and apprentices, excluding their wives from participation in the trade.[106]

The gradual separation of home and work meant reduced opportunities for women to learn skills or contribute equally to their family's economic well-being. Women's trades passed into male hands. In addition, although new industries were created, women were excluded from them. Sally Alexander details a host of occupations in which women did not work by the 1820s.[107] When women did work, they participated in "women's" jobs like domestic and household labor, child care and training, the distribution and retail sale of food and other articles of regular consumption, and manufacturing based on the sexual division of labor in the household. Industrial work was primarily "slopwork," in which a division of labor broke jobs into semi- and unskilled tasks and then exploited cheap labor. Women were especially exploited here, with long hours and extremely low wages. Slopwork also contributed to the demise of women's occupations because it occurred in trades that had previously been occupied by skilled women, trades like dressmaking and needlework. Overall, then, the rise of slopwork, the increase in out-of-home work, the exclusion of women from new trades and occupations, and the competition of slopwork with traditional women's trades, led to both declining wages for women and an overall reduction in the range of work available to women in London. Between 1700 and 1900, women in England lost their ability to contribute equally to the household and became economically dependent upon men. Additional study of the role of women in the economies on the Continent is required to see if this is a general pattern that can be related to the trend of women's involvement in crime.

Thus, in the eighteenth-century transition from feudal household modes of production to capitalist forms, some of the patriarchal controls over women were weakened. Over the next century, the sexual division of labor in the working class underwent significant changes. Some women continued to work in their husband's trade as full participants in the household economy or pursued their own trades. Others had to look for wage work. From a situation of martial partnership in a household economy, women moved to a weaker economic partnership working out of the household, and finally to no economic partnership and economic dependence on men. This transition, which took place over the course of the eighteenth and early nineteenth centuries, coincided with a decline in female involvement in criminality.

During this early transitional period, it is likely that patriarchal control was weakened. Women had the power that economic contribution gave them vis-à-vis male household heads, but they increasingly worked outside of household controls. This period was relatively short-lived, however, because in the course of the transition to capitalism men took over the full range of productive work and women were relegated to the home.

Women and Reproduction

The early eighteenth century was a period in which patriarchal controls in areas other than production were weaker. For instance, as Stone notes, the century witnessed the acceptance of the idea of the "companionate marriage," in which marriage came to be regarded as a decision to be made by the couple in accordance with their own feelings. More generally, he identifies other changes in sexual changes as well:

Until about 1700 . . . among the lower class . . . sexuality was channelled and controlled, partly by the legal pressure of Puritan magistrates and the propaganda pressure of Puritan preachers, and partly by the successful internalization of ideas about chastity and virginity. The result was a society in which a late marriage pattern co-existed with low rates of illegitimacy and of pre-marital pregnancy. . . .
    The second state, which began in about 1700, was characterized by continued intimate courting, but a sharp rise in pre-marital intercourse, and consequently in the proportion of pregnant brides. This was caused by the collapse of the Puritan movement, the decay of institutional religion, the weakening of kin protection, the rise of a landless laborer class, which placed less value on virginity than on fertility, the rise of a rural cottage industry which made it economically easy to marry if pregnancy occurred, and perhaps a revival in the belief that the decisive ceremony was the betrothal not the wedding. Moral controls over intimate courting were greatly weakened, but local community pressure, exercised through moral suasion and legal compulsion, was still strong enough to enforce marriage on all except a handful of couples. This handful was increasing rapidly, however, and as a result the illegitimacy ratio was rising fast. This was caused by the weakening of the social controls over the seducer previously exercised by the neighbors, the parish clergy and the local community, caused in part by the isolation of migrant and propertyless young people in big cities.[108]

Hill's discussion of courtship relations among the laboring classes (which were differ from middle and upper class women) concludes that women in the lower classes seem to have enjoyed a good deal of freedom in choosing a mate. A real period of courtship occurred in which couples evaluated each other's character and ability to contribute economically to the marriage. Because there was no property to be inherited, however, the laboring classes had a more tolerant view of premarital sex than did the propertied classes, and thus had higher illegitimacy rates, as reported by Stone.

Over the course of the nineteenth century, however, sexual controls over women tightened.[109] As children were removed from productive work, women were obligated to spend increasing amounts of time in childrearing duties. And as women were removed from productive work, their responsibilities in the home and restrictions over their sexuality were increased. Thus, both economic historians examining changes in the structure of the eighteenth century economy and social historians examining changes in attitudes and institutions of "moral authority" point to similar conclusions.

In his study of the family in England between 1500 and 1800, Lawrence Stone proposes that one test of changes in the nature of the control of women would be shifts in women's crime rates. "[W]hether or not the crimes they committed were similar in scale and type to those of men" would be, he asserts, a test for the "independence displayed by women."[110] With this test in mind, he concludes that for the late sixteenth century women were not independent, but rather "submissive" and "dependent," because as compared to men they had a minimal share in crimes of theft, commercial fraud and violence. He goes on to note that in this period, a part from showing some independence in leading food riots and adhering to dissident religious opinions, women involved in violence were typically only "aiding their menfolk."[111] While this argument that female criminality is a test of female independence sounds like the modern liberation hypothesis, his comments that female criminality may differ when there are shifts in patriarchal controls is consistent with the concern of this chapter.

Stone's characterization of women's involvement in crime in the sixteenth century is quite different from the picture we have found for the early eighteenth century. This is not an anomaly, but is due in part to the changes that Stone and others have documented for England and elsewhere. Not only was this a period when women were more involved in "productive activities," and more highly valued as economic assets, but it was also a time in which patriarchal controls were lessened and women constituted a higher proportion of those involved in the criminal process. Throughout the eighteenth and nineteenth centuries, however, a new version of the family was constituted, one that was far more private and patriarchal. Over this same period, women's criminality appears to have declined. We cannot, of course, say conclusively that women began to commit fewer criminal offenses. But patriarchal control theory would suggest that the numbers we have found reflect real differences in female criminality as well as men's willingness to involve them in public criminal justice institutions.

I do not wish to be interpreted as arguing that women in the eighteenth century were "emancipated," for surely they were not. The fact that they were relatively uninvolved in violent crimes throughout the eighteenth and nineteenth century—and almost all the data that addresses this issue point to this conclusion—may be one measure of this.[112] However, the data from the several studies reviewed earlier in this paper show substantially greater female involvement in the criminal process during a period when patriarchal controls were in flux or transition. Further research obviously needs to be conducted to determine if the patterns suggested above hold upon close inspection.

NOTES

This article is part of an ongoing inquiry on variation in the level of women's involvement in the criminal process over time. I am deeply indebted to Christine Boerdam of Erasmus University who shared some of her unpublished materials, and to Professor Herman Soly of the Free University of Brussels who directed me to a number of important sources. My biggest debt, however, is to Kristel Beyens of the Institute of Criminology at the Free University of Brussels, whose assistance was invaluable. I also profited enormously from comments I received when I presented an earlier version at the Social History Conference, Luton, England, January 3–5, 1994. Needless to say, I assume final responsibility for the arguments put forward in this paper. Finally, I wish to acknowledge the support of the Committee on Research at the University of California at Berkeley.

1. Michael R. Gottfredson and Travis Hirschi, *A General Theory of Crime* (Stanford, 1990), 45.

2. For a recent review see Alfred Blumstein et al., *Criminal Careers and Career Criminals* (Washington, D.C., 1986), 40, reporting on a review of the literature and an analysis sponsored by the National Academy of Sciences.

3. See Caeser Lombroso and William Ferrero, *The Female Offender* (New York, 1895); W. I. Thomas, *Sex and Society* (Boston, 1907), and *The Unadjusted Girl* (New York, 1967); and Otto Pollak, *The Criminality of Women* (New York, 1961). For an excellent recent analysis of nineteenth-century views of women's deviance, see Lucia Zedner, *Women, Crime and Custody in Victorian England* (Oxford, 1991).

4. See Alfred Blumstein et al, *Criminal Careers*.

5. There is, of course, an older Continental tradition on which this work rests—the work of William Bonger, *Criminality and Economic Conditions* (Boston, 1916); Lombroso, Ferrero, and others. But these theories, too, are largely about male behavior.

6. See Gareth Stedman Jones, "From Historical Sociology to Theoretical History," *British Journal of Sociology* 27 (1976): 295–305.

7. See Stephen Box, *Power, Crime and Mystification* (London, 1983); Darrell J. Steffensmeier, "Development and Female Crime: A Cross-National Test of Alternative Explanations," *Social Forces* 68 (1989): 262; Darrell J. Steffensmeier, "Sex Differences in Patterns of Adult Crime: A Review and Assessment," *Social Forces* 58 (1980) 964–77; Darrell Steffensmeier, "Crime and the Contemporary Woman: An Analysis of Changing Levels of Female Property Crime, 1960–1975," *Social Forces* 57 (1978): 566–84; and Yael Hassin, "Female Criminality: Israel as a Testing Ground of Feminist Theoretical Perspectives" (Institute of Criminology, Hebrew University, May 1993).

8. Carol Smart, *Women, Crime and Criminology: A Feminist Critique* (London, 1977), 70.

9. The exceptions, discussed below, are Helen Boritch and John Hagan, "A Century of Crime in Toronto: Gender, Class, and Patterns of Social Control, 1859–1955," *Criminology* 28 (1990): 567; Malcolm M. Feeley and Deborah L. Little, "The Vanishing Female: The Decline of Women in the Criminal Process, 1687–1912," *Law and Society Review* 25 (1991): 719–57; Zedner, *Women;* John M.

Beattie, *Crime and Courts in England 1660–1800* (Princeton, 1986); and David Greenberg, "The Gendering of Crime in Marxist Criminology" (Department of Sociology, New York University, 1992).

10. For discussions of this issue, See V.A.C. Gattrell, Bruce Lenman, and Geoffrey Parker, eds., *Crime and the Law: The Social History of Crime in Western Europe Since 1500* (London, 1980); and James Sharpe, *Crime in Early Modern England, 1550–1700* (London, 1984).

11. Feeley and Little, "Vanishing Female," 724–32.

12. Greenberg, "Gendering of Crime."

13. Thereby controlling for the possibility that changes in the proportion of women are a function of informal jurisdictional shifts in the handling of cases, personal communication. I am indebted to Dr. Beattie for his continuing help on my project, and for sharing his research findings with me.

14. See Feeley and Little, "Vanishing Female," 729–30.

15. Zedner, *Women.*

16. Ibid., 1.

17. Ibid., 33–50.

18. Ibid., 33–36.

19. Ibid., 38.

20. Ibid., 39.

21. "Judicial Statistics," *Parliamentary Papers* (1857–1913).

22. See Feeley and Little "Vanishing Female," 731.

23. Trying to make sense of trends is a challenge. One of the most formidable tasks is determining where to begin and end one's trend line. Zedner, for instance, focuses on the period 1857–1913, and accounts for the downward trend in women's involvement in terms of the emergence of a new scientific approach to women's deviance that treated them as mad rather than bad, and thus shifted them from courts and prisons to hospitals and asylums. Alternative explanations that she fails to consider sufficiently are that the decline is a result of the constriction of the jurisdiction of the crown courts in ways that disproportionately affected women (she acknowledges that this occurred, but does not examine the implications carefully). Also, she both begins her analysis of declining female involvement in the mid-nineteenth century and offers a theory based on mid-nineteenth-century developments (the medicalization of women's crime), and thus ignores a very important point, namely, that a decline had been taking place since at least the early eighteenth century, and that indeed the greater decline in the proportion of women took place roughly 100 years before the Victorian era. Using Victorian-era social developments to account for this decline is of course problematic.

24. See Feeley and Little, "Vanishing Female."

25. David Phillips, *Crime and Authority in Victorian England* (London, 1977).

26. Sharpe, *Crime in England,* 1984.

27. John Langbein, "Shaping the Eighteenth-Century Criminal Trial: A View from the Ryder Sources," *Univ. of Chicago Law Rev.* 50 (1983): 1.

28. Sjoerd Faber, *Strafrechlspeging en Criminaliteit te Amsterdam, 1680–1811* (Ph.D. dissertation, Vrije Universiteit te Amsterdam, 1983); and Herman Diederiks, "Criminality and its Repression in the Past: Quantitative Approaches—A Survey," *Economic and Social History in the Netherlands* 1 (1990): 86.

29. Diederiks, "Criminality," 79.

30. Lotte C. van de Pol, "Vrouwencriminaliteit in Amsterdam in de tweede helft van de 17e eeuw," *Tijdschrift voor Criminologie* 5 (1987): 148–55.

31. Pieter Spierenburg, *The Spectacle of Suffering* (Cambridge, 1984).

32. Christine Boerdam, letter to the author, 1 Nov. 1993. I am deeply indebted to Ms. Boerdam for sharing her work in progress with me.

33. Els Kloek, "Criminaliteit en sekse in de confessieboeken van Leiden, 1678–1794," *Achtste Jaariboek van Vrouwengeschiedenis Vrouwenlevens 1500–1850* (Summer 1987): 145.

34. Herman Diederiks, "Quality and Quantity in Historical Research in Criminality and Criminal Justice: The Case of Leiden in the 17th and 18th Centuries," *Historical Social Research* 15 (1990): 57–77.

35. Excepting the years of World War I.

36. Diederiks, "Criminality," 80.

37. A. M. Roets. "Vrouwen en criminaliteit in Gent in de achttiende eeuw," *Tijdschrift voor Yeschiedenis* 95 (1982): 363–78.

38. Nanon Borgerhoff, *Vrouwen en Criminaliteit in Tongeren: 1700–1789* (M. A. Thesis, Vrije Universiteit Brussel, 1993).

39. N. E. H. Hull, *Female Felons: Women and Serious Crime in Colonial Massachusetts* (Urbana, Ill., 1987).

40. Helen Bortich and John Hagan.

41. Perhaps the highest figure is reported by Zedner, who found that at one point in the early nineteenth century women constituted 40 percent of those charged with murder. This finding appears to be exceptional. More typically the levels are 10 percent or lower, perhaps two to two and a half times as large as the twentieth-century levels, but far short of the fourfold decrease that was found for more frequently committed property offenses.

42. Work in progress.

43. See Feeley and Little, "Vanishing Female," 724–32.

44. This is not to say that shifting jurisdiction does not account for some—even a great deal—of the decline. Indeed, I believe that it does. See ibid., 724–32, for a discussion of the decline in indictments of women in the nineteenth century.

45. See also Douglas Hay et al., *Albion's Fatal Tree* (New York, 1975); and John Beattie, *Crime and the Courts in England, 1660–1800* (Princeton, 1986).

46. Especially John Beattie's ongoing work.

47. For an elaboration on this issue, see Smart, *Women*.

48. Zedner, *Women*, 264–96.

49. Ibid., 264.

50. Ibid., 296.

51. My own work on the Old Bailey suggests that the greatest changes took place during the eighteenth and early nineteenth centuries, and indeed that many of the changes that occurred later in the nineteenth century are probably due to shifting jurisdictions and are thus not "real" drops.

52. See David Garland, *Punishment and Welfare* (Gower, 1985).

53. This discussion was briefly outlined in Feeley and Little, "Vanishing Female."

54. Freda Adler, *Sisters in Crime: The Rise of the New Female Criminal* (New York, 1975). I use the recognized division between sex and gender in this paper.

Sex refers to the biological characteristics of males and females. Gender is the set of socially defined characteristics and behaviors associated with the two sexes.

55. Smart, *Women.*

56. See also Steffensmeier, "Female Crime."

57. Rita James Simon, *Women and Crime* (Lexington, Mass., 1975).

58. Steffensmeier, "Female Crime"; Peggy C. Giordano and Stephen A. Cernkovich, "On Complicating the Relationship Between Liberation and Delinquency," *Social Forces* 26 (1979): 467; Stephen Box and Chris Hale, "Liberation and Female Criminality in England and Wales," *British Journal of Criminology* 23 (1983): 35; and Carol Smart, "The New Female Criminal: Reality or Myth," *British Journal of Criminology* 50 (1979): 50.

59. For example, Box and Hale, "Liberation," argue that differential opportunity theory requires that women be given meaningful opportunity to engage in both legal and illegal activity. They claim that women's restrictions to primarily low-wage, low-power jobs may restrict their opportunity to engage in the most prevalent forms of work-related crimes.

60. Juliet Mitchell, "The Longest Revolution," *New Left Review* 40 (1966).

61. Sylvia Walby, *Theorizing Patriarchy* (Oxford, 1990).

62. See, for example, Heidi Hartmann, "Capitalism, Patriarchy and Job Segregation by Sex," in E. Abel and E. K. Abel, eds., *The Signs Reader: Women, Gender and Scholarship* (Chicago, 1983), (control of female labor power in production and the family); Nancy Chodorow, *The Reproduction of Mothering: Psychoanalysis and the Sociology of Gender* (Berkeley, 1978) (socialization and the family); and R. W. Connell, *Gender and Power: Society, the Person, and Sexual Politics* (Cambridge) (production and the family).

63. John Hagan, John Simpson, and A. R. Gillis, "Feminist Scholarship, Relational and Instrumental Control, and a Power-Control Theory of Gender and Delinquency," *British Journal of Sociology* 39 (1989): 301.

64. Ibid., 301.

65. Ibid., 302.

66. Meda Chesney-Lind, "Girl's Crime and Woman's Place: Toward a Feminist Model of Female Delinquency," *Crime and Delinquency* 35 (1989): 5.

67. Box and Hale, "Liberation"; and Frances Heidensohn, *Women and Crime* (New York, 1985).

68. Travis Hirschi, *Causes of Delinquency* (Berkeley, 1969).

69. See Box and Hale, "Liberation." The attempt to analyze female crime within control theory points to some variation in the concept of control. As theorized by Hirschi, one looks to the processes by which individuals are induced to cooperate in society. Some feminist analysis of crime looks to the processes by which women are especially induced to cooperate. An analysis of patriarchy, however, changes the unit of analysis, focusing not on individuals but on society as a whole.

70. Heidenshon, *Women and Crime,* 174–95. Specifically, she discusses (1) domestic constraints—restriction of women to motherhood and housewifery within a nuclear family, marital violence, and the deferential and hierarchical relationship between husband and wife; (2) public propriety—controls over women's behavior in public, ranging from "reputation" and the ideology of separate spheres to the male monopoly over legitimate and illegitimate means of force; (3) work—male

authority through a structure of occupational job segregation, sexual harassment, and the requirement of the "double shift" for women; and (4) social policies—state policies that maintain and reinforce the dependent housewife/mother position of women.

71. John Hagan, John Simpson, and A. R. Gillis, "The Sexual Stratification of Social Control: A Gender-Based Perspective on Crime and Delinquency," *British Journal of Sociology* 30 (1979): 25.

72. Eileen Boris and Peter Bardaglio, "The Transformation of Patriarchy: The Historic Role of the State," in Irene Diamond, ed., *Families, Politics and Public Policy: A Feminist Dialogue on Women and the State* (New York, 1983); Carol Brown, "Mothers, Fathers and Children: From Private to Public Patriarchy," in Lydia Sargent, ed., *Women and Revolution* (Boston, 1981).

73. Walby, *Patriarchy*.

74. See Hay, *Albion's Tree;* and E. P. Thompson, *Whigs and Hunters* (New York, 1975).

75. David Phillips, "A Just Measure of Crime, Authority, Hunters and Blue Locusts: The 'Revisionist' Social History of Crime and the Law in Britain, 1780–1850," in Stanley Cohen and Andrew Scull, eds., *Social Control and the State* (Oxford, 1983); and Paul Rock, "Law, Order and Power in Late Seventeenth- and Early Eighteenth-Century England," in Cohen and Scull, *Social Control*.

76. Beattie, *Crime*, 229.

77. Ibid., 229–37. Although detailed occupational data is not always (carefully) reported in the various studies reviewed earlier in this chapter, it does appear that the vast majority of those caught up in the criminal process were of the poor and laboring classes. Some worked as domestics, others as unskilled and casual laborers, and others in assorted crafts and trades. Very few records detail the employment status of women, except for the occasional notation as a domestic worker. For extended discussions of this issue for England, see also Clive Emsley, *Crime and Society in England 1750–1900* (London, 1987).

78. Dorothy M. George, *London Life in the Eighteenth Century* (New York, 1965).

79. There is an additional important question we must also address: What was the nature and level of women's involvement in crime prior to the mid-seventeenth century. Existing studies available to this author rarely go back further than the mid-seventeenth century, and there is no clear indication as to what the pattern of women's involvement was prior to this period. As reported earlier in this paper, there is some evidence to suggest that there was a rise in women's involvement during the late seventeenth and early eighteenth century. But before anything can be asserted with confidence, a still longer time span must be considered. The problem is crucial for the development of theory: Is the issue, (1) What factors contributed to the decline of the level of women's involvement in crime in the eighteenth century? or (2) What contributed to the rise and subsequent decline of the level of women's involvement? Unfortunately, we cannot now even ask the right question, let along offer convincing answers!

80. Alice Clark, *Working Life of Women in the Eighteenth Century* (London, 1919, repr. 1982).

81. Ibid., 7.

82. Ibid., 5.

83. Ibid., 32.

84. Ibid., 301.

85. Hans Medick, "The Proto-Industrial Family Economy: The Structural Function of Household and Family During the Transition from Peasant Society to Industrial Capitalism," *Social History* 1 (1976): 311.

86. Louise A. Tilly and Joan W. Scott, *Women, Work and Family* (New York, 1978).

87. George, *London*, 168.

88. Tilly and Scott, *Women*.

89. Sonya Rose, "Gender Antagonisms and Class Conflict: Exclusionary Strategies of Male Trade Unionists in Nineteenth Century Britain, *Social History* 13 (1988): 191.

90. Lawrence Stone, *The Family, Sex, and Marriage in England: 1500–1800* (New York, 1977), 200.

91. Tilly and Scott, *Women*.

92. Ivy Pinchbeck, *Women Workers and the Industrial Revolution, 1750–1850* (London, 1930, repr. 1969).

93. Ibid., 148.

94. Ibid., 257.

95. Ibid., 126.

96. Ibid., 117.

97. See also Bridget Hill, *Women, Work and Sexual Politics in Eighteenth-Century England* (Oxford, 1989); Chris Middleton, "Women's Labour and the Transition to Pre-industrial Capitalism," in L. Charles and L. Duffin, eds., *Women and Work in Pre-Industrial England* (London, 1985).

98. Clark, *Working Life*, 302.

99. Ibid., 302.

100. Hill, *Women*.

101. Ibid., 262.

102. Ibid., 259f1.

103. Ibid., 263.

104. See Hartmann, "Capitalism"; and Sonya Rose, "Gender Antagonism and Class Conflict: Exclusionary Strategies of Male Trade Unionists in Nineteenth Century Britain," *Social History* 13 (1988): 191. There is substantial debate over the reasons female unionists tried to exclude women and the participation/agreement of working-class women in these struggles. However, the fact of their increasing exclusion from production remains.

105. Sally Alexander, *Women's Work in Nineteenth Century London: A Study of the Years 1820–1850* (London, 1983).

106. George, *London*.

107. These included shipping industries, public utilities, transport, semi-processing and extractive industries (i.e., London's factory trades), professions, civil service, clerical work, scientific trades, and the old craft guilds. See Alexander, *Women's Work*.

108. It should be emphasized that, unlike the economic historians discussed earlier, Stone adamantly rejects any "argument that these developments can be attributed in some way or other to capitalism." Stone, *Family*, 646. Rather, he links these changes to the decline of Puritanism and the rise of secular individualism.

109. As is well known, sexual controls also tightened during the Victorian era. These controls were evident in our data for the Old Bailey. The latter part of the nineteenth century saw a rise in the numbers of prosecutions for sexual offenses, especially sexual assaults of minor girls and homosexuality. But it appears that the shift in controls that most fully accounts for the decline of women's involvement in the criminal process took place long before the Victorian era.

110. Stone, *Family*, 201.

111. Ibid.

112. The data reviewed in this paper support the argument that women's lower participation in violent crime or offenses against persons is a historical constant. Much of this crime is "private," between individuals who know each other, often occurring in the home or neighborhood. Patriarchal control of women in the private sphere also seems to be a constant, in that women have historically been subject to male control of their reproductive labor power. Even as individual males have seen their private power over individual women lessened, women have experienced a shift from control by their husbands/fathers to control by the state. See Boris and Bardaglio, "Transformation of Patriarchy." If patriarchal controls explain female noncriminality, the fact that women are always expected to labor in the private (family as opposed to market or polity) sphere, coupled with the constant existence of these controls (which while shifting in intensity have never completely disappeared), may begin to account for women's lower participation in violent crime. In contrast, women's participation in production has varied historically as has their participation in property crime (which occurs primarily outside the home).

Book Review Essay
The Postmodern Prostitute: A
Thematic Review of Recent Research

Augustine Brannigan
University of Calgary

COMPETING AGENDAS AND THEIR LEGAL FRAMEWORKS

For the past two decades there has been tremendous public concern over prostitution in Canada, Britain, and Australia. This has been associated with growth both in the sex trade and in the law reforms designed to deal with it.[1] In the Third World, particularly Thailand and the Philippines, there has been a great concern with sex tourism and the exploitation of young women and girls by men from the industrialized countries.[2] Attention has also been drawn to the plight of poor women working in brothels in India and Central and South America.[3] The demise of the Soviet Bloc has also been associated with a sharp rise in the sex trade, making prostitution a worldwide problem in the 1990s.[4]

In the common law countries, there is widespread optimism that "something can be done" about the prevalence of prostitution and the victimization of prostitutes by making and enforcing appropriate criminal laws. The legal objectives of such laws are not always consistent nor well defined, and as a result they often have contradictory effects. By way of example, there is virtually universal agreement that no one should be forced into the sex trade involuntarily by a pimp or retained in "the life" against her will. Laws against procurement, controlling the movement of prostitutes, doping a person for illicit intercourse, and living on the avails are directed at this issue. There is also widespread concern over violence against, and the murder of, so-called "sex trade workers" by pimps, "johns," and others. In Canada since 1985, there have been over thirty murders recorded of females working as prostitutes.[5] Even in the absence of such violence, in Canada the acquisition of the sexual services of, and living on the avails of, an adolescent prostitute are viewed as child sexual abuse and can be punished with lengthy periods of imprisonment—a maximum of five years imprisonment for the former, fourteen years for the latter. Although these provisions have been exercised very rarely, the objective of these kinds of laws has been to stem the harms to prostitutes. These laws are based on a victimological perspective.

Nuisance represents a different concern. In urban areas where street prostitution occupies a stroll frequented by numbers of sellers and their customers, it is widely accepted that the street trade is a source of serious disturbance to the community, that it injures the peace and security of the neighborhood, and results in unwanted litter in the form of discarded condoms and needles, high volumes of late night traffic, intrusions onto or near private property for the transaction of "dates," and unwanted solicitation of females who are not prostitutes by male curb crawlers. In Canada, nuisance is controlled primarily by a law that makes communication for the purposes of prostitution a summary conviction offense for both sellers and clients. This law derives from a delinquency perspective. Ironically, nuisance is not an element of the offense of communication. It is meant to protect communities and is the single most frequently laid charge related to prostitution in Canada—resulting in recent years in some 10,000 arrests annually. In the past, the charge has tended to be laid more frequently against prostitutes (including adolescents at risk of sexual abuse), although recent civic concern over street prostitution has resulted in a significant increase in arrests of "johns." The delinquency approach inadvertently aggravates the level of victimization of prostitutes arising from other sources of stress—bad dates, abusive pimps, drug dependency, and so forth. For the johns, the courts have shown uncommon leniency, typically disposing of convictions with discharges or small fines. As a consequence, the communication law has little deterrent effect.

There are also contradictory considerations that operate at the level of the institution of prostitution which reflect ideological considerations. Conservatives view it as a threat to moral integrity and family and community values,[6] while feminists equate it with female degradation and sexual exploitation.[7] Both condemn it. However, conservatives like to blame the prostitutes while feminists blame the johns. A different occupational perspective comes from advocates of the sex business, who find the criminal, moral, and ideological intrusions into their work offensive and unjustified. Along with Pheterson's earlier *Vindication of the Rights of Whores,* this is the space explored by Jenness's book on the prostitutes' rights movement— *Making It Work: The Prostitutes' Rights Movement in Perspective.*[8] From the occupational perspective, prostitution is a service industry that reflects personal choices in acquiring an income through the marketing of intimate contact.

Jenness's account is decidedly removed from the day-to-day practices of prostitution in major North American cities. There is no discussion of pimping, no discussion of the sexual, physical, or emotional trauma in the backgrounds of prostitutes, no discussion of inner-city kids and runaways sexually exploited by middle-class, middle-aged gentlemen from the suburbs, no discussion of the appalling levels of assault and murder of prostitutes, no discussion of the various venues in which prostitution occurs (street, bar, brothel, massage, escort, trick pad, etc.), and no discussion of the ideological and sexist foundations of the sex trade. What Jenness concentrates on is the struggle by COYOTE ("Call Off Your Old Tired Ethics") and similar groups to legitimize the provision of sexual access to strangers as a matter of human rights. This study records the social movement created by advocates to gain public affirmation in spite of the stigma associated with commercial sexual relationships. Such groups have been most successful where community response has been favorable—notably in San Francisco, where the gay and lesbian communities have been powerful political allies. They have also experienced some success related to education on the issues of health and STD (sexually transmitted disease) transmission both among prostitutes and in the wider community. In Canada, one of the most prominent prostitution advocacy groups, POWER (Prostitutes and Other Women for Equal Rights) has received provincial funding in Manitoba for an outreach service that distributes condoms and needles to street people.[9] One of the limitations that arise from this approach is that public concerns with prostitution tend to become confined to public health issues—as though prostitution would be more acceptable if no one contracted a disease from engaging in it. If we go beyond the advocacy groups, there is more to deal with than that.

In fact, we appear to have five separate agendas here: victimology, delinquency, ideology, occupation, and public health. With five competing perspectives on the issue, what are the consequences in terms of the legal framework? Do the laws conflate protection of working prostitutes under one set of considerations (antipimping) with a condemnation of prostitution per se via another set (anticommunication)? In Canada, prostitution per se in not unlawful, nor was it unlawful in the English common law. However, massive action against nuisance, particularly with respect to communication charges against the female sellers, and rather spartan use of the laws devised to protect prostitutes, creates an imbalance. Suppression overshadows protection. This contradiction follows from the conflicting perspectives that motivate discourses in this area—victimology, delinquency, ideology, service, and public health.

We have initiated this discussion by outlining some of the contradictory views that arise over prostitution and the potential for legal miasma that results from these competing agendas. In the balance of this discussion we will review some of the key alternatives that have arisen in critiques of prostitution law in the recent literature: criminalization, legalization, and decriminalization. These policies are based on competing social objectives and appear to oversimplify the optimal legal frameworks that could be evolved to deal with the various issues. At the heart of the matter are (1) ambiguities about the nature of prostitution itself, what the work consists of, and who engages in it; (2) complexities of the niches in which prostitution flourishes; and (3) the resulting competing and contradictory legal objectives behind the respective laws. Before we turn to these matters, the historical record of law reform offers some sobering reminders about the deficiencies of simple legal panaceas.

HISTORICAL IMPACT OF REFORM MOVEMENTS ON PROSTITUTION LAW

To appreciate the contradictory forces behind antiprostitution legislation, it is helpful to examine the role of the prostitution reform movements in the late nineteenth and early twentieth century. According to Musheno and Seeley, "progressive era feminists supported severe state suppression of prostitution."[10] Unfortunately, the consequences were extracted on the suffragists' "fallen" sisters. Prior to this period, Ronald Walkowitz argues that citizens accepted the right of working-class women to sell sexual access without police harassment.[11] In the 1880s, parallels were drawn between the enslavement of Africans and the enslavement of women. Entry into prostitution or "white slavery" was attributed to pimps, Jews, and swarthy Eastern Europeans who kidnapped unsuspecting females and forced them to perform as sexual slaves imprisoned in brothels. As John McLaren notes, the Canadian court statistics record that the vast majority of persons convicted under the draconian antipimp laws created by the white slave campaign were other female prostitutes—usually madams renting premises to younger workers.[12] Kathleen Daly draws a parallel between contemporary efforts to suppress the commercialized sex trade and the efforts of the "progressive era" in which the white slavery stereotype was promulgated: "however well intentioned, such efforts are fraught with the potential to criminalize the most vulnerable parties: women."[13]

While feminists in both periods identified with the vulnerability of the sex trade workers, K. A. Holmes points to another agenda of the middle-class reformers. Part of the nineteenth-century women's intent was to protect the middle and upper class from the perceived promiscuity of the "dangerous classes," with all the implications for medical and moral infection that that promiscuity portended.[14] The campaign against "white slavery" overlapped with the "purity movement," which adopted "a single standard of chastity," so that prostitution was not suppressed solely to minimize victimization, but to extirpate promiscuity itself and to upgrade what were viewed as the questionable inclinations of the lower orders of society.[15] Victimization and ideology dominated the agenda—the occupational perspective never saw the light of day.

DEBATING CONTEMPORARY LEGAL SOLUTIONS

Fran Shaver outlines three basic approaches to contemporary prostitution control: criminalization, legalization and decriminalization.[16] Criminalization represents the current policy. It outlaws communication, procuring, living on the avails, controlling the movements of a prostitute, and, in most jurisdictions, the act of prostitution itself. Legalization is characterized as a matter of regulation, which confers formal recognition of prostitution as an occupational niche. On this point, it is unclear why Shaver refers to the federal criminal code as the enabling legislation for licensing, as health, business considerations (including licensing), and labor standards are entirely provincial matters, and may in fact fall under municipal or county jurisdiction. She rejects legalization, quoting an activist who says that it would be "tantamount to slavery," and recommends decriminalization as the most appropriate policy. Her decriminalization classification is similar to that of Susan Hatty, who refers to "prohibition, regulation and un-monitored approaches." Presumably, decriminalized prostitution would be equivalent to "unmonitored" prostitution. Bennetts et al. also call for de-criminalization since the current laws oppress the women they are designed to protect. Jeffrey Reiman calls for decriminalization of both prostitution and heroin addiction—not because these are socially desirable ends, but because the criminal law is an inappropriate method to deal with what he calls "alienated desires"—the desire for anonymous sex or narcotic stupor. Belinda Cooper calls for "legalization," while acknowledging that women are generally in an exploited status—a view shared by Carolyn Smart, who finds that the preoccupation with prostitution overlooks "the larger social forces that foster and maintain . . . the sexual inequality and oppression of all women."[17]

While most of the authors mentioned here reject the criminalization option since it compounds the oppression of women, Mathews applauded proposals from the UK Criminal Law Revision Committee to control certain aspects of the street trade by criminal prohibition. The proposals would have made it illegal to solicit anyone from a car, to persistently solicit on a street, or to solicit a woman "in a manner likely to cause her fear."[18] Notably, most of these provisions would punish the customers of street workers. Carol Pateman also appears reluctant to abandon the use of law to condemn prostitution in a philosophical analysis that argues that women in an oppressed status cannot be said to willingly enter into a pros-titution "contract"; their compliance with a more permissive framework (legalization) would be illusory.[19] However, P. Connelly argues the same would be true for female entry to *any* occupation.[20] Disparities in feminist opinion are obviously reflective of the larger disparities in perspectives noted earlier. Baslow and Campile report another dimension: college women who accept feminist values tend on the whole to be much less tolerant of prostitution than other women, a finding that, if true, might explain the failure of university feminists to establish much common ground with active prostitutes.[21]

Is the legal standing of prostitution consequential for the welfare of prostitutes? On this matter, it is an open question whether the stigma attributed to prostitution from a middle-class perspective derives from its criminal labeling, or whether a change in perceptions would follow its removal from criminal law prohibition. R. W. Smith suggests that where deviance is not prohibited by law (Nevada), the public tends to have a more tolerant attitude toward it, although which came first is an open question.[22] A. J. Velarde argues that the negative publicity attached to the massage parlor industry in the 1970s produced "secondary deviation" among the masseuse professionals, leading them to adopt a conception of themselves as deviants.[23] This suggests that the welfare of the prostitutes is at least in part a reflection of the status attributed to them by society. Arguing in a consistent vein, Eileen McLeod reports that public debate by the Program for Reform of the Law on Soliciting (PROS) encouraged destigmatization of prostitutes and reduced their liability to imprisonment for soliciting.[24] However, the power of such public lobbying is questionable in the view of L. Dominelli. It "ultimately fails to challenge the existing social relations and the distribution of power between men and women."[25] Why the onus to achieve this should revert particularly to the suppliers as opposed to the consumers is unexplored. The reasons for the lobby failure may be that prostitutes simply cannot—or have not—mustered the political capital to effectively articulate their case. COYOTE's attempts to shift the rhetoric that surrounds prostitution from one of sin and crime to one of "work, choice and civil rights," appear to have had little impact on public opinion. Ronald Weitzer in a piece called "Prostitutes' Rights in the United States: The Failure of a Movement," argues that because of "chronic deficiencies of material and human resources," the prostitutes' rights movement was unable to prop up a campaign that had little moral capital to start with.[26] As a result, most observers accept the victimization framework and call for decriminalization of prostitution in order to minimize the aggravation of prostitutes, but stop short of envisioning prostitution as an occupation.

FALSE DICHOTOMIES?

What can be concluded about the contemporary debates on the legal framework? Most writers acknowledge that prostitution is bad (as an institution), but that the criminalization of it is worse (for the practitioners). Nothing is said of the quality of service delivery, as though this were ancillary to the entire question. A *"Consumer Reports"* on customer satisfaction and service reliability seems to be out of the question. That "complex convergence of lust and bitterness" of which Gustave Flaubert wrote in

1853 is unexamined territory.[27] Perhaps a better indication of popular attitudes is that expressed in a Canadian editorial in one of the local Calgary papers in which the sex trade was described simply as "garbage" promoted by a "hag ridden" trade of "sullen faced harlots." Associate editor Catherine Ford was not talking about nuisance, nor a credible occupation.[28] The policy issues tend to be framed from either the perspective of vulnerable sex trade workers—a victimological perspective—or the sick sexual inclinations of the johns—an ideological perspective.[29] Again, it is significant that the occupational perspective is occluded. The sex trade enjoys about as much credibility as an occupation as mercenary services. Both groups get paid for what they do but few people view the "work" as legitimate. And where many soldiers of fortune were motivated by jingoistic anticommunist ideologies, few women providing sexual access for money are motivated by the ideals of sexual liberation and the "free love" movement of the 1960s.

In reviewing specific policy alternatives, it is difficult to credit the distinction between decriminalization and legalization for several reasons. First, if we can borrow from another illustration—abortion—it appears that when abortion was struck from the Canadian criminal code in the *Morgentaler* case, it was not merely decriminalized.[30] By default it became a matter of provincial health services. Similarly, if the laws with respect to brothels were removed from the criminal code, by default all the usual laws that are associated with businesses would apply. These would not be unmonitored underground rackets operating outside the law, and if they were, would they not justifiably attract the attention of the revenue police? Decriminalization cannot escape regulation. Businesses created by decriminalization would have to make decisions about site location, building codes, recruitment, advertising, labor standards, and so forth. If a legitimate masseuse who works in a chiropractic office requires a license, why would a prostitute be different? And in what sense is the licensing of either practitioner equivalent to slavery? The observation about slavery from Shaver appears to suggest that the workers would not or do not like their work. If we take the occupational perspective seriously, why should we be alarmed if people do not like their jobs, for who does? Why should prostitution be different from other mind-numbing vocations? It is impossible to discuss the occupational perspective seriously without thinking about its regulatory framework, for surely it is within such a framework that we would address workplace grievances, stresses, and hazards.

A second point is that criminalization and legalization are falsely dichotomized. Simply because enabling legislation existed for, say, brothels, it does not follow that one would decriminalize street soliciting. Nuisance would still be a concern. The reason for this is that not all those who might want to work as prostitutes would necessarily be permitted into the legal venue. As a consequence, they would tend to gravitate back to an illegal venue. Because of age, HIV infection, drug dependency, serious criminal record, or similar attributes, many applicants would be unfit for licensing. In Victoria, Australia, where the antibrothel laws were struck from the Police Offences Act and made part of the Town Planning (Brothels) Act in 1984, criminal legislation continued in place to suppress street soliciting. Concerns about the victimization of prostitutes was maintained in the Prostitutes Regulation Act of 1986.[31] In other words, both criminalization and legalization exist side by side, the former deriving from the delinquency and victimization perspectives (nuisance and violence against prostitutes), the latter from the occupational perspective. Neither criminalization nor legalization is a panacea.

A third observation about the policy alternatives outlined above is that different levels of government can enact different sorts of laws, some of which suppress and some of which permit the activity. This is the case in escort services in several Canadian cities whose policies expedite what federal laws were designed to suppress. The practitioners are treated as though they are involved in legitimate dating and dining introductions, but it is common knowledge that such agencies are fronts for prostitution. These operations survive because the communication takes place in private where it is not contrary to law, and because in Canada prostitution per se is not unlawful.[32] If we are correct about this, these policies are not a case of "either/or" (criminalization/legalization) but "both/and" (i.e., federal proscription and municipal acceptance).

THE POSTMODERN PROSTITUTE: PROBLEMS IN DEFINING PROSTITUTION

Why is there so much ambiguity surrounding the legal framework, making a simple legal solution so difficult? Clearly, the conflicting conceptions of what requires attention play a role (victimization, delinquency, etc.). Increasingly, researchers are recognizing that the problem also has to do with the ambiguity in the nature of prostitution itself. It might prove useful to turn briefly to that point. The "modern" image of prostitutes as fallen women, the images of the whore versus the virgin, the harlot, and so forth, provided clear stereotypes of good and evil women. These were nineteenth-century images that grounded the legal framework that survives today. Now we read of Mayflower Madams and the Beverley Hills "sex broker" to the stars.[33] Are the nineteenth-century images adequate? Many authors think not. The postmodern prostitute is a pastiche of competing images, with prostitution inhabiting a variety of sites and taking a variety of forms. Edward Armstrong writes that "the difference between prostitution and conventional behavior is provisional. . . . The distinction must be dissolved. . . . The concept of prostitution fails to organize and interpret data of direct observation in a coherent and comprehensive fashion."[34] In a critique of articles on prostitution in the *Journal of Sex Research,* Gail Pheterson criticized the research for "reinforcement of classical stereotypes. . . . The category 'prostitute' is based more on symbolic and legal representations of the bad woman or whore than on an actual set of characteristics. . . . Deconstruction of the category 'prostitute' is therefore necessary."[35]

Something of what Pheterson has in mind is suggested by a study of female prostitutes conducted in Colorado Springs. John Potterat, an officer with the Public Health Office concerned with venereal diseases, classified 52 percent of those in his sample as "evanescent."[36] In other words, the plurality of his sample were not seasoned pros, but young amateurs who had merely a fleeting exposure to the street, and whose "master status" ("mistress status"?) was probably not one of prostitute in the traditional sense. Linda Hancock makes equally telling observations in her study of juvenile prostitutes in Melbourne, Australia. She argues that prostitution extends beyond the stereotype of "common" streetwalkers seeking money in exchange for sex. It includes "acts involving the provision of sexual services in return for goods or services such as drugs, food or accommodation and/or acts involving indiscriminate sexual promiscuity often motivated by desires for approval, attention or affection."[37] By way of explanation, indiscriminate sexual promiscuity referred to young people who were not just sexually active (as this may include many young people), but who had engaged in "indiscriminate sexual relations with a succession of partners, often not knowing them by name." Fred Mathews refers to adolescent prostitution as "survival sex" pursued on a transitory, short-term basis by runaways without immediate resources. Mathews stresses that it is not prostitution at all, but the sexual exploitation of children.[38]

The complexity of the concept is further suggested in studies of massage parlors. Bryant and Palmer reported that the female workers who provided "special massages" for male customers rejected "the occupational label and role of prostitute, but were willing to assume the responsibility and self-image of 'hand-whore.'"[39] Presumably, prostitution would involve some kind of penetration. Armstrong goes further. Writing with an unspecified coauthor who worked as a masseuse, he suggested that "unlike a brothel where sexual gratification is the purchased commodity, only 67% of the massage parlor customers desired these 'extras,' and only 42% of these customers actually received them. . . . The decision to engage in sexual activity is more often the result of a complex set of spontaneous factors, over which the parlor worker retains considerable control."[40] So much for a guaranteed encounter—aside from a lot of naked squeezing, rubbing, hand chopping, and flesh pinching of a nonsexual kind. And as for the issue of penetration, this is probably less frequent in massage than we think, but in the sector characterized by bondage and domination it is completely out of the question; yet all these venues are described as prostitution.

If massage parlors are a stereotypical form of prostitution, the utilization of highway rest stops by local gay men and straight truck drivers is something of a surprise—especially since the transactions often occur without tangible remuneration. This work was reported by Corzine and Kirby, but several studies of prostitution involving professional drivers, particularly truckers and heterosexual liaisons contacted over CB radios, have been reported.[41] And then there is what Forsyth and Fournet refer to as the "office harlot"—a form of prostitution in which a person receives employment and high wages, does little business-related work, and who is involved in "sexual affairs with a boss or bosses and/or clients of the company."[42] As one approaches this end of the continuum, one is reminded of Engels's description of marriage as a legalized form of prostitution.

Recently, two appeals court decisions in Canada have blurred the line between "exotic entertainment" and prostitution. In Montreal, the provision of small rooms for tête-à-tête encounters between individual customers and exotic dancers, both of whom are permitted to masturbate without any interpersonal contact, was found acceptable in a case that was upheld by the Supreme Court of Canada. In Toronto, "lap dancing," in which exotic dancers bump and grind on the patron's lap, has escaped judicial suppression in the Ontario Court of Appeal. In both cities, the police equate these forms of "exotic entertainment" with prostitution.[43]

Ironically, the leading decision of the Supreme Court of Canada in the area of obscenity—R. v. Butler—permitted the circulation of explicit sex but drew the line at violent and degrading representations.[44] The implications for obscene dancing appear to be that consensual explicit dancing, or what might now be called "lap massage" in a public club, without violence, without underage dancers, and without coercion, would be found permissible. The boundaries of the common law are driven by considerations that most citizens can little identify with. This is a hazard of leaving law reform to the sort of special interest groups that intervened in Butler.

What we are beginning to see is that the concept of who is and who is not a prostitute, whether the work is occupational or transitory, whether it is work at all, and how those who do it perceive themselves—all this is much fuzzier than the case made by Jenness for an occupational perspective. If that is the case, then no single legal solution could ever be expected to successfully cover all the venues, activities, and persons involved. That certainly was one of the main lessons learned from the laws devised to suppress prostitution during the "progressive era." Mark Connelly reports that the national concern over prostitution in North America at the turn of the century "had at least as much to do with anxieties produced by the transformation of American society occurring in the progressive era as with the actual existence of red light districts. . . . Prostitution became a master code . . . for a wide range of anxieties engendered by the great social and cultural changes that [gave] the progressive era its coherence as a distinct historical period."[45] These changes included a rising female autonomy from traditional domestic roles, an increase in female labor markets of commerce and sales, assimilation of foreigners with alien values, and the industrialization of production.

Today, we face a globalization of national economies and a downsizing of the social safety nets, both of which have created massive anxieties about personal and financial security as "jobless growth" and the international flight of capital make traditional employment prospects precarious. Both changes have occurred in a period where changing cultural values have initiated dramatic shifts in the family form, particularly with the rise of single parenting. There is no doubt that many of the young women and girls working as prostitutes, whether in Bangkok or Toronto, are correctly perceived as casualties of these changes. Even if this is true, finding a single legal solution to the issues associated with prostitution is obviously unrealistic. A pastiche of postmodern prostitution laws and regulations, as well as resistance to them by those so governed, appears to be unavoidable.

NOTES

1. *The Report of the Committee on Sexual Offences Against Children and Youths*, Chair, Robin Badgley (Ottawa, 1984); *The Report of the Special Committee on Prostitution and Pornography*, Chair, Paul Fraser (Ottawa, 1985); Criminal Law Revision Committee, *Sixteenth Report: Prostitution in the Street* (London, 1984); Criminal Law Revision Committee, *Seventeenth Report: Off-Street Prostitution* (London, 1985); Marcia Neave, *Inquiry into Prostitution in Victoria, Final Report* (Melbourne, 1985).

2. Erik Cohen, "Sensuality and Venality in Bangkok: The Dynamics of Cross-Cultural Mapping of Prostitution," *Deviant Behavior* 8 (1988): 223–34; Jeff O'Malley, "Sex Tourism and Women's Status in Thailand," *Loisir-et-Société/Society-and-Leisure* 11 (1987): 99–114. Apparently, the exploitation of Third World women was prevalent by Western military personnel in the colonial period. See David J. Pivar, "The Military, Prostitution, and the Colonial Peoples: India and the Philippines, 1885–1917," *Journal of Sex Research* 17 (1981): 256–69.

3. R.A.P. Singh, "Women Trade: Question of Demand and Supply," *Journal of Sociological Studies* 9 (1990): 130–43.

4. *Time*, "Sex for Sale: Special Report" 141 (21 June 1993): 16–31.

5. David Steinhart, "Murdered Woman Worked as Hooker," *Calgary Herald*, 4 Dec. 1992: B1; Greg Owens, "Dead Woman Was Hooker," *Calgary Herald*, 13 Feb. 1993: B10. The Canadian Department of Justice launched investigations in 1994 to determine the causes of violence against prostitutes, and specifically to determine whether the law that forbids communication in public is a contributing factor. The author is participating in one such study.

6. *The Report of the Special Committee on Prostitution and Pornography*, Chair, Paul Fraser (Ottawa, 1985): 348–50.

7. Linda Bell, *Good Girls, Bad Girls, Sex Trade Workers and Feminists Face to Face* (Toronto, 1987).

8. Gail Pheterson, *A Vindication of the Rights of Whores* (Seattle, 1989); Val-

erie Jenness, *Making it Work: The Prostitutes' Rights Movement in Perspective* (New York, 1993).

9. The Mount Carmel Community Clinic of Winnipeg is similar to needle exchange and condom distribution programs found in many large North American cities. The emphasis on needles and condoms suggests that the many clients have narcotic addictions that keep them in "the life."

10. M. Musheno and K. Seeley, "Prostitution Policy and the Women's Movement: Historical Analysis of Feminist Thought and Organization," *Contemporary Crises* 10 (1986): 237–55.

11. J. R. Walkowitz, "The Politics of Prostitution," *Signs* 6 (1980): 123–35 at 123.

12. J.P.S. McLaren, "Chasing the Social Evil: Moral Fervour and the Evolution of Canada's Prostitution Laws, 1867–1917," *Canadian Journal of Law and Society* 1 (1986): 125–66.

13. Kathleen Daly, "The Social Control of Sexuality: A Case Study of the Criminalization of Prostitution in the Progressive Era," *Research in Law, Deviance and Social Control* 9 (1988): 171–206 at 171.

14. K. A. Holmes, "Reflections by Gaslight: Prostitution in Another Age," *Issues in Criminology* 7 (1972): 83–101.

15. Walkowitz, "The Politics of Prostitution," 123.

16. Fran M. Shaver, "Prostitution: A Critical Analysis of Three Policy Approaches," *Canadian Public Policy/Analyse de Politiques* 11 (1985): 493–503.

17. Susan Hatty, "Violence Against Prostitute Women: Social and Legal Dilemmas," *Australian Journal of Social Issues* 24 (1989): 235–48; L. Bennetts, E. Carlton, W. Cutler, L. Humiston, D. Leopold, M. Mann, M. Goldman, A. Bolster, M. Reich, B. Scudder, L. Stewart, S. Cronon, and N. Walker, "Prostitution: A Non-Victim Crime? Women Endorsing Decriminalization," *Issues in Criminology* 8 (1973): 137–62; Jeffrey Reiman, "Prostitution, Addiction and the Ideology of Liberalism," *Contemporary Crises* 3 (1979): 53–68; Belinda Cooper, "Prostitution: A Feminist Analysis," *Women's Rights Law Reporter* 11 (1989): 99–119 at 99; Carolyn Smart, "Researching Prostitution: Some Problems for Feminist Research," *Humanity and Society* 8 (1984): 407–13.

18. Ralph Mathews, "Streetwise? A Critical Review of the Criminal Law Revision Committee's Report on 'Prostitution in the Street,' " *Critical Social Policy* 4 (1985): 103–11.

19. Carol Pateman, "Defending Prostitution: Charges Against Ericsson," *Ethics* 93 (1983): 561–65.

20. P. Connelly, "Female Labour Force Participation: Choice or Necessity?" *Atlantis* 3 (1978): 40–53.

21. S. A. Baslow and F. Campanile, "Attitudes Toward Prostitution as a Function of Attitudes Toward Feminism in College Students: An Exploratory Study," *Psychology of Women Quarterly* 14 (1990): 135–41.

22. R. W. Smith, "Legalized Recreation as Deviance," *Quarterly Journal of Ideology* 10 (1986): 37–42.

23. A. J. Verlade, "Becoming Prostituted: The Decline of the Massage Parlor Profession and the Masseuse," *British Journal of Criminology* 15 (1975): 251–63.

24. Eileen McLeod, "Feminist Action Research and the Criminal Justice System:

Lessons from the PROS Campaign on Prostitution," *Resources for Feminist Research* 14 (1985): 40–41.

25. L. Dominelli, "The Power of the Powerless: Prostitution and the Reinforcement of Submissive Femininity," *Sociological Review* 34 (1986): 65–92.

26. P. A. Roby, "Politics and Prostitution: A Case Study of the Revision, Enforcement, and Administration of the New York State Penal Laws on Prostitution," *Criminology* 9 (1972): 425–47; Valerie Jenness, "From Sex as Sin to Sex as Work: COYOTE and the Reorganization of Prostitution as a Social Problem," *Social Problems* 37 (1990): 403–20; Ronald Weitzer, "Prostitutes' Rights in the United States: The Failure of a Movement," *Sociological Quarterly* 32 (1991): 23–41.

27. Francine du Plessix Gray, "Splendor and Miseries," *New York Review of Books,* 16 July 1992: 31–35.

28. Catherine Ford, "City Needs to Clean Up its Garbage," *Calgary Herald,* 1 Sept. 1992.

29. A. L. Bardach, "A Fever in the Blood," *Vanity Fair,* January 1991: 24–34.

30. *Morgentaler v. R.,* 62 C.R. (3d) 1, 37 C.C.C. (3d) 449, 1988 (S.S.C.).

31. T. L. Bryant, "Planning Town and Country Brothels: Now Red Lights Have the Go-Ahead," *Law Institute Journal* (March 1985): 202–5; "Brothels Revisited," *Law Institute Journal* (May 1986): 442–46; "Planning and Social Issues in the Prostitution Regulation Act," *Law Institute Journal* (Sept., 1987): 903–5.

32. This was examined in some detail for Calgary by Sharon Williams, *Nobody's Business: An Analysis of the Calgary Escort Business* (MA Thesis, University of Calgary, 1992). Also, see the discussion of escort services in Augustine Brannigan, Louis Knafla, and J. C. Levy, *Prostitution on the Prairies: Evaluation of Bill C-49 in Calgary, Regina and Winnipeg,* Department of Justice (Ottawa, 1989).

33. Pam Lambert, "Heidi's High Life: High School Drop Out Madam to the Stars," *People,* 23 Aug. 1993: 50–57; Sydney Barrows, *Mayflower Madam: The Secret Life of Sydney Biddle Barrows* (New York, 1986).

34. Edward G. Armstrong, "The Sociology of Prostitution," *Sociological Spectrum* 1 (1981): 91–102.

35. Gail Pheterson, "The Category 'Prostitute' in Scientific Inquiry," *Journal of Sex Research* 27 (1990): 397–407.

36. John J. Potterat, D. E. Woodhouse, J. B. Muth, and S. Q. Muth, "Estimating the Prevalence and Career Longevity of Prostitute Women," *Journal of Sex Research* 27 (1990): 233–43.

37. Linda Hancock, *The Involvement of Young Persons in Prostitution* (Melbourne, 1985), p. 6.

38. Fred Mathews, "Adolescent Prostitution," Speech to the National Meeting on Prostitution in Canada, Federation of Canadian Municipalities (Calgary, 1993).

39. C. D. Bryant and D. E. Palmer, "Massage Parlors and 'Hand Whores': Some Sociological Observations," *Journal of Sex Research* 11 (1975): 227–41.

40. Edward G. Armstrong, "Massage Parlors and Their Customers," *Archives of Sexual Behavior* 7 (1978): 117–25.

41. T. G. Foltz, "Escort Services: An Emerging Middle Class Sex-for-Money Scene," *California Sociologist* 2 (1979): 105–33; P. K. Rasmussen and L. L. Kuhn, "The New Masseuse: Play for Pay," *Urban Life* 5 (1976): 271–92; J. Corzine and R. Kirby "Cruising the Truckers: Sexual Encounters in a Highway Rest Area," *Urban Life* 6 (1977): 171–92; L. Klein and J. L. Ingle, "Sex Solicitation for Short

Wave Radio," *Free Inquiry in Creative Sociology* 9 (1981): 61–63, 68; J. Luxenburg and L. Klein, "CB Radio Prostitution: Technology and the Displacement of Deviance," *Journal of Offender Counselling Services and Rehabilitation* 9 (1984): 71–87.

42. C. J. Forsyth and L. Fournet, "A Typology of Office Harlots: Mistresses, Party Girls, and Career Climbers," *Deviant Behavior* 8 (1987): 319–28.

43. Kirk Makin, "Strip's Tease Gives Way to Touch: Do People Know or Care?" *Globe and Mail*, 12 March 1994: A1, A10.

44. *R. v. Butler*, 70 C.C.C. (3d) 129 1992 (S.C.R.).

45. Mark Connelly, *The Response to Prostitution in the Progressive Era* (Chapel Hill, 1980), 6.

Book Reviews

John K. Brackett, *Criminal Justice and Crime in Late Renaissance Florence, 1537–1609*. Cambridge: Cambridge University Press, 1992. 160 pp.

This book examines the Florentine system of criminal justice during the Renaissance. It focuses on the celebrated and central institution of justice administration: the *Otto di Guardia* (The Eight); and it situates the analysis in the context of the emergence in sixteenth-century Italy of a centralizing state. Brackett discusses successively the structure of bureaucratic justice (chapter 1), its financial evolution (chapter 2), the functions of *Otto* in policing the city and its hinterland (chapter 3), and the procedure in criminal matters (chapter 4). He underlines the role played by the *Otto di Guardia* in the centralization of criminal justice within the Tuscan state during the late sixteenth and early seventeenth centuries (chapter 5), and concludes by discussing the pattern of crime during the period in relation to the economic, political, and social changes in Tuscany (chapter 6).

By choosing the key of centralizing state development in a European territorial principality, the author follows a well-organized plan, moving from the institutional aspects to the criminal "production," by the various ways of policing the country. Despite the limitation of archival material, he pays particular attention to the financial aspects of the court's management and reveals the leading role of the prince in budgetary policy. The study charts the progressive loss of independence of the citizens' court of the Eight, noting how increasingly from the middle of the sixteenth century it was controlled by ducal administration. Brackett pays particular attention to the financial administration of justice, a topic generally neglected by many scholars. His doubts about the assertion that criminal courts in early modern Europe were sources of profit for the state (p. 29) echo my own conclusions based on an analysis of profits and expenses in a Low

Countries town at the same moment. Particularly interesting are his reflections on the discrepancy between the hopes of sixteenth-century reformers and financial control measures, a discrepancy that can explain the failure to create an effective centralized justice.

Brackett details how the policing power of the *Otto di Guardia* was used particularly in regard to real or perceived enemies among the aristocracy (p. 56). He carefully describes the prison's organization under the Eight's control, and underlines the structural and financial weaknesses of the policing function of the criminal justice system due to the lack of police stations in the various districts. Small in number, poorly paid, and deeply involved in local family networks, the police forces were never as efficient as the grand dukes wished. The evolution of criminal procedure over the period demonstrates the grand dukes' attempts to obtain the final authority to judge criminal cases, and to make "all justice at least potentially the grand duke's justice" (p. 76), using the administration of justice as a tool of absolutism in the dominion. Brackett has no doubt that "the grand duchy did not have enough centralised control over criminal justice to be considered an absolutist state" (p. 78) in Vivens Vives's model of the sixteenth-century absolutist state. "The absolute authority of the prince existed only at the pinnacle of a pyramid of power blocs, comprised by the corporate power of the cities and the feudal power structure in the countryside" (p. 79).

After a detailed description of how the Florentine criminal justice system was organized and how it worked, one might expect a critical analysis of criminal patterns. Unfortunately, this important chapter seems to be limited to a classical enumeration of crimes and criminogenic factors, offering information very similar to other criminal patterns in early modern Western Europe. Because of the lack of quantitative analysis of prosecuted crime, Brackett does not offer a structural evaluation of Florentine crime patterns, nor an idea of the evolution of such patterns during the period 1537–1609. But the biggest weakness of this chapter is its disconnection with the former analysis of the criminal justice system. The crime pattern seems totally monolithic and independent of the various activities of the *Otto's* magistrates (policing, judging, or executing the sentences), or of the grand dukes' policies to extend their administrative power to Florence and its "hinterland."

Furthermore, the lack of comparative data from other territorial states in Italy and the absence of existing "standard" references to early modern European criminal justice (France, Germany, the Low Countries, Switzerland, England) does not allow Brackett to extend his interesting views to a broad reflection on state-building in Europe. One can also regret the absence of any comparison between the sixteenth-century *Otto di Guardia* and medieval Florentine justice. Nevertheless, despite his limited size (160 pages), this book represents a concise and valuable attempt to understand the complex relationship between the evolution of criminal justice and the development of the centralized territorial state in early modern Europe.

Xavier Rousseau
Facultes Universitaires Saint Louis, Brussels

Lincoln B. Faller, *Crime and Defoe: A New Kind of Writing*. Cambridge: Cambridge University Press, 1993. xx + 263 pp., £35.00, $54.95.

Following the unprecedented success of his first novel, *Robinson Crusoe*, Defoe turned for inspiration to the world of crime. In rapid succession he published *Captain Singleton* (1720), dealing with the life of a pirate adventurer; *Moll Flanders* (1722), whose heroine was, according to the original title page, "born in Newgate, and during a life of continu'd variety . . . was twelve times a whore, five times a wife (whereof once to her own brother), twelve years a thief, eight years a transported felon in Virginia"; *Colonel Jack* (1722), in which the hero grows up to be a pickpocket and notorious thief; and finally *Roxana* (1724), the tragic story of a courtesan.

In turning to criminal biography as a model for fiction, Defoe was appropriating one of the most popular narrative genres in early eighteenth-century England. It had emerged only recently, in the second half of the seventeenth century, when accounts of the life histories, characters, and last words of felons hanged at Tyburn, as compiled by the chaplain (known as the "ordinary") at Newgate, began to be published. Originally broadsheets that devoted only a paragraph or two to individual criminals, these criminal biographies had developed by the 1720s into full-scale pamphlets running to forty or more pages and appearing in numerous editions.

In his earlier study of the genre, *Turned to Account* (1987), Lincoln B. Faller argued that these biographies of real-life criminals fell into two main categories: what he called the "morally serious and quasi-realistic" on the one hand, and the "generally frivolous, overtly romantic and often fantastic" on the other. In their different ways, however, the two categories could be seen as discourses that helped people make sense of the activities of criminals and the judicial punishment of their crimes. They were almost invariably devoted to criminals who had been executed; those whose sentences were commuted to transportation, or who had reformed and become honest citizens, almost never attracted the attention of biographers. In that sense, Faller argued, they may be seen as a kind of "supplement" to execution, giving a socially accepted signification to the criminal and helping to place his or her actions in an understandable framework. The "morally serious" accounts sought to demonstrate not only God's providential order in the punishment of the wicked, but also the power of divine grace in bringing them to repentance; and in tracing the stages by which once decent people fell into a life of crime, they offered an explanation of behavior which could otherwise seem incomprehensible. By contrast, "frivolous" rogue biographies tended to present criminals as entertaining fools or monsters whose lives and deaths were unaccountable by ordinary human standards and therefore at a safe distance from the reader's experience.

In the book under review, Faller's aim is to read Defoe's four novels of criminal life both within and against the conventions of criminal biography as it had developed in the early eighteenth century, showing how they exploit, but more significantly depart from, the genre. He begins by demolishing some critical clichés about the nature of Defoe's celebrated "realism," demonstrating conclusively that many of the criminal biographies exhibit much more in the way of "concrete particularity" than is to be found in these novels. What would have made Defoe's fictional criminals seem "realistic" to his original readers was, paradoxically, their very difference from the stereotypical accounts of actual criminals. Thus, for example, where criminal biography, at least of the "serious" kind, was usually processed by the ordinary or some other redactor who would select, filter, and shape the narrative in order to give it coherence, Defoe's novels are seemingly free of a controlling hand. The only vestige of such an authority figure comes in the prefaces, but these are teasingly ambiguous. Under cover of anonymity, Defoe's criminal heroes and heroines can, apparently, speak more fully and freely—a powerful element in their attractiveness.

But what Faller also brings out in a series of persuasive close readings is the variety of ways in which the narrators of these novels do not in fact tell all: Their stories are full of gaps and loose ends that continually prompt the reader toward reflection or invite interpretation. For one thing, the narrators do not know everything about their own lives, and cannot explain their actions fully. They all refuse to go into detail about certain events, particularly of an especially vicious or "unnatural" kind—very different from the criminal biographies, which specialized in relating every gory detail. Of even more importance is the incorporation of dialogue, which gives the reader access to other points of view, and helps us see around or beyond the main character, a point Faller establishes by way of an engrossingly thorough and illuminating analysis of the famous episode where Moll is wrongly (for once) accused by a mercer of shoplifting. But perhaps most significant of all is the fact that the novels lack the usual conclusion to criminal biography. This was clearly something that disturbed readers in the eighteenth century: Abridged versions of *Moll Flanders,* for example, always ended more satisfyingly with Moll dying an unambiguously penitent death in Virginia or Ireland. Faller does not devote much attention to the publishing history of the novels, but a study of the numerous chapbook versions of *Moll Flanders* suggests that these tended to make it conform more closely to the conventions of criminal biography.

Thus, even though Moll was not executed, the chapbooks would often include images of the gallows at Tyburn.

Altogether, Faller has produced a scholarly, attractively written, and largely convincing study that avoids the reductionism of many contextualizing approaches. In showing how the specifically "literary" qualities of his novels enabled Defoe to open up for his readers some of the more troubling moral and intellectual issues raised by crime, he contrives also to enrich their significance for twentieth-century readers.

W. R. Owens
The Open University, Milton Keynes

Adam J. Hirsch, *The Rise of the Penitentiary: Prisons and Punishment in Early America*. New Haven: Yale University Press, 1992. xvi + 243 pp.

If there is one question that has guided historians of prisons and punishment in the past twenty years, it is why between 1780 and 1850, in Western Europe and America, the penitentiary was conceived and constructed. Why were public and physical punishments (whipping, branding, and the death penalty) replaced by the less visible, less corporal sanction of imprisonment? Why was it thought that the prison, and other nineteenth-century "asylums," would be a more effective apparatus for the control of society's "undesirables"? If there is one dominant explanation of this revolution in punishment, it is that its origins are to be located less in the humanitarian sensibility of philanthropic reformers, whether secular or religious, utilitarian or evangelical—which an older, "reformist" historiography emphasized—and more in the determination of elite groups to control and isolate deviant members of society, thereby bringing order and discipline to a society in flux. Humanitarian sensibility, according to the "revisionist" historians, must be traced back to its source in economic interest or the will to power.

The American penitentiary found its first and most accomplished revisionist historian in David J. Rothman. In *The Discovery of the Asylum* (1971), Rothman asked why Americans in the postrevolutionary or Jacksonian period began to construct institutions (the prison, the mental asylum, the juvenile reformatory) for deviant members of the community. His answer to this question was that the asylum represented society's fearful response to the emergence of an expanding, mobile population, no longer bound by the ties of farm and family. The penitentiary was invented to impose order and stability on deviant populations by isolating them from the environment that caused the deviance. The asylum was also meant to restore the moral discipline and ordered community of the colonial past; it was to stand as the very model of a new social equilibrium. Essential to

Rothman's interpretation was, first, a "social control" approach in which the striving for control was located not exclusively in the political elite, but more vaguely throughout American society; and, second, the sudden and uniquely American "discovery" of a solution (the asylum) to a uniquely American problem (the threat to social stability).

Inevitably, Rothman's bold interpretation has experienced the rough and tumble of academic life. He has been taken to task for underestimating the humanitarian and especially religious bases of prison reform, and for neglecting entirely the European and especially English precedents for the American penitentiary. A moment's attention to English experience, or to the evidence of communication between evangelical sects active in prison reform on both sides of the Atlantic, would have revealed, say his critics, that the Jacksonian prison was neither an exclusively American "discovery," nor a uniquely American response to a uniquely American problem. It has become evident, too, that the American lunacy reform movement also drew heavily upon European ideas and example. And, finally, the folly of describing the history of imprisonment in terms of "discoveries," "inventions," or "transformations"—with the implied notion of radical and abrupt change—has been revealed by historians of the European prison who insist, *pace* Foucault, that the movement from corporal and capital punishment to incarceration was a long, gradual evolution that began in the late sixteenth century with Dutch and English "houses of correction." It is on the foundation of such critiques of Rothman's pioneering study that Adam J. Hirsch, associate professor of law at the Florida State University College of Law, seeks to build.

The Rise of the Penitentiary, based on a Yale Ph.D. dissertation, is a short book by contemporary academic standards. The text consists of only 117 pages, but this is supported by 109 pages of references. It is a rare page of text that does not sport four or five notes, many of which are of paragraph length. (What is it about law departments that leads people to contract, like legionnaires' disease, the excessive endnote compulsion?) It is apparent immediately that Hirsch's intention is to challenge a number of Rothman's main conclusions, and secondarily to provide a rejoinder of sorts to the "critical" analysis of the rise of the penitentiary: the view that those who advocated and built prisons did so out of sectional class interest. The primary evidence for Hirsch's study comes from Massachusetts—the state that established the first program for criminal incarceration in the wake of independence, yet a state that has been neglected in the rush to examine New York and Pennsylvania—where penitentiaries were established that would ultimately attract European attention. In 1805, Massachusetts opened the state prison at Charlestown, built for 300 inmates, all offenders sentenced to imprisonment. Where, asks Hirsch, did this penitentiary come from? For an answer, he travels to England, and documents the varied strands that made up what he calls English carceral ideology.

Hirsch examines three strands of thought: "rehabituation," "reclamation," and "rationalism." The first refers to the "habit of industry" that "houses of correction" imposed on vagrants, and increasingly on criminals, from the late sixteenth century onward. In the rehabituation of criminals, these "workhouses" looked to establish disciplinary routines, not to change moral values. In contrast, the "philanthropists" (like John Howard) who advocated reclamation looked to inmates' spiritual needs and to an inner change in the offender's character. For those who espoused rationalism, the offender's hedonistic responses to work, and hence to crime, were to be corrected by hard labor. Jeremy Bentham's Panopticon plan, for example, called for solitary labor within cells. Returning to America, Hirsch contends that the postrevolutionary moves toward criminal incarceration in Massachusetts "owed their inspiration primarily to the rehabituative tradition of the ancient workhouse" (p. 23). Neither reclamation nor rational ideology (which Rothman stressed) had more than secondary impact. Hirsch also illustrates that the workhouses in colonial Massachusetts, based on English example, already embodied the rehabituative paradigm; that the Puritan creed was not, as Rothman asserted, inimical to criminal rehabituation; and that American advocates of incarceration were under no illusion that they had invented a new institution.

But why, asks Hirsch, was it in the 1780s and 1790s that the penitentiary idea came into its own? Because it was in these decades, he argues, that alarm over the level of crime and the associated ineffectiveness of traditional penalties reached a pitch sufficient to impel state legislatures first, to extend existing sanctions, including hard labor in the workhouse, and second, to establish systems of imprisonment. The rise of the penitentiary was not influenced to any great degree, however, by the birth of the Republic, a connection posited by Rothman. Even after the Revolution, American criminologists carried on a lively debate about prisons with their English counterparts. Republican political rhetoric had little or no impact upon the discussion of penal change. And a number of colonies examined or passed prison programs in the decades before independence. Hirsch concludes, therefore, that the Revolution, if anything, delayed the rise of the American penitentiary. Only in England, he speculates, did the Revolution move the penitentiary forward, due to the loss of the colonies as a dumping ground for English convicts.

At first, the postrevolutionary prisons followed the rehabituative paradigm. There ensued, however, under English influence, an animated struggle between advocates of rehabituation and advocates of reclamation, the latter stressing solitary confinement more than hard labor. In Pennsylvania, Philadelphia's Walnut Street Prison realized the ideal of reclamation; in New York, Auburn prison stood for the rehabituative ideal (associated hard labor by day, separate confinement at night). Massachusetts followed the Auburn plan, as indeed did most other states. In the 1830s, European criminologists and administrators inspected the prisons of New York and Pennsylvania. The influence, at least in terms of prison design, now went the other way across the Atlantic. The structure and routines of London's Pentonville, opened in 1842, were modeled on Pennsylvania's Eastern State Penitentiary. But Hirsch asks that this not mislead us: "The Jacksonians reared the penitentiary; they did not conceive it" (p. 113). The rehabituative ideology, he reiterates, derived from sixteenth-century England, not Jacksonian America. Hirsch's other main conclusions are equally challenging. The adoption of the prison was shaped less by Beccarian or Benthamite reasoning and more by a social reality that made urgent the need for change. And reformers were never so indulgent as to believe that they had created in the prison a template for American society. For most of its advocates, the penitentiary was simply a practical instrument of crime control.

To this closely researched evaluation of the rise of the American penitentiary, the author adds two final chapters comparing penitentiary discipline and slavery. They are not without interest. After all, the penitentiary arose in an age of slavery. The two institutions were alike in many ways. As Hirsch shows, moreover, many of the same people who pressed for the penitentiary, in both England and America, were prominent in the antislavery movement. Hirsch tries to understand how these reformers reconciled adherence to prison discipline with opposition to slavery, and what united the two movements. Unfortunately, the contrasts and connections uncovered by Hirsch add little depth to our understanding of the penitentiary. Far more useful would have been an evaluation of the realities of penitentiary life, particularly the interior regime of the new prisons.

The merit of the book resides, therefore, in the gauntlet it throws down at the feet of revisionist historians. In particular, it substantiates the proposition that the American penitentiary was no sudden discovery of the 1820s. American reformers borrowed heavily from English penal theory and (even more so) penal practice, both before and after independence. Only by exploring these European precedents, along with the slow evolution of punishment in the colonial era, can the rise of the American penitentiary be entirely explained. One doubt remains, however. Were prison reformers so exclusively practical in bent, responding alone to insistent social realities? In this respect, Hirsch is closer to Rothman than he might realize. Both are fairly dismissive of the religious springs of prison reform, despite Hirsch's introductory plea to listen carefully to reformers' ideas and ideals. In fact, we are given little opportunity to listen to the likes of Thomas Eddy, New York Quaker and disciple of John Howard; or the Reverend Louis Dwight, Boston Calvinist, secretary of the Prison Discipline Society, and proponent of carceral discipline being applied to schools and even to large families. Other prison activists were similarly influenced by religious sensibilities. The rehabilitative ideal, moreover, was predicated, at least in part, on religious persuasion and training. And, of course, one of the most renowned observers of the period, Alexis de Tocqueville, was firmly of the view that the character of prison reform was in essence religious. Hirsch disappoints, then, in failing to explore more sensitively the religious underpinnings of the penitentiary.

This criticism aside, *The Rise of the Penitentiary* is a worthy addition to the rich corpus of work on the history of punishment in Europe and America. It is written in an elegant and economical style. If the notes are a mite indulgent, the text is sleek and flat-bellied. While not all historians will accept Hirsch's descriptive and explanatory account of the origins of imprisonment, probably few will disagree with his concluding judgment that the penitentiary persists to this day, "a monument to failure, hallowed only by time" (p. 117). I have much less confidence, however, in his pronouncement that history is coming full circle after 200 years of a failed experiment, in the move toward noninstitutional, communal punishments. The population of American prisons has quadrupled in the last twenty years. There are presently more than a million people behind bars, making the United States the world's biggest per capita incarcerator. More ominously, the Clinton administration's crime bill, and the Senate's amendments to it, presage the expansion of mandatory minimum sentences, the introduction of three-strikes laws, and thus the inexorable expansion of prison populations and the penal estate.

Victor Bailey
University of Kansas

Jean-Claude Farcy, *Guide des Archives Judicaires et Pénitentiares, 1800–1958*. Paris: CNRS Editions, 1992. 1,175 pp. 650 French Francs.

E. M. Palmegiano, *Crime in Victorian Britain: An Annotated Bibliography from Nineteenth-Century British Magazines*. Westport, Conn: Greenwood Press, 1993. 165 pp.

Bibliographies and guides to archives make the researcher's life immeasurably easier. Farcy's *Guide* and Palemegiano's *Bibliography*, while vastly different in scope and size, will both be boon companions.

Farcy's *Guide* is encyclopaedic. It weighs in at several pounds and its 1,175 pages constitute a complete guide to the judicial and penal archives for the whole of France and its overseas territories from the First Empire to the Fourth Republic. The book is divided into five parts. The first, and briefest, surveys the present state of research into the history of the French criminal justice system, and the richness and variety of the judicial and penal sources, most of which, in spite of growing interest in the area, remain unexplored. There follows an account of the development and the jurisdictions of the different courts and penal institutions; as a work of reference and quick guide to, for example, *les conseils de prud'hommes, les jurisdictions spéciales de l'Occupation, les peines subies dans les colonies,* the seventy pages of this section are invaluable. The third part, almost 200 pages, is a subject nomenclature of judicial and penal documents describing their content, location and, where relevant, giving reference to the relevant sections of the legal code. Parts 4 and 5 are detailed inventories, respectively, of the judicial and penal documents in the national and departmental archives. The entries for each department are supplemented with select bibliographies ranging from master's theses to monographs.

Anyone intending to carry out research into the criminal justice system in, or more generally, the social history of France between 1800 and 1958 will need to consult this *Guide.* It will serve generations of historians, and no self-respecting university library that services people working on France can afford to be without it. Farcy is to be thanked, and warmly congratulated on his achievement and industry.

The periodical literature of the nineteenth century is a vital source to anyone researching Victorian crime. But it is hard graft working through the lists of contents of runs of serials looking for anything that appears relevant, and then reading what promises to be a gem and finding it to be paste. E. M. Palmegiano's annotated bibliography will dramatically reduce the graft of wading through contents pages; unfortunately, there is little that can alleviate the second problem.

Palmegiano begins her volume with a rather breathless and wordy introduction, which many researchers might choose to bypass. What, for example, does "Forgery was in the air, but fraud was an anathema" really mean as a sentence on "types of crime"? Nevertheless, this introduction does have the virtue of pinpointing, and briefly surveying, the shifting attitudes to different elements of the Victorian criminal justice system and to different kinds of offenders. It also has the virtue, foreign to many North American academics, of recognizing that there were four separate entities— England, Scotland, Wales, and Ireland—constituting the United Kingdom. The real value of the book, however, comes in the 120 closely typed pages surveying over 1,600 articles drawn from fifty-five magazines in the period 1824–1900. There is a brief note on each magazine, and a sentence or two describing the content of each of the individual articles. These range from "The Ethics of the Turf" and "The Morality of Advocacy" to "The Policeman—His Health" and "Autobiography of a Thief in Thief's Language." An author index and a detailed subject index complete the volume.

Clive Emsley
The Open University, Milton Keynes

Paula J. Byrne, *Criminal Law and the Colonial Subject: New South Wales, 1810–1830*. Cambridge: Cambridge University Press, 1993. xiv + 301 pp. £37.50 or $65.00.

How do you govern a convict colony? In the Australian case, there were many who advocated harsh discipline backed by a strong military presence. Certainly in the years before 1840 the structures to maintain such an order were in place—military forces, a pass system to differentiate convict from free men, colonies of secondary punishment for the refractory, liberal use of the lash, and the "legal" sanction of torture to extract a confession in criminal cases. Courts until 1823 were primarily military tribunals and many magistrates, responsible for day-to-day discipline, were prominent landowners determined to maintain the privileges of their class. The image of the early Australian convict colonies as hellish, brutalized, and repressive is well established and still popular, if the success of Robert Hughes' recent account, *The Fatal Shore,* is any measure.

In recent years, however, a number of historians have sought to question this conventional representation of the convict period. Historians such as Atkinson, Sturma, Daniels, Neal, and Hirst have uncovered abundant evidence of convict resistance to authority and a rich culture of petty subversion. More controversially, Hirst has argued that the convicts were able to forge various "freedoms" within the convict system, to the extent that the structures of a free society were already present at the foundation of the convict colonies. David Neal has also charted new territory with his recent study of the "rule of law" in the convict period, demonstrating that convicts and ex-convicts used the law for their own ends—extracting concessions from employers, complaining about the harshness of their treatment, and prosecuting those who infringed their person or stole their property. Paula Byrne's new book, *Criminal Law and the Colonial Subject,* is a welcome addition to this rich strand of revisionist history.

Byrne's focus is the early nineteenth century, a period of transition in the criminal justice system from the centralized, authoritarian rule of the governor and the military to the emergence of a system more closely approximate to that in Britain, where the "rule of law" and the institutions for its maintenance were paramount. Byrne charts this transition with care and insight. But she also does much more. For Byrne, the law is an open and contested field, to be used for and against established authority, where there are gaps and weaknesses to be exploited by different parties and in which social relations were produced (following Foucault) rather than repressed. She explores important themes such as policing, bushranging, law and labor relations, the surveillance of private space, policing the body and sexuality, and popular uses of the law. The range of themes and insights is impressive. Like Hirst, she sees the law as an arena in which convicts successfully fought to modernize work and labor relations. Unlike other historians of the convict system, however, she has looked behind the door to the private sphere and investigated relations between mistress and servant, intraclass household burglary, domestic violence, and murder. Moreover, she finds that working-class women were more likely to seek redress through legal means than men. Her evidence is a sharp rebuttal of the rather rosy picture of the life of female convicts painted by historians such as Portia Robinson. Her work on bushranging is equally impressive, exploring the evidence for the emergence of gangs, their ethical codes (only rob from the rich) and their ambivalent place in the wider community—outlaw, popular hero, and yet also betrayed by working-class informants. Disappointingly, however, she fails to consider, confirm, or contest the arguments of McQuilton that bushrangers (following Hobsbawm) were "primitive rebels."

These issues are explored with resort to the rich load of court depositions still extant for this period. The sources have been viewed with justified suspicion by crime historians in Britain, but Byrne does not fall into the simplistic trap of seeing the deposition statements as simple reflections of society. Rather, she seeks to use them as ritual statements, as language and symbol, as performance, and as sites of cultural meaning. Drawing on the work of ethnographic historians such as Greg Dening, she looks beyond the obvious for the deeper cultural norms and meanings that structured ritualized court statements. This is dangerous territory, but in the right hands it can be illuminating. Byrne has used the technique well and has offered a complex and nuanced study of the convict period.

The most innovative sections of the book concern her arguments over the body and subjectivity. Here her use of the ethnographic method is less certain. She does much to establish that the criminal law saw men and women differently and treated them differently, but there is nothing startling in that, although her empirical evidence is interesting. But to shift to exploring the body and the construction of subjectivity is more difficult, and here far less convincing than other arguments in the book. Too often these difficult arguments are swamped by case descriptions, and too often the identification of the different treatment of men and women before the courts is taken as evidence that the court constructed male and female bodies and identities differently. The link is too neat here; the relationship is asserted rather than argued. Relations between legal rulings, bodies, and subjectivities are more problematic and complex than this study suggests.

Nonetheless, Byrne has made a very valuable contribution to understandings of British criminal law and the convict period in Australia. She has opened up new lines of inquiry, drawn on a rich load of case material, and done much to illuminate the lives of the convicts and ex-convicts who turned to the law to assert their legal rights.

Stephen Garton
University of Sydney

David Walker with Stephen Garton and Julia Horne, eds., *Crimes and Trials: Australian Cultural History*. Faculty of Arts, Deakin University, Geelong, Victoria, 1993. $13.

The appearance of this volume reflects the convergence on the object of crime of different disciplines in recent years. David Garland's articulate exposition of the cultural dimensions of punishment in his recent survey of the sociology of punishment firmly located the field of crime and its punishment as a subject of substantial interest for the student of society. Social historians have been active in the field now for two decades and more, although their concerns have often been more limited than the broader ambitions of a general cultural history of society might expect. This volume of papers from the annual conference on Australian Cultural History often approaches the subject from outside the speciality of the social history of crime, and the benefits as well as the limits of other disciplinary insights are evident.

The collection is necessarily heterogeneous, though for the most part the focus on specific crimes and their social and juridical contexts as suggested by the title "crimes and trials" is retained. Exceptions to the "case study" are the essays of Judith Allen on abortion, Anne McFeath on the colonization of Australian Aborigines, Stephen Knight on Australian crime fiction, and Hilary Maddocks on Aboriginal art and copyright law. All draw on well-established expertise in their areas. Knight's valuable survey of an extensive range of crime novels from the mid-nineteenth century forward draws lessons from a comparison with other national fictions, especially American and English: The close attention to the way in which crime novels use "place" leads Knight to the theme that a peculiarly Australian phenomenon is the sense of location in this fiction as always "some kind of displacement," though the meanings of such displacement have been varied (p. 157). It would be good to see this idea explored with attention to something more than the rather intratextual approach, which represents a limit on this contribution's links to other themes in the book.

McGrath tackles colonialism with a sobering exploration of the criminalizing effects of colonial dispossession on the country's indigenous people. This overview will be the more valued as one of the rare treatments of the history of Aboriginal involvement with the criminal justice system, a subject that is likely to benefit from comparative historical study with conditions in Canada, New Zealand, and elsewhere. When she asks, however, why so few Aborigines pleaded not guilty in lower courts in the 1950s and 1960s (p. 109), the limitations of an analysis that takes place largely without reference to other analyses of criminal justice processes are evident.

The major contribution of feminism to the social and cultural study of crime is also registered in this collection in a number of articles. Judith Allen's article on abortion explores the complex relation between criminalization and its social and cultural effects on women as agents and victims in the process of a widely practiced but criminalized offense in the late nineteenth and first half of the twentieth century. Allen goes beyond this to speculate on the cultural significance of abortion in a history of sexual relations between women and men, a history, she argues, that needs to consider matters of sexual negotiation and corporeal experience.

Three other articles deploy a variety of historical, feminist, and other perspectives to examine specific criminal cases involving women as offenders or victims. In the most innovative essay in the collection, Juliet Peers uses her skills as an art historian to explore the cultural contexts of the furious public debates over one of Australia's most notorious criminal law cases. The gang rape in 1886 at Mt. Rennie in Sydney of Mary Jane Hicks by a group of youths, members of a "larrikin push," led to the trial, conviction, and execution of a number of the youths. The debate over the horror of the rape was quickly displaced by a sustained public campaign against capital punishment, in which the colonial misogyny of the Sydney press and its bohemian culture was well in evidence. Peers moves outwards from the contemporary black-and-white art of the popular press to explore its links to other cultural motifs, then and later, which contextualize the ambiguous place of women as rape victims in colonial society. It is an essay that shows the rich rewards that may be gleaned from the application of the methods of a broadly based cultural history and use of visual evidence in exploring the culture of crime and punishment.

More briefly, and in the only non-Australian case in the collection, Ann Schofield examines the historical and cultural texts constructed around the case of Lizzie Borden, alleged murderer of her parents in 1890s New England. In its careful attention to the "specific historical situation" in which woman as offender or victim is placed, Schofield's analysis acts as something of a foil to the following essay on a notorious recent Queensland murder of a middle-aged man by a group of four women, the so-called "Lesbian Vampire" case. Attempting to explore the meanings of women's place in criminology, jurisprudence, and the popular discourse of crime, Sue Davies and Andrea Rhodes-Little end up with an account that asks many questions but throws little light. The weakness of the single casestudy is demonstrated by this article: It is difficult to see how "the marks of men's *desire*" are always, in jurisprudence, "the poetic and normal manifestations of sovereign individuality affirming itself" (p. 27). A comparison of the media and other discourses around offenders in this case with those of another recent act of violence, such as the notorious Anita Cobby rape and murder in Sydney, would seem necessary to test the generalizations and essentialisms of this paper.

In the wittiest paper of the collection, Stephen Garton observantly re-reads the press coverage of the Graeme Thorne kidnapping case of 1960. The way in which a criminal event becomes the focus and reflection of its time and place is reviewed through mundane detail: "Freda Thorne's clothes became a metaphor for these ideas. . . . Brown and green seemed to dominate in contrast to the later reports of the kidnapper's lemon yellow socks" (p. 31). Bumbling police, obsessive lay volunteers and hoax-callers, the crowds of women at the trial of the kidnapper—the colorful and al-lusive mix of elements that make up a major crime event are all called up in this reprise. The case, with its reference point being the Opera House lottery that Thorne's parents had won, is picked up again by Noel Sanders in a less crime- than culture-oriented exploration of the rise of a TV and gambling culture in postwar Australia.

Crime associated with gambling is also a concern of papers by Richard Waterhouse on the circumstances of a horse-swapping racing scandal of the 1980s, and by John Perry with Peter Mewett in an analysis of profes-sional foot-racing at the Victorian town of Stawell. The links of these three papers with the collection's themes are more tenuous, with the promise, for example, of an anthropological insight into the Stawell Gift as an instance of relations between power, law, and custom not quite realized. Fiction writer Frank Moorhouse completes the issue with a somewhat rambling but critical piece on the responses of academics and intellectuals to the Azaria Chamberlain (the Ayers Rock infant disappearance) case of the 1980s.

The diversity of the papers in this collection points to the immense reach of the subject of crime and punishment into the interstices of the culture. Few of the papers are by researchers from the field of criminal justice his-tory. But the value of nonspecialist contributions lies in the insights that new methods and different ways of looking at this rich cultural domain can contribute.

Mark Finnane
Griffith University

John McLaren, Hamar Foster and Chet Orloff, eds., *Law for the Elephant, Law for the Beaver: Essays in the Legal History of the North American West*. Regina: Canadian Plains Research Center/ Pasedena: Ninth Judicial Circuit Historical Society, 1992. ix + 322 pp. USA $19.95, Canada $24.

Do borders really matter in legal history? This is one of the questions ad-dressed in this collection of essays emanating from a "transboundary" con-ference held in 1991 at the University of Victoria. The title borrows from John Phillip Reid's 1980 study of property and "law mindedness" on the nineteenth-century Oregon and California trails. "Seeing the elephant" meant experiencing the hardships of the overland trail; Reid uses the elephant as a metaphor to describe legality on the frontier.[1] The beaver, a Canadian national symbol, refers to the fur trade era, dominated by the Hudson's Bay Company, that shaped the history and legal development of the Canadian West.

Region, over the past twenty-five years, has become a respectable and valuable unit of historical analysis. The eleven essays in this volume, although not totally representative of legal scholarship, explore similarities and differences in Western American and Canadian legal experience. Canadian historians have always been sensitive to external influences on their society and institutions, and have been chastized for borrowing from American historiographic trends. Despite differences, both real and perceived, between the two nations, Canadian law and legal institutions have been influenced in both positive and negative senses by the United States. In many cases a common legal culture, shared by lawyers, judges, police, legislators, and regulatory agencies—combined with similar economic and social factors (agriculture, immigration, mining, ranching, urbanization)—made for slight differences between national jurisdictions. Yet there will also be distinctly Canadian or American characteristics in transboundary legal history.

In his masterful overview, "The Layers of Western Legal History," John Phillip Reid describes the discipline, in contrast to the more developed literature on Southern legal history, as an academic frontier that has suffered somewhat from popular culture's fascination with tales of the Wild West. Reid identifies six "layers" of potential research on the law in the West: frontier legal history (he discusses the difficulty of defining this concept); topics unique to the West (such as the law of the Mexican-American borderlands); the law of cattle drives and the open plains (without the romanticized gloss); Mormon legal history; the law of the fur trading companies (whose records have greatly benefited Canadian research); and mining law. The latter, Reid contends, illustrates the legal-mindedness of miners on the frontier in both British Columbia and California. He concludes with some thoughts on the importance of, and the difficulties in researching, Indian law.

The remainder of the book consists of four pairs of thematically linked essays and two contributions that stand on their own. Richard Maxwell Brown and R. C. Macleod discuss the culture and ideology of justice. In "Law and Order on the American Frontier," Brown argues that the social and class violence of the antebellum West was part of the resistance to the "incorporating" of America by capitalism. Gunfighters and vigilantes, it appears, were not carrying out personal or communal vendettas, but were actors in a protracted civil war among various political and economic groupings. Macleod, in contrast, downplays theories of frontier violence,

explaining that the Canadian frontier was settled in a manner that minimized native-white conflict. He also reaffirms his earlier positive assessment
of the North-West Mounted Police, but is less sweeping in his claims as to
their influence on legality.

The next two articles deal with aboriginal rights, a topic that the conference apparently highlighted. Paul Tennant, author of an excellent mon-
ograph on the subject, discusses the West Coast anomaly to Canadian
aboriginal rights. From the time of Governor James Douglas onward, suc-
cessive governments of British Columbia refused to recognize the principle
of aboriginal title established by the Royal Proclamation of 1763. B.C.
natives, with the exception of those in the northeastern corner of the province, made no treaties on the mainland. Thus, as Native groups began to
organize and lobby in the 1960s, the land issue rose to the forefront. Tennant describes Chief Justice McEachern's 1991 land claims decision, which
went against the Gitskan-Wet' suwet' en band, as "a stunning defeat" that
also denigrated Indian life and culture. Stephen Haycox's piece on aboriginal land rights in modern Alaska looks behind the scenes at a 1955 U.S.
Supreme Court case that reversed a judicial trend toward compensating
Native Americans for lost or abandoned land and resources. Alaska natives,
like those to the south in British Columbia, had signed no treaties with the
national government. The litigation of the Tee-Hit-Ton Indians, as Haycox
details, for all its importance, was instigated by a lone Native leader who
sought compensation for individuals. This approach later was rejected by
Native groups who saw the wisdom of pursuing claims on a group basis.

A pair of essays by John Wunder and John McLaren will interest social
historians. Wunder's survey of anti-Chinese violence in the American West
reminds us that on racial issues the region was violent indeed. California
had the greatest incidence of sinophobia, ranging from legislative harassment to arson, assault, and murder. The article is more descriptive than
analytical, and could benefit from a wider discussion of racism and nativ-
ism. McLaren's examination of early B.C. judges and the Chinese Question
is a welcome addition to legal and social history. In four out of five Supreme Court decisions between 1878 and 1886, B.C. judges struck down
discriminatory provincial statutes aimed at the Chinese. In the face of
strong anti-Chinese opinion, the judges invoked the rule of law in well-
researched, rational decisions. They were influenced by American judicial
thinking and were motivated not so much by human as economic rights.
McLaren does not mention that Justice John H. Gray, as a New Brunswick
barrister, supported the Confederacy during the Civil War and probably
saw not only Chinese, but blacks, as a servant class.

The other contributions to the volume include essays on the legal ordering of water rights in the Canadian West, constitution-making in the
American West, and shared legal jurisdiction in the nineteenth- and twentieth-century Northwest. This transboundary enterprise hopefully will

spawn imitators and make American researchers and readers more aware of Canadian historiography. The frontier era and process will generate comparative work for a long time to come. Why not compare and contrast other regions and themes, such as New France and New England, Ontario and the Great Lakes states, or the Maritimes and New England? Similarly, we would benefit from conferences or anthologies on comparative policing, Native policies, criminology, penology, and law reform. This volume is for the most part a pleasure to read, but pedants would be helped by an index, and Easterners by the inclusion of maps.

NOTE

1. John Phillip Reid, *Law for the Elephant: Property and Social Behaviour on the Overland Trail* (Salt Lake City, 1980).

Greg Marquis
Halifax, Nova Scotia

Maeve E. Doggett, *Marriage, Wife-Beating and the Law in Victorian England*. London: Weidenfeld and Nicolson, 1992.

Judith R. Walkowitz, *City of Dreadful Delight: Narratives of Sexual Danger in Late-Victorian London*. London: Virago, 1992.

Maeve E Doggett's *Marriage, Wife-Beating and the Law in Victorian England* appears as part of Weidenfeld and Nicolson's "Law in Context" series, which is aimed at bringing academic legal writing to a wider audience. In the work, Doggett focuses directly on the circumstances and results of the 1891 *Jackson* decision, which made it illegal for a man to beat and imprison his wife, drawing on a wide range of legal and historical sources to explain the broader social changes that led up to such a decision being taken, and to interpret why, prior to 1891, the rights of men to beat and imprison their wives were allowed to survive intact for so long. She achieves this through a detailed study of two interdependent legal phenomena. Coverture, which she defines as "a collective label for the legal disabilities attendant on wifehood" (p. 34), and the fiction of martial unity, the process through which a wife became legally assimilated into her husband upon marriage.

Within her study, Doggett is not confined by a traditional chronological approach, but instead moves back and forth through centuries of history, happily juxtaposing examples separated by hundreds of years. To identify the roots of the fiction of unity, for example, she takes us back to Anglo-Saxon society, where it existed within theological writings; through the Norman Conquest, when it passed into common law (specifically with regard to divorce); and finally to the nineteenth century. Such a broad time-scale is not in itself problematic, although it does result in the title's mention of Victorian England becoming somewhat redundant on occasions, such as when she identifies the late seventeenth century as the time that the fiction of unity began to play an important social function. Here, she explains, amidst the social and political upheavals of the century, arose the principle of individualism, a principle that opposed any schematic subordination of one individual by another. Simultaneously, the modern state emerged with its attendant middle classes. It is at this point, Doggett explains, that what she calls the "power principle," the legitimization by the state of men's power over women, first developed. In return for accepting the power of the state, men were granted both a civil position and power over their wives. The advantage of this to men is obvious, while the state was safeguarded from the worst excesses witnessed in revolutionary Europe, which included the extreme feminist demands of Jacobinism. What women gained from the arrangement is less apparent, and led to a series of critiques from individuals such as Wollstonecraft, through to groups of radical women such as the Owenites. However, Doggett believes that just at the moment when it "looked as if the game was up for the fiction of marital unity" (p. 90), by the early nineteenth century, the emergence of the ideology of separate spheres and the cult of domesticity combined to give it a new lease of life, which was not wholly ended even by the *Jackson* decision.

Although writing as a lawyer rather than a historian, Doggett does make some attempts to explain the links between the fiction of marital unity and the many aspects of coverture, ranging from divorce laws to the right of men to beat and imprison their wives. Rather than simply deriving from marital unity, she regards coverture as a by-product of the power principle, and its relationship with the fiction as being more one of mutual dependence, reflecting broader social developments and concerns. This is an interesting argument, and one that is quite convincing. However, although claiming to investigate the relationship between social and political changes on the one hand, and legal changes on the other, she appears unwilling to engage in a detailed examination of how laws come to be changed, apart from acknowledging that they alter as a result of "changing attitudes" (p. 147). Thus, although she mentions feminist law reformers, she gives little or no account or description of the minutiae of their campaigns. The 1884 Matrimonial Causes Act and the Married Women's Property Acts of the 1870s, 1880s, and 1890s are touched on as examples of the law responding to changes in social opinion. But legal changes such as the Contagious Diseases Acts, which represented further erosion of women's rights and were met with large and angry feminist campaigns, are not mentioned. Similarly, while she acknowledges the role played by many Victorian women in spreading the ideology of separate spheres via their writing of prescriptive literature, she fails to see this work as representative of anything other than a negative, secondary role, neglecting to examine how many women were exploiting the rhetoric of separate spheres, as Sarah Ellis put it, to "place (themselves), instead of running the risk of being placed, in a secondary position,"[1] deriving personal power and satisfaction from controlling the moral sphere of their home. Doggett does devote some space to an explanation of those occasions when coverture worked in a wife's favor, acknowledging that while the law did occasionally treat women more harshly as wives, it usually benefited them, allowing advantages such as the defense of marital coercion. However, even in the area of crime, Doggett sees women's role as mainly prescribed by and subordinate to men's. Women rarely use the law in her study. The most interesting example she presents of a woman who does attempt to use it to her own advantage is Mrs. Georgina Weldon, who, in an interesting subversion of the norm, attempted to obtain a decree against her husband for the restoration of conjugal rights. Yet in Doggett's portrayal, she appears as a sad and desperate figure, refusing her husband's reasonable attempts at financial settlement in an attempt to force him back under her roof. From the unfortunate Emily Jackson, who gave her name to the *Jackson* case, although it was actually brought not by her but by her family, to the other beaten wives, confined and abused at will, the majority of women in this book appear as passive victims.

Much more active, although not necessarily always victorious, are the women who throng the narrative of Judith Walkowitz's *City of Dreadful Delight,* a study of the late Victorian London that created Jack the Ripper. Walkowitz believes that although individuals are products of their own culture and society, they nevertheless, as Marx pointed out, "make their own history, albeit under circumstances they do not . . . fully control" (p. 9). Using a variety of sources, ranging from archives and parliamentary papers to the lurid excesses of the nineteenth-century tabloid press, Walkowitz shows all sides of a geographically and socially divided Victorian London, from the splendid new shopping malls, where "shopping dolls" enjoyed a freedom of movement unimagined by their mothers, to the teaming slums of the East End, where the more socially aware middle-class women could practice settlement work. She illuminates this by examining discourses on sexuality and sexual danger produced in locations as various as the courtroom and the music hall.

The work is bounded chronologically by two main events: the 1885 publication of W. T. Stead's exposure of child prostitution, "The Maiden Tribute of Modern Babylon" in the *Pall Mall Gazette,* and the 1888 Whitechapel murders of Jack the Ripper. Between these two dates, other events are studied; including the debates on sexual practices, political disputes, and scandalous court cases. Both of the main boundary events involve criminal actions by men toward women, in the obvious murderous actions of the Ripper, and also in the more subtle purchase by Stead from her mother of the young virgin Eliza Armstrong, "Lily" in the *Pall Mall Gazette,* a criminal abduction for which he eventually served a term in prison. However, Walkowitz does not portray women as passive, nor as subordinate to men. Of great interest is her account of the notorious case of the spiritualist Georgina Weldon, who also figures in Doggett's book. Here, she is presented quite differently, as a woman who not only successfully escaped an attempt by her husband to have her confined to an asylum, but also happily used the new powers given to her under the 1882 Married Women's Property Act to sue the doctors who signed her lunacy certification. Not only did she use the courts, she also appeared on her own behalf, eschewing legal counsel and being dubbed the "Portia of the Law Courts" by the popular press. Here, her action against her husband to force his return to the martial bed appears the triumphant act of an independent woman, wryly subverting the existing law to use it against the husband who had attempted to curtail her chosen life as a spiritualist long after their legal separation. Although clearly an exceptional woman, Georgina Weldon is by no means unique within Walkowitz's text. Striking matchgirls, the "Hallelujah Lasses" of the Salvation Army, Octavia Hill and her settlement workers, Eleanor Marx Aveling on her many platforms—these and many more populate the work, sometimes disadvantaged by class or gender, but never disillusioned.

Readers who are most familiar with Walkowitz through her earlier studies of prostitution will expect to find some familiar themes returned to here, in view of her selection of an exposé of the extent of child prostitution, and popular reporting of Jack the Ripper's murder of prostitutes. However, this is far more than simply an extension of her previous work on the subject. Walkowitz sets the scene for us by showing a London that is geographically divided between its East and West ends, but through which certain figures, the " *flaneurs*" in Baudelaire's terminology, moved freely, often using the need for social study or social reform as an excuse to mask their true mission of voyeurism. Through the eyes of these "Urban Spectators," the tensions of class and gender surrounding sexuality and sexual practice are revealed. Through the narratives that the urban spectators produced, and through the columns of the Victorian popular press, Walkowitz presents us with a multilayered view of prostitutes and prostitution. For example, she locates the increase in the sensationalized reporting of sex crimes, interestingly including reports of police attacks on women falsely accused of prostitution, as coinciding with the confusion caused by the increased public mobility of the many, often young "New Women" about the capital. The new women sought out and claimed fresh public spaces, travelling alone on the omnibus to school, waiting about for public transport, or parading through the new department stores. Within these new spaces, adopting newer modes of dress, their social position became unclear, especially as the West End shops were increasingly frequented by prostitutes. Such blurring of identities passed into the humor of popular culture, as in the case of a lady pestered by a clergyman who sharply informed him, "you're mistaken. I am not a social evil, I am only waiting for a bus" (p. 50). Yet while acknowledging that these freedoms were mainly enjoyed by middle-class women, Walkowitz is keen to extend her analysis of women as social actors to working-class prostitutes, presenting even the victims of Jack the Ripper as "part of an intense female network," not separate or condemned in their own community, whose choice of prostitution as an industry did not preclude them from enjoying its respect nor the companionship of friends or lovers. Such an interpretation means that this particular account of the Ripper murders, despite drawing on some of the most sensationalized contemporary accounts available, avoids much of the sense of voyeurism that has run through previous accounts of the crimes and has left readers feeling somewhat uncomfortable.

The epilogue chapter moves the book beyond simply being an additional, if significant, contribution to the history of British women at the turn of the century. Here, Walkowitz picks up the narratives of male violence against women surrounding the Whitechapel murders, and shows us how they were returned to almost a century later during the Yorkshire Ripper killings. Similarities between the two events are startling, especially when attempts were made to place the crimes into alternative (i.e., non-bourgeois) geographical locations, and to examine what was presented as the culpability of the prostitute victims through reports that constantly classified only those victims who were not prostitutes as "innocent women." The main difference highlighted is in the reaction of women to the murders. In her conclusion, Walkowitz charts women enthusiastically engaging in a series of criminal actions—stealing and burning pornography, carrying out acts of criminal damage against sex shops and cinemas showing nonpornographic, but nevertheless sexually violent films—as a response to the murders. These actions are replayed, along with a detailed account of the debates they precipitated among the feminist movement, leading into the still-unresolved pornography debate, where Walkowitz's knowledge of similar discussions from the previous century highlights some of the dangers of "social purity" approaches.

Each of these books takes as its central narrative an account of criminal actions by men against women, and then explores the broader social and cultural settings around these actions. However, they differ widely in their interpretations of the women themselves. Doggett believes that the cultural forces pushing women toward housekeeping and childcare in the domestic sphere were so great that they prevented the daughters, and even the granddaughters, of late Victorian women from actually using their new legal rights. Walkowitz, by contrast, is aware of the dangers of what she calls a "reliance on an iconography of female victimization" (p. 245), both historically and for contemporary feminists. The women of the *City of Dread-*

ful Delight fight against this on many levels. As prostitutes, they are pitied as "fallen" or despised as criminal within middle-class narratives, then reestablished as autonomous individuals through those of their own communities. As social workers, they use images of unprotected womanhood to fight for social and legal changes that will advantage all their sex.

NOTE

1. Mrs S. Stickney Ellis, *Mothers of England, Their Influence and Responsibility* (quoted in L. Davidoff and C. Hall, *Family Fortunes* (London, 1987), 183.

Krista Cowman
University of York, Heslington

P. Moczydlowski, *The Hidden Life of Polish Prisons.* Bloomington and Indianapolis: Indiana University Press, 1992. xvi + 190 pp., index.

Having survived the rigors of communist government for nearly half a century, Poland, in common with other post-communist countries, is currently benefiting from the experiences of what the inhabitants of east-central Europe have for some years regarded as "normal" societies. These include growing socioeconomic inequality, unemployment, political battles over growing state budget deficits, cuts in social services, and a rising crime rate. While conditions in ordinary community prisons (let alone those of the Gulag variety) were hardly mild, the strains of post-communist socioeconomic change have made their own contribution to the problems of the Polish prison service. Prison revolts, by no means absent during the communist period, have made their presence felt in more recent years. In mid-1993, 63,000 Poles (mostly) inhabited the country's 209 prisons, in excess of the official 60,000 limit. This worked out at 160 in detention per 100,000 of the population, way above the equivalent 42 in Sweden, 80 in France, and 95 in Britain—the latter itself not much of a model for a modern prison service. On the European scale, then, the extent of Poland's prison population constituted a major social problem.

The Polish prison service had, nevertheless, experienced periods of severe crisis—and, indeed, adopted measures to cope with them—before Moczydlowski's appointment as Director General of prisons in April 1990. His experience of prison conditions and the process of collection of the data used as a basis for this book, however, extend back before that date. An academic scholar, Pawel Moczydlowski was a frequent prison-visitor in the 1970s and early 1980s. His experience provided the basis for the psychosocial study of the prison situation and the institutional conditioning of the prison inhabitants that constitute the focus of this study. At that stage,

Polish prisons held some 100,000 people and were reckoned to be in a critical state. By 1986, however, the prison population had reached 116,000. By a stroke of irony, radical measures to rectify this situation were taken by the communist government some years before the more general political reforms enacted by the post-communist authorities in 1989 and afterwards. By the end of 1989, the prison population had already fallen to 40,000 and has, in fact, thus been rising during the years of Moczydlowski's stewardship. Conditions in Polish prisons have therefore been subject to considerable change over a lengthy period of time. This study, originally published in a limited Polish edition in 1982, depicts a situation somewhat more severe in terms of prison overcrowding than current conditions suggest, but that was actually to worsen before remedial action was taken.

Relating closely to the conditions that prevailed in Polish society as the forces that gave rise to the original Solidarity movement erupted, this study paints a rare and graphic picture of a closed community subject to intense pressure. It was "hidden," not just from the bulk of Polish society, but also—as was much of communist society—from the view of the West, and may thus be doubly welcomed for the perspective it offers on patterns of institutional behavior. As Moczydlowski outlines in chapter 2, a "conspiracy of ignorance," prevailed, which meant that staff were committed to keeping the number of official misdemeanors as low as possible, and that the higher officials had most to gain from the image of institutional peace. It was of course the prisoners, those at the bottom of the heap, who had the most to lose.

The prisoners' social structure was correspondingly intricate and code of behavior highly complex in order to safeguard their status and enhance their personal security. Some of Moczydlowski's descriptions carry an anthropological charge that seems to refer to a tribal culture far more exotic than one might expect to find in sectors of a European society. He relates how a new inmate, when admitted to his cell, proceeded to touch his genitals and dipped his hands into a bowl of cottage cheese placed on the table. He then stretched out his hands and, lightly shaking them, approached each of those present in the cell in turn to gauge their response. This was the action of a seasoned member of the prison population whose strategy for claiming privilege and achieving a relatively secure status was perfectly rational in terms of the prevailing norms. Some of the folkways described, it should perhaps be pointed out, are considerably less salubrious: It will, for example, be difficult to regard the idea of having a "flutter on the Derby" in quite the innocent light that we are generally accustomed to.

Neither is the account without its lighter side. Those committed to a quiet way of life and who had declared their wish for noninvolvement were, of course, called the Swiss. The "embassy" was composed of "ambassadors" who were rarely subject to attack, and were able to circulate with relative freedom because they had taken jobs such as cooks, barbers, and librarians. Their cells were less frequently searched while, naturally enough, the ambassadors received more rewards than the average prison resident. While the anthropological folklore is strikingly depicted and presented at some length, it is somewhat unfortunate that what Moczydlowski alludes to as his basic thesis in the preface to the book—that the differentiation of social relations in the hidden life of Polish prisons is a derivative of their economic organization—is presented in a concluding chapter only five pages in length. Processes of barter and exchange, and aspects of economic differentiation within prison society, are of course not absent from earlier discussion, but a longer concluding discussion would have given the indefatigable Moczydlowski more leeway to ponder the interesting question he poses of whether Poland's "hidden" prison life was more determined by features of its economic organization than that in other countries.

Paul G. Lewis
The Open University, Milton Keynes

Clive Emsley, *The English Police: A Political and Social History.* Hemez Hempstead: Harvester Wheatsheaf, 1992. xiii + 253 pp.

Clive Emsley is well-known to all historians of modern crime and criminal justice for his important books *Policing and Its Context 1750–1870* (1983) and *Crime and Society in England 1750–1900* (1987), and a number of articles relating to police history in both the nineteenth and twentieth centuries. Now he has added substantially to these with this "political and social history" of the English police in the same centuries. Emsley is much more than just a "police historian"—he is a social historian with a through knowledge of modern English social history who happens to be interested in policing issues. This means that his histories are always written with a full social context—by no means the case with many police histories.

Emsley is rightly critical of the "Whig historians" of the English police— Melville Lee, Charles Reith, T. A. Critchley, David Ascoli—who wrote uncritical teleological history based on the firm belief that the English police were self-evidently the best in the world. But he is also skeptical of the view that the police were established and maintained as an instrument of class power to discipline and control the industrial proletariat and any potentially subversive groups. This puts him into a moderate category, somewhere between these two poles; some critics may see this as "wishy-washy liberal" and accuse him of accepting the image of the traditional friendly Bobby, which ignores sustained criticism and evidence on modern issues of racism and partisanship in the policing of public order. But Emsley, as he shows in this book, is one of the most effective critics of that traditional image, discussing how it was invented and has been sustained. His supporters can claim that to be in the middle between two extremes is no bad position for a historian who can produce evidence and careful discussion to support all his points.

The first eight chapters of the book deal with the development of the police chronologically, from the eighteenth century to the present; the last two discuss the police thematically—who they were, what was involved in police work, how the "police culture" has developed, how they have been controlled and disciplined. The conclusion considers the English police in a comparative context with the French police and similar paramilitary *gendarmeries*. The first three chapters take the story to the mid-nineteenth century, when the entire country was covered with three types of police forces—metropolitan, borough, and county. Readers familiar with police history are not going to find anything new here, but students will appreciate the clear and succinct way Emsley sets out his history, and are likely to prefer this clear exposition to the lengthy and complex accounts of Sir Leon Radzinowicz or Stanley Palmer, or the conservative pieties of Critchley.

The next five chapters take developments through the late nineteenth century and into the twentieth, including the effects of the two World Wars, police unionism and strikes, and the policing of strikes and political demonstrations, in the interwar period and since the 1960s. This section is more original and includes more new material, since this area of police history has been much less written about in academic histories, and Emsley is able to draw on a number of published memoirs by, and oral interviews with, policemen. He does a good job of combining content, analysis, and balance in these chapters, and keeps them relatively short and clear. One of the themes that he carefully develops through the book is the gradual but inexorable increase of centralization and uniformity in the English forces: In 1856 there were 231 separate forces in England; by 1964 they were down to just 41, with the Home Office taking over much of the control formerly exerted by local authorities. Chapters 7 and 8 offer an opportunity for a thematic social history of policemen over the whole period from 1829, giving some sense of who became policemen, and what it meant to become a policeman in the different periods.

There is nothing very dramatic in the book—nothing to give comfort to strongly pro-police or anti-police proponents arguing about the policing of the British miners' strike under Margaret Thatcher or about "the thin blue line" as society's only defense against rising crime. But in a quiet, understated way, Clive Emsley has achieved a notable success. He has drawn on a wide range of sources, both archival and published, to present the history of the English police in a way that is clear, balanced, and easily readable— and that places the development of the Bobby in a clear political and social context over this period. This is a book to which one can refer students or

newcomers to the area, with confidence that they will receive a good introduction to the topic, the issues, and the evidence, and a good source of
material for citation or for further research.

David Philips
University of Melbourne

Gerry R. Rubin, *Durban 1942: A British Troopship Revolt.* London and
Rio Grande: The Hambledon Press, 1992. x + 148 pp. £25.

Nearly eighty years after the event, the House of Commons is still preoc-
cupied with the administration of military justice during World War I.
Prime Minister Major, in a recent statement to an inquisitive backbencher,
declined to de-classify the court martial records for the war years or make
himself party to any attempt to rewrite the nation's past. In France, too,
the conduct of courts-martial during the Great War remains controversial.
The article by G. Meynier, "Pour l'example, un sur dix! Les dénonciations
en 1914," which appeared in the journal *Politique aujhourd'hui* (Jan.–Feb.
1976), was a radical critique of the military justice system of 1914–1918
from an antimilitarist perspective. It was also a forceful challenge to a
revisionist scholarship that argued that, in general, the defects of the system
had been exaggerated and that insufficient attention had been devoted to
the moderation of the courts and the leniency of the sentences imposed.

Nowhere has the postmortem been so extensive or so anguished as in
Germany. Here, though, it is the administration of military justice in the
Wehrmacht rather than in the Imperial German Army that gives continuing
cause for concern. The disciplinary system of the Kaiser's armies—tame by
comparison with those enforced by the British, Belgian, or French com-
mands—was, indeed, identified by the Nazis as one of the principal causes
of the military collapse of 1918. Hitler and his generals, determined to
prevent the repetition of any such turn of events, applied a system that in
its brutality and violence equalled the worst excesses of the armies of an-
tiquity. Whereas the French army in World War II carried out just over
100 death sentences, the Wehrmacht, by 1945, had carried out an estimated
15,000. The British army, by contrast, seemed a veritable haven of peace
and tranquillity. Official statistics reveal that courts martial of World War
I imposed 3,080 death sentences, of which 346 were carried out, compared
with the forty death sentences (thirty-six for murder, three for robbery, and
one for treason) carried out in World War II. Figures compiled by army
psychiatrist Robert H. Ahrenfeldt show that the average incidence of de-
sertion was much lower in World War II than in World War I: 10 percent
(per year per thousand men) in 1914–1918 compared with 7 percent in
1939–1945.[1] Either the British soldier between the wars had become better

behaved or gone soft, or the military justice system become less lethal and more understanding. Whichever, the framework of British military law and the functioning of the courts martial do not, on the face of it, raise questions analogous to those posed by the German experience of total war.

Of course the British, having been on the winning side and having fought a "clean war," have nothing to atone for and no past to come to terms with. The angst-ridden forces that drive the work of a Streit, a Wegner, a Müller, or a Walle do not in the main effect British historians.[2] The unease felt about aspects of our glorious past tends to emanate from an Oh-What-a-Lovely-War-tradition of criticism centered on the alleged wrong-doings of the military courts of World War I. Work in this sphere has at one and the same time been sustained and frustrated by the secretive culture of the British bureaucracy. Convinced that there is something sinister in our past, something unwholesome to conceal and cover, the great unlearned have issued forth from the media and other creative quarters to produce a considerable literature which, though racy and readable, too often displays an inverse relation between its popularity and its scholarship.[3] Serious students, deterred by the difficulties of the documentation, have turned to the more accessible features of mass industrialized warfare. The qualitative differences consequent upon a less restrictive approach to the public records is immediately evident from a glance at the superiority of French scholarship in connection with World War I and of German scholarship in respect of World War II. In Britain we have nothing comparable in stature with Pedroncini's monographs and articles on indiscipline in the French armies in World War I,[4] and next to nothing on the military justice system of World War II. If ever there was a vacancy for a scholar, this is it. Who will do for the British military what Messerschmidt and Wullner have done for the Wehrmacht?[5]

The vacancy is not filled with Gerry Rubin's interesting study of a minor kerfuffle in a British troopship in 1942. The incident, which took place on the quayside at Durban, South Africa, involved 300–400 Royal Air Force ground-crew personnel en route for the defense of Singapore. The men took umbrage against the unsatisfactory state of the 8,000-ton *City of Canterbury*, which they refused to board. The ship sailed without them. The protesters were detained and preparations made to try them for mutiny. This book, based upon departmental records and interviews with some of the surviving participants, examines the judicial process and consequences of the courts martial hearings, and tries to relate the episode to other examples of unrest in the armed forces. All of this, footnotes and bibliography included, is contained within a volume of 140-odd pages. Much of the text is taken up with a narrative of the events preceding the protest. The walk-out itself, a modest affair, provoked by the cramped conditions on a filth-ridden rust-bucket, was similar in character to other, less well-documented, protests that occurred during the war. Gerry Rubin tells the story, and tells it well.

What light do these various acts of insubordination throw on the nature of war service radicalism? The political content of such incidents, it must be said, was fairly minimal. In form and method these actions bear a striking resemblance to the routines of collective industrial protest. This will come as no great surprise unless you are of that school, influenced by the cultural and literary historians of World War I and the primary group theorists of World War II, that emphasizes the discontinuous nature of modern war service, the isolating character of combat, and the alleged changes in personality attendant thereupon. Rubin's mutineers, far from being the bearers of a new outlook, reaffirm in their defiance their traditional identities as workers and civilians.

More interesting, in many respects, are his observations on the operation of the military courts. Rubin, an expert in labor law, is at his best when taking us through the workings of the military legal system—the peculiar status of the act of mutiny, the functions of the courts martial, and the politics of punishment. The presentation of this material, though, is unfortunate. I know it is fashionable to take obscure happenings and try to show how they illuminate larger social processes—Martin Guerre, Montaillou, and who have you. But, as with all good things, you can go too far. It is to be hoped that this study will not give rise to subsequent book-length accounts of every piddling act of defiance and disobedience during World War II. Enough of sideways glances! What we read is a full frontal view of the criminal justice system in the military. I can think of no one better equipped to provide such a view than Gerry Rubin himself.

NOTES

1. Robert H. Ahrenfeldt, *Psychiatry in the British Army in the Second World War* (London, 1958), 273.

2. Christian Streit, *Keine Kumeraden: Die Wehrmaht und die sowjetischen Kriegsgefangenen 1941–1945* (Studien zur Zeitgeschiete, 13: Stuttgart, 1978); Bernd Weger, *The Watten-SS* (Oxford, 1990); Ingo Müller, *Hitler's Justice, The Courts of the Third Reich* (Cambridge, Mass, 1991); Heinrich Walle, "Individual Loyalty and Resistance in German Military The Case of Sub-Lieutenant Oscar Kusch," in Francis R. Nicosia and Lawrence D. Stotes, eds., *Germany Against Nazism: Nonconformity, Opposition and Resistance in the Third Reich* (New York and Oxford, 1991).

3. The brouhaha created by the screening of the BBC television drama series *The Monocled Mutineer* presents an instructive commentary; see David Englander, "Mutiny and Myopia," in *Bulletin of the Society for the Study of Labour History* 52: I (1987): 5–7.

4. D. Pedroncini, *Les mutineries de 1917* (Paris; 1967); "Les cours mar tiules pemdent la Courde Guerre," *Revue historique* 252 (1974).

5. Manfred Messerschmidt and Fritz Wullner, *Die Wehrmachtjustiz im Dienste des Nationalsozialismus: Zerstorung einer Legende* (Baden-Baden, 1987).

David Englander
The Open University, Milton Keynes

Greg Marquis, *Policing Canada's Century: A History of the Canadian Association of Chiefs of Police.* Toronto: University of Toronto Press, 1993. xv + 459 pp., photographs, appendix, notes, and index. $45.

In 1905, as a result of the increasing turn toward professional and occupational organization within both Canadian and American society, approximately fifty of Canada's senior municipal police officials formed the Chief Constables' Association of Canada. Among its goals were the desire to promote professionalism within the rank and file, to lobby for greater national awareness of local police agencies and their myriad problems, to encourage uniform administrative procedures throughout Canada's many police organizations, and generally to foster greater fraternity between Canada's municipal police agencies. To a large degree, these goals still predominate the organization, now known as the Canadian Association of Chiefs of Police (CACP). Over 700 members comprise the association.

Historian Greg Marquis sees the organization as a bellwether of Canadian policing policies and practices and has written *Policing Canada's Century,* among other things, as a means to battle popular misconceptions about Canadian police. For too long the general population has held an overly romantic (and inaccurate) view of Canada's police forces, mainly because of the nineteenth-century exploits of the Royal North-West Mounted Police (RNWMP), of which, it should be noted, this work *is not* a history. Marquis feels, rightly so, that it is a mistake to view Canadian police history as synonymous with that of either the RNWMP or the RCMP. Thus, Marquis maintains, historians and criminologists interested in gauging Canadian criminal justice more accurately should look closely at the local and municipal police forces whom the CACP represents. Indeed, Marquis argues that the CACP story is one that "mirrors the social and intellectual history of policing in twentieth-century Canada" (p. 3).

Through his analysis of the CACP's convention records, official publications, speeches, legal and political briefs, correspondence, and related secondary literature, Marquis adduces four broad themes within a chronological framework. First, his study emphasizes the technological changes in the twentieth century that, in Marquis's view, have allowed the police better "methods of managing the population" (p. 4), namely, through informational storage and retrieval technologies. Undoubtedly, these technologies have been the most significant developments in the ability of Canada's local police to manage crime (and, as the author suggests, the population; unfortunately, Marquis does not acknowledge the more insidious aspect of his observation). Second, Marquis traces the politicization of the CACP from its inception, and measures the varied rate of success the organization has had on lobbying the national government on a variety of issues and shifting agendas. Third, the author examines the evolution of what he terms "practical criminology"—how well the police have adapted to changing social conditions and attitudes, and have internalized and incorporated social opinions about crime and punishment and the expanding legal rights of the accused later in the century. Finally, Marquis examines the changing nature of the organization's ongoing quest for greater professionalism in its nine-plus decades of existence, and how the organization (and by extension the municipal forces) has refashioned its self and public images several times over to meet both societal expectations and political exigencies. Earlier in the century local police were much more familiar with their constituency; they walked a beat in many areas and were generally regarded as pillars of the community. The prevailing philosophy of chief constables entailed instilling loyalty and obedience among the rank and file to the organization primarily; training was minimal. Yet with the complications posed by modern society and the spread of urban crime, current Canadian police philosophy is aimed at crime prevention, fostering greater awareness within its members of the complexities of society, social analysis, education, and responsiveness to public demands.

The main limitations of this work—which the author partially admits— are twofold. First, the work is a commissioned history and thus, despite Marquis's best intentions and careful research, he nonetheless accentuates certain issues and personalities at the expense of others. The CACP was nativist and antiradical, to the point of being reactionary during the interwar years; the organization, similar to others during the Cold War era, was infected by anti-Communist hysteria to the detriment of many innocent individuals; and the leadership has marched, even when it was not politically expedient to do so, to a rigid, law-and-order ideology through most of its history. Much of this, to his credit, Marquis notes, though not necessarily unflinchingly, Again, this is a commissioned history—funded by the very organization this history is describing, the CACP. Although Marquis has been meticulous in his research and mostly objective, the CACP is placed in the most favorable light and the tough questions, such as open sexism within the ranks and the lack of minority and gender equity, though hinted at, are mostly ducked. Second, this work is constructed solely from the perspective of the elite (from the top down). Though Marquis does provide a fascinating glimpse at crime and local police response in nineteenth-century Canada, he has virtually excluded the local rank and file in his work, concentrating exclusively on the leadership cadre. Much more historical work can and should be produced on the local police and constabulary forces, both in Canada and the United States, with an eye toward uncovering local attitudes concerning crime and crime prevention, the respective races and ethnicities of criminals incarcerated, and local police unions and their power (or lack thereof) at influencing politics and policies. *Policing Canada's Century,* though useful in illuminating the history of a powerful and select group, nevertheless only provides one piece of a still to be constructed puzzle.

Keith Edgerton
Washington State University

Writing a history of policing in twentieth-century Canada offers any author a considerable challenge. Perhaps the greatest difficulty arises from the nation's size and the multiplicity of police forces. Consistent with the English tradition of local control, Canadian police were organized by town, city, or county administrators, a pattern that in turn produced considerable variation in approach and method. Further, the political evolution of Canada, with its robust regional identities, encouraged still more diversity between provincial police departments once they, in turn, were established. The institution of a number of national police forces added yet another variable to an increasingly diverse and sometimes fragmented police culture. Finally, as the pace of modern life accelerated, the demands placed on these various forces multiplied accordingly and, in the process, provide the prospective author with an ever-widening range of concerns and issues. Yet despite these and other obstacles, Greg Marquis has endeavored to write such a history. In the end, while *Policing Canada's Century: A History of the Canadian Association of Chiefs of Police* leaves a number of issues unexplored, it nevertheless provides valuable insight into Canadian police history.

Keenly aware that policing in Canada offers an extraordinarily broad canvas covering everything from town by-laws to watching spies, Marquis required a foothold if he was to manage such an immense topic. Fortunately, the Chief Constables Association of Canada (CCAC) and its modern descendant the Canadian Association of Chiefs of Police (CACP) provided such an avenue. The CCAC and CACP afforded a national perspective on issues confronting many police departments while avoiding the tangles of local issues and controversies. Marquis acknowledges that concentrating on these associations and their respective members is not without a cost. Specifically, "[t]he view presented in this book is from the top down; the focus here is the concerns and activities of senior officials, and no claim is made that such a view is totally representative of those employed at other levels and in the various forces" (p. 4). As such, *Policing Canada's Century* is less a history of nuts and bolts police work than an examination of concerns that animated chiefs throughout the years.

Divided into nine chapters plus an introduction and postscript, Marquis's book chronologically traces the origins and development of the CCAC and CACP through four basic themes. The first addresses how technological change served to complicate police work while also providing novel methods for responding to an expanding variety of criminal activities and a corresponding range of public expectations. Thus, on the one hand, forensic technology such as fingerprinting and the centralization of data on known criminals proved to be useful advances, while on the other, the widespread availability of automobiles, especially to criminals, fundamentally altered police work during the century. On the whole these changes cut both ways for police chiefs and, in the process, created constant pressure to maintain technological sophistication and a balanced budget.

The second theme concerns the relationship between politics and law enforcement. It is fair to observe that for much of the period under consideration Canadian chief constables and chiefs of police were not politically astute. Struggling with limited budgets, a variety of jurisdictions spread over an expansive nation, and a pronounced absence of a professional identity, the two associations were poorly situated to present any level of government with a coherent body of recommendations on a chosen issue for most of the century. For example, Don Cassidy's first report as secretary-treasurer to the CACP in 1966 recommended that the association should "reconsider the often unproductive tradition of simply sending resolutions to the two levels of government." At least part of the problem was that "[a]fter more than six decades of associations activity, most committees met only during the annual conference" (p. 311). Given such an approach, fighting political battles in support of their organization and its viewpoint was simply beyond the capabilities of the chiefs. Significantly and regardless of possible benefits, most chiefs would have probably viewed such behavior as being beneath their individual and group stature.

Another aspect of politics was how the chiefs viewed their departments' responsibilities in regard to allegedly radical groups. The nation's immigration policies, the two world wars, and the Cold War all offered various police forces throughout Canada ample opportunity to address the question of where they stood in regard to radicalism. Considering that the CACP viewed "itself as the guardian of a British country" (p. 149), it is not difficult to imagine how "foreigners" and their supposedly dangerous ideas were viewed. This suspicion extended into a belief that the police should also monitor political activities throughout the nation, especially those perceived as subversive. The result was predictable. As Marquis points out, by the end of the 1930s "a generation of Canadian police officials had grown accustomed to equating communism with criminality." He hastens to add, however, that while much of "this thinking was occupational paranoia, . . . it also reflected the concerns of a great many Canadians" (p. 158).

The book's third theme involves what Marquis terms "practical criminology." As the twentieth century progressed, an increasing number of individuals espoused a faith in intellectual approaches to crime and criminal justice, a development that implicitly threatened the expert status assumed by many chiefs and officers. While the chiefs were usually willing to listen to the latest criminological views on recent developments, the association was inclined toward dismissing "ill-advised civilian reformers" whose sentimentality hamstrung effective police work (p. 8). Marquis notes that most members of the CCAC would have concurred with the anti-intellectual tone of Chief Thompson of Peterborough, who observed: "I have read literary productions of criminologists, but in spite of this fact, I still maintain that if one wishes to write anything of value concerning any given subject, he should depend largely upon his own experience" (p. 102). Specifically, "[m]ost chiefs, after long years of service, believed that crime was rooted not so much in social conditions, but in human nature. And in the case of extremely anti-social individuals, the best deterrent was swift and stern justice" (p. 140). The passing years have done little to alleviate this basic tension between those whose experience is obtained in the field as opposed to the classroom, and it seems evident that the rights consciousness of the post-Charter era in Canada will do little to improve the environment.

The fourth and final theme concerns the ongoing search for professionalism. The attempt to raise the profile of police and improve their image was founded on "improvements in recruiting, training, discipline, salaries and working conditions, and public relations" (p. 10). The stress that underlays this theme is one that runs throughout the book. Perhaps as a product of the English origins of municipal policing combined with a tradition of deference, most of the chiefs of the pre-World War II era in Canada were raised in an environment that encouraged a great deal of respect for police and authority figures. The difficulty was that increasing numbers of individuals began questioning the methods or challenging the actions of police, sometimes because of an overt lack of respect, or worse, because it was evident the police seemed ill-prepared for modern Canada. Thus, while forces across the nation were wrestling with technological changes, political issues, and the growing prevalence of criminological approaches to crime, these same departments were having to continually justify their methods and demonstrate their capabilities in light of all these changes. It remains an unending struggle in which individual departments often seem one step behind.

The greatest strength of Marquis's approach is that through these four themes, he is able to trace the increasing assortment of issues confronting police forces during the twentieth century. Everything from training, police unions, the availability of radio patrol cars, capital punishment, organized crime, the 1960s drug culture, and the effects of the Canadian Charter of Rights finds a place in his discussion. Admittedly, the emphasis on chief constables and police chiefs insures that these issues are placed in a context somewhat removed from grassroots policing, but this perspective from the top does not negate the importance of the view offered. Further, it is quite apparent that while Canadian chiefs believed they were acting in accordance with British traditions and within a context of British justice, the reality of their situation demonstrated that, from the 1920s forward, Canadian policing was wholly shaped by the North American environment. The simple fact was that lines of communication with American police forces, especially the Federal Bureau of Investigation, were of greater value than symbolic ties across the Atlantic.

While the focus on the CCAC and CACP reveals important aspects of Canada's policing history, it also unearths a number of unflattering tendencies. For example, there are occasions when the chiefs do not appear as particularly enlightened or thoughtful individuals and, in so doing, suggest an image of amateurish and heavy-handed police methods. Further, the marked inability to ascend above local or regional identities is also an unavoidable theme in this history, a tendency that still hampers an effective national police voice in Canada. The tension between the Royal Canadian Mounted Police and individual provincial, municipal, and urban forces is but one instance. Finally, it is evident that the position of chief remains largely the domain of white men. Although explanations exist for this characteristic, the simple fact is that women and non-white Canadians have not, until recently, been particularly welcomed as recruits; few recruits insures that few individuals with a non-white, non-male perspective gain the necessary experience to become chiefs.

Marquis has constructed a solid piece of work in exposing these and other blemishes along with the chiefs' accomplishments. The nature of the undertaking required a wide-ranging discussion and, on the whole, Marquis manages the affair with skill. Occasionally he retreats from anecdotes a little too quickly, leaving the reader without a payoff. For example, what came of the royal commission investigation of Canadian Pacific Railway agent Antonio Cardasco who was using immigrant labor for security workers? Or what of Dr. Crippen who, having murdered and dismembered his wife, was subsequently arrested by Canadian Pacific Railway security? (p. 136). Understandably, Marquis may have wanted to avoid too much detail detracting from the national picture, but in most of these instances the anecdote required one more sentence to conclude the story and connect it to the ongoing discussion. Elsewhere, a number of typographical errors have slipped into the final copy. Otherwise, *Policing Canada's Century* meets the usual high standards of all Osgoode Society publications.

On the whole, *Policing Canada's Century* will stand as a welcome addition to a police history that has, heretofore, been dominated by the RCMP. There is little question that the origins and history of the Mounted Police have served to create a particular perspective of law enforcement that does not necessarily correspond to the reality of local and provincial forces. Marquis has done a great service in reminding us of this fact. Predictably, there remains a great deal to explore. Future work will have to tackle the question of how these issues that animated the chiefs filtered down to the average officer. Further, a comparative perspective will always be necessary if we are to chart what is truly distinctive about Canadian policing. At the very least, future work must follow Marquis's lead and endeavor to place Canadian developments within a North American context. Gender issues demand our attention not only in matters of staffing profiles, but also in how the police respond to questions framed by gender. Finally, policing concerns for Canadian minority communities deserve further research, especially in regard to the practical demands of First Nations' police forces. Clearly, there remain a vast number of issues to be addressed in Canada's police history. For those who wish to shoulder that challenge, *Policing Canada's Century* will stand as a thoughtful and well-researched point of departure.

Jonathan Swainger
University of Northern British Columbia, Fort St. John

Terrence Sullivan, *Sexual Abuse and the Rights of Children: Reforming Canadian Law*. Toronto: University of Toronto Press, 1992. xi + 212 pp. $16.95 pb, $45.00 hb.

In Chapter 1 of this book the author, Terrence Sullivan, indicates that "the purpose of this study is to begin to make sense of the unprecedented reform efforts dealing with the sexual status of adolescents in light of the question, Who is gaining and who is losing social power?" (p. 4). His historical analysis attempts to answer the following three related theoretical and practical questions: (1) what can be said of the sexual status of adolescents from the perspective of children's rights? (2) who has the power to define the nature of consensual sex in adolescence, and how is that power shifting? and (3) has the position of young persons as sexual actors been advanced in the recent reforms?

The author systematically pursues the answers to these questions in the chapters that follow. Chapter 2 focuses on how sexual consent is defined in law. Age of consent in relation to reproductive activity such as birth control and abortion is discussed extensively. Factors other than age that are related to the capacity to consent are also considered and documented through American, British, and Canadian legislation and case law. The author concludes from the analysis of precedents in this chapter that there has been some increase in the authority of young persons to exercise consent over their own sexual activity and reproductive choice. However, he questions whether this apparent growth in autonomy to exercise consent actually results in a gain of autonomy. He concludes that the growth in professional authority has clearly replaced declining parental authority.

In Chapter 3, the author tracks the evolution of Bill C-15, An Act to Amend the Criminal Code and the Canada Evidence Act. This act deals with substantive and procedural aspects of sexual assaults against victims seventeen years old and younger. The author documents how this act was developed in response to federal commission reports (particularly the Badgley Committee Report), published commentaries in both the professional literature and the popular media, and submissions made to a legislative committee dealing with Bill C-15. While the act, as well as the preceding material and discussion, focuses broadly on the issue of child sexual assault, the discussion in this chapter focuses primarily on the issue of "adolescent's consent to sexual activity and on the role of other actors in defining this consent" (p. 79). The chapter concludes that "the new legislation appears to grant young persons both more protection and more autonomy with regard to sexual consent" (p. 106), but that "the adolescent is in a precarious place—somewhere between the legally autonomous status of adulthood and the dependent status of childhood" (p. 107).

Chapter 4 examines the interplay of power among children, families, professionals, the state, and the market. Analysis in this chapter focuses on the composition of the Badgley Committee and the fact that it was comprised almost exclusively of professionals. Next, the author presents a historical analysis of the relationship between the state and the family. Finally, an analysis of "the child in this mix of commercialism and professionally driven welfarism which is now part of the modern family" (p. 126) is presented. Trends that point to the increase in the importance and power of professionals versus both the adolescent and the family are the main focus of the above analysis. The chapter concludes with a question, albeit rhetorical, "Can we promote reform in counter-discourse and in law without further reinforcing the role of privileged professional and class interests?" (p. 133).

The final chapter begins with a discussion of children's rights and points to the problem of "rhetoric or rights." The author suggests that there are three questions related to the reform efforts directed at the sexual status of young persons that should be explored:

(1) Are the kind of case-based, judge-made decisions we reviewed in Chapter 2 legitimate ways of pursuing reform in Canada, and, if so, in what manner? (2) It is possible to achieve legislative reforms which acknowledge the status of children as sexual actors without advancing the interests of third-party professionals who act between children and families, and between families and their neighbours? (3) What non-legal, vernacular form of counter-discourse and social action will help us to promote human-scale community involvement in decisions related to the sexual status of adolescents? (p. 142).

In regard to the question of judicial reform, the author concludes that "We can try to improve the position of young persons through advocacy and litigation, but . . . doing so through an adversarial process . . . will want to fix the adversaries as the private family and the child" (p. 149). The conclusions to the second question concerning legislative reform are similarly negative. Here the author concludes that the process of the Badgley Committee and its evolution into Bill C-15 was basically faulty because it was "stuffed with professional opinion rather than with the views of families and their young persons" (p. 153).

In terms of the counter-discourse question, the author concludes that "there is room to challenge the involvement of the law altogether in a number of areas governing sexual status issues in adolescence" (p. 155). Further, "matters of gynecological and contraceptive care for adolescents and of adolescent sexual involvement cannot be reduced to matters of legal or medical judgement" (p. 157). Finally, seven recommendations are listed for policy reform on the sexual status of adolescents.

While this book contains a detailed and interesting documentation of the process of the development of child sexual abuse legislation (i.e., Bill C-15) in Canada, it contains major flaws. First, the title of the book, *Sexual Abuse and the Rights of Children: Reforming Canadian Law,* is misleading. The focus of the book is much narrower than the title suggests. Its sole focus is the consent of adolescents to sexual activity and this is only a very minor component of the problem of child sexual abuse and the legislative response to it.

The most significant problem, as is well documented by the Badgley Report and subsequent assessments of the implementation of Bill C-15,[1] is not adolescents engaging in sexual activities with other adolescents, but rather adults and older adolescents involving children under twelve years of age in activities for the sexual gratification of the much older perpetrator. Moreover, approximately 50 percent of child sexual abuse occurs within the context of the extended family. The author's analysis should have been more balanced by a discussion of the rights of children not to be sexually exploited.

Finally, the author seems to view those who act under the mandates of the law, that is, judges, crown prosecutors, and police, as inflexible, inhumane, and driven by the law. It appears that the author has little understanding of the role of discretion and decision making on the part of the professionals involved.

I agree with the author's conclusion that we need alternatives to the law to deal with illicit sexual activity involving adolescent and child victims. I came to that conclusion, however, from a different argument, that is, that "the scope and complex nature of the problem of child sexual abuse requires a response far broader than a legal response alone."[2]

NOTES

1. Joseph P. Hornick and Floyd Bolitho, *A Review of the Implementation of the Child Sexual Abuse Legislation in Selected Sites* (Ottawa: Department of Justice, Canada, 1992).

2. Ibid., 117.

Joseph P. Hornick
University of Calgary

Katy J. Harriger, *Independent Justice: The Federal Special Prosecutor in American Politics*. Lawrence: University Press of Kansas, 1992. x + 270 pp., tables, notes, bibliography, index. $25.

On 20 October 1973, acting under orders from President Richard Nixon, Solicitor General Robert Bork fired Archibald Cox, who had been appointed the previous spring to serve as a special prosecutor in the Watergate case. Before Bork acted, both Attorney General Elliot Richardson and Deputy Attorney General William Ruckelshaus had resigned rather than comply with the president's demand that they dismiss Cox, whose Watergate Special Prosecution Force was technically part of the Department of Justice. The "Saturday Night Massacre" of Cox, Richardson, and Ruckelshaus ignited a firestorm of public protest, jump-started the impeachment machinery in Congress, and proved to be the beginning of the end for the Nixon presidency. It also inspired Congress to provide in the Ethics in Government Act of 1978 for judicial appointment of special prosecutors who would be largely independent of both the Justice Department and the President. The unique office created by that legislation is the subject of this book by Wake Forest political scientist Katy J. Harriger.

The institution she examines has been controversial ever since Congress devised it. Critics contended from the outset that the concept of a judicially appointed special prosecutor who was not under the control of the president was inconsistent with the separation of powers between the judicial and executive branches of government mandated by the Constitution. The Supreme Court resolved this constitutional issue in *Morrison v. Olsen*, 487 U.S. 654 (1988), upholding the independent counsel provisions of the Ethics in Government Act.

Although Harriger devotes a chapter to this constitutional controversy, "The purpose of this book is to assess the practical political consequences of creating an independent prosecutorial body separate from established law enforcement arrangements" (p. 8). Her objective is to determine "how federal special prosecutors have actually operated within the system of separation of powers" (p. 9). In order to do that, Harriger attempts to answer a series of questions about their office. The first is how the statutory independent counsel differs from the special prosecutors appointed on an ad hoc basis to investigate past political scandals. Next, Harriger probes the legislative reaction to Watergate, congressional monitoring of the implementation of the Ethics in Government Act, and amendments to that law, in seeking to determine what Congress hoped to achieve and why it chose the particular institutional arrangements that it adopted. After devoting a chapter to constitutional issues, she turns to the role of the attorney general in the independent counsel process, asking whether the creation of the position of special prosecutor has actually gotten rid of the conflict of interest that arises when the executive investigates itself, which the Ethics in Government Act was supposed to eliminate. In chapter 7, Harriger explores the issue of how accountable special prosecutors are, and in chapter 8 she asks how effective the independent counsel arrangement is in reassuring the people that officials accused of misconduct are being impartially investigated. After discussing whether this institutional innovation represents good public policy, she concludes with some suggestions for improving it so that it will better serve the public interest.

Although her approach sometimes leads Harriger to recross ground she has covered previously, it results in a thorough investigation of all relevant issues and yields conclusions that are generally well supported. For example, by examining the interaction of special prosecutors with the Department of Justice, investigative agencies, the judiciary, defense attorneys, the White House, Congress, and the press, she establishes that, despite the lack of formal constraints on independent counsel, there are actually a number of very meaningful limitations on their power. The book becomes somewhat speculative only when it tries to explain the continued use of the special prosecutor provision, something Harriger attributes to a combination of broad-based elite support (rooted in the memory of Watergate and in the way the arrangement serves an array of institutional and organizational interests) and public support derived from this elite backing. That judgment is based on inferences drawn from general literature on public opinion, post-Watergate poll data on public attitudes about government, and indirect evidence from news coverage. Although it is really just an educated guess, the chapter in which Harriger makes this argument is perhaps the most thoughtful and interesting in the book.

Her analysis is impressive, but some readers may find her bottom-line conclusions unsatisfying. As Harriger herself acknowledges, she is somewhat ambivalent about the special prosecutor. Consequently, her conclusion is rather indecisive. "This study finds," she says, "that in practice, the independent counsel is neither so bad as its critics paint it nor so good as its supporters believe it to be" (p. 12).

Although unlikely to cause anyone to mount the barricades either to defend or destroy the office of special prosecutor, this somewhat wishy-washy conclusion rests on a mountain of evidence. Besides consulting the usual secondary sources, published congressional hearings and reports, judicial opinions, and law reviews, Harriger has examined unpublished documents in three manuscript collections, among them the Leon Jaworski Papers at Baylor University. In addition, she has conducted over fifty interviews with special prosecutors, Justice Department lawyers, judges, defense attorneys, and other actors in the ongoing drama of the special prosecutor. If there is a weakness in her research, it is her failure to talk with more than one of the nine targets of special prosecutor investigations. Since she interviewed lawyers who represented the other eight, however, this is at most a minor problem.

Another minor problem is the somewhat plodding prose that characterizes much of *Independent Justice*. The book, however, makes up in substance for what it lacks in sparkle. Harriger offers her readers a unique perspective on the separation of powers, providing them with a bottom-up view of issues too often examined from the top down, based on evidence of how things work in practice rather than on abstract constitutional theory. Perhaps more importantly, *Independent Justice* provides valuable insights into a subject that has received far too little attention from students of the American legal system: the interaction between politics and the criminal law. American history is replete with examples of politically motivated prosecutions, and of situations where the judicial process has been manipulated by those in control of the government to serve political ends. Unfortunately, most of what we know about the politicization of criminal justice comes from historical monographs and articles that supply in-depth accounts of particular cases but fail to provide a theoretical framework for their accounts. Harriger not only offers a different perspective on the interaction between law and politics, but also takes the more analytical and less narrative approach one expects from a political scientist. That makes *Independent Justice* a valuable book, not only to those in her own discipline, but also to scholars bent on enriching their understanding of criminal justice history.

Michal R. Belknap
California Western School of Law, San Diego

Index

Contributors

VICTOR BAILEY is associate professor of modern British history at the University of Kansas. He is the editor of *Policing and Punishment in Nineteenth Century Britain* (1981), and author of *Deliquency and Citizenship: Reclaiming the Young Offender, 1914–1948* (1987). He has contributed "The Fabrication of Deviance: 'Dangerous Classes' and 'Criminal Classes' " to *Protest and Survival: Essays for E. P. Thompson* (1993), and is currently working on essays concerning Victorian suicide and Edwardian prisons.

DAVID E. BARLOW is assistant professor of criminal justice at the University of Wisconsin, Milwaukee. He received his doctorate in criminology from Florida State University. His recent work includes "Long Economic Cycles and the Criminal Justice System in the U.S." with Melissa Hickman Barlow and Theodore G. Chiricos in *Crime, Law and Social Change* 19 (1993), and forthcoming articles on the media and the police in multicultural communities in *J. of Crime and Justice,* and cultural diversity awareness training in criminal justice in *Social Justice.* His current projects include an ethnographic study of the Menominee tribal police.

MICHAL R. BELKNAP teaches criminal law, constitutional law, and Amercian legal history at California Western School of Law in San Diego. He is the author of *Cold War Political Justice* (1977), and *Federal Law and Southern Order* (1987), as well as the editor of *American Political Trials* (1981).

AUGUSTINE BRANNIGAN is professor of sociology at the University of Calgary, Canada. He has published extensively on the history of morality laws, delinquency, and crime comics, including "Mystification of the Innocents: Crime Comics and Delinquency in Canada, 1931–1949," *CJH* 7 (1986), and coauthored *Prostitution on the Prairies: Evaluation of Bill C-49 in Calgary, Regina and Winnipeg* (1989). He is currently studying the rise and fall of the Canadian prairie provincial police forces, and the policing of immigrants during prohibition.

IAN BRIDGEMAN is lecturer in history, University of Luton, England. His publications include *A Guide to the Archives of the Police Forces of England and Wales* with Clive Emsley (1989), and he is currently preparing his doctoral dissertation for publication as *Policing Rural Ireland*. His research projects include the Nottinghill and Nottingham race riots of 1958, and the policing of Belfast, 1850–1914.

MICHAEL BROERS is lecturer in history at the University of Leeds, England. He is the author of several articles on the history of Napoleonic Italy, including "Revolution as Vendetta: Patriotism in Piedmont, 1794–1821," *Historical J.* 33 (1990), and has two forthcoming books this year: *Piedmont in the Age of Revolution, 1789–1821* (Edwin Mellon), and *Napoleonic Europe, 1799–1815* (Cambridge).

PHILIPPE CHASSAIGNE graduated from the universities of Bordeaux and Paris IV-Sorbonne, and is currently lecturer in modern British history at the University of Orléans. His doctoral dissertation, "Le meurtre à Londres à l'époque Victorienne: Structures sociales et comportements criminels, 1857–1900" (1991), has been followed by several articles. He is currently working on law-breaking and enforcement in nineteenth-century England and the cultural representations of criminals and criminality.

KRISTA COWMAN is a graduate student in the Center for Women's Studies at the University of York, England. She is currently completing a thesis on women in political organizations in Merseyside, c. 1890–1920.

JAMES M. DONOVAN is associate professor of history at the Mont Alto campus of Pennsylvania State University. Recent publications include "Justice and Sexuality in Victorian Marseille, 1825–1885," *J. of Social History* 16 (1987), and articles on abortion, infanticide, and juries, 1825–1913, in *Criminal Justice History* 9 (1988) and *J. of Family History* 16 (1991). He is currently working on a book on the influence of juries on the French criminal justice system since 1791.

KEITH EDGERTON teaches in the American Studies program at Washington State University, Pullman. He has published a book on the history of the Montana Highway Patrol, and is currently working on the related issues of power, punishment, and the development of democracy in the nineteenth-century Pacific Northwest.

CLIVE EMSLEY is professor of history and codirector of the European Center for the Study of Policing at the Open University, Milton Keynes, England. Among his publications are *Crime and Society in England 1750–1900*, and *The English Police: A Political and Social History*. He is currently working on a study of gendarmes and peasants in nineteenth-century Europe.

DAVID ENGLANDER is senior lecturer in European Humanities and co-director of the Booth Research Group at the Open University, Milton Keynes, England. He is the author of *Landlord and Tenant in Urban Britain 1838–1918* (1983), and has just published a study of Charles Booth. He is currently completing a comparative study of mass armies and politics in twentieth-century Europe.

MALCOLM FEELEY is at the Institute for Advanced Studies, Hebrew University, Jerusalem, Israel, and the School of Law, University of California, Berkeley. His study here is a major expansion of his coauthored article with Deborah Little on "The Vanishing Female: The Decline of Women in the Criminal Process, 1678–1912," *Law and Society Review* 25 (1991), on which he has been engaged in further work for several years.

MARK FINNANE is associate professor and dean of the faculty of humanities at the University of Griffith, Brisbane, Australia. He is the author of *Insanity and the Insane in Post-Famine Ireland*, and editor of and contributor to *Policing in Australia: Historical Perspectives*. He is currently completing a history of imprisonment in Australia, and is embarking on a comparative study of violence in Australia, Britain, and the West Indies in the nineteenth century.

STEPHEN GARTON is associate professor of history at the University of Sydney, Australia. He has published *Medicine and Madness: A Social History of Insanity in New South Wales 1880–1940* (1988), and *Out of Luck: Poor Australians and Social Welfare 1788–1988* (1990). He is currently working on the cultural history of crime in Australia.

JOSEPH P. HORNICK is Director of the Institute for Law and the Family at the Faculty of Law, University of Calgary, Canada. He has served on federal government royal commissions examining children and children's rights at law, and has authored several papers in this area.

LOUIS A. KNAFLA is professor of history at the University of Calgary,

Alberta, Canada. He has published books and articles on the legal history of early modern England and of nineteenth-century and Western Canada. He currently has two books in press: *Law, State and Society: Essays in Modern Legal History* (University of Toronto Press) and *Kent at Law 1602* (Her Majesty's Stationery Office).

PAUL G. LEWIS is senior lecturer in government at the Open University, Milton Keynes, England. An expert in contemporary Polish politics, his publications include *Eastern Europe: Political Crisis and Legitimation* (1985), and *Political Authority and Party Secretaries in Poland 1975–1985* (1989). He is currently working on contemporary politics in Eastern Europe, with particular reference to Poland.

NELLA LONZA is assistant lecturer in Croatian legal history at the University of Zagreb Law School. She has published articles on penal procedure in medieval Dalmatia, including *Anali Zavoda za povijesne znanosti Hrvatske akademije znanosti i umjetnosti u Dubrovnike* 30 (1992). She is currently working on a dissertation on criminal justice in eighteenth-century Dubrovnik.

GREG MARQUIS received his doctorate from Queen's University, Kingston, Ontario, and has taught at a number of Canadian universities. He has written several articles on Canadian legal history, both theoretical and particular; a book on *Policing Canada's Century: A History of the Canadian Association of Chiefs of Police* (1993); and has in press an examination of the police archives of the Canadian municipalities in *Essays in Modern Legal History* (Toronto, 1995). He is currently researching the impact of the American Civil War on the maritime provinces.

ANTHONY McELLIGOTT is lecturer in modern history at the University of St. Andrews. A specialist in the social history of Weimar and the Third Reich, he is coauthor of a study of the Nazi seizure of power in Hamburg (Hamburg, 1984), and author of the forthcoming *Contested City: Municipal Politics and the Rise of Nazism in Altona 1917–1937* (Ann Arbor). He is currently writing a history of German society and politics from the 1890s to the 1950s.

W. R. OWENS is subdean of the faculty of arts and codirector of the Defoe Research Group at the Open University, Milton Keynes, England. His publications include *The Canonisation of Daniel Defoe* with P. N. Furbank (1988). He works on English literature of the seventeenth and eighteenth centuries in its historical context.

DAVID PHILIPS is associate professor of history at the University of Melbourne, Victoria, Australia. His recent publications include an article on the associations for the prosecution of felons in England 1760–1860 in Hay and Snyder, *Policing and Prosecution in Britain 1780–1850* (1989), and on "Crime, Law and Punishment in the Industrial Revolution" in Quinault and O'Brien's *The Industrial Revolution and British Society* (1993). He is currently co-editing a volume of essays on *A Nation of Rogues? Crime, Law and Punishment in Colonial Australia* (Melbourne), and writing a book with Robert Storch on the origins and establishment of the English county police forces in the 1830s and 1840s.

XAVIER ROUSSEAU is a research fellow at the University of Saint Louis, Brussels, Belgium. He has published several articles on criminal justice history in the Netherlands, and more recently coauthored "Etats, justice pénale et histoire, bilan historigraphique et relecture," *Droit et Société* 20/21 (1992), and a major bibliography on criminality in Europe, 1250–1850, in the 1993 volume of this *Annual*. He is currently working on state formation and criminal justice in northwest Europe 1750–1850.

JONATHAN SWAINGER is assistant professor in history at the Fort St. John campus of the University of Northern British Columbia, Canada. He has recently published an article on the judiciary of Quebec, as well as several articles on the criminal law in central Alberta and capital crimes in nineteenth-century British Columbia. He is currently completing a full calendar of criminal cases in the judicial district of Red Deer, 1907–1914, with Louis Knafla, and is beginning research into the legal history of the Canadian North.

ROGER SWIFT is Director of Victorian Studies at Chester College of Higher Education, Chester, England. He has published widely on aspects of crime, policing, and popular protest in Victorian Britain, and is the co-editor of *The Irish in the Victorian City* and *The Irish in Britain 1815–1939*. He is currently editing a book on culture and society in Victorian Chester.

Submissions

Notes on Submissions:

The general rule guiding authors and editors is that submissions should follow as closely as possible the formats of the most recent publication. Therefore, the previous volume of *Criminal Justice History* should be consulted for guidance. The basic format used is the University of Chicago Style Manual.

Editorial correspondence and submissions:

Professor Louis Knafla
Department of History
University of Calgary
Calgary, Alberta
Canada T2N 1N4
FAX 403-289-8566

Books for review, proposals to review, and reviewer registrations should be sent to the appropriate review editor:

U.S.A. and Canada

Professor Julia Kirk Blackwelder
Department of History
University of North Carolina
Charlotte, NC 28223
U.S.A.

Other areas and transnational:

Professor Clive Emsley
European Centre for Policing
The Open University
Milton Keynes MK7 6AA
England

ISBN 0-313-28737-6